Worth's Income Tax Guide
for
Ministers

2017 Edition
(For Preparing 2016 Tax Returns)

B. J. Worth

WORTH
PUBLISHING

Worth Financial Service

P.O. Box 242
Winona Lake, IN 46590

To Order call: 574-269-2121 or
Or Fax: 888-483-7350
Order on line - *www.worthfinancial.com*

ISBN 978-0-9912192-6-1

NOTICE
This book is also available in digital format on CD-Rom disk.
ISBN 978-0-991292-7-8
For more information, please contact Worth Publishing.

This publication is designed to provide accurate and authoritative information in regard to the subject matter covered. If legal advice or other expert assistance is required, the services of a competent professional person should be sought. It will be most important to check for any changes in interpretations, rulings, or technical corrections made by Congress and the IRS.

Printed in the United States of America

Items Worth Noting

IRS Mileage Rates for 2016 & 2017:

Business rate:	**2016 - 54¢**	The rate for 2017 - **53½¢**
Medical & moving mileage rate:	**2016 - 19¢**	The rate for 2017 - **17¢**
Contribution rate:	**2016 - 14¢**.	The rate for 2017 - **14¢**

Volunteers can be reimbursed at the business rate if they adequately account to an organization. We have included a volunteer reimbursement agreement in Chapter Three.

Chapter Seven includes tax return examples of Rev. Pious, who is provided a parsonage. We show a return in which he is subject to social security, and another one in which he is exempt from social security. The earned income credit calculation is also shown for both situations.

Effective for 2017: New Law Allows Small Employers to Pay Premiums for Individual Policies. On November 30, 2016, the House of Representatives passed H.R. 34, the 21st Century Cures Act. The Small Business Healthcare Relief Act (SBHRA) was contained within the 21st Century Cures Act in Section 18001. The Senate passed this legislation on December 7, 2016. The President signed on December 13, 2016. Small employers, less than 50 full-time employees, can use Health Reimbursement Arrangements to assist employees with individual health insurance and related medical costs. Benefits can not exceed $4,950 for single coverage or $10,000 for family coverage. **Relief from the ACA $100 a day penalty for small employers.** There's transition relief retroactive for all plan years beginning on or before December 31, 2016 that the onerous penalties announced by the IRS in Notice 2015-17 are no longer in effect.

The Affordable Care Act: Chapter One, pages 19-27 provides a summary of what is in the Act. New forms, subsidy adjustments, and penalties for not having health insurance have been implemented.

For those who qualify for the Premium Assistance Credit or **Subsidies** the definition of "household income" **does not include** a minister's provided parsonage or a designated parsonage allowance. Household income is Adjusted Gross Income, plus any exclusions for Sec. 911, plus tax exempt interest, plus portion of social security income that is not taxed.

Employers of one full-time employee: An employer can reimburse for the premiums of the individual policy without a plan document. According to Technical Release N. 2013-03 a **"One Person" HRA written plan** that can reimburse for qualified medical expenses such as co-payments, deductibles and individual health insurance premiums can be established.

Employers of two or more full-time employees: According to IRS Notice 2013-54, beginning in 2014, The Affordable Care Act does **not allow** an employer of two (2) or more full-time employees to reimburse them for insurance obtained on the marketplace exchange or for any individual policy. Employers of two (2) or more full-time employees must obtain **group insurance coverage**. Because of the Affordable Care Act, an arrangement that reimburses employees (two or more) for insurance obtained on the marketplace or any individual policy fails to satisfy the market reforms. Employers may be subject to a **$100/day excise tax per applicable employee (which is $36,500 per year, per employee)** under section 4980D of the Internal Revenue Code.

Because the Affordable Care Act is anything **but affordable** and the Federal Exchange or marketplace **is proving to lack security for your personal information**, it is advisable to participate in a **healthcare sharing ministry**. Obtain information from four Co-op's websites (page 20). They are available for individuals who attend worship services 75% of the time. Members of your congregations who are self-employed or do not have employer provided coverage can participate

The Parsonage Allowance challenge has been filed again: The Freedom From Religion Foundation renewed its challenge against the IRS Sec. 107 in a federal lawsuit filed on April 6, 2016, in the Western District of Wisconsin. Freedom From Religion Foundation's nonbelieving directors' challenge of the parish exemption giving preferential tax benefits to "ministers of the gospel" continues. They are an atheist organization. You can follow their court activity by going to their website: **www.ffrf.org**, then enter "parsonage allowance" in their search engine.

We Encourage you to Utilize the Internal Revenue Services's Web Site. At **www.irs.gov**, click on "IRS Publications and Forms". Any time you see a web site in our text, you can access more in depth forms and information.

Federal Payroll Deposits: Employers must **use EFTPS** or the telephone to make deposits since 2011. The 8109 deposit coupons are no longer available. However, if an employer accumulates less than $2,500 tax liability for the quarter, no deposit is needed and payment can be made by check with the tax return for the quarter.

January 31st is new deadline for filing W-2s with the IRS. In an effort to combat fraud, The Protecting Americans from Tax Hikes (PATH) Act of 2015 revised the filing deadline for Form W-2 and Form 1099-Misc with income reported in Box 7.

The Trade Preferences Extension Act of 2015 made steep increases in information form reporting penalties in **Sec. 6721 for 2016**. If filed after August 1st of any year, the penalty is **$250** a return, maximum of $3,000,000 a year If corrected by the 30th day after the due date, the penalty is **$50** a return, maximum of $500,000 a year. If filed or corrected more than 30 days late but by August 1, the penalty is **$100** a return, maximum of $1,500,000 a year.

Child Tax Credit: In addition to the 2016 exemption of $4,050 for each dependent child, the Child Tax Credit of **$1000** per child is usually a non-refundable credit against federal taxes. An eligible child must be **under the age of 17 by the close of the year** in which the credit is claimed. The child must also be your dependent child, grandchild, stepchild, or foster child. The child tax credit is refundable for 2016 to the extent of 15% of earned income in excess of $3,000. American Taxpayer Relief Act of 2012 made the $1000 child tax credit permanent.

Qualified Retirement Plans for Churches: A 403(b) written plan document should contain all the terms and conditions for eligibility, benefits, limitations, the form and timing of distributions and contracts available under the plan and the party responsible for plan administration. A review of Mutual fund vendors found some who provide a written plan for churches and non-profit organizations, some who require a TPA or third party administrator, and some who no longer offer 403(b) plans.

We recommend small employers consider establishing a 408(p) SIMPLE Plan. See Chapter One, pages 29-32 for the new rules.

Contribution Substantiation

A donor must have a bank record, cancelled check, or written communication from a charity for **any** monetary contribution before the donor can claim a charitable contribution. The name of the donee organization, the date of the contribution, and the amount of the contribution, must be shown on the documentation.

A donor is responsible for obtaining a **written acknowledgment** from a charity for **any single contribution of $250** or more before the donor can claim a charitable contribution on his federal income tax return. Each contribution is viewed separately. All contributions made on the same date, however, should be combined for purposes of determining if the donor has exceeded the $250 level. Recipient organizations typically send written acknowledgements to donors no later than January 31 of the year following the donation. The taxpayer donee must be given the contemporaneous statement by the donor the **earlier** of: the date on which the donor actually files his tax return or the due date (including extensions) of the return.

Required written statement:

(1) name of organization,

(2) amount of cash contribution,

(3) description (but not the value) of non-cash contribution,

(4) Statement that no goods or services were provided by the organization in return for the contribution, if that was the case,

(5) One of these statements: "Only intangible religious benefits were received by the donor," **or** "Value of tangible benefit donor received was $_____."

Non cash contributions of clothing or a household item must be in good used condition or better to be deductible. A contribution deduction of clothing or a household item that has minimal monetary value, such as used socks and undergarments are not allowable. Non cash contributions with a value of $5,000 or more requires a qualified appraisal to be attached to the return.

IRS Publication 526, "Charitable Contributions" and **IRS Publication 1771,** "Charitable Contributions Substantiation and Disclosure Requirements," have complete details. Treasurers and members of an organization's financial board **must download and read** these IRS Pubs from **www.irs.gov** every year.

Contribution Substantiation for Vehicles Donated to Charity - A charitable deduction under Sec. 170(a) will be denied to any taxpayer who donates a vehicle, boat, or airplane and fails to obtain a written acknowledgement from the charity. **IRS Publications 4303** " A Donor's Guide to Vehicle Donations" and **4302** "A Charity's Guide to Vehicle Donations" explain the requirements. You must obtain the written acknowledgment from the charity within 30 days from the date of the vehicle's sale, or if an exception applies, within 30 days of the date of the donation.

Form 1098-C: If you contribute a vehicle and claim the value of the vehicle is more than $500, the charity is required to provide a contemporaneous written acknowledgment to the you. Form 1098-C, *Contributions of Motor Vehicles, Boats, and Airplanes* can be used to make the acknowledgement. The charity must provide Form 1098-C to the donor and to the IRS by January 31st.

If the charity sells the vehicle, generally your deduction is limited to the gross proceeds from the sale.

If the charity retains the vehicle for its usage, the amount deductible will be the **fair market value** determined by the donor.

Non-Church Small Exempt Organizations Are Required to E-File Form 990-N

Under the Pension Protection Act of 2006, most small tax-exempt organizations whose gross receipts are normally $50,000 or less ($25,000 for tax years ending on or after December 31, 2007 and before December 31, 2010) must file Form 990-N or the e-Postcard on the IRS website by May 15th (if on a calendar year.) The form must be completed and filed electronically. There is no paper Form 990-N available. Before this law was enacted, these small organizations were not required to file annually with the IRS. The first filings were due in 2008 for tax years ending on or after December 31, 2007.

Exceptions to this requirement include: (1) Organizations that are included in a group return, **(2) Churches**, their integrated auxiliaries, and conventions or associations of churches, and (3) Organizations required to file a different return

If you do not file your e-Postcard on time, the IRS will send you a reminder notice. There is no penalty assessment for late filing the e-Postcard, but an organization that fails to file required e-Postcards (or information returns – Forms 990 or 990-EZ) for three consecutive years will automatically lose its tax-exempt status. The revocation of the organization's tax-exempt status will not take place until the filing due date of the third year.

Foreword

Meet B. J.

Mrs. Beverly J. Worth is recognized as one of the foremost authorities in the area of Income Tax as it relates to ministers and religious workers. Beverly is a successful tax consultant, instructor and author.

Her seminars are in constant demand by churches, missions, accounting organizations and seminaries. She has authored the annual publication "**Worth's Income Tax Guide for Ministers**" since 1973, the "**Professional Tax Record Book**" since 1981. The "**Auto Log**" book contains the two auto sections from the "Professional Tax Record Book".

A graduate of Calvary Bible College, Beverly was honored as a distinguished alumnus in 1988. The NRCC Business Advisory Council presented to Beverly a "2004 Businesswoman of the Year" award. She is a member of the National Association of Enrolled Agents, National Society of Tax Professionals, National Association of Tax Practitioners. Her husband, Jack, is a pastor and they have two children and two grandchildren.

Our two-fold goal is to teach ministers how to keep their taxes to a minimum and to maximize their earning power. When congress passes new tax legislation in complex language, it is important that you as a taxpayer find a professional tax preparer to help you through the maze.

It is necessary to update "**Worth's Income Tax Guide for Ministers**" each year. So we must strongly encourage you to READ EACH NEW EDITION carefully in order for you to be able to apply the law changes to your situation.

A minister quite often has difficulty teaching and communicating to the church officials how they, the employer, can assist him in paying the least amount of tax legally possible. A one hour audio CD presentation of "**Minister's Compensation Package, Tax & Financial Planning,**" is available to share the basic information with your financial committee.

You will find references to Internal Revenue Code Sections, Revenue Rulings, court cases, IRS Publications, etc. throughout this publication. Quotations of important portions of tax law and regulations **are included to give you confidence** in what you read and learn.

We would love to meet you in person at one of our seminars.

- B.J. Worth, EA, ATA, CTP

Table of Contents

TABLE OF CONTENTS

Income and Fringe Benefits

Employees of churches and integral agencies of churches are divided into two classifications: the dual-status minister and the lay employee. It is important to determine the proper status of each employee when they are employed. To qualify for the unique **dual-status** tax treatment an employee of a church or an integral agency of a church must be performing ministerial duties. These duties include preaching, teaching, evangelism, conduct of worship, administration, baptisms, weddings, funerals, and communions. In J.M. Ballinger, U.S. Court of Appeals, 10th Circuit, No. 82-1928, 3/7/84, it was stated, "We interpret Congress' language providing for an exemption for any individual who is 'a duly ordained, commissioned, or licensed minister of a church' to mean that **the triggering event** is the assumption of the duties and functions of a minister." Therefore, with or without formal credentials, the date of hire by a church or an integral agency, becomes an important date at which the unique dual-status tax treatment begins.

Dual-status tax treatment means that the minister is an **employee** for income reporting, fringe benefit and expense deducting purposes, and **self-employed** for social security purposes. There is an opportunity to make a decision to become exempt from paying Social Security on ministerial earnings. Parsonage allowance can be designated in advance and to the extent used, it is free from income tax. **It is mandatory** to treat a dual-status minister as self-employed for social security purposes, according to the regulations. When an employer withholds and matches social security for a dual-status minister, it is wrong.

The employer of a dual-status minister does not have to withhold federal income tax, it is optional.

Employees of churches and integral agencies of churches who are not performing ministerial duties are **lay** employees. Employees of non-integral agencies are lay employees, even if they are formally credentialed, unless their church or denomination "assigned or designated" them to the position.

There are definite tax advantages to being a dual-status minister. A close examination of court cases and letter rulings reflect a very friendly definition of who is entitled to the unique dual-status tax treatment. A full discussion with quotations and citations is in Chapter Two.

Where to Report Income

Dual-Status Minister

Ministers employed by churches and integral agencies of churches have a dual-status treatment in the Internal Revenue Code. They are to be treated as employees for income tax reporting according to "common law rules" in Reg.31.3401(c)-1; and as self-employed for social security reporting Sec. 1402(a)(8). A dual-status minister's Form W-2, Wage and Tax Statement, Box 3, for social security wages and Box 5, for medicare wages should be left blank. The **chart shown in Chapter Six, page 113**, is a good guide indicating what is considered taxable income to be entered on Form W-2, Box 1.

Withholding of income tax for the dual-status minister is not required according to Sec. 3401(a)(9); it is optional. If the dual-status minister did not file Form 4361, it is necessary for social security to be computed on Schedule SE of his personal tax return. If a minister has filed Form 4361, "Application for Exemption from Self-Employment Tax for Ministers," and has received an approved copy, he is exempt from social security on earnings from the ministry and needs to indicate that by writing "Exempt---Form 4361" on the self-employment line of Form 1040, page 2.

Ministers are considered employees for income reporting, expense deducting, and fringe benefit eligibility. Unreimbursed or reimbursed without "an accountable plan," automobile, travel, and professional expenses are allowed only as miscellaneous itemized deductions on Schedule A. They are also subject to limitations: (1) meals & entertainment are reduced by 50%, then combined with other miscellaneous deductions, (2) only the percentage of unreimbursed expenses spent in earning the taxable salary are allowable, and (3) they are further reduced by 2% of the Adjusted Gross Income.

Lay Employees

Lay Employees are employees for both income and social security purposes. A lay employee's Form W-2, Box 1 will show his salary, Box 3 will show the social security wage, and Box 5 will show the medicare wage. Until the end of 1983, a nonprofit organization or church was exempt from withholding and matching social security on their lay employees, unless they chose to cover them by filing Form SS-15. As a part of the Social Security Amendments Act of 1983, social security coverage was extended on a **mandatory** basis to all lay employees of nonprofit organizations as of January 1, 1984. The Tax Reform Act of 1984 provided for an election by a church or qualified church-controlled organization that is opposed for religious reasons to the payment of social security taxes, not to be subject to such taxes. By filing Form 8274 lay employees of churches that make the election **are liable for paying social security** on their personal returns on Schedule SE, Section B. Electing church employers have the responsibility of withholding income tax, filing quarterly reports, and preparing a W-2 for each employee. It is very important that the employer educate the staff of their responsibility to pay their Social Security on Schedule SE and include it with their Form 1040. (See complete discussion in Chapter Four and the examples of the W-2 in Chapter Six.)

Unreimbursed or reimbursed without "an accountable plan," automobile, travel, and professional expenses are allowed only as miscellaneous itemized deductions on Schedule A. They are also subject to limitations: (1) meals & entertainment are reduced by 50%, then combined with other miscellaneous deductions, and (2) they are further reduced by 2% of the Adjusted Gross Income.

Employed Ministers Are Not to Use Schedule C For Reporting Salary

Employed ministers are definitely self-employed for social security purposes. However, for income reporting, expense deducting, and fringe benefit provision purposes, the Internal Revenue Code speaks clearly about their status being that of an employee. IRS publications on the issue have historically presented the dual-status treatment for ministers performing services for a church or an integral agency of a church. To ignore the historic IRS position and report a minister's salary and deduct their professional expenses on Schedule C will often cause an audit and an assessment of additional tax liability by moving expenses from Schedule C to Schedule A. Thousands of employed ministers have been audited and have experienced additional tax liability because they used Schedule C.

"Worth's Income Tax Guide for Ministers" is happy to have clearly focused our efforts on educating church employers and their ministers on how to establish an accountable reimbursement plan for employee business expenses to produce the **desired lower tax liability without conflicting with existing IRS code and regulations.** Ministers who have prepared their returns as dual-status ministers have experienced a much lower audit risk. If their return is audited they will not be assessed an additional tax liability because of how they reported their ministry income and expenses.

● **Historic IRS Position**

The IRS's position that an employed minister is an employee for income reporting purposes is well defined in the following quote from IRS Publication 517, page 4:

"EMPLOYMENT STATUS FOR OTHER TAX PURPOSES

Even though all of your income from performing ministerial services is subject to self-employment tax for social security tax purposes, you may be an employee for income tax or retirement plan purposes in performing those same services. For income tax or retirement plan purposes, your income earned as an employee will be considered wages.

Common-law employee. *Under common law rules, you are considered either an employee or a self-employed person. Generally, you are an employee if you perform services for someone who has the legal right to control both what you do and how you do it, even if you have considerable discretion and freedom of action. For more information about the common-law rules, see Publication 15-A, Employer's Supplemental Tax Guide.*

If a congregation employs you and pays you a salary, you are generally a common-law employee and income from the exercise of your ministry is wages for income tax purposes. However, amounts received directly from members of the congregation, such as fees for performing marriages, baptisms, or other personal services, aren't wages; such amounts are self-employment income for both income tax purposes and social security tax purposes.

Example. A church hires and pays you a salary to perform ministerial services subject to its control. Under the common law rules, you are an employee of the church while performing those services.

If you aren't certain whether you are an employee or a self-employed person, you can get a determination from the IRS by filing Form SS-8."

Before requesting a determination from the IRS, study a copy of the full text of Rev. Ruling 87-41. It states, "If the relationship of employer and employee exists, the designation or description of the relationship by the parties as anything other than that of employer and employee is **immaterial**." To draft a contract or an agreement to state that an independent contractor relationship exists when facts and circumstances indicate an employer/ employee relationship actually exists would be an exercise of futility. It also does not matter how payments are measured or paid, what they are called, or whether the employee works full or part time.

Wages earned as an employed minister are to be reported on Form W-2 for income tax purposes, but no social security taxes are withheld. This is because you are treated as self-employed for social security purposes. You must pay self-employment tax on those wages yourself unless you request and receive an exemption from self-employment tax. Your Form **W-2, Box 3** for social security wages and **Box 5** for medicare wages **should be left blank**.

For a minister who is serving part-time and is not fully supported by the employer, it is possible to designate all or 100% of his salary as parsonage allowance. Since parsonage allowance is not required to be shown on Form W-2, a **Form W-2 generally does not need to be prepared**. You may report a designated parsonage allowance in a separate statement.

- ### *The 20 Common Law Rules*

As an aid to determining whether an individual is an employee under the common law rules, twenty factors have been developed based on an examination of cases and rulings. In applying the IRS twenty-factor test, there is no set number of factors that make the payee an employee. Each case is evaluated on its own merits. Some of the factors that indicate the presence of **"the right to control"** weigh more in importance on the scale of determining if an employer/employee relationship exists. The threshold level of control necessary to find employee status is generally lower when applied to professional services than when applied to nonprofessional services. Ministers are professionals. If enough of the factors indicate there is an employer/employee relationship and the employer does not treat the employee correctly, the IRS penalties are substantial.

In Rev. Ruling 87-41,CB 1987-1, 296, we find a list of **THE TWENTY COMMON LAW FACTORS**. This list, along with our explanations, is as follows:

(1) ***Compliance with instructions;*** A payee who MUST OBEY the payor's instructions about when, where and how he is to do the work is apt to be an employee. Even if no instructions are given, the control factor is present if the employer has the right to control how the work results are achieved. A minister paid by a church or organization is generally required to hold a certain theological position and maintain an honorable lifestyle and hold worship services at set times, teach classes, etc.

(2) ***Training required;*** The use of an employee handbook or staff meetings would be a factor of control and indicative of employee status. A payee who is an independent contractor ordinarily receives no training from the payor.

(3) ***Integration of services into business operations;*** How closely related to the work of the payor is the work of the payee? It would seem rather difficult to prove a church or organization's purpose and ministry is not closely integrated with the purpose and ministry of the minister hired to perform ministerial duties. A minister has the responsibility to lead a local church in conformance with the beliefs of the church. This is another factor that indicates control. A payee who is an independent contractor would have a separate line of business from the payor.

(4) ***Services rendered personally;*** If the payor requires a payee to physically perform the services himself, this shows control by the payor over the payee. An independent contractor would have the right to hire a substitute without getting the payor's consent.

(5) ***Hiring, supervising, and paying assistants;*** When the payor hires, trains and pays the staff working with the payee it indicates control by the payor and employee status. Independent contractors must have the right to hire assistants at their own discretion, regardless of payor's wishes.

(6)   ***Continuing relationship;*** An ongoing long term relationship between the payor and the payee indicates an employee status. A continuing relationship may exist even if work is performed at recurring, although irregular, intervals. An independent contractor will finish an assignment project and work for several payors.

(7)   ***Set hours of work;*** A payee's ability to schedule his activities according to his own desire merely demonstrates that less supervision is necessary in connection with a professional. When the payor sets regular hours of work it is a definite indication of control and an employee status. An independent contractor will schedule a job and have the right to change the date and time and give scheduling priority to other jobs.

(8)   ***Full time required;*** When a payee must work full time for one payor, it indicates control and employee status. An independent contractor is free to work when and for whom he wishes.

(9)   ***Work done on premises;*** When the payor provides the premises for a payee to perform the work to be done it indicates an employee status. When the employing church or organization owns the worship location or office in which the professional minister performs most of his duties it indicates the factor of control.

(10)   ***Services performed in order or sequence set;*** When the payor has the right to establish the schedule and routines of the payee, an employer/employee relationship exists. A church employer has regular worship services, committee meetings, etc., that a minister must plan for and lead as scheduled. A minister does not have the ability to unilaterally discontinue the regular services of a local church. An independent contractor evangelist schedules meetings any day or evening of the week he may choose.

(11)   ***Oral or written reports;*** An employee is usually required to give reports or an accounting of his time and accomplishments. An independent contractor submits invoices to the payor.

(12)   ***Payment by hour, week, month;*** When a payee is paid by the hour, week, month, mile, etc., this is an indication of employee status. An independent contractor estimates his cost of labor and materials and receives payment from the payor by the job.

(13)   ***Payment of business and/or traveling expenses;*** This factor weighs as light as a feather. It is good tax planning for either an employee or an independent contractor to "adequately account" to the employer or payor and be reimbursed for job related expenses. An employee who does not establish an accountable plan with his employer can only deduct the expenses on Schedule A if he itemizes his deductions. An independent contractor is able to deduct his job related expenses on Schedule C.

(14)   ***Furnishing of tools and materials;*** When the payor provides the necessary tools and materials for a payee to carry out his duties, an employer/employee relationship is indicated. An independent contractor owns, repairs and takes with him from job to job the tools necessary for his trade.

(15)   ***Significant investment;*** When the payor provides the work facilities and the payee performing the services is not required to make an investment, an employer/employee relationship is indicated. A church provides the church building for holding services and an office in which to perform administrative services and often buys religious materials for the minister. To voluntarily purchase books, tapes, computer equipment, furnishings for a home office, etc., does not count as required significant investment.

(16)   ***Realization of profit or loss;*** An employee is shielded from risk of loss. If a payee is subject to a real risk of economic loss due to significant investments and bona fide liabilities it indicates an independent contractor status. An independent contractor evangelist could incur travel and advertising expenses and experience economic loss if he failed to secure adequate engagements.

(17)   ***Working for more than one firm at a time;*** A payee who performs services for more than one firm at a time could be a part-time employee of each firm. However, if a payee works or consults with many clients and customers simultaneously, it would be a strong indicator of an independent contractor status.

(18) ***Making service available to general public;*** To the extent of honorariums received from individuals for ministerial services (weddings, funerals, etc.), outside speaking engagements, writing, etc., a minister receives independent contractor income to be reported on Schedule C. There are many ways of holding one's self out to the public such as: business cards, a business name at the top of an invoice, a business listing in a phone book, distribution of a brochure, advertisements in a newspaper or trade journal, placement of business name on key chains or jackets, etc.

(19) ***Right to discharge;*** An employer has the ability to fire an employee. An employer exercises control through the threat of dismissal, which causes the worker to obey the employer's instructions. A payee serving as a minister of a church or organization is accountable to the payor to maintain certain theological positions, an acceptable lifestyle and an acceptable performance of his duties. This is true in a denominational connectional church polity as well as in an independent autonomous church polity. That in a connectional church polity a bishop or overseer appoints the minister to a church and the church usually pays the minister for services rendered indicates more control and is a substantial indication of a co-employer/employee relationship. While the congregation of a connectional church cannot fire a minister, they can certainly seek dismissal for just cause through the bishop or overseer. An independent contractor, on the other hand, can not be fired so long as the independent contractor produces a result that meets the contract specifications.

(20) ***Right to terminate relationship without incurring liability.*** When a payee has the right to terminate his relationship with the payor at any time he wishes without incurring liability, it indicates an employer/employee relationship. An independent contractor agrees to complete a specific job and is responsible for its satisfactory completion or is legally obligated to make good for failure to complete the job.

• *Additional Factors to Consider*

To be eligible for "Tax Free" fringe benefits such as medical insurance, group term life insurance, etc., an individual must be a common law employee. Hypothetically, if a minister could be considered as an independent contractor and use Schedule C for reporting salary and expenses, **he would have to report as taxable income** the value of any fringe benefits provided by a payor.

When the source of income is from a nonprofit organization: Payment for services performed on a regular and continuous basis is to be treated as salary, not independent contractor income. To be a nonprofit corporation, it is important that individuals do not personally benefit or inure from funds and assets acquired. **If a minister actually had complete control of funds and assets of a church, it would no longer be a nonprofit organization or church.**

A business owner who creates a for-profit corporation becomes its employee when paid for services rendered. Rev. Ruling 71-86 states that a president and sole shareholder, who sets his own hours, duties, salary and was not responsible to anyone else, was an employee for income tax withholding, social security and federal unemployment tax purposes. Similarly, Rev. Ruling 73-361 treats an officer performing substantial services as an employee.

When the source of income is from individuals for whom a service was performed, reporting the income on Schedule C is correct. Honorariums received for performing weddings, funerals, baptisms and counseling are correctly reported as self-employment income on Schedule C.

Preparer penalties: Tax preparers are subject to negligence penalties if they knowingly prepare a return incorrectly. After a careful study of the citations just presented, tax preparers who disregard the position of the IRS by not preparing an employed minister's tax return as dual-status would be guilty of negligently understating the minister's tax liability. Sec. 6694(b) provides for a $5,000 penalty per return prepared with an intentional disregard of rules or regulations.

Churches who fail to prepare W-2's for their employees are subject to many penalties. Providing a Form 1099 to an employed minister rather than a W-2 can result in a $250 penalty as **it is necessary to prepare "correct" informational returns to avoid penalties.** It is very important to learn what the law requires and carefully meet those obligations. Chapter Six, page 105, discusses Sec. 6721 penalties for failing to prepare informational returns or failing to file them timely. Penalties have increased greatly for 2016.

Statutory employee status cannot be used by ministers: It is a status limited to **four occupational groups.** Generally, statutory employees receive a W-2 and are able to deduct their business expenses on Schedule C. Because of this ability, some ministers have attempted to claim this status. (IRS Publication 15, page 10)

The four specific occupational groups deemed to be statutory employees regardless of whether they are employees under the usual common law guidelines are: (1) An agent (or commission) driver who delivers food, beverages, laundry or dry cleaning for someone else. (2) A full-time life insurance salesperson who sells primarily for one company. (3) A home worker who works by guidelines of the person for whom the work is done, with materials furnished by and returned to that person or to someone that person designates. (4) A traveling or city salesperson who works full time for one firm or person getting orders from customers. The orders must be for merchandise for resale or supplies for use in the customer's business.

- *WHY all the Confusion over Status and Contention with the IRS?*

Often a church treasurer or board will ask their minister what tax status they prefer as if it is an optional decision. Our theological colleges and seminaries do a very poor job teaching ministerial students about tax law and how it applies to them. Due to inadequate knowledge of tax law, many wrong decisions have been made.

Many clergy tax advisors, accountants, and publications have continued to recommend or show examples of using Schedule C for **employed ministers**. The "fight for the right to use Schedule C" that has caused thousands of ministers to be audited and assessed additional tax liabilities is unfortunate.

If you call the IRS "800" number six times and ask for information concerning the correct status of a minister, you may get six different answers. (That is if they answer.) It is unfortunate that some of the confusion concerning the minister's correct status has been caused by uninformed IRS employees and the courts. Going against the historic position stated in IRS publications results in taxable fringe benefits and **increases the IRS audit exposure**. Most ministers claiming to be independent contractors cannot afford legal representation to pursue their case through the courts.

- *An Important District Court Case - Weber v. Commissioner, 103 T.C. 378, 386 (1994)*

In North Carolina the IRS audited several hundred United Methodist ministers' tax returns that reported their salary income and professional expenses spent to earn that income on Schedule C. Legal counsel of the United Methodist denomination required Methodist churches to provide Form 1099 to their ministers, rather than a Form W-2. A tax liability was assessed when the professional expenses were changed from Schedule C to Schedule A, Itemized Deductions. These audits resulted in a District Court Case in North Carolina, Weber v. Commissioner, in January, 1993. The case was well represented by Rev. Weber's denomination and the written result was released on August 25, 1994. An appeal was filed and the final decision was received on July 31, 1995. (U.S. Court of Appeals, 4th Circuit, 94-2609, 7/31/95) **The IRS position stands.** This case was a test case for the United Methodist ministers as to the issues it contains. Petitioners in many of the pending cases agreed to be bound by the final decision in this case.

Special Trial Judge John J. Pajak, seemed to have carefully read the Book of Discipline of the United Methodist Church. He decided that the "right to control" test was of primary importance and found that Weber was subject to significant control. The court stated, "generally a lower level of control applies to professionals. Petitioner is a professional minister." He was required to work at the church to which he was assigned and was required to attend meetings. He had to explain the position of the Discipline on any topic he chose to present in his sermons. He did not have the authority to unilaterally discontinue the regular services of a local church. Though the church did not give him a Form W-2, the court gave that factor little weight. The Court found that Reverend Weber's position was intended to be permanent as opposed to transitory and that the fringe benefits provided by the Church indicated an employment relationship.

Methodist ministers, spouses, and dependents are covered by life insurance and contributions are made to the General Board of Pensions of the United Methodist Church which provides payments upon retirement. Ministers are expected to make voluntary contributions to the pension plan equal to 3 percent of their salary. As an employee, Rev. Weber was entitled to tax free treatment of these fringe benefits.

A more recent U.S. Tax Court decision in Radde v. Commissioner, T.C. Memo 1997-490 upholds the Weber decision that as a minister Rev. Radde was an employee. In Private Letter Ruling 9825002, a United Methodist minister, who served as a presiding elder, **was denied his request** to be considered an independent contractor.

• *Other Tax Court Cases have Resulted in Conflicting Decisions.*

The tax courts have added to the confusion by giving conflicting decisions. On the same day that Rev. Weber's District Court Case was released, another judge in Florida gave a conflicting opinion in Shelley v. Commissioner, T.C. Memo 1994-432. The church Rev. Shelley pastored was a member of the International Pentecostal Holiness Church. The judge's opinion that Rev. Shelley was an independent contractor is a decision by a small Tax Court that the IRS will not follow. However, Weber v. Commissioner was a decision of a District Court that was agreed to be a precedent setting case.

On December 2, 1996, in Greene v. Commissioner, T.C. Memo 1996-531, it was determined that an Assembly of God missionary to Bangladesh was an independent contractor rather than an employee. On June 20, 1997, Alford v. United States, U.S. Court of Appeals for the eighth circuit, No. 96-3287 also determined that an Assembly of God minister was an independent contractor rather than an employee. Both IRS and the District Court determined that Alford was an employee. The District Court concluded that Alford was an employee of not only the local church but also of the district and national organizations. If this decision had not been appealed it would have exposed the district and national organizations to unnecessary liability. The U.S. Court of Appeals correctly determined that there was no employer/employee relationship with the district or national organizations. However, they wrongfully determined that there was no employer/employee relationship with the local church.

NOTE: The Assembly of God national organization's recommendation is to disregard the Alford decision and to accept the employer/employee relationship when the facts and circumstances support it.

• *What to do if your employer gives you Form 1099 instead of Form W-2?*

After gathering all the facts and circumstances of the relationship between a payor and a payee, based on the common-law guidelines, determine what the payee's correct status is. If an incorrect informational return has been issued by the payor, **it is important** to educate the payor why an employer/employee relationship exists. Making the corrections according to step #1 below will reduce the audit exposure for the employee and result in the correct returns being prepared in the future.

1. Have the payor prepare a corrected Form 1099 with -0- income shown. Then prepare a Form W-2 correctly reporting the taxable salary in Box 1.

2. When an employed dual-status minister receives Form 1099 rather than a Form W-2 **and the payor will not prepare corrected forms,** we recommend the following procedure for preparing Form 1040:

   a. Enter the amount shown as income on the Form 1099 on Schedule C as gross income because IRS computers will scan the informational return and expect it to be there.

   b. Subtract the same amount as "wages taken to Form 1040, line 7" in the expense section of Schedule C to have a net result of zero on Schedule C to the extent of the salary. Any honorariums received will remain as taxable on the Schedule C.

   c. Then enter the amount as income on Form 1040, line 7 as though it were wages reported on a W-2. IRS computers will accept an amount on line 7 that is greater than the total wages reported on W-2s attached to the return.

   d. Use Form 2106 and Schedule A to deduct any unreimbursed employee business expenses.

There will be a higher audit exposure if the return is prepared according to Step 2 because Schedule C income from one Form 1099 appears to the IRS computers as a potential misclassification of status. However, if audited, there will be no additional tax assessed for an incorrectly prepared Form 1040.

Taxable Sources Of Income

Important Definition of Income: Gross income, according to Sec. 61, includes all income (cash, value of property, or value of services) from whatever source, unless it is specifically excluded by a section in the Internal Revenue Code. It is important to understand that regardless of what a payor or payee calls a sum of money, property or value of service; facts and circumstances will determine whether it is taxable or not. **Any income that is received because services are performed is taxable.** Generally, the employee will be taxed on all remuneration from a payor that is not a qualified fringe benefit (Chapter One), housing allowance (Chapter Two), or reimbursement for professional expenses under an accountable plan (Chapter Three).

According to Rev. Ruling 68-67, whether a missionary receives support from an organization or from individuals directly, the dominant reason for such payments is that the missionary performs ministry services.

Voluntary contributions, irrespective of their designation as "gifts," made directly to missionaries are includible in gross income. Furthermore, voluntary contributions, which are designated for a specific missionary, made by individuals or groups and transmitted directly to the mission, should be included in the mission's receipts and included on the missionary's Form W-2, Box 1.

It is wrong to conclude that if a donor cannot deduct the gift to a minister or missionary's support, that it is not necessary for the recipient to report the gift as taxable income. The payee receiving taxable support and the payor deducting a Schedule A contribution are two separate acts. According to Commissioner v. Duberstein, 363 U.S. 278, 285 (1960), the Supreme Court holds that **when the contribution is for services rendered it is irrelevant that the payor derives no economic benefit**. Contributions must be paid directly to a qualifying organization in order for the donor to be able to deduct them on Schedule A. Contributions paid directly to an individual are never allowable as Schedule A deductions.

Professional Income

Fees, offerings, or gifts for speaking, performing weddings, funerals or baptisms are considered professional income. An independent contractor, evangelist, or missionary receives professional income from the churches to which he ministers as well as from individual supporters. When as a minister you have provided a service and the person receiving the benefit of your ministry gives you money, it should be considered as earned professional income according to Reg 1.61-2(a)(1). **Pastor appreciation gifts or "love gifts"** received from individuals should be reported on Sch C.

When as an independent contractor you personally receive your support from individual contributions, it becomes necessary to show these amounts on Schedule C and to deduct the expenses of doing ministry to arrive at net income. Reporting large amounts of support for work projects on Sch C and deducting them as expenses, is a greater exposure to an IRS audit. **The ideal solution for this Schedule C problem is for the independent missionary to establish an employer/employee relationship with a church.** (See complete discussion of this recommendation in Chapter Six.)

Income received from writing, lecturing, radio or television appearances, etc., are additional types of professional income. The income or royalties and expenses of selling religious tapes and books are to be shown on Schedule C as professional income, according to Rev. Ruling 59-50. For ministers not exempt from social security, the net profit will be considered social security earnings.

If honorariums and fees for weddings, funerals, etc., are paid directly to the employer and not personally received by the minister, they would not be taxable to him.

Salary From Employer

Compensation or salary, for services rendered, received from an employing church is to be reported in the W-2, Box 1. When an employer gives a **bonus, pastor appreciation gift or "love gift"** to an employee it is simply additional salary and should also be **included in the W-2, Box 1.** Payments of severance pay are continued salary and can be designated as parsonage allowance. Honorariums or gifts that are received by the minister from individuals to whom he ministers or from whom he receives support are to be included on Schedule C.

Two court cases, Banks v. Commissioner, T.C. Memo 1991-641 and Goodwin v. United States Court of Appeals, KTC 1995-479 (8th Cir. 1995), involved ministers who had received three or four large special occasion offerings each year on a regular basis and had not included them on their tax returns. Both ministers were assessed large sums of income tax and Social Security tax for three years plus many penalties and several years of interest by the time the court decisions were final.

Because of **The Affordable Care Act**, if an employer has **two or more full-time employees** the only type of medical insurance they can provide as a tax free fringe benefit is a group policy. If a group medical insurance is provided, there can also be an integrated HRA plan provided. Extra salary paid for an employee to obtain an individual policy results in taxable salary for income tax purposes and social security purposes.

The **Affordable Care Act** does not apply to an employer with **one full-time employee**. An employer can reimburse for the premiums of the individual policy without a plan document. An employer of one full-time employee is allowed to establish a **"One Person" HRA written plan** that can reimburse for qualified medical expenses such as co-payments, deductibles and individual health insurance premiums. (Technical Release No. 2013-03) The cost of paying a benefit specialist or a TPA for establishing and maintaining the plan for one employee can be greater than the tax savings of being reimbursed for the additional medical expenses.

Transfers of property other than cash should be considered at their fair market value (FMV) and, if received from the employer, included in the W-2. Transfers of property received from individuals are to be included on Schedule C.

Congregations who own the parsonage and decide to **sell it at a bargain price or transfer the ownership** of the parsonage outright to their minister are actually paying him a considerable amount of "extra" compensation. The difference between the amount paid and the amount of its fair market value at the time of the transfer is taxable according to Reg. 1.61-2(d)(2). To avoid an excessive tax burden in the year of transfer we suggest the following: The employer should loan the employee the amount of the difference between the FMV and the amount paid by the employee and, over a period of time, forgive a portion of the loan each year. The annual income would be the amount of forgiveness and if the loan is secured by the home, it would be principal payment that can be parsonage allowance expense. Interest at the rate of the Applicable Federal Rate (AFR) must be stated in the contract. If absent, a complicated calculation of imputed interest must be done. (See discussion of "Loans from employers" in Chapter Two)

Benevolence to an employee or a family member: When an employer helps an employee or a member of an employee's family with crisis needs it will result in taxable compensation to the employee. **To avoid this, we recommend** that a local non-employer, nonprofit organization (such as Red Cross) be utilized to raise funds for the crisis needs of an employee.

Only small gifts of merchandise are non-taxable: According to Rev. Ruling 59-58, "The value of a turkey, ham or other item of merchandise purchased by an employer and distributed generally to each of the employees engaged in his business at Christmas, or a comparable holiday, as a means of promoting their good will, does not constitute wages." The ruling also states **that this rule "will not apply** to distributions of cash, gift certificates, and similar items of readily convertible cash value, regardless of the amount involved." This tax-free provision of giving small non-cash gifts of merchandise to your minister might include T-bone steaks, a neat tie, or a package of golf balls.

Social Security Paid By the Employer

When an employer agrees to provide extra payment to a dual-status minister to pay all or part of his social security tax, **it must be shown as taxable salary** according to Rev. Ruling 68-507. Dual-status ministers are treated as self-employed taxpayers when computing their social security on Schedule SE. Their combined rate of social security tax and medicare tax is 15.3% less adjustments. It may be convenient to have the employer pay this amount to the minister on a quarterly basis, to coincide with the due dates of his estimated tax payments.

On Schedule SE the gross social security base is adjusted to allow one half of social security as a deduction. On Form 1040, page 1, an adjustment for one half of the social security paid by the self-employed taxpayer is allowed. This is similar to the way employees are treated under the tax laws, because the employer's share of the Social Security tax is not considered wages to the employee.

The wage base for the two parts of the social security tax (social security and medicare) are different. **The 7.65% combined rate** is made up of 6.2% rate for social security and 1.45% rate for medicare.

Here is the schedule of what has happened since 2006

YEAR	SOCIAL SECURITY WAGE BASE	MEDICARE WAGE BASE	EMPLOYEE RATE FICA	Medicare	SELF-EMPLOYED RATE FICA	Medicare
2006	$94,000	No limit	6.20%	1.45%	12.40%	2.9%
2007	$97,500	No limit	6.20%	1.45%	12.40%	2.9%
2008	$102,000	No limit	6.20%	1.45%	12.40%	2.9%
2009	$106,800	No limit	6.20%	1.45%	12.40%	2.9%
2010	$106,800	No limit	6.20%	1.45%	12.40%	2.9%
2011	$106,800	No limit	4.20%	1.45%	10.40%	2.9%
2012	$110,100	No limit	4.20%	1.45%	10.40%	2.9%
2013	$113,700	No limit	6.20%	1.45%	12.40%	2.9%
2014	$117,000	No limit	6.20%	1.45%	12.40%	2.9%
2015	$118,500	No limit	6.20%	1.45%	12.40%	2.9%
2016	**$118,500**	**No limit**	**6.20%**	**1.45%**	**12.40%**	**2.9%**
2017	$127,200	No limit	6.20%	1.45%	12.40%	2.9%

Insurance

The cost of regular term and permanent life insurance (whole, universal, etc.), paid by the employer is a taxable fringe benefit if the minister names the beneficiary of his choosing. Any premium paid for group term life insurance **over $50,000** coverage is also taxable. The Table from Reg. 1.79-3(d)(2), shown on page 18, is to be used to compute the amount to be included in an employee's income, even though the employer's actual premium may be more or less.

Housing

Sec 107 housing: We recommend that the dual-status minister "over estimate" his parsonage allowance that is required to be designated in advance by his employer. When filing the tax return, any unused parsonage allowance becomes taxable income and is to be entered on Form 1040, line 7, as "excess parsonage allowance." Both the value of a parsonage provided and/or a parsonage allowance are subject to social security and medicare tax, unless the minister has become exempt by filing Form 4361.

Sec 119 housing: The lay employee who is provided living quarters that are not on the premises of the employer, nor for the convenience of the employer, nor a requirement of the job, must show as taxable income the value of the living quarters provided. This value is also subject to social security tax. (Sec. 119 qualifications are not met.) (See discussion of Sec. 119 housing on page 35 of this Chapter)

Non-Accountable Allowances

If you are paid a non-accountable expense allowance or reimbursement and are not required to submit your records and receipts to your employer, the income has to be shown on your Form W-2, Box 1. For example: when an employee receives $400 a month for his auto expenses and is not required by a written accountable plan to submit a mileage log to his employer as substantiation, the auto allowance must be reported on Form W-2, Box 1.

It is very important to establish a written accountable reimbursement plan and "adequately account" to your employer in order not to lose some or all of the deduction for your professional expenses. A complete discussion of how to establish an accountable reimbursement plan is in Chapter Three.

Personal Use of Auto Provided by Employer

Strict regulations require the **value of personal use** of an employer owned auto to be included in the W-2 as a taxable fringe benefit. The amount to be included in income is to be reduced by any amount the employee pays the employer for the taxable fringe benefit. (See complete discussion in Chapter Three.)

Non-Taxable Sources of Income—Exclusions

Fringe Benefits

Gross income, for tax purposes, includes all income from whatever source unless specifically excluded by an Internal Revenue Code Section. Many code sections provide rules on how to establish **qualified tax-free** fringe benefits. Any **non-qualified** fringe benefits provided by an employer are taxable fringe benefits that must be included as wages on Form W-2, box 1. Before establishing employee fringe benefits that are **subject to nondiscrimination rules**, seek the assistance of a benefits specialist or a TPA. With congressional changes happening often, existing plans must be continually examined and revised to meet new requirements.

Fringe benefits are available for either dual-status or lay employees of nonprofit employers and employees of for-profit employers. Providing qualified fringe benefits in an employee's "pay package" reduces the base upon which both income tax and social security tax are paid.

To be qualified, most fringe benefit options must meet nondiscrimination tests. **There is one fringe benefit that is free from the nondiscrimination tests for church employers.** If provided for some of the staff but not everyone on staff, it is still a tax-free fringe benefit for the recipient employee: That tax-free fringe benefit is certain church plans providing **group term** life insurance to employees.

The **Affordable Care Act** has completely changed the tax-free treatment of employer provided medical insurance. See complete discussion later in this Chapter.

Group Term Life Insurance

An **exemption** from the **nondiscrimination rules** of Sec. 79 applies to certain church plans providing group term life insurance to employees. Premiums paid by an employer for group term life insurance on the first **$50,000** coverage are not to be included in income according to Sec. 79. Any coverage for group term life insurance over $50,000 is taxable. Use the Table from Reg. 1.79-3(d)(2) to compute the amount to be included in an employee's income, even though the employer's actual premium may be more or less.

The only time premiums paid by the employer for regular term or Permanent life insurance are not taxable is when the employer is named as beneficiary.

Cost Per $1,000 of group term life insurance protection for 1-Month Period Reg. 1.79-3(d)(2)	
Age	Cost
Under 25	5¢
25 through 29	6¢
30 through 34	8¢
35 through 39	9¢
40 through 44	10¢
45 through 49	15¢
50 through 54	23¢
55 through 59	43¢
60 through 64	66¢
65 through 69	$1.27
70 and above	$2.06

Accident And Health Plans & The Effect of ACA

In the area of employer provided medical insurance and other medical plans the Affordable Care Act has produced volumes of changes and regulations. For churches and small businesses, many of the changes were effective on January 1, 2014.

Our limited discussion of the fringe benefit provisions of health insurance, HDHPs, HSAs, HRAs, and Cafeteria plans with FSAs, is but a small fraction of the ambiguous massive law and regulations produced by the Congress and the IRS.

PAST HISTORY: Rev. Ruling 61-146 and Rev. Ruling 2002-3 allowed an employer to reimburse an employee for premiums for an individual health insurance policy as a tax free fringe benefit.

The basic IRS Code Sec. 106 reads the same:

106(a)General Rule.—Except as otherwise provided in this section, gross income of an employee does not include employer-provided coverage under an accident or health plan.

This is an arrangement that provides benefits for your employees, their spouses, their dependents, and their children (under age 27) in the event of personal injury or sickness. The plan may be insured or self-insured by an employer.

Employers of two or more full-time employees:

According to IRS Notice 2013-54, beginning in 2014, The Affordable Care Act does **not allow** an employer of two (2) or more full-time employees to reimburse them for insurance obtained on the marketplace exchange or for any individual policy. Employers of two (2) or more full-time employees must obtain **group insurance coverage**.

When the group insurance coverage is an HDHP (High Deductible Health Plan) that is **qualified** for establishing an HSA (Health Savings Account), the employer can also contribute to the HSAs of their employees. Some HDHP plans however are not qualified to establish an HSA. So it is important to inform your agent that you want a qualified HDHP.

With the help of a benefits specialist or TPA, an employer that provides group insurance coverage (that is not a HDHP plan) can provide an integrated HRA. An HRA is not treated as integrated with other employer primary health coverage unless the HRA is available only to employees who are actually enrolled in the employer-provided primary group health plan coverage.

Because of the Affordable Care Act, an arrangement that reimburses employees (two or more) for insurance obtained on the marketplace or any individual policy fails to satisfy the market reforms. **Employers may be subject to a $100/day excise tax per applicable employee (which is $36,500 per year, per employee) under section 4980D of the Internal Revenue Code.** Fortunately, Notice 2015-17 provided limited transition relief for coverage provided by an employer of less than 50 full-time employees. The effective date of the $100 a day excise tax per employee was changed from January 1, 2014 to after June 30, 2015.

If an employer of two (2) or more full-time employees wishes to increase the employee's salary so they can pay for their own coverage, they **must not say in writing** that the reason for the increase is to pay for insurance. An employer can simply pay the employee additional compensation without any requirement that the amount be used for insurance premiums. The employee must be free to do with the extra compensation whatever they choose. The employee, in losing a wonderful tax-free fringe benefit will experience considerable increase in income tax and 15.3% social security tax if he does not have an approved Form 4361.

Employers of one full-time employee:

Code Sec 9831(a)(2) states that the Affordable Care Act does not apply when there is less than 2 full-time employees. Therefore, when an employer has only one full-time employee, Rev. Ruling 61-146 is still applicable. The reimbursement for premiums on an individual policy can be treated as a tax-free fringe benefit. **Medicare B, D, and a supplement premium are considered individual plans, not group. Therefore they can be reimbursed by an employer of one full-time employee.**

An employer can reimburse for the premiums of the individual policy without a plan document. An employer of one full-time employee is allowed to establish a **"One Person" HRA written plan** that can reimburse for qualified medical expenses such as co-payments, deductibles and individual health insurance premiums. (Technical Release No. 2013-03) The cost of paying a benefit specialist or a TPA for establishing and maintaining the plan for one employee can be greater than the tax savings of being reimbursed for the additional medical expenses.

- ### Retired Employee Reimbursement

An employer's continuation of health care plan coverage for an employee that is laid off or retired is tax free, according to Rev. Rul. 62-199 & Technical Release N0. 2013-03. Medical coverage provided to the family of a deceased employee is tax free since it is treated as a continuation of the employee's fringe-benefit package. If you are age 65 or older, Medicare premiums and supplemental policies paid or reimbursed to you by your former employer qualifies as a "tax free" fringe benefit. A stand-alone HRA plan may be created just for retirees to reimburse all or certain eligible Code § 213 medical expenses of the retirees.

- ### *Discrimination Testing coming for Sec. 106*

The Affordable Care Act contains a new nondiscrimination requirement for insured group health plans that potentially applies to all employers, regardless of the number of employees. According to **IRS Notice 2011-1** the IRS, DOL and HHS collectively stated that they **would not require compliance** with this rule "until after regulations or other administrative guidance or general applicability has been issued." **No regulations have been issued to date.** In the notice announcing the enforcement delay, the IRS promised that there would be ample time to come into compliance once final rules are issued. When this new nondiscrimination rule becomes effective, any employer that sponsors an insured group health plan for its employees could be subject to substantial monetary penalties if the insured plan improperly discriminates in favor of certain highly-paid employees.

Self-insured medical reimbursement plans have been required to be nondiscriminatory since 1978. Sec. 105(h)

- ### *Fraternal Medical Co-ops - Affordable Care Act provides a waiver for Co-ops!!*

This approach satisfies the **individual mandate** in the recent Federal Health care law (Compilation of Patient Protection and Affordable Care Act (May 2010)Sec. 1501, page 148 or Sec. 5000A (d)(2)(B))" To constitute as a health care sharing ministry — and therefore be exempt from the Affordable Care Act requirements — the nonprofit has to have been in existence since 1999. They must also have an independent accounting firm conduct a publicly available annual audit.

Because the Affordable Care Act is anything but affordable and the Federal Exchange or marketplace **is proving to lack security for your personal information**, it is advisable to participate in a healthcare sharing ministry. Obtain information from the four Co-op's websites. They are available for individuals who attend worship services 75% of the time and commit to living a Christian lifestyle. Members of your congregation who are self-employed or do not have employer provided coverage can participate

Fraternal form of non-insurance carriers, such as The Christian Care Ministry (**www.mychristiancare.org**), Samaritan Ministries (**www.samaritanministries.org**), Christian Health Care Ministries (**www.chministries. org**), Liberty Health Share **(www.libertyhealthshare.org)**, etc, are not incorporated under state insurance laws as are insurance companies. Being an "Accident and Health Plan" that reimburses participants for actual hospital and medical expenses, according to Sec. 106(a), the share amounts have the same tax treatment as payments for insured plans.

When paid by an employed individual that is not reimbursed, share amounts are Sch A Medical deduction. When paid by a self-employed individual, share amounts are an adjustment on Form 1040. Ministers are employees and **do not qualify** for the adjustment on Form 1040, line 29.

Employers of one full-time employee may reimburse the employee for their share amount as a tax-free fringe benefit. The ACA Market Reforms do not apply.

Employers of two or more full-time employees cannot reimburse for the individual share amounts. Of the four co-ops listed above, Christian Health Care Ministries (www.chministries.org) provides membership in CHM Gold + Brother's keeper that mostly satisfies ACA mandates. They have an Employee Benefit Attorney that has developed a group health plan that meets the guidelines of the Affordable Care Act.

The share amounts are definitely not allowable as a contribution deduction on Sch A. If the Co-op publishes needs for individuals that are not covered, and when a participant "gifts" an extra payment for those needs, it would qualify for Sch A contribution deduction.

According to Samaritan Ministries "If you are a committed Christian, you do not have to violate your faith by purchasing health insurance from a company that pays for abortions and other unbiblical medical practices. You can live consistently with your beliefs by sharing medical needs directly with fellow believers through a non-insurance approach."

HSA - Health Savings Accounts & HDHP - High Deductible Health Plans

Health Savings Accounts are relatively untouched by The Affordable Care Act. Accordingly, HDHPs remain not only viable, but a very effective way of helping employers curtail the growth in the costs of their benefit plans. The passing of the Affordable Care Act, appears to be accelerating the speed at which large employers are moving away from more traditional major medical coverage.

An individual HDHP plan is available on marketplace exchanges or from an insurance company. Some HDHP plans however are not **qualified** to establish an HSA. So it is important to inform your agent that you want a **qualified** HDHP. Read your policy statement. If it is qualified for an HSA, it will be stated on the policy.

IRS Publication 969 is the best resource for HSAs information. Since 2004, Health Savings Accounts (HSAs), designed to help individuals save for future qualified medical and retiree health expenses on a tax-free basis have been available according to Sec. 223. A HSA is a tax-exempt trust or custodial account that you set up with a qualified HSA trustee to pay or reimburse certain medical expenses you incur. A qualified HSA trustee can be a mutual fund, bank, insurance company, or anyone already approved by the IRS to be a trustee of individual retirement arrangements (IRAs).

To be an eligible individual and qualify for an HSA, you must:

1. have a qualified high deductible health plan on the first day of the month.
2. have no other health coverage except long term care, vision care, dental care, or disability. Participation in a health Flexible Spending Arrangements (FSA) or a Health Reimbursement Arrangement (HRA) generally prevents an individual from making contributions to a HSA.
3. not be enrolled in Medicare.
4. not be claimed as a dependent on someone else's tax return.

When an employer provides a HDHP for an employee, contributions to the employee's HSA can be made by the employer or the employee, or both.

Employment Taxes: Amounts contributed by the employer directly or amounts the employee elected to contribute through a cafeteria plan are not subject to employment taxes. The employer's activity will be included on the employee's Form W-2, Box 12 with code W. Amounts contributed directly by the employee are an adjustment on page 1 of Form 1040, and thus not subject to income tax. However they do not reduce Social Security and Medicare tax liability.

An eligible individual or family can establish both a qualified HDHP and an HSA for themselves. Each spouse who is an eligible individual who wants an HSA must open a separate HSA. You cannot have a joint HSA.

Amounts contributed to an HSA belong to individuals and are completely portable. Every year the money not spent will stay in the account and gain earnings tax-free, similar to an IRA. Unused amounts remain available for later years

Distributions from an HSA reported on Form 1099-SA **are tax free** when used to pay for qualifying medical expenses. **Form 8889** must be included with your Form 1040 showing **all activity**. Report deductible contributions made as an individual and by your employer. If you receive distributions for other reasons, the amount you withdraw will be subject to income tax and may be subject to an additional 20% tax.

Qualified medical expenses that HSAs can be used for are those expenses that would generally qualify for the medical and dental expenses deduction. Examples include amounts paid for doctors' fees, prescription medicines and necessary hospital services not paid for by insurance. After December 31, 2010, according to Section 9003 of the Affordable Care Act, only prescribed medicines or drugs (including over-the-counter medicines and drugs that are prescribed) and insulin (even if purchased without a prescription) will be considered qualifying medical expenses. Dietary supplements that are merely beneficial to general health **are not** reimbursable.

HSA Contribution Limits

	2016	2017
HDHP Minimum Deductible Amount		
Individual	$ 1,300	$ 1,300
Family	$ 2,600	$ 2,600
HDHP Maximum Out-of-Pocket Amount		
Individual	$ 6,550	$ 6,550
Family	$13,100	$13,100
HSA Statutory Contribution Amount		
Individual	$ 3,350	$ 3,400
Family	$ 6,750	$ 6,750
Catch-Up Contributions (age 55 or older)	$ 1,000	$ 1,000

Most plans obtained by individuals on the marketplace are HDHP plans. Carefully choosing a HDHP plan that is qualified for an HSA account will have two possible tax advantages. (1) An employer cannot contribute to the employee's HSA directly, but can pay the employee extra salary. When the employee contributes to his HSA, he will have an adjustment which **lowers the AGI** on his tax return. (2) Depending on the size of the employee's family and his AGI, if he qualifies for a subsidy, it will be greater.

Health Reimbursement Arrangements - (HRA)

Under a health reimbursement arrangement (HRA), an employer funds an account for employees from which employees are reimbursed tax free for qualified medical expenses up to a maximum dollar amount for a coverage period. Under the arrangement, the HRA: (1) is paid for solely by the employer and not provided through a salary reduction arrangement or cafeteria plan; (2) reimburses the employee for medical care expenses incurred by the employee and the employee's spouse and dependents; and (3) provides reimbursements up to a maximum dollar amount for a coverage period with any unused portion of the maximum dollar amount carried forward to increase the maximum reimbursement available in later coverage periods. HRAs are excludable from an employee's gross income.

HRAs generally are considered to be group health plans within the meaning of Code § 9832(a), § 733(a) of the Employee Retirement Income Security Act of 1974 (ERISA), and § 2791(a) of the Public Health Service Act (PHS Act) and are subject to the rules applicable to group health plans. **Therefore, your plan document for an HRA must be drafted by a benefits specialist or a TPA to include compliance with all of the departments requirements**.

Beginning in 2014, The Department of Labor states that an HRA with 2+ participants must be "integrated" with a group health plan such that the combined benefit meets the requirements of the Affordable Care Act. An HRA that is offered apart from group health insurance (a "standalone" HRA") does not comply.

One-person HRA plans may continue to reimburse for qualified medical expenses such as co-payments, deductibles, and personal health insurance premiums. The ACA Market Reforms only apply to HRAs with 2+ participants. (Technical Release 2013-03) However, the cost of establishing a one-person HRA may not be cost effective.

After December 31, 2010, according to Section 9003 of the Affordable Care Act, only prescribed medicines or drugs (including over-the-counter medicines and drugs that are prescribed) and insulin (even if purchased without a prescription) will be considered qualifying medical expenses.

Effective for 2017: New Law Allows Small Employers to Pay Premiums for Individual Policies. On November 30, 2016, the House of Representatives passed H.R. 34, the 21st Century Cures Act. The Small Business Healthcare Relief Act (SBHRA) was contained within the 21st Century Cures Act in Section 18001. The Senate passed this legislation on December 7, 2016. The President signed on December 13, 2016. Small employers, less than 50 full-time employees, can use Health Reimbursement Arrangements to assist employees with individual health insurance and related medical costs. Benefits can not exceed $4,950 for single coverage or $10,000 for family coverage. Employees who obtain an individual policy from the marketplace, and receive a subsidy, will have their subsidy reduced by the amount an SBHRA reimburses them.

Relief from the ACA $100 a day penalty for small employers: There's transition relief retroactive for all plan years beginning on or before December 31, 2016 that the onerous $100 a day penalties announced by the IRS in Notice 2015-17 are no longer in effect.

Sec. 125 - Cafeteria Plans

A cafeteria plan, including a flexible spending arrangement (FSA), is a written plan that allows your employees to choose between receiving cash or taxable benefits instead of certain qualified benefits for which the law provides an exclusion from wages. If an employee chooses to receive a qualified benefit under the plan, the fact that the employee could have received cash or a taxable benefit instead will not make the qualified benefit taxable. An employee can generally exclude from gross income up to $5,000 salary reduction for benefits.

A cafeteria plan is a separate written benefit plan maintained by an employer or a third party administrator. Both employers and employees receive significant tax savings. For plan years beginning after December 31, 2012, a cafeteria plan may not allow an employee to make salary reduction contributions to a health flexible spending arrangement (FSA) in excess of **$2,550** for 2016 The dollar limitation is adjusted annually for inflation and is $2,600 for 2017.

A plan must offer both a cash benefit and at least one statutory nontaxable benefit. Nontaxable benefits include accident and health benefits, flexible spending arrangements (FSA), group term life insurance up to $50,000 coverage, dependent care assistance, adoption assistance, disability benefits, and group legal services.

Benefits are of the **"use it or lose it"** nature and therefore should be set conservatively. A plan may allow either a grace period or a carryover, but it cannot allow both. The plan can provide for a grace period of up to 2½ months after the end of the plan year or allow up to $500 of unused amounts remaining at the end of the plan year to be paid or reimbursed for qualified medical expenses you incur in the following plan year.

Since 2011, eligible employers meeting contribution requirements and eligibility and participation requirements can establish a simple cafeteria plan. Simple cafeteria plans are treated as meeting the nondiscrimination requirements of a cafeteria plan and certain benefits under a cafeteria plan according to Sec. 125(j).

Caution: Reimbursing an employee for the extra medical expenses typically not covered by an insurance policy, without an established Sec. 125 Cafeteria plan in place, results in taxable income for the employee. **It is wise to seek the assistance** of an benefits specialist or a TPA to draft a qualified Cafeteria plan.

The Patient Protection and Affordable Care Act (March 23, 2010) and

The Health Care and Education Reconciliation Act of 2010 (March 30, 2010)

Beginning in 2014, the IRS began to play a pivotal role in the administration and implementation of healthcare reform. The IRS has undergone massive internal changes that are necessary for this undertaking. Much of the healthcare reform is being phased in over a period of years with changes and delays on the fly. The IRS website has questions and answers on several portions of health care reform. As regulations are developed by the IRS, there has been more guidance at this website:

http://www.irs.gov/uac/Affordable-Care-Act-Tax-Provisions

● *A Supreme Court Case -King v. Burwell*

On June 25, 2015, in a 6-3 ruling, the Court rejected the ACA's challengers' arguments. In an opinion authored by Chief Justice Roberts, the Court held that tax credits are available to individuals in states that utilize a federally-facilitated Exchange. With this ruling, the Court affirmed the understanding of the ACA that has been held by state governments and members of Congress since the Act's inception—that tax credits are available to eligible citizens for insurance purchased on any Exchange created under the ACA, be it state-run or federally-facilitated.

● *Minimum Essential Health Benefits Required by ACA*

1. Outpatient care - the kind you get without being admitted to a hospital
2. Emergency services
3. Hospitalization
4. Maternity and newborn care
5. Mental health and substance use disorder services, including behavioral health treatment
6. Prescription drugs
7. Rehabilitative and habilitative services and devices
8. Laboratory services
9. Preventive and wellness services and chronic disease treatment
10. Pediatric services, including dental care and vision care for children under the age of 19.

● *Health Care Benefits Provided With Respect to Children Under Age 27*

The Affordable Care Act requires group health plans and health insurance issuers that provide dependent coverage of children to continue to make such coverage available for an adult child until age 26. This provision was implemented on September 23, 2010, effective on March 30, 2010. The new policy applies only to health insurance plans that offer dependent coverage in the first place: while most insurers and employer-sponsored plans offer dependent coverage, there is no requirement to do so.

The new policy providing access for young adults applies to both married and unmarried children. This provision includes a child of the employee who is not the employee's dependent within the meaning of § 152(a). Thus, the age limit, residency, support, and other tests described in § 152(c) do not apply with respect to such a child for purposes of § 105(b).

● *Catastrophic Health Plans (not sold on Market Place)*

To qualify for a catastrophic plan, you must be under 30 years old OR get a "hardship exemption" because the Marketplace determined that you're unable to afford health coverage. Catastrophic health insurance plans have low monthly premiums and a high deductible — $2,000 to $5,000. They may be an affordable way to protect yourself from worst-case scenarios, like getting seriously sick or injured. Catastrophic plans **are not eligible for subsidies**. Catastrophic plans cover 3 primary care visits per year, and certain preventive services, at no cost. Once the deductible is met, the catastrophic plan will cover the essential health benefits.

● *Healthcare Employer Insurance Reporting Requirements on Form W-2*

The Affordable Care Act requires employers to report the cost of coverage under an employer-sponsored group health plan. Employers that are subject to this requirement should report the value of the health care coverage in Box 12 of the Form W-2, with **Code DD** to identify the amount. There is no reporting on the Form W-3 of the total of these amounts for all the employer's employees. In general, the amount reported should include both the portion paid by the employer and the portion paid by the employee.

For more information, see the chart provided by the IRS at this website:

http://www.irs.gov/uac/Form-W-2-Reporting-of-Employer-Sponsored-Health-Coverage

The IRS released drafts of several new healthcare forms (and instructions) to help employers comply with the reporting requirements under the Affordable Care Act.

Form 1095-B, Health Coverage

Form 1095-C, Employer Provided Health Insurance Offer and Coverage

Form 1094-B, Transmittal of Health Coverage Information Returns

Form 1094-C, Transmittal of Employer-Provided Health Insurance Offer and Coverage Information Returns

Form 8941, Credit for Small Employer Health Insurance Premiums

• *Small Business Health Care Tax Credit*

The small business health care tax credit is designed to encourage both small businesses and small tax-exempt organizations to offer health insurance coverage to their employees for the first time or maintain coverage they already have. (Notice 2010-82)

Form 8941, Credit for Small Employer Health Insurance Premiums, and revised Form 990-T, are now available on IRS.gov. This IRS website is designed to help small employers correctly figure and claim the credit:

https://www.irs.gov/affordable-care-act/employers/small-business-health-care-tax-credit-and-the-shop-marketplace

Small businesses can claim the credit for 2010 through 2013 and for any two years after that. For tax years 2010 to 2013, the maximum credit was 35 percent of premiums paid by eligible small businesses and 25 percent of premiums paid by eligible tax-exempt organizations. Within three years statute of limitations, amended returns can be filed.

Beginning in 2014, the maximum tax credit increased to 50 percent of premiums paid by eligible small business employers and 35 percent of premiums paid by eligible tax-exempt organizations. The credit is available to eligible employers for two consecutive taxable years. However, **you have to purchase insurance through the SHOP Marketplace** (or qualify for an exception to this requirement) to be eligible for the credit for tax years 2014 and beyond.

The maximum credit goes to smaller employers, those with 10 or fewer full-time equivalent (FTE) employees, paying annual average wages of $25,000 or less. The credit is completely phased out for employers that have 25 or more FTEs or that pay average wages of $50,000 or more per year. Because the eligibility rules are based in part on the number of FTEs, not the number of employees, employers that use part-time workers may qualify even if they employ more than 25 individuals.

Eligible small businesses will first use Form 8941 to figure the credit and then include the amount of the credit as part of the general business credit on its income tax return.

Tax-exempt organizations will first use Form 8941 to figure their refundable credit, and then claim the credit on Line 44f of Form 990-T. Though primarily filed by those organizations liable for the tax on unrelated business income, Form 990-T will also be used by any eligible tax-exempt organization to claim the credit, regardless of whether they are subject to this tax.

Subject to sequestration, refund payments processed on or after Oct. 1, 2014, and on or before Sept. 30, 2015, issued to a tax-exempt taxpayer claiming the Small Business Health Care Tax Credit under section 45R will be reduced by the fiscal year 2015 sequestration rate of 7.3 percent.

• *Medicare Tax Changes*

Effective on January 1, 2013, the following medicare tax changes occurred:

(1) **3.8%** Medicare tax on net investment income if modified adjusted gross income (MAGI) exceeds $200,000 (or $250,000 for joint filers). In general, investment income includes, but is not limited to: interest, dividends, capital gains, rental and royalty income, non-qualified annuities, income from businesses involved in trading of financial instruments or commodities and businesses that are passive activities to the taxpayer (within the meaning of section 469). IRS states, "Amounts collected under section 1411 are not designated for the Medicare Trust Fund". Thus the word "Medicare" in the name of this tax provision is misleading. A better name for this tax provision would be the Net Investment Income Tax, which is the phrase used by the IRS on tax Form 8960.

(2) **0.9%** increase to the current 1.45% (2.35% total) in medicare taxes on earned income, including net self-employment income. The income threshold amounts are $250,000 for married taxpayers who file jointly, $125,000 for married taxpayers who file separately and $200,000 for all other taxpayers. An employer is responsible for withholding the Additional Medicare Tax of 0.9% from wages or compensation it pays to an employee in excess of $200,000 in a calendar year.

- **Changes to Itemized Deduction for Medical Expenses**

Beginning Jan. 1, 2013, you can claim deductions for medical expenses not covered by your health insurance when they reach **10%** of your adjusted gross income. There is a temporary exemption from Jan. 1, 2013, to Dec. 31, 2016, for individuals age 65 and older and their spouses who can continue to use the **7.5%** limitation. For 2017 and subsequent years, taxpayers age 65 and over will be subject to the same 10% AGI threshold as all other taxpayers.

- **Individual Responsibility Mandate - Form 8965 and Instructions**

The Patient Protection and Affordable Care Act added Sec. 5000A. It states that every applicable individual must obtain minimum essential coverage for themselves and their dependents or pay a penalty. It became effective January 1, 2014. Applicable penalties are calculated as additional tax on the individual's Form 1040 starting with the 2014 tax year. **Form 8965 must be completed for each member of the tax household.** All the IRS can do to collect an unpaid mandate tax is to offset a tax refund otherwise owed to a taxpayer.

2014, the penalty, or tax, was the **greater of**
- (a) a per-person tax of $95 per adult and $47.50 per child, up to a maximum of $285, **or**
- (b) 1 percent of income above filing threshold.

2015, the penalty, or tax, was the **greater of**
- (a) a per-person tax of $325 per adult and $162.50 per child, up to a maximum of $975, **or**
- (b) 2 percent of income above filing threshold.

2016, the penalty, or tax, is the **greater of**
- (a) a per-person tax of $695 per adult and $347.50 per child, up to a maximum of $2,085, **or**
- (b) 2.5 percent of income above filing threshold.

2017, the penalty, or tax, will be the **greater of**
- (a) **(adjusted for inflation)** a per-person tax of $695 per adult and $347.50 per child, up to a maximum of $2,085, **or**
- (b) **(adjusted for inflation)** 2.5 percent of income above filing threshold.

All persons are applicable individuals for each month unless one of the following exemptions applies:

(1) Religious conscience. Religious Order members who have filed Form 4029. You are a member of a religious sect that is recognized as conscientiously opposed to accepting any insurance benefits. The Social Security Administration administers the process for recognizing these sects according to the criteria in the law. (Must obtain an Exemption Certificate Number from the Marketplace)

(2) **Health care sharing ministry.** You are a member of a recognized health care sharing ministry. Such as The Christian Care Ministry (www.mychristiancare.org), Samaritan Ministries (www.samaritan-ministries.org), Christian Health Care Ministries (www.chministries.org), Liberty Health Share (www.libertyhealthshare.org).

(3) Indian tribes. You are a member of a federally recognized Indian tribe.

(4) Income below the filing threshold — Your gross income or your household income was less than your applicable minimum threshold for filing a tax return.

(5) Short coverage gap. You went without coverage for less than **three consecutive months** during the year.

(6) Coverage considered unaffordable — The minimum amount you would have paid for premiums is more than 8% of your household income

(7) Incarceration. You are in a jail, prison, or similar penal institution or correctional facility after the disposition of charges against you.

(8) Citizens living abroad - qualify for either physical presence or bona fide residency. Not a U.S. citizen, not a U.S. national, and not an individual lawfully present in the U.S.

(9) **HHS Hardship Exemptions include: (Must obtain an Exemption Certificate Number from the Marketplace)** Homeless; evicted in past 6 months; received shut-off notice from a utility company; recently experienced domestic violence; death of close family member; experienced fire, flood or other natural or human-caused disasters; filed for bankruptcy in last 6 months; unable to pay medical expenses in last 24 months; unexpected increase in necessary expenses due to caring for ill, disabled, or aging family member; dependent child denied coverage; eligible appeals decision; ineligible for Medicaid; current health insurance plan cancelled; and another hardship in obtaining health insurance.

• *Premium Assistance Credit or Subsidies - Form 8962*

The Premium Assistance Credit (PAC) is a refundable income tax credit available on a sliding scale basis to qualifying taxpayers with household incomes between 100% and 400% of the federal poverty guidelines for the family size involved and who **do not receive** coverage through either the taxpayer's employer or the spouse's employer.

The **good news** for dual-status ministers is that value of parsonages provided and/or parsonage allowance used, **is not to be added** to the Adjusted Gross Income, and will qualify them for more Premium Assistance Credit.

Household income is defined as the sum of:

(1)   the taxpayer's modified adjusted gross income, plus

(2)   the aggregate modified adjusted gross incomes of **all other individuals** taken into account in determining that taxpayer's family size (but only if such individuals are required to file a tax return for the tax year) (Code Sec. 36B(d)(2)(A); Reg. Sec. 1.36B-1(e)(1)).

Modified adjusted gross income is defined as adjusted gross income increased by:

(1) the amount (if any) normally excluded by Code Sec. 911;

(2) any tax-exempt interest received or accrued during the tax year; and

(3) an amount equal to the portion of the taxpayer's social security benefits which is not included in gross income.

When you get health insurance through the marketplace, and qualify for advance payments of the Premium Assistance Credit, the credit goes directly to your insurer. The remaining lower premium is all you personally pay for. For any tax year, if you receive advance credit payments in any amount or if you plan to claim the premium tax credit, you **must file a federal income tax return for that year**.

When you file your tax return, you will subtract the total advance payments you received during the year from the amount of the premium tax credit calculated on your tax return. If the premium tax credit computed on the return is more than the advance payments made on your behalf during the year, the difference will increase your refund or lower the amount of tax you owe. If the advance credit payments are more than the premium tax credit, the difference will increase the amount you owe and result in either a smaller refund or a balance due. The amount you'll have to pay back depends on your 2016 family income. If your 2016 income is below 400% of the federal poverty level, there is a cap on the amount you'll have to pay back, even if you received more in assistance than the amount of the cap. However, at higher income levels, you'll have to pay back the entire amount you received. See FPL chart @ **http://familiesusa.org/product/federal-poverty-guidelines**

	Single	All other statuses
Less than 200% of Federal Poverty Line	$300	$600
At least 200%, but less than 300% of FPL	$750	$1,500
At least 300%, but less than 400% of FPL	$1,250	$2,500
400% or more of FPL	No Limit	No Limit

• *Applicable Large Employer (ALE) Mandate*

The Affordable Care Act employer mandate/employer penalty, originally was set to begin in 2014. The employer mandate began in 2015 for employers of 100 or more full time equivalent (FTE) employees. The employer mandate begins in 2016 for employers of 50 or more full time equivalent (FTE) employees. The employer mandate is a requirement that all businesses with over 50 full-time equivalent (FTE) employees provide health insurance that meets minimum value for 95% of their full-time employees, or pay a per month "Employer Shared Responsibility Payment" on their federal tax return. The employer will determine its status as an applicable large employer using the rules that generally apply (that is, based on the number of full-time employees and full-time equivalents that the employer employed in the preceding year). The FTE calculation is essentially a formula for converting part-time employees into hypothetical full-time employees. The hours of the part-time employees are used solely for purposes of determining whether an employer meets the ALE requirements. Even if an employer is classified as an ALE, the employer is only required to offer health plan coverage to its full-time employees. It is not required to offer coverage to its part-time employees.

Under the Employer Shared Responsibility provisions, if an ALE employer does not offer affordable health coverage that provides a minimum level of coverage to their full-time employees (and their dependents), the employer may be subject to an Employer Shared Responsibility payment if at least one of its full-time employees receives a premium tax credit for purchasing individual coverage on the individual Marketplace.

Employers with over 50 employees but less than 100 can obtain their employee health insurance using **SHOP** (Small Businesses Health Options Marketplace).

If insurance isn't offered by an ALE the annual mandate penalty is **$2,000** per employee (the first 30 full-time employees are exempt).So an employer with fifty workers that doesn't provide insurance will be fined $2,000 x (50-30) = $40,000. An employer with 100 employees will be fined $2,000 x (100-30) = $140,000.

If at least one full-time employee receives a premium tax credit because coverage is either unaffordable or does not cover 60 percent of total costs, the employer must pay the lesser of $3,000 for each of those employees receiving a credit or $750 for each of their full-time employees total.

The shared responsibility payment for employers not offering coverage is referred to as the Sec. 4980H(a) penalty. Unlike employer contributions to employee premiums, the Employer Shared Responsibility Payment is **not tax deductible**. The IRS will contact employers to inform them of their potential liability and provide them an opportunity to respond before any liability is assessed or notice and demand for payment is made. Employers will not be required to include the Employer Shared Responsibility payment on any tax return that they file.

The ACA has fundamentally changed the health care landscape, affecting premiums, small business wages, and employment.

• *HIPAA - Health Insurance Portability and Accountability Act of 1996*

HIPAA provided for improved access, portability and renewability of health insurance coverage. A good by-product of HIPAA was that **pre-existing condition exclusions are reduced** by the employee's period of creditable coverage as of the enrollment date, so long as the person does not have more than a 63-day break in coverage.

The Administrative Simplification provisions of the Affordable Care Act of 2010 (ACA), build on the Health Insurance Portability and Accountability Act of 1996 (HIPAA) with several new, expanded, or revised provisions.

Disability Insurance

Premiums for disability insurance paid by the employer are not taxable income according to Sec. 105(e). The income from a disability plan provided by the employer is taxable as sick pay. Either the employer or the third party payor must report benefits as salary on Form W-2, subject to the appropriate withholding requirements. Benefits received by a dual-status minister will be subject to social security on Schedule SE, unless he is exempt as an individual.

However, if the **employee pays** the premium for a private disability insurance policy, the cost of the premium is not deductible, and the income from the plan is **not taxable**.

Qualified Moving Reimbursement

Unreimbursed qualified moving expenses to move the family when there is a change of job location is an above-the-line deduction subtracted from gross income in arriving at adjusted gross income under Sec. 62(a). Reimbursed qualified moving expenses from an employer **with** an accountable plan are excludable from an employee's gross income as a qualified fringe benefit under Sec. 132(a)(6). Reimbursed qualified moving expenses from an employer **without** an accountable plan are to be included in an employee's gross income. The employee can then deduct the qualified moving expenses as an adjustment. Having an accountable plan for moving reimbursement requires the same three rules that are discussed fully in Chapter Three for reimbursed professional expenses.

Qualified moving expenses are limited to the reasonable cost of:
1. Moving household goods and personal effects from the former residence to the new residence; (includes cost of packing, crating, transporting your goods; also includes the cost of storing and insuring your goods for any period of 30 consecutive days after the day your things are moved from your former home), and
2. Traveling, including lodging during the period of travel from the former residence to the new place of residence. Auto travel can be the actual gas and oil expenses for the trip or the **2016** IRS mileage allowance for moving **19¢**. (2017 - 17¢) You can add parking fees and tolls to the amount claimed under either method. Use travel expenses for only one trip for yourself and members of your household. However, all of you do not have to travel together or at the same time.

The following costs of moving are unqualified and **nondeductible**: meals, temporary living expenses, pre-move house hunting trips, expenses of sale or lease of a home, and expenses of purchase or lease of a home. An employer reimbursement to an employee for costs of moving that are not allowable is taxable salary and must be reported on Form W-2.

Two requirements of **Sec. 217** must be met for moving expenses to be allowable. The new place of work must be at least **50 miles** farther from the former home than was the former place of work. Employment in the new area must be full-time for **39 weeks** during the 12 month period immediately following the move.

Self-employed persons must be working 78 weeks during a 24-month period immediately following the move. **Employed ministers** are subject to the 39 week work requirement.

If the employer expects the employee to satisfy the 50 mile and 39 weeks of work requirements for deduction, the allowable moving reimbursement is not subject to income tax withholding or social security. Dual-status ministers and lay employees do not pay social security on allowable moving reimbursements.

If the employer knows that the requirements of Sec. 217 **will not be met**, the nonqualifying moving reimbursement is subject to both income tax and social security tax withholding for the lay employee. Nonqualifying moving expense reimbursement paid to a dual-status minister is subject to income tax and social security tax and the additional tax liability should be included in his estimate or optional withholding.

Educational Assistance Programs

An educational assistance program is a plan established and maintained by an employer under which the employer provides educational assistance to employees. Education expenses that improve or develop the capabilities of an individual, not limited to courses that are job related or part of a degree program, qualify under Sec. 127. The annual excludable amount for educational assistance is **$5,250**.

Since 2013 Sec. 127 exclusion was made permanent. Since 2001 graduate level courses qualify for the exclusion.

Notice in **Chapter Three that educational expenses that are job related** can be reimbursed by an employer as business expenses or deductible on Schedule A if unreimbursed.

Qualified Tuition Reduction

Employees of qualified educational organizations described in **Sec. 170(b)(1)(A)(ii)** can exclude from gross income qualified tuition reduction, including cash grants. An educational organization is described in Sec. 170(b)(1)(A)(ii) has as its primary function the presentation of formal instruction, and it normally maintains a regular faculty and curriculum and normally has a regularly enrolled body of pupils or students in attendance at the place where its educational activities are regularly carried on.

This fringe benefit is **not available** for any other type of nonprofit organizations according to Rev. Ruling 78-184. A church that provides tuition payments for employee's children must treat the payments as **a taxable fringe benefit**, as payment for services. (Private Letter Ruling 9226008)

According to **Sec. 117(d)(2)**, the exclusion applies to tuition for education provided at the employer's school as well as at any educational institution. The exclusion is limited to education below graduate level. A special rule applies to graduate students at eligible educational institutions who are engaged in teaching or research activities for the institution.

Qualified tuition reduction applies to: (1) an individual currently employed by the educational institution; (2) a person separated from service with the institution due to retirement or disability; (3) a widow or widower of an employee who died while employed by the institution, (4) spouses and dependent children of the above.

The nondiscrimination rules under Sec. 414(q) apply to a qualified tuition reduction plan.

Qualified Scholarships

While scholarships are typically provided to non-employees, we felt it important to include the following "non-fringe benefit" discussion, following the educational topics we have just discussed.

Sec. 117(a) provides for qualified scholarships given to degree candidates to be excluded from income to the extent amounts are used for "qualified tuition and related expenses." Related expenses include fees, books, supplies, and equipment required for courses of instruction. Additional amounts for room, board, or incidental expenses are not excludable. So that recipients understand their tax liabilities, they should be formally advised in writing that amounts granted for expenses incurred are taxable income if the total amount exceeds tuition and fees required for enrollment and related expenses according to IRS Notice 87-31. Add the taxable amount to any other amounts on Form 1040, line 7. Then write "SCH" and the taxable amount on the dotted line next to line 7.

To establish a private foundation that can grant qualified scholarships requires legal assistance. Rev. Procedure 76-47 and 80-39 (amplified by 94-78) establishes seven conditions and a percentage test or a facts and circumstances test for a qualified scholarship program. IRS Publication 4221-PF gives further guidance. The program must impose minimum eligibility requirements that limit the independent selection committee's consideration to those children of employees who meet the minimum standards for admission to an educational institution. No more than 10% of the program's recipients can be employee's children.

National Clergy Renewal Program - Lilly Endowment

Recognizing the importance and necessity for busy pastors to have an opportunity to take an extended break for renewal and refreshment, Lilly Endowment in 2000 introduced a competitive grants program. Annually the Lilly Endowment provides as many as 146 grants of up to $50,000 each. Applicants must be ordained and have an M.Div degree from a seminary accredited by ATS. Since 2012 the Lilly Endowment program is administered by Christian Theological Seminary, more information is available on their website:

www.cts.edu

The primary goal of the program is to ensure a period of rejuvenation for a pastor and congregation. Continuing education is not recommended. Therefore, the break for renewal is often planned to be of a personal nature. In the budget presented in the application, Lilly Endowment allows for up to $5,000 to be requested for the income tax and social security tax for the taxable personal nature of the grant. It is possible that a portion of the renewal break would be eligible for education or business expense reimbursement.

The employing church receives the grant. The employer is required to report the personal portion **as salary** on the minister's Form W-2.

Qualified Retirement Plan Contributions

For retirement plan purposes, the Internal Revenue Code **considers the salaried minister as an "employee."** It is important to inform your financial advisor of your correct status. There are qualified plans for employees and there are qualified plans for self-employed individuals. To establish the wrong qualified retirement plan will create "excess contributions" which are subject to 6% penalty each year, until withdrawn. An employer cannot establish and make contributions to more than one plan during a year.

The Employee Retirement Income Security Act of 1974 **(ERISA)** is a federal law that sets minimum standards for most voluntarily established pension and health plans in private industry to provide protection for individuals in these plans.

Distributions from qualified retirement plans to which contributions were based on wages earned while performing ministerial duties can be designated 100% as "housing allowance". To the extent the retired minister incurs housing expenses, distributions are tax-free. (See Suggested Wordings in Chapter Two)

• *Sec. 401(a) - Employer Qualified Retirement Plan*

A qualified pension, profit-sharing, or stock bonus plan is a definite written program and arrangement which is communicated to the employees and which is established and maintained by an employer. It has a vesting schedule and is expensive to establish and maintain. Many large corporations have abandoned their Sec. 401(a) plans and have set up Sec. 401(k) plans instead. Annual contributions in **2016** by an employer to a qualified retirement plan on the behalf of an employee cannot exceed the lesser of (1) **$53,000**, or an additional **$6,000** if age 50 or older by end of the year, or (2) 25% of the employee's compensation for the year. (2017 - $54,000 annually with an additional $6,000 available if age 50 or over by end of year.)

• *Sec. 401(k) - Salary Reduction*

Since 1997, nonprofit organizations are allowed to establish 401(k) or CODA plans. 401(k) plans **are subject** to nondiscrimination testing. The maximum amount that an employee can defer under all 401(k) plans in **2016** is 100% of compensation limited to **$18,000** annually, with an additional **$6,000** available if age 50 or over by end of year. (2017 - $18,000, with an additional $6,000 available if age 50 or over by end of year.)

• *Sec. 403(b) - Tax Sheltered Account (TSA)*

TSAs are available for employees of nonprofit organizations or public schools according to Sec. 403(b). IRS Publication 571 contains additional information on TSAs. An employee of a qualified organization can make an election to reduce their taxable salary and request that the employer make Non-ERISA (employee is always 100% vested) contributions to a Sec. 403(b) plan.

If a taxpayer continues to work after 70½, Sec. 403(b) accounts can receive contributions and are not required to begin distributions (RMD) until the calendar year in which the employee retires from employment, according to Reg. 1.403(b)-6(e)(3).

Salary reduction contributions to a TSA are not to be shown on the W-2 as income in Box 1. The amount of the contribution is required to be shown in Box 12, Form W-2 with the Code E.

Beginning in years after December 31, 1996, a self-employed minister (evangelist or chaplain) is treated as his own employer that is presumed to be an exempt organization eligible to participate on his behalf in a Sec. 403(b) plan. Ministers employed by non-exempt organizations can participate in Sec. 403(b) plans so long as their duties consist of the exercise of ministry. With the absence of a W-2, the amount of the contribution must be deducted on Form 1040, line 28.

Change in regulations: On July 23, 2007, the first comprehensive regulations for 403(b)s in 43 years were issued. The general effective date was extended for taxable years beginning after December 31, 2009. Previously, individuals controlled their accounts exclusively. Under the new regulations, 403(b)s are established and maintained by the employer. Employers are required to exercise greater oversight and management of their plans.

A 403(b) written plan document should contain all the terms and conditions for eligibility, benefits, limitations, the form and timing of distributions and contracts available under the plan and the party responsible for plan administration. However, church plans that do not contain any retirement income accounts are exempt from having a 403(b) written plan. A review of Mutual fund vendors found some who provide a written plan for churches and non-profit organizations, some who require a TPA or third party administrator, and some who no longer offer 403(b) plans.

There must be an information sharing agreement in place between the plan sponsor and their investment vendor. Vendors typically do not charge for this service.

Two methods of funding are provided in Sec. 403(b). An employer can provide a 403(b) plan that includes **both** ERISA contributions by the employer and Non-ERISA voluntary contributions made by the employee through a salary reduction plan. Or an employer can provide a 403(b) plan that includes either method of funding without the other.

Employer Contributions - ERISA (employee loses if not vested) can be made by the **employer** to a Sec. 403(b)(9) account on behalf of its employees. The maximum limit for a defined contribution plan applies (lesser of **$53,000** or 100% of pay). The cost to establish and administer this type of Sec. 403(b)(9) employer plan that must meet discrimination testing causes it to not be cost effective for an employer with a small staff.

Salary Reduction Contributions - Non-ERISA (employee is always 100% vested) can be made for the employee to a Sec. 403(b)(7) account established by the employer for voluntary salary reduction contributions. For **2016**, an employee can contribute up to 100% of compensation limited to **$18,000** annually, with an additional **$6,000** available if age 50 or over by end of year. (2017 - $18,000, with an additional $6,000 available if age 50 or over by end of year.)

According to **Rev. Ruling 65-208**, contributions are subject to social security tax and medicare tax for the lay employee and must be included on the W-2, Box 3 and Box 5.

According to **Rev. Ruling 68-395,** contributions to a TSA by a dual-status minister are not subject to social security. If you have paid social security on contributions to a TSA as a dual-status minister you should file amended returns for the open years and request a refund.

A Sec. 403(b)(7) retirement annuity or a Sec. 403(b)(7) mutual fund account can be established to accept only **Non-ERISA voluntary** salary reduction contributions. The employer is required to notify all of their employees that they have the opportunity to make voluntary salary reduction contributions to the 403(b)(7) plan. It is not necessary that they all choose to participate.

For tax years after 2005, a Sec. 403(b)(7) plan may include qualified **Roth contributions**. Qualified distributions would not be included in income. For a lay employee with low or no income tax, a Roth 403(b)(7) would be a good choice. However, for a dual-status minister a Roth 403(b)(7) would not be a good choice. Distributions are already treated as non-taxable to the extent they are spent for housing expenses. Roth contributions are not deductible from taxable income and also **not a reduction of Social Security base.**

A special "catch up" election allows a certain long-term employee to "catch up" on the funding of their retirement benefit by increasing their elective deferrals over the **$18,000** limit. An employee who has completed **15 years of service** with a qualified organization can make an additional contribution. If during your church career, you transfer from one organization to another or to an associated organization, treat all this service as service with a single employer. Under the election, the annual limitation is increased by **the smallest of**: (1) **$3,000**; (2) $15,000 minus any elective deferrals made by the organization and previously excluded under the catch-up election; or (3) $5,000 times the employee's years of service minus the elective deferrals made to plans of the organization in earlier taxable years. In effect, elective deferrals for an employee (under 50) who qualifies for the 15 year rule for **2016** is **$21,000**, (over 50 - **$24,000**)

IRS ordering rule. Participants who qualify for the 15 year catch-up contribution and the age-50 catch-up contribution must use the 15-year catch-up contribution first. (IRS Pub 571)

Includible compensation: This is a very difficult area of tax law to comprehend. Includible compensation for the employee's most recent year of service is a combination of income and benefits received in exchange for services provided to the employer that maintains the employee's 403(b) account, and that the employee must include in income. Beginning in 1998, Sec. 403(b)'s definition of includible compensation was expanded to include (1) elective deferrals (your employer's contributions made on your behalf under a salary reduction agreement), (2) amounts contributed or deferred by your employer under a Sec. 125 cafeteria plan, (3) amounts contributed or deferred by your employer under a Sec. 457 plan, and (4) income otherwise excluded under the foreign earned income exclusion.

An employee's most recent year of service is the employee's last full year (ending no later than the close of the taxable year for which the limit on annual additions is being determined) that the employee worked for the employer that maintains a 403(b) account on the employee's behalf. (Sec. 403(b)(4)). The most recent year of service may precede the taxable year by up to five years; thus, contributions may be made for an employee for up to five years after retirement, based on the last year of service before retirement. (Sec. 403(b)(3).

Beginning in 1997, compensation for a self-employed minister (evangelist or chaplain) who is treated as if employed by a nonprofit organization is his **net earnings from self-employment** reduced by contributions to retirement plans and the deduction for one-half of the self-employment tax. This definition for includible compensation for an evangelist clearly takes the combination of **salary and parsonage allowance** from Schedule SE.

Reg. 1.403(b)-1(d)(5) provides for an election to have the exclusion allowance determined under Sec. 415 rules. Such an election to include parsonage allowance would allow for greater contributions and be irrevocable.

In Private Letter Ruling 200135045, the IRS concluded that Sec. 107 housing allowance **was not** includible compensation for an employee because it was not required to be reported anywhere on an informational return by the employer. **However**, in a footnote, the IRS stated, "ministerial services are covered by social security provisions under the Self-Employment Contributions Act (SECA)." Under Sec. 1402(a)(8), Sec. 107 housing allowance **is included** in determining net earnings from self-employment for purposes of SECA. An employee can contribute up to 100% of includible compensation, subject to the annual limitations. The question of whether housing allowance is considered as "includible compensation" or not, affects fewer ministers because they can contribute 100% of includible compensation.

A private letter ruling is directed only to the taxpayer who requested it. Section 6110(k)(3) of the Code provides that it may not be used or cited by others as precedent.

● *Sec. 408(k) - Simplified Employee Pension (SEP)*

Only an **employer or a self-employed person** may establish a SEP. The employer makes contributions directly to a SEP-IRA account or annuity that has been set up for each employee with a broker, bank, mutual fund or insurance company qualified to sponsor an IRA under Sec. 408(k). **2016** contributions are limited to 25% on first **$265,000** of compensation, with maximum of **$53,000**. (2017 - 25% of $270,000 or $54,000) Employer contributions must be made to a SEP for each employee age 21 or over who has worked for the employer for at least 3 of the last 5 years and received annual compensation of **$600** or more. (2017 - $600) Contributions to SEPs must not discriminate in favor of highly compensated employees. Employer contributions must be determined under a definite written allocation formula and withdrawals must be allowed. Because the SEP-IRA is established in the employee's name it is 100% vested and portable.

Employees of tax-exempt organizations and state or local governments **may not** make additional voluntary salary reduction contributions to a Sec. 408(k) SEP. They are eligible for Sec. 403(b)(7) salary reduction plans instead.

● *Sec. 408(p) - Savings Incentive Match Plan for Employees (SIMPLE)*

Employers with less than 100 employees may want to consider establishing Sec. 408(p) SIMPLE plan instead of a 403(b). The IRS has provided the plan document. The contribution limitations are lower than a 403(b) plan and the employer is required to match up to 3% of employee participation.

A SIMPLE retirement plan is a written salary reduction arrangement that allows a **small employer** (an employer with 100 or fewer employees) to make elective contributions to a simple retirement account (IRA) on behalf of each eligible employee. The plan document is provided by the IRS and is *"really"* **simple** to establish and administer by an employer.

Unlike traditional IRAs, the account owner of a SIMPLE IRA may make contributions after age 70½. If a taxpayer continues to work after 70½, Sec. 408(p) accounts can receive contributions. However, RMD distributions are required at age 70½, since they are IRA based plans.

For **2016**, an employee can contribute up to 100% of compensation limited to **$12,500** annually, with an additional **$3,000** available if age 50 or over by end of year. (2017 - $12,500, with an additional $3,000 available if age 50 or over by end of year.) The employer is required to match the employees' contributions on a dollar for dollar basis, up to 3% of compensation, or elect to make 2% nonelective contributions on behalf of all eligible employees. Eligible employees are those who earned at least $5,000 in compensation from the employer during any two prior years and who are reasonably expected to receive at least $5,000 in compensation during the year. The plan document allows an employer to choose between $0 and $5,000 for the compensation requirement and to choose between zero to two prior years for the time requirement.

Form 5304-SIMPLE establishes the plan under which each eligible employee is permitted to select the financial institution for his or her SIMPLE IRA. Form 5305-SIMPLE establishes the plan under which the employer designates the financial institution. Do not file Form 5304-SIMPLE or Form 5305-SIMPLE with the IRS. It remains in the employer's records.

Both the employee contributions and the employer contributions are **Non-ERISA** (employee is always 100% vested). A participating employer is not allowed to maintain any other retirement plan.

When an employer establishes a voluntary salary reduction employer's plan for one employee, **it is required that all of the employees on staff be notified** that they have the opportunity to make voluntary salary reduction contributions. It is not necessary that they choose to participate.

Distributions from a SIMPLE retirement account are subject to IRA rules. However, withdrawals of contributions during the two-year period beginning on the date the employee first participated in the SIMPLE plan are subject to a 25% early withdrawal penalty rather than a 10% penalty.

Additional Information for Qualified Retirement Plans

● *Distributions from Employer Qualified Retirement Plans (QRP)*

Upon retiring, resigning, or disability an employee usually has choices to make as to how he wants the distribution from an employer's Qualified Retirement Plan to be paid out. The choices are provided for in the employer's plan document. **Tax planning is important.** Each taxpayer's tax situation will differ. Obtain help from your tax and financial advisors in regards to the best choice for your situation.

When a minister has a choice of receiving a lump-sum distribution, it is important to "roll over" by transfer trustee to trustee into a qualified retirement plan, including an IRA, **otherwise the vendor is required to withhold 20%** of the distribution for income tax withholding. Some vendors no longer offer transfer 403(b)s. They only offer "rollover" IRAs. To retain the proper identity of earnings from the ministry, and to preserve the opportunity for designated parsonage allowance, **never co-mingle** retirement funds from ministry earnings with retirement funds from secular earnings.

● *Required minimum distributions (RMD)*

Your required minimum distribution is the minimum amount you must withdraw from your account each year. You generally have to start taking withdrawals from your IRA or retirement plan account when you reach age 70½. Required minimum distributions from most qualified plans must begin by April 1 of the calendar year following the calendar year in which you reach 70½. The first year following the year you reach age 70½ you will generally have two required distribution dates: an April 1 withdrawal (for the year you turn 70½), and an additional withdrawal by December 31 (for the year following the year you turn 70½). To avoid having both of these amounts included in your income for the same year, you can make your first withdrawal by December 31 of the year you turn 70½ instead of waiting until April 1 of the following year.

The exact distribution amount changes from year to year. It is calculated by dividing an account's year-end value by the distribution period determined by the Internal Revenue Service. The most commonly used Uniform Lifetime Table can be found at:

http://www.irs.gov/pub/irs-tege/uniform_rmd_wksht.pdf

Once you determine a separate RMD from each of your traditional IRAs, you can total these minimum amounts and take them from any one or more of your traditional IRAs.

RMD distributions **are** required for Sec. 408(p) SIMPLE IRA plans at age 70½, since they are IRA based plans.

RMD distributions **are not** required for Sec. 403(b) plans at age 70½ if the taxpayer **continues to work**. RMD distributions are not required to begin until the calendar year in which the employee retires from employment, according to Reg. 1.403(b)-6(e)(3).

If taxpayer **continues to work** after 70½, Sec. 403(b) and Sec. 408(p) plans can receive contributions.

● *Distributions and Penalties*

Early distributions of voluntary plans before age 59½ or disability are subject to the 10% early withdrawal penalty. To transfer or "roll-over" distributions within 60 days to another qualified tax shelter plan will prevent tax in the year of distribution and the 10% penalty. It is important to "roll over" by transfer trustee to trustee into a qualified retirement plan, otherwise the vendor is required to withhold 20% of the distribution for income tax withholding. **Two ways to avoid the 10% penalty are**: (1) Early distributions can be rolled over to another qualified account or (2) 72(t) distributions under which you may take systematic withdrawals from your account prior to age 59½ and avoid the 10% penalty. Once begun, such distributions must continue for five full calendar years or until you reach age 59½, whichever occurs later.

● *Retired Ministers & Parsonage Designation*

A **retired minister** receiving an otherwise taxable distribution from a qualified Sec. 401(a), Sec. 401(k), Sec. 403(b), Sec. 408(k), Sec. 408(p) or Sec. 414(e) plan may have a **"parsonage allowance"** designated by the former employer or denominational pension board according to Rev. Ruling 63-156. We recommend that a perpetually worded designation state that 100% of the retirement income be designated as parsonage allowance and be tax free to the extent spent for housing. **(See sample wording in Chapter Two)** Language found in the Department of Labor Regulations under ERISA indicate that both types of contributions to a Sec. 403(b) plan (ERISA and Non-ERISA) are considered as contributions to an employer's plan and both types are eligible for parsonage allowance designation.

According to Rev. Ruling 72-249, the parsonage allowance exclusion **is not available** to the surviving spouse who continues to receive retirement income as a beneficiary.

Third party payors of retirement plan distributions will include the gross distribution on Form 1099-R, Box 1. Not being able to determine the taxable amount, Box 2a could be left blank and Box 2b could be checked. As a retired minister receiving distributions from a retirement plan that has been designated as "parsonage allowance," you are to enter the gross amount on Form 1040, line 16a. It is the responsibility of the retired minister to show as taxable on Form 1040, line 16b any designated distributions not spent for parsonage expenses. If all of the distribution has been spent for parsonage expenses enter -0- on line 16b.

"Retired Minister" is recommended to be shown as "occupation" on Form 1040.

● *Retirement Savings Contributions Credit*

Retirement Savings Contributions Credit **has been made permanent**. Low income taxpayers are allowed a tax credit for a portion of contributions made to Traditional IRAs, Roth IRAs, elective deferrals made to a Simple IRA, 401(k), 403(b), 408(p), or 457(b) plan. The maximum credit is 50% of the individual's first $2,000 contributed; thus the maximum credit per each individual is $1,000. However, contributions are reduced by any distributions taken during a 2 year look back period.

The adjusted gross income limitation under Section 25B(b)(1)(A) for determining the amount of retirement savings contribution credit allowed for **2016** is between **$37,000 and $61,500** for married joint, **$27,750 and $46,125** for head of household, and **$18,500 and $30,750** for single and married filing separate. Compute the credit on **Form 8880** and enter the credit on Form 1040, line 50.

● *Effect of Sec. 911 Foreign Earned Income Exclusion*

According to Reg. 1.403(b)-2(b)(11), foreign earned income counts **as includible** compensation if an employee wishes to make contributions to a TSA.

According to Reg. 1.219(b)(3), for IRA purposes compensation **does not include** foreign earned income and/or housing that is excluded from income and contributions to an IRA are not allowed.

● *Decedent's Distributions*

A spouse beneficiary can rollover a distribution from a decedent's qualified plan into an account maintained in the survivor's name or into his or her own IRA. A **nonspouse beneficiary** can rollover distributions from a decedent's qualified plan into an Inherited IRA, established in the name of the decedent.

● **Charitable contributions of IRA Distributions:**

IRA owners who have attained age 70½ are allowed to make charitable contributions of their otherwise taxable IRA distributions. They must be less than $100,000 per year, per person and distributed directly to the charitable organization. This provision was made permanent by the "Protecting Americans from Tax Hikes" (PATH Act)

- *Tax Planning*

When a taxpayer has an income tax liability, it is good tax planning to consider making contributions to a "sheltered" retirement plan. Even when a minister has **no income tax liability**, he may wish to contribute to a Sec. 403(b)(7) Tax Sheltered Account or a Sec. 408(p) Simple IRA account and **reduce his social security base.**

- ## Sec. 408(a) - Traditional Individual Retirement Accounts

In addition to making contributions to an employer's retirement plan, you may also contribute to an IRA. IRS Publication 590 contains detailed information on IRAs.

Total **individual** contributions to all IRAs (regular & Roth) for **2016** cannot exceed **$5,500**, or **$6,500** if you are 50 or older by the end of the year. (2017 - $5,500, plus $1,000 catch up)

The maximum IRA limit for a married couple filing jointly is **$11,000 for 2016**, or **$12,000** if only one of you is 50 or older, or **$13,000** if both of you are 50 or older, as long as your combined compensation is at least that much. Contributions for **2016** must be made by April 17th, 2017. You can set up and make contributions to an IRA if you received taxable compensation during the year and have not reached age 70½ by the end of the year.

According to Reg. 1.219(b)(3), for IRA purposes, compensation does not include Sec. 911, foreign earned income and/or housing that is excluded from income, therefore contributions to an IRA are not allowed.

If an employer makes payments to a regular Individual Retirement Account (IRA) on the behalf of an employee, it is actually just additional salary. It must be shown as salary on Form W-2, Box 1, and will be subject to social security on employee's Schedule SE. The employee will show the IRA contribution as an adjustment on Form 1040, line 32, subject to income limitations.

You will receive a Form 5498 by May 31 from the trustee of your account each year stating the amount you have contributed for the past year. The earnings of an IRA accrue tax-free as long as you do not withdraw them. When you reach 70½, the value of your account on December 31st must be provided by the trustee by January 31. It is that value that will be used to compute the required minimum distribution (RMD).

For those who are active participants in an employer retirement plan, a SEP, a SIMPLE, or a 403(b), contributions to an IRA can still be made but may not be deductible contributions. Active participation in an employer-sponsored plan by one spouse does not prevent the non-participating spouse from making a deductible contribution to an IRA unless their combined AGI reaches the phaseout level between **$184,000** and **$194,000**. For active participants in **2016**, the AGI phaseout range for making deductible IRA contributions for single persons is **$61,000 to $71,000**. For married persons filing jointly the range is **$98,000 to $118,000**. For married persons filing separately, if they lived together for any part of the year, the phaseout range is **$0 to $10,000**. For active participants in 2017, the AGI phaseout range for making deductible IRA contributions for single persons is $62,000 to $72,000. For married persons filing jointly the range is $99,000 to $119,000.

There is a provision that allows you to designate contributions as non-deductible, even if they qualify as deductible. **This prevents "wasted" deductions when there is no tax liability**. It allows the combination of "sheltered" and "non-sheltered" contributions to the same plan. Contributions that you choose to designate as non-deductible can be changed to deductible on an amended return for three open years.

Record keeping for non-deductible contributions to an IRA is **the responsibility of the taxpayer!!** Form 8606 is necessary to be completed and attached to your Form 1040. The non-deductible basis or contributions will be returned to you in retirement as non-taxable. If a taxpayer fails to keep record of the basis of his IRA account, the IRS can treat it as fully taxable upon withdrawal. Keeping copies of your tax returns in a safe place for your total working lifetime is your responsibility. The earnings of non-deductible or designated contributions are sheltered from tax until withdrawal.

10% Penalty free withdrawals from IRAs can be used for qualified higher education expenses and up to $10,000 (lifetime cap) of qualifying "first time" home-buyer expenses. You are a "first time" home buyer if you did not have a present ownership interest in a principal residence in the two year period before the acquisition of a new home. Such distributions would be subject to regular income tax.

- ## Sec. 408A - Roth Individual Retirement Accounts

Contributions to a Roth IRA are non-deductible in the year of the contribution. As with regular IRAs, earnings accumulate within a Roth IRA tax free. Total **individual** contributions to all IRAs (regular & Roth) for **2016** cannot exceed **$5,500**, or **$6,500** if you are 50 or older by the end of the year. (2017 - $5,500, plus $1,000 catch up) For single persons the phaseout range is **$117,000 to $132,000**. For married taxpayers filing a joint return the phaseout range is **$184,000 to $194,000**. For married persons filing separately, if they lived together for any part of the year, the phaseout range is **$0 to $10,000**.

Qualified **distributions** from a Roth IRA **are tax free** and not subject to a 10% penalty. Qualified distributions are those made after a 5 year period, and in addition, made after age 59½, after death to a beneficiary, after becoming disabled or distributed to pay for "qualified first time home buyer expenses." You do not include in your gross income qualified distributions or distributions that are **a return of your regular contributions** from your Roth IRA(s). Nonqualified distributions are includible in income to the extent they exceed total contributions - earnings only - and are subject to a 10% penalty unless an exception applies.

You are not required to take a "mandatory distribution" or a RMD from a Roth at 70 ½).

Roth IRAs are a wonderful choice for the non-tax paying minister's retirement planning. A Roth IRA invested in a mutual fund will capture the long term growth of the capital market.

The conversion of a regular IRA to a Roth IRA is treated as a taxable distribution. A conversion from a regular IRA to a Roth IRA is taxable in the year it is done. In 2010, the $100,000 threshold was lifted. Conversions after 2010 are taxable in year of conversion. All non-deductible regular IRAs that have a basis can be converted to a Roth IRA. The amount taxable will be the gains only. The basis will be non-taxable.

If you have contributed to or converted to a Roth IRA during the year and later become ineligible because you are filing a married separate return, there are provisions for recharacterizing or unconverting back to a regular IRA. Timely recharacterizing can be chosen because you or your tax advisor discover that it was unwise to convert to a Roth IRA and pay tax. Treasury Decision 9056 is the final regulation for conversions and Reg. 1.408A-5 provides rules regarding the recharacterizing of IRA contributions.

● *Self-Employed Retirement Plans*

Salaries received as "employees" **are not eligible** for making contributions to self-employed retirement plans. Only income from honorariums or true independent contractor status qualify as income from which individual SEP or SIMPLE contributions can be made. Contributions and other additions to a defined contribution plan on one's own account or on account of another employee cannot exceed the lesser of $53,000, or 100 percent of the participant's compensation.

Housing Exclusion

Two separate types of housing are provided in the tax law. Dual-status employees **must use Sec. 107 housing**. Lay employees that meet the requirements must use Sec. 119 housing.

However when the employer is a church or an integral agency of a church, a minister may be an administrator serving as manager or camp director and would qualify for dual-status and Sec. 107 housing. (See Chapter Two)

● *Lay Employees - Sec. 119 Housing*

For the lay employee (janitor, dorm parents, caretakers, camp cooks, etc.), the value of employer furnished lodging and utilities is not taxable if:

1. Furnished on your employer's business premises;
2. For your employer's convenience;
3. And as a condition of your employment. Regular and emergency duties must be continuous, on constant 24-hour call.

All three conditions must be met or the value of housing provided is taxable. The exclusion does not apply if an employee can take cash instead of the housing.

"In the case of an individual who is furnished lodging in a camp located in a foreign country by or on behalf of his employer, such camp shall be considered to be the business premises of the employer," according to Sec. 119(c).

Employees of colleges, universities, and other educational institutions described in Sec. 170(b)(1)(A)(ii), can exclude the value of qualified campus lodging, provided they satisfy an adequate rent requirement. The rent must be at least equal to the lesser of:

1. 5% of the appraised value of the lodging, or
2. the average of rentals paid by individuals (other than employees or students) for comparable lodging held for rent by the educational institution.

If the rent paid is less than the lesser of these amounts, you must include the difference in your income. The lodging must be appraised by an independent appraiser and the appraisal must be reviewed on an annual basis. If the rent paid is more, the employee gets to exclude the entire lodging's value according to Sec. 119(d) and IRS Pub 525, page 8.

Originally, Sec. 119 housing had been subject to social security. A Supreme Court Decision (Rowan Companies, Inc. v. United States) and Rev. Ruling 81-222 stated that the IRS cannot have a different definition for wages for the lay employee for income and social security purposes. Therefore, the value of the meals and lodging that had previously been subject to social security, became exempt retroactively.

- *Dual-Status Minister - Sec. 107 Housing*

Dual-status ministers are not taxed for income tax purposes on the parsonage provided them and/or the parsonage allowance paid to them as a part of their compensation. Chapter Two gives full detailed discussion on how to designate in advance and compute tax-free parsonage allowance.

Unfortunately, the Rowan court case has no effect on the Sec. 107 for the dual-status minister. According to Flowers v. Commissioner, TC Memo 1991-542, parsonage provided and/or parsonage allowance paid **are still subject to social security** unless Form 4361 has been timely filed. Some tax advisors have applied the Rowan case to Sec. 107, **out of context**, and the IRS has assessed the preparer the negligence penalty for each return filed in error. If you have failed to pay social security on your housing under Sec. 107, we would advise you to amend your returns and pay the correct amount of social security.

NonTaxable Gifts & Benevolence

According to Sec. 102, gifts and inheritances, received directly from relatives and personal friends for personal reasons are not taxable income. When you **have not performed a service** and someone gives you a gift and **it does not come from an employer**, the gift can be considered non-taxable.

Deacon's Fund or Benevolence Fund: Churches should never hesitate to help people in the community who are unemployed, have a catastrophic illness, been an accident victim, or aged. Benevolent gifts to non-employees that are based on their needs **are non-taxable and are never to be reported** on an information return (Form 1099). Churches should be actively involved in meeting the benevolent needs of their community.

Often a church is asked to "funnel" a designated contribution to a specific individual. If that individual **is involved** in a ministry or missionary endeavor and the church finance committee is given control of the gift and chooses to honor the request, it should be treated as compensation to the individual receiving it, and included in the church's payroll reports. When the gift can be forwarded to a mission organization with which the individual is employed, that organization can include the amount in their payroll reports. If the individual to whom the gift is designated **is not involved** in a ministry, extreme caution must be exercised by the church. When a designated recipient is a relative of the donor and not involved in a ministry, deductible contribution receipts should not be issued. **Deductible contribution receipts should not be issued when the church does not have the right to control the monies.**

Caution: When an employer helps an employee or a member of an employee's family with crisis needs it will result in taxable compensation to the employee, according to Sec. 61. **We recommend** that a local non-employer, nonprofit organization (such as Red Cross) be utilized to raise funds for the crisis needs.

Accountable Reimbursement Plan for Professional Expenses

Auto, travel, and professional expenses that are reimbursed by an employer who has adopted an accountable reimbursement plan according to Sec. 62(2)(A), are not required to be shown on the employee's W-2. The employee must "adequately account" to his employer. Chapter Three contains tax savings and audit reduction reasons for establishing an accountable reimbursement plan with your employer.

Sec. 457 Deferred Compensation Plans

Employees who have fully funded qualified 403(b) tax shelter retirement plans may be able to defer additional taxable income through a Sec. 457 "non-qualified deferred compensation plan." These plans, which frequently use a trust arrangement known as a "rabbi trust," may be adopted with a model rabbi trust published by the IRS in Rev. Proc. 92-64.

To successfully defer taxes under a "non-qualified plan," the compensation deferred must, until actual payment, continue to be owned by the employer and be available to the employer's creditors if the employer becomes bankrupt or insolvent. The **2016** annual limitation for Sec. 457 deferrals is 100% of includible compensation up to **$18,000** with an additional **$6,000** catch up if age 50 or over. (2017 - $18,000 with an additional $6,000 if age 50 or over.)

Distributions from a Sec. 457 plan are wages subject to income tax withholding and are to be **reported on Form W-2**. Social security and medicare taxes should be withheld and matched for a lay employee participant. A dual-status minister participant will be subject to social security and medicare tax unless he has become exempt by filing Form 4361.

Distributions to a beneficiary of a deceased participant under a Sec. 457 plan are reported on Form 1099-R. No income tax withholding is required for distributions from Sec. 457(b) plans to beneficiaries. (IRS Notice 2003-20)

Equity Fund for Ministers Living in a Church Provided Parsonage

When church employers who provide a parsonage for their minister realize the minister does not benefit from the equity growth, they often want to establish an Equity Fund for the minister.

However, the Internal Revenue Code and Regulations **are silent** concerning "Equity Funds" for a minister.

When church employers wish to assist their minister in having "equity" or savings available at retirement for a home purchase, **they can use qualified retirement accounts**. Establishing a Sec. 403(b) or a Sec. 408(p) voluntary salary reduction retirement plan or contributing an additional amount to an existing retirement account will accomplish the desired goal.

Gratuity Payments to a Retired Minister

Payments made by a congregation to a retired minister (because of age or disability), if he is not expected to perform any further services, are non-taxable. Such non-taxable gifts based on gratitude and appreciation can be given after a minister retires in addition to his receiving taxable pension from an established plan. It is also necessary that the payments not be required by an established plan or agreement entered into before retirement and that they are determined in the light of the financial position of the congregation and the needs of the recipient, who had been adequately compensated for his past services. **The payor does not report the gifts on any informational return**.

A statement in Osborne v. Commissioner, T.C. Memo 1995-71: "In Rev. Ruling 55-422, the Service indicated that a payment by a congregation to a retiring clergyman would qualify as an excludable gift where, among other circumstances, there was a closer personal relationship between the recipient and the congregation than is found in secular employment situations."

In all other careers all payments after retirement are taxable to the retiree because of past services. (Sec. 102(c)(1)) **Rev. Ruling 55-422 is a unique special provision for retired clergy**. In Goodwin v. United States, KTC 1995-479, the judge said, "...the legislative history suggests that section 102(c)(1) was enacted to address other fact situations..."

The IRS's Minister Audit Technique Guide states the following: *"There are numerous court cases that ruled the organized authorization of funds to be paid to a retired minister at or near the time of retirement were gifts and not compensation for past services. Rev. Rul. 55-422, 1955-1 C.B. 14, discusses the fact pattern of those cases which would render the payments as gifts and not compensation."*

Gratuity Payments to Widows of Employees

IRC Sec. 102 allows for payments to a widow as a non-taxable gift. A Supreme Court decision in 1960 settled the question for gift v compensation. (Commissioner v. Duberstein, 363 U.S. 278,285 (1960)) "A gift proceeds from a 'detached and disinterested generosity,"...'out of affection, respect, admiration, charity or like impulses." (Rev. Ruling 99-44)

A determination of whether a transfer proceeds from detached and disinterested generosity requires an inquiry into the transferor's intention in making the payment. Insight into a transferor's intention can be gained by examining the factors that the transferor considered in deciding whether to make the transfer and the form of the assistance. (U.S. v Kaiser, 363 U.S. 299,304 (1960)) "In general, a payment made by a charity to an individual that responds to the individual's needs, and does not proceed from any moral or legal duty, is motivated by detached and disinterested generosity."

On the other hand, when an employer has a written plan to pay certain sums to any widows of employees it does become taxable as unqualified retirement proceeds. When the widow actually performs services, it does become taxable as wages. When there is no plan and no services are being performed; gifts made to a widow because she has financial needs, are non-taxable to her. **The payor does not report the gifts on any informational return.**

CHAPTER TWO

Parsonage Allowance

The understanding of this chapter will result in tremendous income tax savings. Some dual-status ministers have spent many years in the ministry and have not been aware of how to "designate" their expenses of providing a home as non-taxable parsonage allowance. Internal Revenue Code Sec. 107 says:

"In the case of a minister of the Gospel, gross income does not include—-

1. **The rental value of a home furnished to him as part of his compensation; or**
2. **The rental allowance paid to him as part of his compensation, to the extent used by him to rent or provide a home and to the extent such allowance does not exceed the fair rental value of the home, including furnishings and appurtenances such as a garage, plus the cost of utilities."**

Are You Entitled to the Parsonage Allowance Exclusion?

The answer to the question, "Are you entitled to parsonage allowance?" is also going to answer another question, "Are you considered self-employed for social security purposes?" **Sec. 107's** regulations refers us to **Sec. 1402(c)'s** regulations for the definition of some important terms. When we determine that you are entitled to tax-free parsonage allowance, we will have also determined that you are to be considered self-employed for social security purposes. **Dual-status means** that you are an **employee** for income reporting, fringe benefit, and expense deducting purposes and **self-employed** for social security purposes.

When we determine that you are not entitled to tax-free parsonage allowance, we will have also determined that you are to be considered as a lay employee for income tax and social security withholding purposes.

Generally, there are three circumstances to be considered. (1) Are you employed by a church or an integral agency of a church? (2) Are you performing ministerial services? and (3) Are you ordained by a church or "the equivalent thereof?" While all three tests must be satisfied for you to be treated as a dual-status minister for tax purposes, court cases and letter rulings reflect a very friendly definition of circumstance #3.

Are You Employed by a Church or An Integral Agency of a Church?

To qualify for minister's tax treatment and tax-free parsonage allowance your employer must be a church or an integral agency of a church. (See "Two Exceptions")

Churches (or a convention or association of churches) are exempt from federal income tax under Sec. 501(a) as a religious organization described in Sec. 501(c)(3) and further described in Sec. 170(b)(1)(A)**(i)**. Churches and their integrated auxiliaries receive an **"automatic"** exemption recognition. A church **is not required to file Form 1023** to be exempt from federal income tax or to receive tax deductible contributions. In many states a church is not required to become incorporated. We feel it is wise for a church to protect individual members and themselves legally by incorporating at the state level. In Rakosi, v. Commissioner, T.C. Memo 1988-149, is the following statement:**"A church is a coherent group of individuals and families that join together to accomplish the religious purposes of mutually held beliefs. In other words, a church's principal means of accomplishing its religious purposes must be to assemble regularly a group of individuals related by common worship and faith."** When a congregation has a membership, separate accounting, and meets regularly for worship services, they are a church. **Many churches do not have and do not need** a determination letter from the IRS. When a church voluntarily files Form 1023 to obtain formal recognition of their exemption they will receive a determination letter. Form 8718 must accompany the Form 1023 and requires either a $400 or a $850 fee to the IRS. Two IRS Publications, **1828** "Tax Guide for Churches and Religious Organizations" and **557** "Tax Exempt Status for Your Organization" are recommended resources.

Religious organizations that are not churches can be under the control of a church or group of churches by drafting their bylaws to meet most of the requirements of **Rev. Ruling 72-606** and be an integral agency of a church.

Organizations that are not integral agencies of a church must file Form 1023. They will receive a determination letter stating that they are an organization described in Sec. 501(c)(3) and further described in Sec. 170(b)(1)(A)**(vi)**. Two well known national non-denominational, non-integral agency organizations are Youth for Christ and Child Evangelism Fellowship.

- *Two Exceptions Available For Those Not Employed by a Church*

Only a church or an integral agency can give authority to a minister to perform the duties of the ministry. Therefore it would be **important for a minister** to have been formally ordained, licensed or commissioned by their church before utilizing either of the following exceptions.

First exception to the requirement that your employer must be a church or an integral agency is provided if you are **assigned or appointed** to perform services at an organization that is not a church by your denomination or church. When you are considering employment by an organization that is not a church or an integral agency, have your church or denomination assign you to the position during the hiring process **before** you accept the position. (See "Qualifying Service Includes" from Reg. 1.1402(c)-5(b), item #7, on page 41.)

The Second exception is provided when the services you are performing is that of conducting religious worship or ministering sacerdotal functions. This exception makes it possible for a **chaplain**, even though he may be employed by a secular organization, or an **evangelist,** who holds engagements in rented auditoriums or stadiums, to qualify for minister's tax treatment. A chaplain or evangelist can have their housing allowance designated by their home church or their denomination. (Reg. 1.1402(c)-5(c)(2)

Definition of Church

The following definitions will help you determine the correct status of your organization. Regulations for Sec. 107 state:

> *"The term, religious organization, has the same meaning and application as is given to the term for income tax purposes."*

The scope of what organizations are included in the definition of "churches" is found in the instructions of **IRS Pub. 557, page 29**. *"Because beliefs and practices vary so widely, there is no single definition of the word "church" for tax purposes. The Internal Revenue Service considers the facts and circumstances of each organization applying for church status."* A separate organization affiliated with a church will be considered an integrated auxiliary if the principal activity of the organization is exclusively religious. Examples of organizations considered to be integrated auxiliaries of a church are a men's or women's organization, a religious school (such as a seminary), a mission society, or a youth group.

A church or organization may be liable for tax on its unrelated business income. Unrelated business income is income from a trade or business, regularly carried on, that is not substantially related to the charitable, educational or other purpose constituting the basis for the organization's exemption. An organization must file Form 990T if it has $1,000 or more gross income from an unrelated business.

The following partial list of organizations that are not required to file an annual information return (Form 990) gives us an **"expanded definition"** of what the IRS deems to be a church to satisfy Sec. 107 and Sec. 1402(c). **(Summary from Pub. 557, page 10)**

1. A church, an interchurch organization of local units of a church, a convention or association of churches, an integrated auxiliary of a church.
2. A school below college level affiliated with a church or operated by a religious order, even though it is not an integrated auxiliary of a church.
3. Church-affiliated mission societies if more than half of their activities are conducted in, or are directed at persons in, foreign countries,
4. An exclusively religious activity of any religious order. (See discussion of "Religious Orders" in Chapter Five.)

No part of an organization's net income may inure to the benefit of any individual.

Integral Agency of a Church

A nonprofit organization with a determination letter showing it is not a church but is described as an organization for charitable, educational, or other purposes in Sec. 170(b)(1)(A)**(vi)**, would be able to treat an employee performing ministerial duties as a dual-status minister for tax purposes and designate parsonage allowance if it meets **most of the requirements** of Rev. Ruling 72-606 to be an integral agency of a church.

Rev. Ruling 70-549 and Rev. Ruling 72-606 clearly state what is required for a school, mission, or other religious organization to be under the control of a church and qualify as an integral agency of a church. The eight criteria listed in **Rev. Ruling 72-606** are:

1. whether the religious organization incorporated the institution;
2. whether the corporate name of the institution indicates a church relationship;
3. whether the religious organization continuously controls, manages, and maintains the institution;
4. whether the trustees or directors of the institution are approved by or must be approved by the religious organization or church;
5. whether trustees or directors may be removed by the religious organization or church;
6. whether annual reports of finances and general operations are required to be made to the religious organization or church;
7. whether the religious organization or church contributes to the support of the institution; and
8. whether, in the event of dissolution of the institution, its assets would be turned over to the religious organization or church.

The only time a nonprofit organization that is neither a church nor an integral agency of a church can treat an employee as a dual-status minister is when he has been assigned or appointed by a church or when his duties are conducting worship or ministering sacerdotal functions. All other employees will be lay employees regardless of their duties.

In the court case, Flowers v. U.S. CA 4-79-376-E, 11/25/81, it was found that Texas Christian University only met two of the possible eight tests of Rev. Ruling 72-606. Therefore, an ordained employee could not have a parsonage allowance as allowed by Sec. 107. Though Texas Christian University has a close relationship with the Disciples of Christ they did not evidence direct or indirect control by the church. TCU had been an integral agency of the Disciples of Christ and had changed their bylaws to become a non-integral agency. Doing so qualified them for favorable financing and bond issues for growth and expansion.

In Private Letter Ruling, 9144047, the teaching staff of a college was allowed to be dual status, because their employing college was deemed to be an integral agency of a church. In Private Letter Ruling 200925001, a university was deemed to be an integral agency of their denomination and the ministers of the denomination who teach or serve in faculty, executive, management, or administrative positions are entitled to parsonage allowance.

We advise any organization that is unsure of their standing to examine their determination letter from the IRS and their bylaws. If it is determined that your organization is a non-integral agency, consider obtaining legal assistance to amend your bylaws to comply with those areas of control and to become an integral agency of a church.

Are You Performing Ministerial Services?

The salary or honorarium you receive for services which are ordinarily the duties of a minister of the gospel is eligible for minister's tax treatment and tax-free parsonage allowance. There is no parsonage allowance exclusion for a minister who volunteers and receives no ministerial income.

As a minister you are not required to be performing all of the duties or even able to perform all of the duties to be a dual-status minister for tax purposes. Since 1978, according to Rev. Ruling 78-301, it is only necessary that a minister be able to perform **"substantially all"** of the duties of the ministry to be a minister for tax purposes.

Regulation 1.107-1 describes the following types of services that a minister in the exercise of his ministry performs:

1. the ministration of sacerdotal functions, **(includes baptism, communion, marriage and funerals)**
2. the conduct of religious worship, **(includes preaching, bible study, evangelism, and music)**
3. service in the administration, control, conduct, and maintenance of religious organizations, including integral agencies, under the authority of a church or church denomination, and
4. the performance of teaching and administrative duties at theological seminaries. **(Includes parochial schools, colleges, and universities which are integral agencies of a church or church denomination according to** Rev. Ruling 62-171.)

*   *Qualifying Services Include (Summary from Reg. 1.1402(c)-5(b).)*
    1. A minister employed as minister of a church is eligible for parsonage allowance. If more than one minister is on the staff, they may all exclude their parsonage allowance as long as their duties are those of ministers of the gospel.

2. Conducting religious worship services or ministering sacerdotal functions are ministerial services whether or not performed for a church or integral agency of a church. This provision makes it possible for a **chaplain** to qualify for dual-status treatment, even though he may be employed by a secular organization.

3. Service performed by a chaplain at either a church-related hospital or health and welfare institution, or a private nonprofit hospital is considered to be in the exercise of his ministry according to Rev. Ruling 71-258.

4. A minister engaged in the control, conduct, and maintenance of an integral agency of a religious organization or church. Members of the executive staff and those serving as departmental managers are performing qualifying ministerial services according to Rev. Ruling 57-129. Duties can include **supervising** all aspects of an organization's finances, fund raising, plant and equipment, kitchen operations and housekeeping according to Private Letter Ruling 8142076.

5. A minister serving on the faculty as a teacher or administrator of a college or seminary which is operated as an integral agency of a church according to Rev. Ruling 71-7.

6. A minister serving on the faculty as a teacher or administrator of an undergraduate or parochial school that is affiliated with a church. (Included in the "expanded definition" of a church)

7. A minister **assigned or designated by a church to perform services for an organization that is not a church,** even though such service may not involve the conduct of religious worship or the ministration of sacerdotal functions, is in the exercise of his ministry. **Example:** A minister assigned to perform advisory service to a printing company in connection with the publication of a book dealing with the history of his church denomination. (Reg. 1.1402(c)-5(b)(v)) *"If your services aren't assigned or designated by your church, they are ministerial services only if they involve performing sacerdotal functions or conducting religious worship."* IRS Pub 517, page 5

8. A rabbi is a minister of the gospel and qualifies for the parsonage allowance. Cantors also qualify according to Rev. Ruling 78-301.

9. A minister who performs evangelistic services at churches away from his permanent home may exclude parsonage allowance paid to him by the host churches according to Rev. Ruling 64-326.

10. Writing or producing religious books, articles, audio or video tapes is considered to be in the exercise of your ministry. Royalty income from their sale is self-employment income according to Rev. Ruling 59-50.

11. Though not able to be treated as self-employed when an employee of a government entity, Sec. 107 parsonage designation was allowed in C.T. Boyd, Jr. v. Commissioner, T.C. Memo 1981-528, by the Church Federation of Greater Indianapolis, Inc., even though Boyd was employed by the Indianapolis Police Department as Senior Chaplain. As a police chaplain he was under the direct supervision of the Chief of Police. However, the Federation retained supervision over Boyd's ecclesiastical performance and maintained day to day contact with him. He was not able to be treated as self-employed while an employee of a government entity. This is **an exception** to Sec. 107 and Sec. 1402(e) qualification being simultaneous.

● *Non-Qualifying Duties Include (Summary from Reg. 1.1402(c)-5(c).)*

1. Ministers who were administrators of nonprofit nursing homes. The nursing homes were not religious organizations nor integral agencies of a church. The services performed by the ministers were not that of conducting worship or performing sacerdotal functions. (Jesse A. Toavs et al., 67 TC 897)

2. If a minister is performing a service for an organization which is neither a religious organization nor operated as an integral agency of a religious organization and the service is not performed following an assignment or designation by his ecclesiastical superiors, then the service performed is not in the exercise of his ministry. **Example**: A minister is employed by a university to teach mathematics and history. The university is not a church nor an integral agency of a church. He receives honorariums from time to time performing wedding and funerals for friends. The honorariums are his only ministerial income.

3. "Routine services performed by secretaries, stenographers, mail clerks, file clerks, janitors, etc., are not in the exercise of ministry according to Rev. Ruling 57-129. Usually the services performed by doctors, nurses, auto mechanics, pilots, carpenters, cooks, computer technicians, etc., are not in the exercise of ministry.

4. A chaplain in the armed forces is specifically denied this exclusion since he is considered to be a commissioned officer, and as such is not a minister in the exercise of his ministry. Military officers are given tax-free housing, therefore, Sec. 107 is not needed.

5. Similarly, service performed by an employee of a State as a chaplain in a State prison or a government owned hospital is considered to be performed by a civil servant of the State and not by a minister in the exercise of his ministry. In Private Letter Ruling 9052001, the chaplain's employment, supervision, evaluation, and termination were strictly the responsibility of the warden. The chaplain's church had designated a housing allowance. However, since written reports or contacts between the chaplain and his church were voluntary, he was not entitled to exclude a housing allowance as a civil servant of the State.

Are You Ordained By A Church Or "The Equivalent Thereof?"

If you are employed by a church or an integral agency of a church and are performing ministerial services, you are considered to be "the equivalent of" ordained at the time you begin your employment. When a church calls or hires you to be their minister, they have informally given you the authority to conduct religious worship and to administer ordinances at the time of employment. You satisfy the "ability to perform services in control, conduct and maintenance of the church" merely by being employed by a church as their minister. In Salkov v. Commissioner, supra, 46 TC at 190 (1966) it was concluded that the congregation's formal selection of the taxpayer as their cantor constituted commissioning him as their minister.

Here is a very important court definition of a "duly ordained, commissioned, or licensed" minister. In J.M. Ballinger, U.S. Court of Appeals, 10th Circuit, No. 82-1928, 3/7/84, it was stated by three judges:

"Not all churches or religions have a formally ordained ministry, whether because of the nature of their beliefs, the lack of a denominational structure or a variety of other reasons. Courts are not in a position to determine the merits of various churches... We interpret Congress' language providing an exemption for any individual who is `a duly ordained, commissioned, or licensed minister of a church' to mean that the **triggering event** *is the assumption of the duties and functions of a minister."*

The minister who is formally ordained, licensed, or commissioned by his church or denomination experiences a very important and meaningful event. However, when he receives formal credentials **after the date of being hired by a church**, it is not an important event for tax purposes. On the **date of being hired** by a church, he was **entitled to ministerial tax status**.

It is very important for a minister who wishes to become exempt from social security to be aware of the date his/her ministry begins. Parsonage allowance must be designated in advance and to the extent used, it is free from income tax. The deadline for a timely filed "Application for Exemption from Self-Employment Tax for Ministers," Form 4361, is the due date of the tax return (including extensions) for the second year in which he/she earns more than $400 from the ministry.

Only a church or an integral agency can give authority to a minister to perform the duties of the ministry. **When a minister is not employed by a church or an integral agency,** it is important for him to have been formally ordained, licensed or commissioned as a minister by a church before being "assigned or designated" to a position with a non-church. When a minister, as **an independent evangelist or a chaplain,** performs worship and/or ministers sacerdotal functions at locations outside of a church, it is also important for him to have been formally ordained, licensed, or commissioned as a minister by a church.

Prior to 1978, Rev. Ruling 65-124 was very strict in stating that a minister had to be able to perform **"all"** the religious functions of the church to be defined as "ordained" for tax purposes.

Since 1978, Rev. Ruling 78-301 modified Rev. Ruling 65-124 and added the word **"substantially"** to the definition in order to allow Jewish cantors to qualify for parsonage allowance. Exactly what was meant by "substantially all" was unclear until 1989. Two tax court cases involving ministers with limited authority who waited until formal ordination to file Form 4361 to become exempt from social security were decided. IRS denied both applications as being untimely filed.

In Private Letter Ruling 9221025 the teaching staff of a school below college level were deemed to be ministers for tax purposes even though they were unable to conduct public adult worship or any of the sacerdotal functions. In Private Letter Ruling 199910055 it was determined that the Minister of Education, Minister of Music and Minister of Stewardship, all ordained deacons, were ministers for tax purposes. Performing ministerial duties and being **recognized as a religious leader** by his church qualifies a minister, administrator or teacher for ministerial tax status.

James S. Wingo, 89 TC No. 64, Docket No. 8613-85: Taxpayer was an ordained "deacon" and licensed as a probationary minister of the United Methodist Church beginning in 1980. He became an ordained "elder" in 1984 and wished to become exempt from social security. The United Methodist Church considers both "deacons" and "elders" as ordained ministers of the Church, and as an appointed full-time minister Rev. Wingo was permitted to administer the sacraments, provide for the organizational concerns of the local church, conduct divine worship, preach the Word, perform marriage ceremonies, and bury the dead. IRS determined that for purposes of applying for the exemption from self-employment tax **under Sec. 1402** or for obtaining the parsonage exclusion **under Sec. 107**, Rev. Wingo was a minister. Because he did not timely file a Form 4361, his application was denied and he was subject to Social Security tax.

John G. Knight, 92 TC No. 12, Docket Nos. 45505-86, 27182-87: Taxpayer was a licentiate of the Cumberland Presbyterian Church and served as a supply minister during 1984 and 1985. He preached, conducted the worship service, visited the sick, performed funerals, and ministered to the needy. Because he was not ordained, he could not moderate the session, administer sacraments, or solemnize marriages. He argued that he was an employee of the church, not a dual-status employee. Under the reasoning of Salkov, Silverman, and Wingo, duties and functions were considered by the court to be appropriate for a "duly ordained, commissioned or licensed minister." Because he did not timely file a Form 4361, his application was denied and he was subject to Social Security tax.

Both **Wingo and Knight** waited until after they received their formal or permanent credentials, they were denied exemption because their applications were untimely filed. Services they performed with temporary or limited credentials were still being performed **with the same employer** when they received their permanent credentials. Not realizing that their initial date of hire was the beginning of their ministry caused them to have their applications disapproved because of untimeliness.

Private Letter Ruling 199910055: A local church requested rulings for three "ordained deacons" whose duties were to assist the senior minister. The Minister of Education's duties included planning and supervising youth, adult, and family activities. He selected the curriculum, scheduled activities, and coordinated lay volunteers. The Minister of Music coordinated all choir and music activities. The Minister of Stewardship performed financial and managerial functions. He encouraged members of the congregation to give their time, talent, and money to the church. They met with the elder to plan the worship services, assist with the sacraments, and officiate at weddings and funerals. All three positions were deemed to be eligible for ministerial tax treatment.

Haimowitz v. Commissioner, T.C. Memo 1997-40: Mr. Haimowitz served for 30 years as an executive director of a temple. He never claimed ministerial tax status or housing allowance during his working years. He eventually performed more religious duties, such as helping students with memorization of blessings, Torah readings, and elocution. He frequently helped plan weddings and participated in the wedding ceremony as a witness to the contract, but he never officiated. After he retired, **never having shown himself to have been recognized as a religious leader** by the temple, he claimed that his pension should be tax-free parsonage allowance. He provided no evidence that a housing allowance had been designated in advance, so it was not allowed and was not appealable.

Private Letter Ruling 9221025: Because some churches allow both genders to be given full authority in the ministry and others extend full authority only to the men, an unequal tax advantage resulted for some women in the ministry. On February 20, 1992, Private Letter Ruling 9221025, gave a positive answer to a major denomination concerning their "commissioned" female teachers being eligible for dual-status treatment. The female staff performed full-time public ministry functions including: classroom teaching; evangelizing; counseling individuals; leading Bible study groups, devotions, worship services for youth, and a congregation's music ministry; giving the children's sermon at the regular Sunday worship service, coordinating lay church workers; caring spiritually for the sick and imprisoned and their families; etc., The female staff could not perform adult worship for both genders and could not perform any sacerdotal functions.

After this decision, the female teaching staff was changed to dual-status tax treatment and parsonage allowance was designated for them.

Private Letter Ruling 200318002: In a Technical Advice Memorandum it was determined that the "date of hire" did not constitute an adequate equivalent of a "duly ordained, commissioned or licensed" minister for the administrators and teachers of a christian school, affiliated with a church.

Cases of Kirk v. Commissioner, 51 T.C. 66 (1968) AFFIRMED, 425 F.2d 492 (D.C. Cir 1970) and Lawrence v. Commissioner, 50 T.C. 494 (1968) were cited. Cases before 1978 reflect the historic IRS position that to be a minister of the gospel one had to be able to perform all of the duties of the ministry. The TAM states that "at a minimum, the person is required to be duly ordained, licensed, or commissioned."

That Rev. Ruling 62-171, Rev. Ruling 78-301, J.M. Ballinger, U.S. Court of Appeals, 10th Circuit, No 82-1928, 3/7/84, and John G. Knight, 92 TC No.12, Docket Nos. 45505-86, 27182-87 were all ignored in the TAM is unfortunate. Though it reflects the attitude of the IRS drafter, **it is disappointing that case history and a very important court definition from the J.M. Ballinger court case were ignored**. As a result, we have Private Letter Ruling 9221025 and Private Letter Ruling 200318002, both addressing the administrators and teaching staff of christian schools, giving us very diverse guidance.

● *Summary Comments*

Making a determination of the correct tax status of an employee at the time he is hired is important. An employee that **qualifies** for dual-status minister tax treatment needs to have his housing allowance designated in advance. If he wishes to consider whether to become exempt from paying social security on his earnings from the ministry, he needs to understand when his ministry begins and file before the due date of the second return in which he earns $400 or more. (See complete discussion in Chapter Four.) A lay employee that **does not qualify** for dual-status tax treatment is subject to withholding of payroll taxes on his wage and matching of social security and medicare taxes by the employer.

When you consider all facts and circumstances of each employer and employee relationship in light of the citations (various regulations, court cases, revenue rulings and private letter rulings), you may discover that your church has not properly classified some of your staff members.

Due to the adverse attitude reflected in **Private Letter Ruling 200318002**, discussed above, a parochial school who has not extended dual-status tax treatment to their administrators and teaching staff may want to first establish a policy of licensing or commissioning them. For a parochial school who has the practice of formally commissioning their administrators and teaching staff, stay on course, continue to treat them as dual-status ministers. There is much solid ground, regulations, rulings and case history to support your position.

The impact of a church, an integral agency of a church or a parochial school making a switch to dual-status tax treatment for their qualifying staff can cause confusion. It is important to inform them of the tax law provisions that apply to them and teach them to keep records for housing allowance for which they are entitled. An employer who has been matching social security and medicare tax should be willing to pay **an additional salary factor** equal to the matching portion to each staff member affected. Otherwise, an employee with little or no parsonage expense would experience an economic loss. Federal income tax savings for $10,000 of parsonage expenses will be $1,000 for those in the 10% bracket, $1,500 for those in the 15% bracket, or $2,500 for those in the 25% bracket. There will be state income tax savings also.

Employees who have been accustomed to having their taxes withheld by their employer will appreciate an employer who will continue to withhold taxes under the optional withholding provisions. Withholding should be adequate to prepay both the reduced income tax and social security/medicare tax at the self-employed rate of 15.3% for 2016. This amount should be shown in Box 2 on Form W-2 as federal income tax withheld.

Whether or not an employee has an opportunity to elect to become exempt from social security will depend on the date they were hired or the date they began performing ministerial duties.

Parsonage Allowance Exclusion Rules

What Does the Parsonage Allowance Exclusion Include?

It includes anything spent to provide a home for the dual-status minister and his family. Regulations for Sec. 107 state that the parsonage allowance does not include food or a maid. Parsonage allowance is the tax-free treatment of a minister's **personal** home expenses on a **cash basis**. Do not use business capital asset rules. Do not depreciate home capital expenses. Parsonage allowance expenses include those for the house, its contents, the garage, and the yard. The following list shows typical expenses that are to be considered in computing the amount of parsonage allowance:

1. Rent or principal payments, cost of buying a home, and down payments.
2. Real estate taxes and mortgage interest for the home. Also deductible again as itemized deductions. **A double deduction,** but allowable by IRS!! (Sec. 265(a)(6)) **An amazing "tax shelter"!**
3. Insurance on the home and/or contents.
4. Improvements, repairs, and upkeep of the home and/or contents. Such as a new roof, room addition, carpet, garage, patio, fence, pool, appliance repair, etc.
5. Furnishings and appliances: dish washer, vacuum sweeper, TV, DVD, stereo, piano, computer (personal use), washer, dryer, beds, small kitchen appliances, cookware, dishes, sewing machine, garage door opener, lawn mower, hedge trimmer, etc.
6. Decorator items: drapes, throw rugs, pictures, holiday decorations, knick knacks, painting, wallpapering, bedspreads, sheets, towels, etc.
7. Utilities - heat, electric, non-business telephone, non-business cell phone, water, sewer charge, garbage removal, cable TV, non-business internet access, etc. (Show long distance business telephone calls, the business percent of cellular phone and internet access usage as a professional expense. Both income tax and self-employment tax will be reduced.)
8. Miscellaneous - anything that maintains the home and its contents that you have not included in repairs or decorator items: cleaning supplies for the home, brooms, light bulbs, dry cleaning of drapes, shampooing carpet, expense to run lawn mower, tools for landscaping, garden hose to water lawn, etc.

The expenses in item No. 8 are often purchased at the grocery or variety store. It is a good practice to buy a supply of household cleaning supplies separately and save the receipt. An easy way to keep record of them is to use the "Housing Expense" section of our **"Professional Tax Record Book."**

Do Not Include the following: Maid (or any labor hired for maintenance such as lawn care), groceries, personal toiletries such as toothpaste, shampoo, deodorant, laundry and dish soap, paper products; personal clothing, coats, shoes, jewelry; toys, bicycles, hobby items, CD's, DVD movies, computer games, personal computer application software, etc.

• *Mechanics of Parsonage Allowance*

Parsonage allowance is free from income tax, **but subject to social security and medicare tax.** Parsonage expense details, receipts, and records are **not to be submitted to the employer.** They are handled differently than the professional business expenses we will discuss in Chapter Three. The personal home expenses can remain confidential. If the designated amount is greater than the amount substantiated, it is the responsibility of the individual minister to show the "excess parsonage allowance" as income on Form 1040, line 7.

• *Double Deduction of Interest & Taxes*

Sec. 265(a)(6) provides for the deduction of home mortgage interest and property taxes on Schedule A even though all or part of the mortgage is paid with funds you get through a nontaxable parsonage allowance. Rev. Ruling 62-212 provided for this amazing "tax shelter" since 1962. In 1983 Congress attempted to end the "double deduction," but Rev. Ruling 83-3 was modified by Rev. Ruling 87-32.

• *Interest*

Interest from loans for the initial purchase of a home, improvements and furnishings can be used for parsonage allowance exclusion. However non-mortgage interest for home purchases will not be allowable on Schedule A as "personal interest." Mortgage and home equity loan interest will qualify as Schedule A "mortgage interest" deduction because the home is used as collateral. Mortgage and home equity loan interest **for the purchase of and improvement of the parsonage** can also be used for parsonage allowance exclusion. Mortgage and home equity loan interest for any other purpose will not be allowable as parsonage allowance exclusion. If a home equity loan is used for home improvements and the purchase of an auto, only the home improvement portion of the interest can be used as parsonage allowance exclusion.

• *Cash Basis*

Since capital expenditures for home principal, improvements, furniture, and appliances are on a cash basis, it is important to understand when to deduct them if the purchase involves borrowed funds. Any purchases with bank charge cards are treated the same as if you paid cash for the item. Any purchases for the home that involves a loan from a bank, store, or individual are treated as not paid for in full. Non-credit card loan **principal** payments for home, improvements, and furniture are to be deducted when payments are made.

● *Sale of Personal Residence*

There is no requirement that the cost of purchasing and improving a residence be adjusted or reduced by the tax-free principal portion of parsonage allowance. Therefore, in reporting the sale of a personal residence, the whole cost basis, for purchase and improvements, is used to determine gain or loss. If the sale of a personal residence results in a loss, it is not deductible from other taxable income.

The Taxpayer Relief Act of 1997 provided for an exclusion of $250,000 of gains on the sale of a personal residence for a single owner and $500,000 for married joint owners. There are two tests:

1. "Once-in-two-years." You must not have used this rule for at least two years prior to the current sale.
2. "Used-as-your-home." In the 5 year period before the current sale, you must have used the property as your home for a total of at least two years.

If you meet the tests, you can exclude the gain. Ministers who have owned their home and relocate to a church that provides them a parsonage can sell without incurring tax on the gain if the two tests are met. If the two tests are not met, the gain is taxable. However, you can claim a reduced exclusion if you sold the home due to a change in health or job transfer by employer. **IRS Publication 523**, "Selling Your Home," explains all the details of selling a personal residence.

The above rules for the sale of a personal residence never apply to the sale of business or rental property. Business property sales will result in taxable gains or deductible losses.

● *First-Time Homebuyers Credit - Form 5405*

The 2008 first-time home buyer credit of up to $7,500 has to be repaid by the taxpayer over a period of 15 years. This started in 2010. You can choose to repay more than the minimum amount with any tax return. If you are required to repay the credit because you disposed of a home you purchased, or that home ceased to be your main home, you generally must repay the balance of the unpaid credit with your current tax return. (See Form 5405 instructions)

How Much of a Minister's Salary Can Be Designated?

IRS Publication 517 historically explained that the "top limit" of any minister's housing allowance was the fair rental value of the home, including furnishings, utilities, garage, etc. Congress codified and strengthened their intent and position by passing the "Clergy Housing Allowance Clarification Act of 2002" on May 20, 2002. The new text Congress added to Sec. 107 is quoted at the beginning of this Chapter. (See "Warren v. Commissioner Tax Court Case")

● *IRS Position as Stated in Publication 517*

Nothing in the Internal Revenue code or regulations establish a "flat" dollar limitation or a percentage of income limitation for the parsonage allowance exclusion. **The amount designated as parsonage allowance must be a specific dollar amount or a specific percentage of salary.** Employers can designate a blanket percentage of their staff's salaries as parsonage allowance. Individuals on their staff who anticipate incurring a greater amount for parsonage expenses should be allowed to ask for a higher amount to be designated.

IRS Publication 517, page 9, gives the **historic** explanation of how much the parsonage allowance can be:

> *"If you own your home and you receive as part of your salary a housing or rental allowance, you may exclude from gross income the smallest of:*
> 1. *The amount actually used to provide a home,*
> 2. *The amount officially designated as a rental allowance, or*
> 3. *The fair rental value of the home, including furnishings, utilities, garage, etc.*
>
> *Excess rental allowance. You must include in gross income any rental allowance that is more than the **smallest** of your reasonable salary, the fair rental value of the home plus utilities, or the amount actually used to provide a home."*

Reasonable salary means that a minister should not be over-compensated for the amount of time spent and amount of work accomplished. Usually the opposite is true, a minister can be **under**-compensated. In Rev. Ruling 78-448, a tax protest minister was considered to have been over-compensated and was not allowed to have 100% of his compensation be tax-free housing allowance **because he did not perform any services to**

earn it. The Revenue Ruling deals with a tax protest situation, and has no application to a legitimate church/minister employment relationship. Some IRS personnel have wrongly claimed that Rev. Ruling 78-448 prevents a minister from using 100% housing designation. In the tax court case, Warren v. Commissioner 114 T.C. 23, fourteen judges agreed that a minister's parsonage allowance **could be 100%** of his compensation.

The salary many bi-vocational ministers receive is often less than they are incurring for parsonage expenses. Since parsonage allowance is not required to be shown on Form W-2, **a Form W-2 generally does not need to be prepared** when a minister has 100% of his salary designated as parsonage allowance. You may report a designated parsonage allowance in a separate statement.

Fair Rental Value: The **"top limit"** that can be claimed by a minister as parsonage allowance exclusion is based on his furnished home's fair rental value, cost of utilities, etc. Actual expenses incurred up to this "top limit" can be used as parsonage allowance exclusion. **Most years** the parsonage expenses incurred are much less than the "top limit" and **it is not necessary to calculate** the "top limit". However, in the year of purchase, or a year in which a major payment of principal or a large outlay for improvements or furniture is made, it is important to carefully compute the "top limit" as follows:

FRV of house + FRV of furniture + decorator items + utilities + miscellaneous

To support the computation of your housing allowance in a year of **major expenditures** we recommend you obtain a professional appraisal of your home's fair rental value. Fair rental value is what it would cost to rent a comparable home in your neighborhood. "rule of thumb" among realtors nationwide is that the fair rental value of a home (without furnishings) amounts to **1% of the appraised fair market value** per month. This formula is fairly accurate. However, **the condition, location, local market demand, and local economic conditions** of your home will need to be considered.

Example: If your home is appraised at $150,000, the monthly FRV could be $1,500. Annual FRV could be $18,000 ($1,500 X 12).

The fair rental value of furniture is more difficult to compute. Based on the amount, age, and condition, we recommend that you estimate your furniture FRV conservatively.

Example: Your furniture annual FRV is estimated to be $6,600 ($550 X 12)

We have included space on the "Worksheet for Form 2106" to compute the top limitation in a year of major expense. FRV of the home would take the place of down payment, closing costs, principal, interest, taxes, insurance and major repairs (line 4 through line 9). FRV of the furniture would take the place of actual furniture purchases (line 10). Actual costs of decorator items (line 11), utilities (line 12), and miscellaneous items (line 13) are to be used in addition to the FRV of the home and the FRV of the furniture.

We have **included an example** of the computation of the "top limit" in Rev. Snodgrass's return in Chapter 7. (See page 124)

When actual expenses exceed the fair rental value limitation or the amount designated as rental allowance, **they are lost**. There are no provisions for carryover of unused portions. Rather than lose the ability to exclude your down payment or major cash home expenses, consider obtaining a second mortgage and spreading the costs over a few years and keep within the "top limit" each year. (See "Tax Plan")

● ***Freedom From Religion Foundation - Renewed Challenge of Parsonage allowance- April 6, 2016***

Freedom From Religion Foundation's nonbelieving directors continue their challenge of the parish exemption giving preferential tax benefits to "ministers of the gospel." They are an atheist organization. You can follow their court activity by going to their website: **www.ffrf.org**, then enter "parsonage allowance" in their search engine.

The Freedom From Religion Foundation renewed its challenge against the IRS U.S.C. § 107 in a federal lawsuit filed on April 6, 2016, in the Western District of Wisconsin. Gaylor v. Lew has case number 3:16-cv-00215. Their request for a housing allowance refund for the year 2012 was denied by the IRS.

On November 13, 2014, the United States Court of Appeals for the Seventh Circuit concluded: "The plaintiffs here have never been denied the parsonage exemption because they have never requested it; therefore, they have suffered no injury. Because the plaintiffs do not have standing to challenge the parsonage exemption, we Vacate the judgment of the district court and Remand with instructions to **dismiss the complaint for want of jurisdiction.**" "You'll hear from us again." FFRF Co-Presidents Dan Barker and Annie Laurie Gaylor said they would continue to seek a way to bring down the discriminatory "parsonage exemption" after an appeals court on Nov. 13 overturned a district court ruling, saying they had no standing to sue. "We call this our David vs. Goliath challenge," said Annie Laurie Gaylor, because virtually all major denominations and many minor congregations—including Unitarians, Muslim and Jewish groups—weighed in with amicus briefs against FFRF's challenge to religious privilege.

- **Warren v. Commissioner Tax Court Case**

In Warren v. Commissioner, 114 T.C. 23, decided on May 16, 2000, it was determined that a minister's parsonage allowance should not be limited by the fair rental value computation. Of the seventeen judges considering the case, fourteen agreed and three dissented. The majority stated that Sec. 107(2) was limited to the amount **used** to provide a home, not the fair market rental value of the home. The case also clearly stated that **a minister's parsonage allowance could be 100% of his compensation.**

The IRS appealed the decision in September, 2000. A serious new issue of the constitutionality of parsonage allowance was raised when Professor Erwin Chemerinsky filed a motion to intervene in the appeal. In 2014, the Freedom From Religion Foundation named him a Champion of the First Amendment.

Congress **acted quickly** with Public Law 107-181, on May 20, 2002. **Congress reinstated the fair rental value limitation as their intent.** The "Clergy Housing Allowance Clarification Act of 2002" added new text to Sec. 107, and it is quoted at the beginning of this Chapter. The Warren v. Commissioner, Tax Court No. 14924-98, August 26, 2002, was dismissed.

Therefore, parsonage allowance really **did not change**, just strengthened, and is still limited by the Fair Rental Value computation.

- **Parsonage Allowance Exclusion Can Only be Used for One Home**

Driscoll appealed to the Supreme Court in August, 2012. The U.S. Supreme Court denied the petition on October 1, 2012 to take up the appeal by Phillip Driscoll, who claimed an income tax exclusion for two homes. So the IRS's position that a minister could only use the expenses of **one home** for his parsonage allowance exclusion stands.

History: Since the IRC of 1954 first used the phrase **"a home"** it has been IRS's position that a minister could only use the expenses of **one home** for his parsonage allowance exclusion. The phrase **"a home"** was not included in earlier IRC versions. Expenses for a permanent vacation or second home was considered not allowable for parsonage allowance expenses. He could only use the "main home" as the one in which he and his family live most of the time.

On December 14, 2010, a U.S. Tax Court had held that nothing in Code Sec. 107, its legislative history or the relevant regulations limited the phrase **"a home"** in Code Sec. 107 to only one home for purposes of the excludible parsonage allowance. (Philip A Driscoll v. Commissioner, U.S. Tax Court, CCH Dec. 58415, 135 T.C. No. 27)

On February 8, 2012, in Commissioner v. Phillip A Driscoll, U. S. Court of Appeals, Eleventh Circuit; 11-12454 the U. S. Tax Court decision **was reversed.**

- **Transition Periods**

During a **temporary period** of changing employers, changing parsonages, or building a parsonage, expenses for two parsonages are allowable according to a tax court case, Fred B. Marine, 47 TC 609 (1967). The temporary period would continue as long as both homes remained personal use. In a slow real estate market or a lengthy building project, the temporary period may easily be a year or more.

When the previous home is converted to rental property, none of its expenses can be parsonage allowance. The rental income and expenses will generally be reportable on Schedule E.

- **Tax Plan**

Loans from employers can be used to spread principal payments over a period of time and avoid losing the benefit of parsonage allowance expenses. It is important that interest be charged if the loan exceeds $3,000 and that the loan be secured by the home and recorded at the courthouse. Sec. 483 rules concerning "below market" interest loans require that the **Applicable Federal Rate (AFR)** (published monthly by the IRS) be charged for loans over $3,000. Based on the date of the loan, apply that month's rate for the duration of the loan. (A browser search for "**IRS AFR**" will quickly give you their website with the monthly rates since January 2000!)

Often the minister's employer would rather not charge him interest for a loan. But Sec. **483 says interest is required**. This requirement has a **positive tax benefit** for the minister employee. Secure the loan with the home and record it at the courthouse. The interest will then qualify for deductible "home interest" on Schedule A and also as a part of tax-free parsonage allowance. Therefore, we recommend the following procedure: (1) pay an additional salary factor to equal the correct interest (annually or monthly);

(2) increase the designated parsonage allowance as needed; (3) accept the interest payment from the minister (annually or monthly). The amount of interest deductible on Sch A reduces the minister's taxable income, while the extra salary is tax-free housing, subject only to social security.

Loan principal forgiveness: In the event the employing church who loans their minister money for a down payment or major improvement desires or decides to forgive the principal of a loan we recommend the following procedure: (1) secure the loan with the home and record it at the courthouse; (2) forgive a portion of the loan principal each year so that the "top limit" is not exceeded; (3) increase the designated parsonage allowance as needed; (4) treat the amount of principal forgiven as income.

According to Sec. 7872, loans not involved with real or personal property with "below-market interest rates," require that the Applicable Federal Rate be charged for loans over $10,000.

Good tax planning for a minister is to "overdesignate" his parsonage allowance and allow for unexpected expenses and increases in utility costs to be covered. Any "unused parsonage allowance" will be shown as income on Form 1040, line 7.

- *Bi-Vocational and Part-Time Ministers*

For a minister who is serving part-time and is not fully supported by the employer, it is possible to designate all or 100% of his salary as parsonage allowance. Since parsonage allowance is not required to be shown on Form W-2, a **Form W-2 generally does not need to be prepared**. You may report a designated parsonage allowance in a separate statement.

When a minister is employed outside the church and a new or small congregation cannot fully support him, it is good tax-planning for the minister to make substantial Schedule A contributions to the church. The church will then have the funds to pay an adequate salary, designate it as parsonage allowance, and allow him to take full advantage of Sec. 107 parsonage allowance. The minister who is not exempt from social security will be subject to social security taxes on the parsonage allowance.

- *What If Your Home Is Debt Free?*

Obtaining a new mortgage or equity line of credit that is used for major home improvements is always allowable principal and interest for parsonage allowance. However to refinance and use the proceeds for investments or any non-home purchases, payment of the principal and interest will not be available for parsonage allowance.

In Swaggart v. Commissioner, TC Memo 1984-409, the taxpayer argued that rental allowance was fully excludable from gross income regardless of how the funds were spent.... In rejecting such argument, the court concluded that Congress intended to exclude from the minister's gross income only that portion of his compensation paid by the church which was **actually used** by the minister for providing a home for himself. In a previous case, Reed et al, 82 TC 208, the court had also restricted tax-free parsonage to out-of-pocket expenses. For the minister whose home is paid for or nearly so, the allowable parsonage allowance is limited to actual expenses for taxes, insurance, upkeep, utilities, etc.

Private Letter Ruling 9115051: The IRS tells us their position in regards to "refinancing the debt-free parsonage." (It is important to understand that Sec. 6110(j)(3) of the Code provides that a letter ruling may not be used or cited as precedent.)

The IRS was asked to respond to these questions: "Are payments made on a home equity line of credit (secured by the debt-free home) expenses for which a parsonage allowance may be granted by the church? Would taking out a loan secured by a mortgage on the home result in expenses for which a parsonage allowance may be granted by the church?"

The response of IRS was: "Neither the payments made on the home equity line of credit nor on the mortgage secured by the house are being used to rent or provide a home as required by Sec. 107 and the regulations. Therefore, amounts designated by the church to pay for these expenditures are not excludable from the minister's gross income as a parsonage allowance under Sec. 107."

What is Meant By "Official Designation"?

"Official designation" means that the employer designates, by official action, **IN ADVANCE**, the amount the dual-status minister expects to spend for all the expenses of his home. The designation can be done by the official board or the congregation, and should be recorded in their minutes. **The amount designated as parsonage allowance must be a specific dollar amount or a specific percentage of salary.** Reg. 1.107-1(b) says:

"The term 'rental allowance' means an amount paid to a minister to rent or otherwise provide a home if such amount is designated as rental allowance pursuant to official action..... taken in advance of such payment by the employing church or other qualified organization.

The designation of an amount as rental allowance may be evidenced in an employment contract, in minutes of or in a resolution by a church or other qualified organization or in its budget, or in any other appropriate instrument evidencing such official action. The designation referred to in this paragraph is a sufficient designation if it permits a payment or a part thereof to be identified as a payment of rental allowance as distinguished from salary or other remuneration."

Because the IRS will accept **a perpetually worded designation**, we recommend using a perpetual clause as a **safety net.** Example: "As long as .....the above amount....shall apply to all future years until modified." We recommend that a minister "tax plan" annually and consider if the amount designated needs to be modified for the coming year. The amount designated as parsonage allowance **must be a specific dollar amount or a specific percentage of salary.**

If you were not aware of how to designate your parsonage allowance or you have had an inadequate amount designated, there is no way to fix the problem for the past. **Now** is the time to designate an adequate parsonage allowance for the future or the rest of the year. In advance of paying for a major expense or a changing from a parsonage provided to buying your own home, do not hesitate to **modify and increase** your designation.

● *Qualified Organization*

This regulation requires that an independent party make the designation and prevents "self-designation." A qualified organization does not have to be a religiously affiliated entity to be able to designate parsonage allowance. Nor is it necessary that the designation come from the payor of a minister's compensation. In C.T. Boyd, Jr. v. Commissioner, T.C. Memo 1981-528, the advance designation requirement was considered to be met by designation of the Church Federation of Greater Indianapolis, Inc., a nonprofit corporation, even though Boyd was employed by the Indianapolis Police Department as Senior Chaplain. As a police chaplain he was under the direct supervision of the Chief of Police. The Federation retained supervision over Boyd's ecclesiastical performance and maintained day to day contact with him.

IRS Letter Ruling 9052001 involved a chaplain employed by a state prison. The chaplain's employment, supervision, evaluation and termination were strictly the responsibility of the warden. The chaplain's church had designated a housing allowance. However, since written reports or contacts between the chaplain and his church were voluntary, he was not entitled to exclude a housing allowance as a civil servant of the State.

● *Ministers Who Own*

Ministers who own their homes will want to designate an amount to cover the total cost of owning, cost of their furnishings, cost of decorating, utilities, and etc.

When the title to the home and the real estate mortgage is in the minister's name, the employer should not make the payments for him. Pay the minister enough salary to pay all the home expenses, and designate an adequate amount as parsonage allowance. **Keep it simple.** The minister who owns his own home should pay his payment and all of the home expenses himself.

Hybrid arrangements where the employer pays some of the expenses and the minister pays others, cause confusion and may result in an inadequate designation of parsonage allowance.

When the home is being purchased by the minister it will be subject to real estate tax. When the home is owned by the employing church it is not subject to real estate tax.

Do not do this: Any attempt to creatively place the minister's home in the name of the church to avoid paying real estate tax is absolutely wrong. A future transfer of the title to the minister who has paid for the home may result in the FMV of the home to be taxed as salary and subject to social security tax.

● *Ministers Who Rent*

Ministers who rent their homes will want to designate an amount to cover the actual rent paid, cost of their furnishings, cost of decorating, insurance, utilities, and etc.

● *Church Owns The Parsonage (See Sample Return for Rev. Pious on page 133)*

If the employer provides the home and/or pays the utilities, its value is **automatically free** from income tax. The minister then needs to estimate how much he expects to spend in all of the other categories of home expenses and have that amount of his cash salary designated. It is important to understand that the minister living in a church-owned parsonage has **"two pieces"** to his parsonage allowance. The value of parsonage provided and the amount of parsonage allowance designated for his additional home expenses are **both subject to social security**.

    1. the value of a parsonage provided and

    2. the amount designated as parsonage allowance for the additional home expenses.

- **Evangelists**

According to Rev. Ruling 64-326, a traveling evangelist may exclude amounts he receives from various churches or meetings as tax-free parsonage allowance. There are two ways to handle the designation in advance: (1) A supporting or home church could designate an annual amount even though they do not pay or handle the honorariums, or (2) individual host churches can designate a portion of his honorarium as parsonage allowance. This involves communicating with the various churches in advance and sending them a statement requesting that they take action to "designate" a portion of your honorarium as parsonage allowance. We recommend that you get signed photocopies of the "Statement of Parsonage for An Evangelist". Each church on your itinerary can keep a copy and easily provide you a copy.

A traveling evangelist or conference speaker with a permanent home will incur deductible travel expenses for lodging and meals while on the road and use parsonage allowance exclusion for his permanent home. If he lives in a motor home or travel trailer and does not have a permanent home, his lodging and meal expenses **will not be** deductible as business travel expenses. His tax home for tax purposes is wherever he "hangs his hat." He may treat the motor home as his parsonage but his meals will not be deductible. The cost of transportation between engagements would qualify as business transportation expense.

An evangelist who forms his own nonprofit corporation, will be an employee of the corporation. An evangelist, as long as the services he performs is that of conducting worship and the ministration of sacerdotal functions, is a dual-status minister for tax purposes. The organization's board can easily designate his parsonage allowance.

- *Missionaries*

Sec. 911 foreign earned income exclusion allows most missionaries serving outside of the United States to be able to earn as much as $101,300 in 2016 and pay no income tax. If they do not qualify to use the $101,300 exclusion, the mission should definitely designate the parsonage allowance for the dual-status missionary. Missionaries who are dual-status ministers should always designate a parsonage allowance so that their home expenses will be excluded while on furlough or sick leave. Chapter Five contains a detailed discussion of the special tax situation for missionaries serving outside of the United States.

- *Retired Ministers & Parsonage Designation*

A **retired minister** receiving an otherwise taxable distribution from a qualified Sec. 401(a), Sec. 401(k), Sec. 403(b), Sec. 408(k), Sec. 408(p) or Sec. 414(e) plan may have a **"parsonage allowance"** designated by the former employer or denominational pension board according to Rev. Ruling 63-156. We recommend that a perpetually worded designation state that 100% of the retirement income be designated as parsonage allowance and be tax free to the extent spent for housing. **(See sample wording in this Chapter)** Language found in the Department of Labor Regulations under ERISA indicate that both types of contributions to a Sec. 403(b) plan, ERISA and Non-ERISA, are considered as contributions to an employer's plan and both types are eligible for parsonage allowance designation.

According to Rev. Ruling 72-249, the parsonage allowance exclusion **is not available** to the surviving spouse who continues to receive retirement income as a beneficiary.

Some vendors no longer offer transfer 403(b)s. They only offer "rollover" IRAs. To retain the proper identity of earnings from the ministry, and to preserve the opportunity for designated parsonage allowance, **never co-mingle** retirement funds from ministry earnings with retirement funds from secular earnings.

Third party payors of retirement plan distributions will include the gross distribution on Form 1099-R, Box 1. Not being able to determine the taxable amount Box 2a could be left blank and Box 2b could be checked. As a retired minister receiving distributions from a retirement plan that has been designated as "parsonage allowance" you are to enter the gross amount on Form 1040, line 16a. It is the responsibility of the retired minister to show as taxable on Form 1040, line 16b, any designated distributions not spent for parsonage expenses. If all of the distribution has been spent for parsonage expenses enter -0- on line 16b.

"Retired Minister" is recommended to be shown as "occupation" on Form 1040.

Steps in Designating & Deducting Parsonage Allowance

1. The dual-status minister is to estimate the amount he expects to spend for the coming year and present this to his employer. It is good to overestimate and allow for unexpected expenses and utility cost increases. In advance of a major unexpected expense, or a change from a parsonage provided to buying your own home, do not hesitate to "amend" and increase your designation for the balance of the year.

2. The employer then makes an official written designation based on the dual-status minister's estimate. You may use the suggested wordings we provide.

3. At the close of the tax year, the dual-status minister then compares his actual expenses with the amount designated. If he has incurred any major expenses he will compute the FRV limit. The smallest amount is allowed as his parsonage allowance exclusion.

Parsonage expense details, receipts, and records are **not to be submitted to the employer.** They are handled differently than the professional business expenses we will discuss in Chapter Three. The personal home expenses can **remain confidential**. If the designated amount is greater than the amount substantiated, it is the responsibility of the individual minister to show the "excess parsonage allowance" as income on Form 1040, line 7. Use the "Worksheet for Form 2106" provided in this publication to compute taxable unused parsonage allowance, if any.

A minister who moves and/or changes amounts of parsonage allowance during the year should allocate the annual designations by the week. For example: You were at ABC Church for 17 weeks and your annual parsonage allowance was $15,600. You were at XYZ Church for 35 weeks and your annual parsonage allowance was $23,400. Compute as follows:

$$\$ 15{,}600 \div 52 = \$300 \times 17 \text{ weeks} = \$ \ 5{,}100$$
$$\$ 23{,}400 \div 52 = \$450 \times 35 \text{ weeks} = \$15{,}750$$

Total parsonage allowance for the two positions would be:

$$\$5{,}100 + \$15{,}750 = \$20{,}850.$$

Once the parsonage allowance has been timely designated, there is no need to attach a copy of the official designation to the tax return itself. Merely show the amount properly designated on the "Worksheet for Form 2106." In the event you are chosen for an audit, the IRS will ask for a verification of the timely official designation from the church records.

Suggested Wording of the Official Designation

● *When The Church Owns The Parsonage*

The chairman informed the meeting that under the tax law, a minister of the Gospel is not subject to federal income tax on "the parsonage allowance paid to him as a part of his compensation to the extent used by him to rent or provide a home."

The parsonage is owned by the church and the actual utility expenses will be paid by the church.

After considering the estimate of Rev. _____ of his additional home expenses, a motion was made by _____, seconded by _____ and passed to adopt the following resolution:

Resolved that of the total cash salary for the year, $_____ (or _____%) is hereby designated as parsonage allowance.

Resolved that as long as Rev. _____ is our employee the above amount of designated parsonage allowance shall apply to all future years until modified.

● *When A Minister Owns Or Rents His/Her Own Home*

The chairman informed the meeting that under the tax law, a minister of the Gospel is not subject to federal income tax on "the parsonage allowance paid to him as part of his compensation to the extent used by him to rent or provide a home."

After considering the estimate of Rev._____ of his home expenses, a motion was made by _____, seconded by _____ and passed to adopt the following resolution:

Resolved that of the total cash salary for the year, $_____ (or _____%) is hereby designated as parsonage allowance.

Resolved that as long as Rev. _____ is our employee the above amount of designated parsonage allowance shall apply to all future years until modified.

• *When A Minister Is Employed By A School, College, Or Mission*

Most teachers and administrators working for a church or integral agency of a church have an annual contract of employment with that organization. It is convenient to include the necessary written designation within the contract itself. An "Agreement for the Designation of the Parsonage Allowance" could be worded as follows:

According to the provisions in income tax law, a minister of the Gospel is not subject to federal income tax on the "parsonage allowance paid to him as part of his compensation to the extent used by him to rent or provide a home."

Based on Rev. _____ estimate of his home expenses, it is agreed to officially designate $_____ (or ____%) of his total cash salary as parsonage allowance.

Resolved that as long as Rev. _____ is our employee the above amount of designated parsonage allowance shall apply to all future years until modified.

• *Statement Of Parsonage For An Evangelist*

Evangelists can have a supporting or home church designate an annual amount of the honorariums they will receive as parsonage allowance or they can send a statement to churches on their itinerary and have a portion or all of the honorarium designated as parsonage allowance, in advance of the engagement. **Get a signed photocopy of the following statement for your records:**

According to the provisions in income tax law, a minister of the Gospel is not subject to federal income tax on the "parsonage allowance paid to him as a part of his compensation to the extent used by him to rent or provide a home."

After considering the request of Rev._____, our evangelist, to designate $_____ (or ____%) of his honorarium as parsonage, a motion was made by _____, seconded by _____ and passed to adopt the following resolution:

Resolved that of the total cash honorarium paid to our evangelist, we hereby designate $_____ (or ____%) as parsonage allowance.

Name of Church _____*Date* _____

Signature _____*Title* _____

• **When A Retired Minister Receives Pension and/or Honorariums**

According to the provisions in income tax law, a retired minister of the Gospel is not subject to federal income tax on ministerial retirement distributions or honorariums designated as parsonage allowance to the extent used by him to rent or provide a home.

Resolved that 100% of any retirement distributions, honorariums, or interim salaries are hereby designated as parsonage allowance for Rev. _____.

Resolved that the above amount of 100% of designated parsonage allowance shall apply to all future years.

Name of Church _____*Date* _____

Signature _____*Title* _____

Computation of Parsonage Allowance -"Worksheet For Form 2106"

• *Value of Parsonage Provided by Church*

Enter the value of a home and utilities provided by the employer in the box provided. It is subject to social security tax. Though it seems to be contradictory, we do not have to use the same formula we used earlier in the chapter for computing the "top limit" for the minister who owns his own home. The fair rental value of the parsonage provided should be reasonable, but has historically been allowed to be a conservative amount in audits. **Do not be guilty of understating your rental value** below a reasonable amount and thereby under-state your social security tax liability.

You may wish to consult a local realtor for an appraisal, or make inquiries of local landlords. **The condition, location, local market demand, and local economic conditions will help you to determine a reasonable value.** The fact that you must live in a particular home as a part of your employment, gives reason for a more conservative estimate of the value of a parsonage provided.

We would like to refer you to the guidelines in Sec. 119 for qualified campus lodging. (See discussion in Chapter One, Lay Employees - Sec. 119.) The guidelines for Sec. 119 are not necessarily applicable to Sec. 107, but they do represent guidelines for housing in another setting. A "bare minimum" rental value should be at least 5% x the appraised value of the home provided. Example: 5% x $150,000 = $7,500 annual FRV of home including utilities. The guidelines for Sec. 119 further require that the appraised value be determined at the end of each year by an independent appraiser, not the employer. However, it is intended that the appraisal be reviewed annually without undue cost to the employer.

A conservative, but realistic rental value estimate of Rev. Snodgrass's $150,000 home including utilities, considering all the facts and circumstances stated above, might be **$13,000 to $15,000** a year.

• *If You Own Your Home - See Rev. Snodgrass's Sample Worksheet on page 124*

Enter amounts for all parsonage allowance expenses the minister pays or provides for himself on a cash basis in column B. The actual expenses of the home, furniture, utilities, decorating, and miscellaneous expenses are to be entered in Column B. Enter their total on line 14 of the worksheet.

In a year of incurring **major** expenses, enter the computation of fair rental value of furnished home, decorating, utilities, and miscellaneous expenses in Column A. Examine the sample computation we have shown on Rev. Snodgrass's return in Chapter Seven, page 124. Enter the lesser of line 14, Column A or Column B on line 15.

Enter the amount that has been officially designated as parsonage allowance by the employer on line 16. If line 16 is greater than line 15, enter the "excess parsonage allowance" on line 17 and as income on Form 1040, line 7.

Parsonage allowance, as an exclusion, **is not to be included on Form W-2, Box 1 according to IRS Publication 15-A, page 10-11.** When the parsonage allowance is included in error on Form W-2, Box 1, we recommend that a corrected Form W-2c be prepared. Otherwise, if it becomes necessary to deduct a large negative parsonage allowance amount on Form 1040, line 7 or line 21, IRS audit exposure is greatly increased.

You may report a designated parsonage allowance in a separate statement or in Box 14 on Form W-2.

Computation of Social Security Base -"Worksheet For Form 2106"

Parsonage allowance is free from income tax, but subject to social security and medicare tax. Enter the value of parsonage provided and/or the amount of parsonage allowance designated from line 16 on the lines provided. A minister who has elected to be exempt from social security and has an approved Form 4361 does not have to compute this value for Schedule SE.

Earned income credit may be available for some ministers who did not qualify in the past. We refer you to the final page of text in Chapter Three, "Definition of Earned Income for Ministers," for the changed definitions.

Professional Expenses

In any profession, the ordinary and necessary expenses incurred in order to be able to earn income are deductible according to Sec. 162. In this chapter we will explain how to have an accountable reimbursement plan. The IRS provides very detailed regulations on how to handle reimbursed employee business expenses. It is good stewardship to take the time to learn the rules and legally reduce income tax by adopting a written accountable plan for professional expenses. But first we need to discuss two non-business expense categories.

- ### *Contributions ARE NOT Allowable as Professional Expenses - Always Sch A Deductions*

Contributions, tithes, or offerings paid to a nonprofit organization are always Schedule A itemized deductions. Therefore, regardless of a person's occupation, contributions and tithes are **always** deductible on Schedule A as an itemized deduction.

CAUTION: Over the years we have heard and read **creative illegal proposals** concerning how a minister's contributions could be a salary reduction or reimbursed as a business expense. The concept was especially attractive to ministers who live in parsonages provided by employing churches and are unable to itemize their Schedule A deductions. Computing social security and medicare tax on the reduced income was also attractive. Even if a contract or other arrangement states that excessive dues must be paid by the employee to retain their position, examination of the facts and circumstances will generally determine that taxable compensation has been wrongly reduced.

The following citations are very clear; contributions are Schedule A deductions:

According to Sec. 61, the assignment of income rule, "Income received for personal services is taxable to the person who earns it, even though he assigns it to another."

The Audit Technique Guide for Ministers, (4/09), an IRS training manual for their auditors, contains this comment on page 15, *"Ministers often pay a small annual renewal fee to maintain their credentials, which constitutes a deductible expense. However, ministers' contributions to the church are not deductible as business expenses. They may argue that they are expected to donate generously to the church as part of their employment. This is not sufficient to convert charitable contributions to business expenses."*

The business expense code Sec. 162(b) specifically states that contributions are Schedule A deductions: *"No deductions shall be allowed under subsection 162(a) for any contribution or gift which would be allowable as a deduction under section 170 (Schedule A) were it not for the percentage limitations, the dollar limitations or the requirements as to the time of payment, set forth in such section."*

- ### *Babysitting Expenses Are Not Allowable as Professional Expenses*

The cost of babysitting for your children is never a business expense. According to Sec. 21, child care incurred while both parents are working results in a potential credit to be computed on Form 2441. When an employer pays for an employee's child care, it is generally a taxable fringe benefit and should be included as income on the employee's Form W-2, Box 1. (Exception: a qualified Sec. 129 Dependent Care Assistance Program or a qualified Sec. 125 Cafeteria plan that provides the choice of dependent care assistance.)

- ### *Different Tax Treatment for Parsonage Expense and Professional Expense*

It is important to separate in our thinking the parsonage expense from professional expense since their tax treatment is very different.

Parsonage expense details, receipts, and records **are not to be submitted to the employer.** The personal home expenses can remain confidential. If the designated amount is greater than the amount substantiated, it is the responsibility of the individual minister to show the "excess parsonage allowance" as income on Form 1040, line 7.

Professional expense details, receipts and records **must be submitted** to the employer for reimbursement when there is an "accountable plan." The limitations on deductibility of employee business expenses may be avoided if the church adopts an "accountable plan." An IRS regulation requires there to be a written reimbursement plan between an employer and an employee.

● *Professional Expense Rules are not Unique to Ministers*

The professional expenses discussed in this chapter are available to all employees, both the dual-status minister and lay employee. All of the information in this chapter about auto, travel, and professional expenses is also applicable to for-profit employers and their employees. Independent contractors or evangelists may also adequately account their expenses to a payor.

● *Volunteer Workers*

When a volunteer receives no income as a volunteer for a qualified organization, but incurs out-of-pocket expenses, they are deductible as contributions on Schedule A. Any miles driven for charitable work are deductible at the rate of **14¢** per mile or actual cost of gas and oil. The miles driven to regular church services for personal worship cannot be deducted. Do not deduct any value for your time, it is not allowable. Travel away from home expenses are limited to actual cost of lodging, meals and transportation.

Volunteer workers can be reimbursed at the business mileage rate. A volunteer must adequately account to the organization making the reimbursement to be a "bona fide volunteer" according to IRS INFO 2000-0235, released August 24, 2000. The **2016** rate is **54¢** (2017 rate is 53½¢)

See suggested wording for reimbursement agreement on page 64.

If a volunteer does not submit diaries and receipts to the organization, the organization will be required to treat the payments as compensation, prepare Form W-2, and withhold taxes.

Recordkeeping a Must!!

We recommend a careful reading of **IRS Publication 463**, "Travel, Entertainment, Gift and Car Expenses." Recordkeeping rules have always existed. Adequate records or sufficient evidence must be available to support deductions for auto and professional expenses. A record of the elements of an expense made at or near the time of the expense, supported by sufficient documentary evidence, has more value than a statement prepared later, when generally there is a lack of accurate recall. A log maintained on a **weekly basis** is considered a record made at or near the time of the expense. It can not be stressed enough — **adequate records and receipts must be kept to substantiate all expenses.** Good stewardship means keeping good records!

IRS regulations require that careful and adequate records be kept to submit to the employer for reimbursement. "Adequate accounting" means you will give your employer the same type of records and supporting information that you would be required to show to the IRS if they questioned a deduction on your return during an audit. There is **no relief** from keeping adequate records! Receipts are always required for lodging. Receipts are also required for other expenses of $75.00 or more. You may maintain an **account book or diary** for any **expense under $75.00.** If you prepare a record on a computer, it is considered an adequate record. (IRS Publication 463, pages 25-28)

According to Rev. Ruling 2003-106, if you charge business expense items on your employer's credit card or charge account, you must submit a record of the details as required in Sec. 274. Employees can be provided a monthly printout of their transactions, add the required details, and submit back to the employer with receipts for lodging and items costing $75.00 or more.

We have available a **"Professional Tax Record Book"** for ministers, missionaries, and professional individuals. It is designed to provide a convenient and efficient way to keep the auto, travel, and professional expense record details required by the IRS. Monthly summary pages are provided. You can easily photocopy the pages and receipts and submit them to your employer for reimbursement. For those who only need to keep records for auto business miles and auto expenses, we have available an **"Auto Log."** Information for ordering these books is given in the back of this publication.

Unreimbursed Professional Expenses

There is no dispute that in order to adopt a written accountable reimbursement plan both the employer and the employee must understand the rules. Therefore, the following results of not establishing such a plan will hopefully provide the motivation to do so and save tax dollars legally. **It is good stewardship** to reduce income tax by **adopting a written accountable plan** for professional expenses!

Unreimbursed professional expenses, other than auto and travel, carry the extra burden of being "required by your employer" and as "a condition of your employment". Establishing an accountable plan and becoming reimbursed by your employer is a good way to show these requirements are met.

If an employer chooses to provide an expense allowance arrangement that **does not meet** the accountable plan requirements, the employer **must report all amounts paid** under the non-accountable plan **as wages** on the employee's Form W-2, Box 1, even though an employee might voluntarily substantiate expenses to the employer and return any excess amounts to the employer. Such allowances paid to lay employees are subject to withholding of income tax and social security withholding and matching. The dual-status minister will incur additional income tax, but can still reduce his social security base by the amount of unreimbursed business expenses.

Tax Savings Illustrated: Our sample return for Rev. Snodgrass in Chapter Seven is computed "without reimbursement" and "with accountable reimbursement." The difference of **$1,198.00** in tax liability illustrates the value of establishing an accountable reimbursement plan.

If You Do Not Adequately Account To Your Employer

Reg. 1.162-17(c) says, **"Expenses for which the employee is not required to account to his employer. If the employee is not required to account to his employer for his ordinary and necessary business expenses, e.g., travel, transportation, entertainment, and similar items, or, though required, fails to account for such expenses, he must submit, as a part of his tax return, a statement showing the following information:"**

All amounts received as advances or reimbursements from his employer, that were not adequately accounted for, must be included as income on Form W-2, Box 1. In order to deduct non-accounted professional expenses on his tax return, he must complete Form 2106 based on his records and supporting evidence.

The following consequences happen when there is no accountable plan:

1. The expenses become "below the line" deductions on Form 2106 and Schedule A. Meals and entertainment are first reduced by 50%, then combined with other miscellaneous expenses, and further reduced by 2% of the employee's Adjusted Gross Income. With higher standard deductions, many taxpayers do not have enough deductions to itemize. **Unless...**they adopt a written reimbursement plan and adequately account to their employer and become reimbursed for all their professional expenses they may lose the income tax deduction entirely. The standard deduction for **2016** is **$12,600** for a joint return and **$6,300** for a single return. Reimbursed auto, travel, and professional expenses are not reduced by 2% of AGI. Employees can be 100% reimbursed for meals. Employers deduct only 50% of reimbursed meals & entertainment as a business expense. Nonprofit employers are not affected since they have no tax liability.

2. A large amount of unreimbursed professional expenses deducted on Schedule A causes many employees to be audited. It is a high "DIF" score area of a tax return. Establishing an accountable reimbursement plan with your employer could prevent the time consuming trauma of proving your expenses to an IRS auditor.

3. Many states do not allow itemized deductions. Therefore, unreimbursed professional expenses cause additional state income tax.

4. Items such as earned income credit, refundable child tax credit, deductible IRAs, percentage of medical deduction limitation, percentage of child care credit allowable, educational credits, taxable social security benefits, etc, are all affected by the amount of the Adjusted Gross Income figure. Establishing a written accountable reimbursement plan with your employer may qualify you for other deductions and credits. **Parents of college students may qualify for more financial aid.**

5. For lay employees the social security base for both the employer and the employee is greater when there are unreimbursed professional expenses. Establishing an accountable reimbursement plan with your employer will allow the employer to compute social security withholding and matching on just the salary. Dual-status ministers have always been able to reduce their social security base by unreimbursed business expenses.

6. When a dual-status minister's income is a combination of taxable salary and Sec. 107 non-taxable parsonage allowance only the percentage of **unreimbursed** professional expenses that were spent in earning the taxable salary are allowable. The percentage of expenses spent in earning the non-taxable parsonage allowance are not allowed. Read the following explanation.

Sec. 265 - Proration of Unreimbursed Expenses

If you establish a written accountable expense reimbursement plan and are adequately accounting to your employer for your auto, travel, and professional expenses, the Sec. 265 limitation **WILL NOT affect you.** Your employer's reimbursement of 100% of your employee business expenses will be non-taxable.

A 1988 court case, Melvin H. Dalan & Lillian J. Dalan, Docket No. 8278-87, T.C. Memo 1988-106, filed March 9, 1988, resurrected an old IRS application of Sec. 265. Unreimbursed ministerial trade or business expenses are not deductible to the extent they are spent to earn non-taxable housing.

Example: A minister receives $40,000, including $16,000 housing allowance. His unreimbursed professional expenses amount to $4,000. ($16,000 divided by $40,000 = 40% X $4,000 = $1,600) $1,600 is the amount of the unreimbursed expenses spent to earn the non-taxable housing that he would not be able to deduct. The proration of unreimbursed expenses is to be computed on Form 2106 and Schedule A for the employed minister and on Schedule C for the self-employed evangelist.

History of the issue goes back to the David E. Deason case, Docket No. 3993-62, January 10, 1964. During the 60's and early 70's we prorated and did not deduct a minister's expenses spent to earn his non-taxable housing allowance. In 1977, the Internal Revenue Manual Audit, 45(11)3 said that the interpretation of the Service was that Sec. 265 should not be applied to a minister's unreimbursed employee business expenses. The promise of a Rev. ruling in the 1977 Memo never happened. Instead, the memo seems to have vanished. Therefore several decisions, such as the Dalan case, were made that were contrary to the IRS's 1977 position. A 1992 court case, Robert H. McFarland and Georgia W. McFarland, Docket No. 28246-90, T.C. Memo 1992-440, filed August 4, 1992, upheld the Deason and Dalan cases. Likewise, a 2005 court case, Johnny J. and Brenda D. Young, Docket No. 18021-02S, T.C. Summary 2005-76, Sec. 265 proration was upheld and applied.

• *The Official Position of the IRS*

The official position of the IRS since 1988 has been to follow the Deason and Dalan Court Cases. **IRS Publication 517**, page 10, contains the published position of the IRS: unreimbursed ministerial trade or business expenses are not deductible to the extent they are spent to earn non-taxable housing. If you receive a tax-free rental or parsonage allowance and have ministerial expenses, you must attach a statement to your tax return showing how you computed the percentage of unreimbursed expenses that are not allowed. In Publication 517, pages 13 through 25, a comprehensive example of a completed minister's tax return illustrates the allocation computation.

Our sample return for Rev. Snodgrass, "Without Reimbursement," in Chapter Seven shows the computation for prorating unreimbursed expenses, using the "Worksheet to be Used With Form 2106, Part B."

Reimbursed Professional Expenses

An employee may deduct from gross income, to arrive at adjusted gross income, only those expenses paid or incurred by him in connection with his employment that are reimbursed under a reimbursement or other expense arrangement with his employer.

To be an accountable reimbursement plan, the plan must meet the following three requirements:
(1) business connection,
(2) adequate accounting, and
(3) return of any excess reimbursement.

A written reimbursement plan allows both the employer and employee to have a clear understanding of their responsibilities. (**Sample policy wording** is provided later in this chapter.) Reg. 1.62-2(d)(1) requires that the payment for an "adequately accounted reimbursement" be identified either by **making a separate payment** or by specifically indicating the separate amount if both wages and the reimbursement are combined in a single payment. If an employer includes salary, housing, and professional expense reimbursement in one check, they must identify the different amounts on the check and in their accounting.

We recommend that an employee submit his substantiation of employee business expenses for reimbursement no less often than **monthly**. If an employee has a cash flow problem and needs to be reimbursed more often, allow him to submit his records on a **weekly** basis.

CAUTION: When an employer and employee have established an accountable reimbursement plan, it is important to be careful to submit all allowable expenses. An employee cannot deduct expenses on his tax return that he failed to submit to the employer for reimbursement (Drury v. Commissioner, T.C. Memo 1977-199).

CAUTION: When an employer reimburses an employee for non-business meals, overseas travel that does not qualify as business, or personal family members travel expenses it must be reported as **income** on the employee's Form W-2, Box 1.

Tax Law & Regulations

Sec. 62(a)(2)(A) says, **"General Rule. ....the term `adjusted gross income' means, in the case of an individual, gross income minus the following deductions:....**

(A) Reimbursed expenses of employees. The deductions allowed by part VI (section 161 and following) which consist of expenses paid or incurred by the taxpayer, in connection with the performance by him of services as an employee, under a reimbursement or other expense allowance arrangement with his employer...."

Sec. 62(c) says, **"Certain Arrangements Not Treated as Reimbursement Arrangements: For purposes of subsection (a)(2)(A), an arrangement shall in no event be treated as a reimbursement or other expense allowance arrangement if:**

(1) such arrangement does not require the employee to substantiate the expenses covered by the arrangement to the person providing the reimbursement, or

(2) such arrangement provides the employee the right to retain any amount in excess of the substantiated expenses covered under the arrangement.
The substantiation requirements of the preceding sentence shall not apply to any expense to the extent that substantiation is not required under section 274(d) for such expense by reason of the regulations prescribed under the 2nd sentence thereof."

Regulation 1.62-2(d)(3) says: **"Reimbursement requirement   (i) In general. If a payor arranges to pay an amount to an employee regardless of whether the employee incurs (or is reasonably expected to incur) business expenses of a type described in paragraph (d)(1) or (d)(2) of this section, the arrangement does not satisfy this paragraph (d) and all amounts paid under the arrangement are treated as paid under a nonaccountable plan."**

Business Connection

The Past: (Before 1991) Employees of nonprofit organizations have often had to absorb the "cost of doing ministry business." Especially small to medium size congregations have said, "Pastor, we understand you will incur auto and professional expenses and we will include enough in your salary to cover them. Just do not bother us with the details." Before 1991, temporary regulations permitted the employer to subtract an employee's adequately accounted business expenses from the gross salary and only report the remaining portion as taxable salary. **It was not necessary to change the "cash flow."** This was recharacterization.

The Present: (Since January 1, 1991) Your expenses must have a business connection, that is, you must have paid or incurred deductible expenses while performing services as an employee of your employer.

The Audit Technique Guide for Ministers, page 9, says: *"As long as the minister is entitled to receive the full amount of annual compensation, regardless of whether or not any employee business expenses are incurred during the taxable year, the arrangement does not meet the reimbursement requirement."*

An employer must provide two separate budget categories: salary & expense reimbursement. The budget established for expense reimbursement can only be used to reimburse adequately accounted business expenses. Any unused budget amount remains in the employer's account. **There must be the possibility of a change in overall "cash flow."** (See Chapter Six, "Steps in Establishing a Compensation Package")

The tax benefits and reduced audit exposure gained by having an accountable reimbursement plan should convince employers and their employees to carefully meet the requirements of an accountable plan. There are two choices for the employer: (**Sample policy wording** is provided later in this chapter.)

1. **"Salary plus Unlimited reimbursement:"** If the employer is willing to bear the burden of the "cost of doing ministry business" they can adopt a policy to fully reimburse the employee for all adequately accounted business expenses incurred. The amount the employer budgeted for expenses may be more or less than the actual amount reimbursed.

2. **"Salary plus Fixed limit reimbursement:"** If the employer feels that they can not assume the unknown amount of the "cost of doing ministry business" they can adopt a policy to reimburse the employee for adequately accounted business expenses up to a fixed limit. If the employee does not incur enough employee business expenses to **"use"** all of the fixed limit amount, he can not be paid the difference nor can it be carried over from one calendar year to the next. This **"use it or lose it"** nature of an accountable reimbursement plan is similar to the tax treatment that applies to Sec. 125 cafeteria fringe benefit plans. If the employee incurs extra expenses, he can deduct them on his Form 2106.

● *How to Start a New Reimbursement Policy or Fix a Partial Reimbursement Policy Already in Place*

It is important to understand that it can be accomplished without **any additional cost to the employer**. It is also possible that the employer will want to **increase** the employee's compensation package by **providing "new money"** for the reimbursement policy for business expenses.

Make a conservative estimate of the amount of business expenses expected to be incurred for the year. When available, examine the employee's past business expense records and deductions on his past two or three years of tax returns. After a determination of the average business expenses incurred in the past, consider if there will be any changes or major expenses for the coming year. From the current amount of compensation, including any partial reimbursements being paid, subtract this **conservative** amount. The reduced salary and the amount available for business expense reimbursement become two completely separate budget amounts.

Employers who initially adjust the employee's salary and adopt an "unlimited" policy will simply reimburse the employee each year for the actual expenses adequately accounted.

Employers who initially adjust the employee's salary and adopt a "fixed limit" policy, according to Private Letter Ruling **9822044** can, prior to the start of a calendar year, determine the amount the "fixed limit" will be in the succeeding year. It is acceptable policy to readjust the "fixed limit" amount for the following calendar or fiscal year according to Private Letter Ruling **200930029**. To be an accountable reimbursement plan, the policy must state that the employee will not receive any unused portion and that any unused portion will not be carried over to another year.

When a "fixed limit" policy is adopted this is what happens:

1. If the employee's expenses are greater than the fixed limit amount, he can deduct what was not able to be reimbursed as "below the line" Schedule A itemized deductions, subject to limitations.

2. If the employee's expenses are less than the fixed limit amount, the difference between the expenses and the fixed limit amount can not be received by the employee and can not be carried over from one calendar year to the next.

Because of the **"use it or lose it"** nature of an accountable reimbursement plan, we recommend that an accountable reimbursement plan be carefully planned and not be overstated.

● *Examples*

Example (1). Community Church pays its minister $500 per week or $26,000 annually. $10,400 has been designated as parsonage allowance. At the end of the month he adequately accounts his employee business expenses of $265 for the month. Community Church designates $265 of the $500 as paid to reimburse the minister's employee business expenses. Because Community Church would pay the minister $500 a week regardless of whether the minister incurred employee business expenses, the arrangement **does not satisfy** the reimbursement requirement of Reg. 1.62-2(d)(3)(i). Community Church must report ($26,000 - $10,400) $15,600 as wages on Form W-2. (This plan would have been an accountable plan for years ending before 1-1-1991.)

Example (2). Community Church pays its minister $500 per week or $26,000 annually. Community Church initially adjusts its minister's salary to $23,000, designates parsonage allowance of $10,400 and adopts a fixed limit reimbursement plan of $3,000. Each month the minister received an expense reimbursement check for the amount of employee business expenses he adequately accounted to his employer. At the end of the year, Community Church had paid their minister expense reimbursements of only $2,400. They decided that they would give him a bonus of $600. The entire $3,000 must be included on Form W-2. Community Church must report ($26,000 - $10,400) $15,600 as wages on Form W-2. The plan **does not satisfy** the reimbursement requirement of Reg. 1.62-2(d)(3)(i)

Example (3). Community Church pays its minister $500 per week or $26,000 annually. Community Church initially adjusts its minister's salary to $23,000, designates parsonage allowance of $10,400 and adopts a fixed limit reimbursement plan of $3,000. Each month the minister received an expense reimbursement check for the amount of employee business expenses he adequately accounted to his employer. At the end of the year, Community Church had paid their minister expense reimbursements of $2,400. Community Church correctly included ($23,000 - $10,400) $12,600 on Form W-2 for their minister. Their reimbursement plan **does satisfy** all the conditions of an "accountable plan."

Example (4). Community Church pays its minister $500 per week or $26,000 annually. Community Church initially adjusts its minister's salary to $23,000, designates parsonage allowance of $10,400 and adopts an unlimited reimbursement plan for employee business expenses. Each month the minister received an expense reimbursement check for the amount of employee business expenses he adequately accounted to his employer. At the end of the year, Community Church had paid their minister expense reimbursements of $3,600. Community Church correctly included ($23,000 - $10,400) $12,600 on Form W-2 for their minister. Their reimbursement plan **does satisfy** all the conditions of an "accountable plan."

Adequate Accounting

- ### *Definition Of Adequate Accounting*

    Reg. 1.274-5A(e)(4) says, **"Definition of an 'adequate accounting' to the employer.... means the submission to the employer of an account book, diary, statement of expense, or similar record maintained by the employee in which the information as to each element of an expenditure is recorded at or near the time of the expenditure, together with supporting documentary evidence, in a manner which conforms to all the 'adequate records' requirements of paragraph (c)(2) of this section."**

Regulations further instruct us that a responsible person other than the employee must verify and approve the records and amounts of expense. Such a person should be careful not to allow personal expenses to be submitted. Employers are to maintain or keep records of reimbursed business expenses for at least three years after the due date of the employee's tax return. Even though it is not required, we would recommend that the records and receipts be photocopied and that both the employee and the employer keep the records. Our **"Professional Tax Record Book"** contains monthly summary pages that are easily photocopied, and has been designed to make it easy to adequately account to your employer. **The instructions for each section of the record book outline the requirements of Sec. 274 and the necessary details to record for each category of expense.**

The details of time, place, destination, business purpose, business discussion, etc., are very important details to record at or near the time of the business expense or trip. Each type of business expense and Sec. 274 requirements that apply to it are discussed in more detail later in this chapter. A record of the elements of an expense made at or near the time of the expense, supported by sufficient documentary evidence, has more value than a statement prepared later when generally there is a lack of accurate recall. A log maintained on a **weekly basis** is considered a record made at or near the time of the expense. If you charge business expense items on your employer's credit card you must submit a record of the required details and receipts for lodging and expenses of $75.00 or more to your employer.

You must have **actual receipts** for **lodging** and any other **professional expense of $75.00** or more. Request and get receipts. Keep credit card receipts and/or statements that are itemized. Consider using duplicate style checks because bank and credit unions no longer return canceled checks. You may maintain an **account book or diary** that includes all of the required details for any **expense that is less than $75.00.** If you prepare a record on a computer, it is considered an adequate record. (IRS Publication 463, page 25-28)

It is **not sufficient** if an employee merely groups expenses into broad categories such as "travel" or reports individual expenses through the use of vague, non descriptive terms such as "miscellaneous business expenses," according to Reg. 1.62-2(e)(3).

- *If You Do Adequately Account To Your Employer*

  Reg. 1.274-5A(e)(2) says, **"Reporting of expenses for which the employee is required to make an adequate accounting to his employer (i) Reimbursements equal to expenses. For purposes of computing tax liability, an employee need not report on his tax return business expenses for travel, transportation, entertainment, gifts, and similar purposes, paid or incurred by him solely for the benefit of his employer for which he is required to, and does make an adequate accounting to his employer and which are charged directly or indirectly to the employer (for example, through credit cards) or for which the employee is paid through advances, reimbursements, or otherwise, provided that the total amount of such advances, reimbursements and charges is equal to such expenses."**

  If you do adequately account to your employer the following will occur:

  1. You do not report on your tax return the reimbursement for professional business expenses when you establish an accountable reimbursement plan with your employer.

  2. You do not have to keep records for possible IRS audit. You do not have to substantiate your expense account for the IRS auditor as you have already done so with your employer. The employer must retain the records and receipts submitted by you. If your return is audited, show the IRS auditor a copy of the written accountable reimbursement plan you established with your employer.

  3. The employer does not include the reimbursements on the W-2, Box 1.

  Other references to support the above discussion of reimbursement policies are Reg. 1.62-2 and Reg. 1.162-17.

  Accountable plan rules not met. Even though you are reimbursed under an accountable plan, some of your expenses may not meet all the rules. Those expenses that fail to meet all the rules for accountable plans are treated as having been reimbursed under a nonaccountable plan according to Reg 1.62-2(j) Example(2)

  It is possible for an employer to have a combination of "accountable" and "nonaccountable" reimbursements for the same employee. The nonaccountable portion is to be reported as taxable salary on Form W-2, Box 1.

- *Adequate Accounting Requirement Is Satisfied by Mileage Allowance & Per Diem*

  Adequate accounting requirement is satisfied when:

  1. The amount of reimbursement is based on the auto mileage allowance of **54¢** per mile and the employee's log of business miles, date, place, and purpose.

  2. The amount of reimbursement for travel away from home is based on the per diem allowance of **$275 or $185** per day and the employee's record of number of days, place, and purpose of travel. (see IRS list of eligible high cost cities on page 81 of this chapter)

  3. The amount of reimbursement for meals away from home (incurred without cost of lodging) is based on the city by city M&IE rate from the IRS tables per day and the employee's record of number of days, place, and purpose. (Notice 2016-58 and Rev. Proc. 2011-47)

  Per diem rates are adjusted for inflation and cover a convenient calendar year time period now. Employee mileage allowances and per diem travel subsistence allowances that are not in excess of IRS-set maximums may relieve difficulty of substantiation and generate a deduction that is greater than actual travel expenses. You must use the same method of accounting for the whole year. We will give more detailed discussion under "TRAVEL" later in this Chapter. Compare the options shown in our discussion of "travel," and use the method that allows the greater deduction.

  Notice 2015-137 announced the **54¢ mileage allowance rate for 2016**. With or without a reimbursement plan, taxpayers are allowed **54¢** per mile for all of their business miles.

  IRS has announced the **53½¢ mileage allowance rate for 2017 in IRS Notice 2016-169**.

- *When Actual Auto Expenses Exceed The Cents Per Mile Computation*

  If you are incurring more than **54¢** per mile to operate your auto, it may be beneficial to submit your business percentage of actual expenses to your employer. Otherwise, any unreimbursed excess expense becomes a Schedule A deduction subject to the 2% of AGI limitation and the Sec. 265 limitation. **Annually** choose to become reimbursed for actual expenses **or** mileage allowance. Rev. Proc 2010-51, Sec. 6, describes a fixed and variable rate (FAVR) allowance that is acceptable to the IRS. However, we recommend the following procedure of computing actual:

1. Compute auto depreciation for year and divide by 12.
2. Total actual monthly expenses for gas, oil, repairs, etc., (omit auto payment).
3. Estimate what your annual percentage of business use will be or use the business percentage that you recorded for previous year.
4. Multiply business percentage by the total of depreciation and expenses for the month and submit to your employer for reimbursement.
5. At the end of the year: Divide business miles by total miles for the year to know what your ACTUAL business percentage is.
6. Multiply actual business percentage by the total of depreciation and expenses for the full year.
7. Submit the difference between the annual auto expense computed and what has been reimbursed during the other 11 months of the year to your employer for December's reimbursement.

Return of Amounts Exceeding Expenses

If you are advanced more than your allowable expenses, you must return the excess reimbursement to your employer within a reasonable time. Reg 1.62-2(f)(2) states: in cases when an employee is reimbursed by the employer on **the basis of a per diem or auto mileage allowance up to the IRS-specified rates,** there is deemed to be **no excess retained** by the employee. An "above the line" deduction is allowed up to the IRS-specified rate. Any reimbursement to an employee in excess of the IRS-specified rates can be treated by the employer as "above the line" deductions when the employee submits proof of actual expenses that equal the amount of reimbursement.

An accountable plan must generally require the employee to return any amount paid under the arrangement over and above substantiated expenses within a reasonable period of time. Advances for expenses must be reasonably calculated to not exceed anticipated expenses and any excess must be returned to the employer within a reasonable period of time after receipt. Under the "fixed date method," the following are treated as having occurred within a reasonable period of time:

1. an advance made within 30 days of when an expense is paid or incurred,
2. an expense substantiated to the payor within 60 days after it is paid or incurred, or
3. an amount returned to the employer within 120 days after an expense is paid or incurred.

We recommend that nonprofit employers **avoid adopting a plan that allows for payment of "advances."** If an "advance" is not paid to an employee this more complex bookkeeping procedure is automatically satisfied. Employers who have volunteer treasurers should choose the **simplicity** of periodically reimbursing their employees for actual expenses and/or IRS-specified rates as they are submitted.

Although the "reasonable time" periods do not specifically apply to plans without "advances," we do recommend that an employee account for his expenses within the guidelines. We also recommend that an employee submit his substantiation of employee business expenses for reimbursement no less often than **monthly**. If the employee has a cash flow problem and needs to be reimbursed more often, allow him to submit his records on a **weekly** basis.

Adopt One of the Following Reimbursement Plans

One of the following plans should be adopted for each employee. An employer does not have to have the same plan for all employees. An accountable reimbursement plan is very important to your employees' economic health! **A written reimbursement plan** allows both the employer and employee to have a clear understanding of their responsibilities.

If you and your employer do not have a written reimbursement plan, you must report your expenses as "unreimbursed" on Form 2106 and Schedule A. A plan is not able to be retroactive; it becomes effective for the future at the time it is adopted. Adopting a reimbursement plan on a calendar year basis causes less confusion than a fiscal year plan.

You may customize one of the following policies to clearly state the agreement between the employer and the employee. For example, if you wish to state that the amount of reimbursement will be at the IRS-specified mileage allowance and/or per-diem allowances for travel, add a sentence that clearly states this in your agreement.

Salary Plus Unlimited Reimbursement

The chairman informed the meeting that according to Sec. 62(a)(2)(A), an employee that adequately accounts to the employer the details of their professional expenses, is allowed a deduction from gross income. Sec. 62(c) further requires an employee to return any excess reimbursement or advance to the employer within a reasonable time. Reg. 1.62-2(d)(3) further requires that no part of our employee's salary be recharacterized as being paid under this reimbursement arrangement.

A motion was made by_____ seconded by_____and passed to adopt the following resolution:

Resolved that in addition to the salary provided our employee, we will reimburse him/her for auto, travel and professional expenses considered ordinary and necessary for him/her to carry out his/her duties. (Add special modifications here.)

It is further understood that a person other than the employee will examine the adequately accounted records and that the records will be kept for at least four years by the employer.

Salary Plus Fixed Limit Reimbursement

The chairman informed the meeting that according to Sec. 62(a)(2)(A), an employee that adequately accounts to the employer the details of their professional expenses, is allowed a deduction from gross income. Sec. 62(c) further requires an employee to return any excess reimbursement or advance to the employer within a reasonable time. Reg. 1.62-2(d)(3) further requires that no part of our employee's salary be recharacterized as being paid under this reimbursement arrangement.

A motion was made by_____, seconded by_____and passed to adopt the following resolution:

Resolved that in addition to the salary provided our employee, we will reimburse him/her for auto, travel and professional expenses considered ordinary and necessary for him/her to carry out his/her duties up to a fixed limit of $_____. (Add special modifications here.) If his/her actual expenses are less than this fixed limit, he/she cannot be given the difference as bonus or salary, nor can it be carried over to the next year. If his/her actual expenses are greater than this fixed limit, he/she will be required to deduct the extra expenses on Form 2106 and Schedule A.

It is further understood that a person other than the employee will examine the adequately accounted records and that the records will be kept for at least four years by the employer.

Suggested Wording for Volunteer Reimbursement Policy:

The chairman informed the meeting that according to IRS INFO 2000-0235, volunteer workers can be reimbursed by the church for expenses incurred in ministry. Travel away from home expenses are limited to actual cost of lodging, meals and transportation. Volunteer workers can be reimbursed at the business mileage rate.

A motion was made by_____, and seconded by_____ and passed to adopt the following resolution:

Resolved that we will reimburse our volunteers for auto, travel and professional expenses considered ordinary and necessary for their volunteer ministry.

It is further understood that a person other than the volunteer will examine the adequately accounted records and that the records will be kept for at least four years by the church.

Typical Professional Expenses for a Minister

Auto Expense

The cost of business transportation is the largest employee business expense that a minister typically incurs. Therefore, it is very important to understand how to arrive at the "largest" deduction or reimbursement that is allowable. We encourage you to read **IRS Publication 463,** "Travel, Entertainment, Gift and Car Expenses."

- *Effect of Employer Reimbursement Plans*

When you **lease an auto and you adequately account to your employer** for your business mileage, you do have the **choice** of being reimbursed at the IRS mileage allowance rate or the business percentage of your actual expenses. If the business percentage of the cost of your lease (**reduced** by inclusion factor discussed later), combined with other operating expenses, is greater than the IRS mileage allowance rate, you will want to adequately account to your employer the business percentage of your actual expenses.

When you **own an auto and you adequately account to your employer** for your business mileage, you have the **choice** of being reimbursed at the IRS mileage allowance rate or the business percentage of your actual expenses.

Log Your Business Miles

Dedicate one auto for business use when possible. Because of depreciation limits placed on less than 50% business use autos, it is advisable to concentrate business use to one auto at a time to keep the percentage of business use above 50%. Because the sale or trade of your auto used for business is a reportable transaction, a separate mileage log for each auto used in business must be kept to prove the business percentage of each auto's basis. It is not easy to **keep a log of miles traveled** for business, **but you must.** When you experience the amount of tax savings generated by being able to fully deduct your business mileage expense, you will agree that keeping a business mileage log is very worthwhile.

Rev. Ruling 1999-7 clarifies the circumstances under which daily trips between a residence and a work location will be deductible as business mileage. In general, daily trips incurred in going between your residence and a work location is **nondeductible commuting expense**. However, the following circumstances permit deductible business miles:

1. Daily trips between your residence and a **temporary** work location outside the metropolitan area where you live and normally work qualify as business miles. Daily trips between your residence and a temporary work location within that metropolitan area are not deductible as business miles unless (2) or (3) below applies.

2. If you have one or more regular work locations away from your residence, you may log as business miles the distance between your residence and a temporary work location in the same trade or business, regardless of the distance.

3. If your residence is your principal place of business according to Sec. 280A(c)(1)(A), you may log as business miles the distance between your residence and another work location in the same trade or business, regardless of whether the other location is regular or temporary and regardless of the distance.

Multiple trips between your residence and work location during the day are all non-deductible commuting miles. The distance between your residence and the **first business stop** of the day and/or between the **last business stop** of the day and your residence are non-deductible as commuting miles. Careful planning of your itinerary and daily entries in your mileage log may legally lessen your non-deductible commuting for some days according to Shea v. Commissioner, T.C. Memo 1979-303.

Rev. Ruling 1999-7 defines a "temporary work location" as one that is expected to last (and does in fact last) one year or less.

How to Log Business Miles: One entry in your mileage log is sufficient to record a daily business trip consisting of several stops without interruption or a business trip consisting of several days away from home. De minimis personal use, such as a lunch stop between two business stops, is not an interruption in business use. Our **"Professional Tax Record Book"** and our **"Auto Log"** have been designed to make it easy to record all the details necessary for your mileage log and actual auto expenses. Your mileage log should contain the following information:

1. Date
2. Odometer reading at beginning of trip
3. Odometer reading at end of trip
4. Business miles driven for the day
5. Place and purpose of the trip

Sale Or Trade Of Business Auto

It is very important that you keep a record of your auto's basis because, upon sale or trade, you must properly compute the gain or loss. The only way to accurately compute each auto's basis is to keep **separate** mileage records for each auto used.

Regardless of whether you have used optional mileage allowance or actual expense method, the sale or trade of an auto with business use results in a reportable transaction on Form 4797 or Form 8824. **A sale** will result in **a gain that is taxable** or **a loss that is deductible** on Form 4797. **A trade** will affect the basis of the new auto, according to Sec. 1031. Form 8824, Like Kind Exchanges, is required to be attached to your tax return to report a trade transaction. We have included an example of an auto trade and Form 8824 in Chapter Seven for Rev. Snodgrass.

Knowing the basis of your auto makes it possible to tax plan. If the potential value of your auto would cause a **gain upon sale**, generally it would be **best to trade autos.** If the potential value of your auto would cause a **loss upon sale**, generally it would be **best to sell the auto outright,** deduct the loss and buy the replacement auto outright. (IRS Publication 463, page 24-25)

• *Depreciation Adjustment to Basis*

If the actual cost method and MACRS method of depreciation are chosen in the first year, you must use the Modified Accelerated Cost Recovery System (MACRS) depreciation for the life of the auto. Even if your employer reimburses you under an accountable plan at the optional rate, you still must use your choice of MACRS to determine your basis.

If the optional mileage allowance method to deduct the business use of your auto is chosen for the first year your auto is placed in service, an optional depreciation factor reduces the basis of your auto in determining the adjusted basis when you dispose of it. All business miles should be multiplied by the factor to determine the optional depreciation factor.

The rate for **2016** is **24¢**. The rate for 2015 was **24¢**. The rate for 2014 was **22¢**. The rate for 2013 and 2012 was **23¢**. The rate for 2011 was **22¢**. The rate for 2010 was **23¢**. The rate for 2009 and 2008 was **21¢**. (2017 is 25¢)

Exception: If the actual cost method is used to deduct the business use of your auto for **any year other than the first year**, you must use 5 year straight line as the depreciation method. You will combine the optional factor for years of mileage allowance method with the actual depreciation for years of actual expense method to determine your basis.

We have designed a **"Worksheet to Compute Auto Basis."** The backside of the worksheet contains the technical rules that we are detailing in this chapter. We advise you to enter your auto information on our worksheet each year, unstaple it each year and bring it forward to the current return. In a year of sale or trade you will have the necessary information to make the required basis calculations. Information for ordering this form is given in the back of this publication. We feel the best way to illustrate the basis computation on the worksheet is to include an auto trade situation in our sample problem for Rev. Snodgrass in Chapter Seven.

When gathering your information for the preparation of your tax return, please provide the type of information you see on the form and **copies of prior year tax returns** showing how your auto basis has been handled.

Auto Interest & Personal Property Tax

Auto interest and personal property tax are not available as an employee business expense. Do not become reimbursed for the business percentage of auto interest and personal property tax. Interest on an auto for an employee is considered "personal interest" and is not deductible on Schedule A. Personal property or excise tax is deductible on Schedule A by employees. Sales tax for the purchase of an auto used in business is to be added to the cost basis as a capital expense. The personal portion of sales tax may be deducted on Schedule A.

Self-employed business use or farm use have the advantage of being able to deduct the business percentage of interest and personal property tax on Schedule C or F. Based on Rev. Ruling 80-110, Sec. 1402(a) and Sec. 62(1), it is correct to **use the business percentage of auto interest and personal property tax as a subtraction from a minister's social security base**.

The portion of tax preparation fee that is attributable to the reporting of ministry transactions can also be a subtraction from a minister's social security base according to Rev. Ruling 92-29.

Lease or Own

Although leasing an auto is subject to luxury limitations, it could be advantageous to lease rather than to own. Lease payments may generate more deduction since auto interest is considered to be nondeductible personal interest for the employee. **The question of whether to lease or own is a difficult question to answer.** Our advice is to shop and negotiate for the best deal that provides you with dependable and comfortable transportation. Be sure to read the "fine print" conditions of the lease. There is usually a limit as to how many miles you can drive the leased auto before an extra charge per mile is assessed.

Spending additional dollars for transportation because it is tax deductible is not sensible. To spend an additional $500 and be in the 15% tax bracket would only reduce your tax by $75. The difference of $425 is a real cost out of your pocket.

Choose the Best Method of Deducting Auto Expenses

There are two methods of computing the deduction for the cost of operating your auto for business. It is important to keep records of your actual expenses so that you can compare optional method with actual cost method. You are allowed to use the method that results in the largest deduction. In the past, due to the luxury auto limitations on depreciation and better gas economy, fewer taxpayers benefited from the actual cost method. If you incur high cost of insurance or have large repairs for your business auto, the actual cost method may be greater than the optional method.

For tax years beginning after December 31, 2005, an **alternative motor vehicle credit (AMVC)** is available according to Sec. 30B. The original use must begin with the taxpayer. Form 8910 is used to figure the credit. The credit was extended to include certain vehicles purchased in 2015 and 2016.

• *Bonus Depreciation*

As the result of the Small Business Jobs Act of 2010, the first year depreciation limit of $8,000 was extended for qualifying vehicles purchased during 2010.

As the result of the "Tax Relief, Unemployment Insurance Reauthorization and Job Creation Act of 2010," the first year depreciation limit of $8,000 was extended for qualifying vehicles purchased before January 1, 2013.

As the result of "American Taxpayer Relief Act of 2012" the first year depreciation limit of $8,000 is extended for qualifying vehicles purchased before January 1, 2014.

The Tax Increase Prevention Act of 2014 Congress passed an extension of first year **$8,000** depreciation limit for 2014.

The Protecting Americans From Tax Hikes Act of 2015, retroactively extended bonus depreciation for 2015, and also extended it for **2016**.

• *Luxury Auto Limitations*

The luxury auto limitations are now split into two categories: passenger auto and trucks/vans (mini-vans and SUVs). Different tables are provided for each category. Generally new vehicles with a gross unloaded weight of more than **6,000 pounds,** SUVs, trucks, vans, and other vehicles that don't qualify as passenger automobiles, are not subject to the IRS depreciation limits. Using bonus depreciation and/or Section 179, you may be able to deduct all or most of the cost of such a vehicle in a single year—a potentially enormous deduction. Effective since October 22, 2004, Sport Utility Vehicles (SUVs), not weighing more than 14,000 pounds fully loaded, are limited to **$25,000** Sec. 179 expensing according to Sec. 179(b)(5)(B).

Mileage Allowance Method

The IRS allows you to be reimbursed or deduct **54¢** a mile for all business miles. In addition, you may be reimbursed or deduct your actual business tolls and parking fees. A daily log book of miles driven must be kept in order to use this method. The IRS mileage allowance may be used if you own or lease an auto.

IRS mileage allowance rate for **2017 is 53½¢** according to **IRS Notice 2016-169**.

You cannot use the standard mileage rate for unreimbursed business use if you:

1. Operate five or more autos at the same time (as in fleet operations).
2. Claimed a depreciation deduction using ACRS or MACRS in an earlier year,
3. Claimed a Sec. 179 deduction on the auto.
4. Claimed the special depreciation allowance on the car,
5. Claimed actual auto expenses after 1997 for a car you leased, or
6. Are a rural mail carrier who received a qualified reimbursement.

Actual Method

This is an itemized list of your actual auto expenses such as: gas, oil, lubrication, repairs, parts, tires, batteries, tune-ups, auto washes, insurance, auto club dues, licenses, parking fees, tolls, and auto depreciation or auto lease.

If the actual cost method and MACRS method of depreciation is chosen in the first year, you must use the MACRS depreciation for the life of the auto. Even if your employer reimburses you under an accountable plan at the optional rate, you still must use your choice of MACRS to determine your auto's basis.

If the actual cost method and optional straight line method of depreciation is chosen in the first year, you will have left open the option to choose actual cost method or optional method on an annual basis. You will combine the optional factor for years of optional method with the actual straight line depreciation for years of actual method to determine your basis.

If the actual cost method is used to deduct the business use of your auto for **any year other than the first year**, you must use 5 year straight line ADS as the depreciation method. You will combine the optional factor for years of mileage allowance method with the actual depreciation for years of actual expense method to determine your basis.

Auto Depreciation Rules

Methods and limits of depreciation apply to autos according to the date placed in service. Follow the same column of the depreciation table **applicable in the year placed in service** until you change autos.

• *Listed Property - Deductions Limited For Less Than 50% Business Use*

When business use is less than 50%, listed property is considered as not predominantly used for business. Listed property includes **autos, computers,** etc. When less than 50% use of listed property is business, depreciation is limited and the auto's basis must be recovered over five years using the straight-line method. Bonus depreciation and/or Sec. 179 expensing is not available.

• *Depreciation Recapture*

Depreciation recapture is to be computed when an accelerated depreciation method is used in the year placed in service and business use drops below 50% in any future year during the 5 year life. Recapture means "pay back." If you used your auto more than 50% in your business in the year you placed it in service, but 50% or less for business in a later year, you must include in gross income the difference between depreciation and all Sec. 179 expensing claimed and the amount of depreciation recomputed at the 5 year straight line method. You must continue using 5 year straight line ADS even if business use rises back above 50%.

The recapture amount is shown as a memo on Form 4797, Part IV. Employees report the recapture amount on Form 1040, line 21. Dual-status ministers also include the recapture amount on Schedule SE. Self employed evangelists report the recapture amount as other income on Schedule C.

• *Deductions Limited For Luxury Automobiles*

When an automobile is used more than 50% for business purposes, the law places further limits on the amounts of annual depreciation deductions that could be taken on automobiles. The amount of annual limits are based on 100% business use. If the business use is less than 100%, the maximum annual limits must be reduced to reflect the actual business use percentage. The depreciation limit amounts apply to regular depreciation and Sec. 179 expensing. The limits are indexed for inflation.

• *MACRS Depreciation for Autos Purchased After 12-31-86*

Luxury Limits for Vehicles Since 2012

Date Passenger Auto, Truck, & Van, Placed in Service During 2012 and After

		Passenger Autos					Trucks & Vans				
		1-1-12 thru 12-31-12	1-1-13 thru 12-31-13	1-1-14 thru 12-31-14	1-1-15 thru 12-31-15	1-1-16 thru 12-31-16	1-1-12 thru 12-31-12	1-1-13 thru 12-31-13	1-1-14 thru 12-31-14	1-1-15 thru 12-31-15	1-1-16 thru 12-31-16
1st Year	$8,000 Bonus Depreciation	$11,160	$11,160	$11,160	$11,160	$11,160	$11,360	$11,360	$11,460	*$11,460	$11,560
	No Bonus Allowance	$3,160	$3,160	$3,160	$3,160	$3,160	$3,360	$3,360	$3,460	$3,460	$3,560
2nd year		$5,100	$5,100	$5,100	$5,100	$5,100	$5,300	$5,400	$5,500	$5,600	$5,700
3rd year		$3,050	$3,050	$3,050	$3,050	$3,050	$3,150	$3,250	$3,350	$3,350	$3,350
4th - 6th		$1,875	$1,875	$1,875	$1,875	$1,875	$1,875	$1,975	$1,975	$1,975	$2,075

Under Modified Accelerated Cost Recovery System (MACRS) autos are 5-year Class property. The percentage method is based on 200% declining balance method. The alternative recovery method is 5 year straight-line. If business use is 50% or less in year of purchase, then the auto's basis must be recovered over five years using the straight-line method and the half-year convention. The most depreciation allowed per year, regardless of your auto's basis, is the business percentage of the luxury auto limits shown above, including **$8000** Bonus Depreciation. MACRS allows depreciation deduction in the year of sale. The IRS depreciation tables have computed the mid-year and mid-quarter factors for the year of purchase automatically.

Mid-year convention allows one half of the annual percentage available in the year placed in service and in the year of sale.

Mid-quarter convention allows the mid-quarter computation percentage depending on which quarter the purchase or sale occurs. If more than **40% of the year's** depreciable assets are placed in service in the **final quarter**, then all non-realty assets for that year **must** be depreciated using "mid-quarter" convention instead of the normal mid-year convention.

The percentages for both mid-year and mid-quarter for autos and other 5-year class equipment are listed below.

Depreciation Table - MACRS 5-year Class Property

Year	Mid-year	Mid-quarter			
		(1st)	(2nd)	(3rd)	(4th)
1	20.00%	35.00%	25.00%	15.00%	5.00%
2	32.00%	26.00%	30.00%	34.00%	38.00%
3	19.20%	15.60%	18.00%	20.40%	22.80%
4	11.52%	11.01%	11.37%	12.24%	13.68%
5	11.52%	11.01%	11.37%	11.30%	10.94%
6	5.76%	1.38%	4.26%	7.06%	9.58%

Leased Automobiles

Autos leased after December 31, 1997 can use the IRS mileage allowance. When you lease an auto for business use, you can choose the greater of the IRS mileage allowance (**54¢**) a mile for all business miles driven in **2016** or the business percentage of the actual cost of the lease, gas, oil, etc. You cannot deduct any part of a lease payment that is for commuting or other personal use of the auto. When you lease an auto for business use, the **luxury auto limitations** are applied by the computation of an **income inclusion factor**. **IRS Publication 463** contains special tables to compute the income inclusion factor.

Enter the rental cost on line 24(a), Part II, of **Form 2106**. The inclusion amount is prorated for the number of days of the lease term included in the tax year. The amount computed would be shown on line 24b. The net amount of vehicle rental expenses will be shown on line 24c. There is **no** additional inclusion amount if you have 50% or less business use for this period. **Easy to use tables are in IRS Publication 463,** pages 39 thru 48 for regular autos, trucks & vans, and electric autos.

Employer Provided Autos

The value of an employee's personal use of an employer provided vehicle must be included in his income minus any reimbursement he made to his employer. **IRS Publication 15-B,** pages 22 to 27, "Employer's Tax Guide to Fringe Benefits," contains instructions for the employer providing this "working condition" fringe benefit. **Reg. 1.61-21(c),(d),(e), and (f)** is a thorough presentation of the "working condition" fringe benefit.

It is best for the employer providing the auto to pay for all costs or all costs except gasoline. Hybrid arrangements cause confusion and cause the employee to pay tax on a value he did not receive. Regulations only allow for a gasoline factor of **5½¢** a mile to be added if the employer pays for the gasoline or omitted if the employee pays for the gasoline.

In order for an employer to exclude from the employee's gross income the value of an employer-provided vehicle, the **employee must keep** a log of business miles and submit the log to the employer. If the employer does not receive such a log of business miles, the whole value of the vehicle is to be reported as income on Form W-2. Please **do not let this happen**.

- ### General Valuation Rule

Whenever an employer does not choose one of the special valuation rules by a timely notification to the employee, **the value of the fringe benefit must be determined** under the general valuation rule. Under the general valuation rule, FMV is the amount your employee would have to pay a third party to lease the vehicle in the geographic area where he uses the vehicle.

If you want to adopt one of the three Special Valuation Rules to calculate the value of personal use to report as income for your employee, **you must adopt in writing** what rule you have chosen by the first day you make the vehicle available to the employee.

Three special valuation rules are available:

● *(1) The Automobile Lease Rule*

The value of availability of an auto to the employee must first be determined. This value of availability is then reduced by the percentage of business use to determine the value of the employee's personal use of the auto to be treated as compensation.

1. Employer must request from the employee a statement as to the business mileage and the total mileage driven by the employee. Where the employee supplies such statement or record within a reasonable period of time, the employer must compute the personal use percentage and the amount of payroll taxes to withhold on the basis of such information.

2. Determine the FMV of the automobile on the first date the automobile is available to any employee for personal use. Use the Annual Lease Value Table (shown below) to determine an annual value. When an automobile is provided for only part of a year, the value is determined by multiplying the annual lease value by a fraction (days automobile is available to the employee divided by 365).

3. The figures in the annual lease value table are applicable for a four-year period starting on the date on which the special rule is applied and ending on December 31st of the fourth full year following that date. After that period, the annual lease value for each calendar year is based on the fair market value of the auto on January 1st of the applicable year.

4. If an employer provides fuel; its fair market value or 5½¢ per mile must be an additional computation.

ANNUAL LEASE VALUE TABLE / Automobile Lease Rule
IRS Publication 15-B

Automobile Fair Market Value	Annual Lease Value	Automobile Fair Market Value	Annual Lease Value
$ 0 - 999	$ 600	$ 22,000 - 22,999	$ 6,100
1,000 - 1,999	850	23,000 - 23,999	6,350
2,000 - 2,999	1,100	24,000 - 24,999	6,600
3,000 - 3,999	1,350	25,000 - 25,999	6,850
4,000 - 4,999	1,600	26,000 - 27,999	7,250
5,000 - 5,999	1,850	28,000 - 29,999	7,750
6,000 - 6,999	2,100	30,000 - 31,999	8,250
7,000 - 7,999	2,350	32,000 - 33,999	8,750
8,000 - 8,999	2,600	34,000 - 35,999	9,250
9,000 - 9,999	2,850	36,000 - 37,999	9,750
10,000 - 10,999	3,100	38,000 - 39,999	10,250
11,000 - 11,999	3,350	40,000 - 41,999	10,750
12,000 - 12,999	3,600	42,000 - 43,999	11,250
13,000 - 13,999	3,850	44,000 - 45,999	11,750
14,000 - 14,999	4,100	46,000 - 47,999	12,250
15,000 - 15,999	4,350	48,000 - 49,999	12,750
16,000 - 16,999	4,600	50,000 - 51,999	13,250
17,000 - 17,999	4,850	52,000 - 53,999	13,750
18,000 - 18,999	5,100	54,000 - 55,999	14,250
19,000 - 19,999	5,350	56,000 - 57,999	14,750
20,000 - 20,999	5,600	58,000 - 59,999	15,250
21,000 - 21,999	5,850	over $59,999	Auto's FMV X 0.25 + $500

EXAMPLE: *An employer makes an auto available for all year. Its fair market value is $16,000; its annual lease value from the table is $4,600. Employee uses the auto 20% for personal use. Thus, the employer must include in the employee's income 20% of $4,600 or **$920**. If fuel is provided by the employer and personal use of 20% was 4,000 miles, (4,000 X 5½¢) an additional **$220** must be included in income.*

● *(2) The Vehicle Cents-per-Mile Rule*

Under this cents-per-mile rule, an employer values the benefit using the standard mileage rate multiplied by the total miles the employee drives the automobile for personal purposes. For **2016**, this rate is **54¢** a mile. (2017 - 53½¢.) All of the following conditions must be met:

1. Employer must request from the employee a statement of the business mileage and the total mileage driven by the employee.

2. This rule cannot be used if the FMV of the auto, as of the first date the auto is made available to any employee for personal use, exceeds **$15,900 or $17,700** for a truck or van.

3. It must be reasonably expected that the auto will be regularly used in the employer's business, or actually driven primarily by employees at least 10,000 (personal and business) miles during a calendar year.

4. The cents-per-mile rule includes all costs of operating the auto. Neither the employer or the employee may adjust the rate for services not provided, such as repairs. The only adjustment allowed is that if fuel is not provided by the employer, the cents-per-mile value may be reduced by no more than **5½¢**.

● *(3) Commuting Rule*

Under this rule, the value of the commuting use of an automobile an employer provides is **$1.50** per one-way commute (**$3.00** for each round trip) for each employee who commutes in the vehicle. An employer can use this special rule if all of the following requirements are met:

1. Employer owns or leases the automobile and provides it to one or more employees for use in his trade or business.
2. For bona fide noncompensatory business reasons, an employer requires the employee to commute in the automobile.
3. Employer establishes a written policy under which they do not allow employees to use the vehicle for personal purposes, other than for commuting or *de minimis* personal use (such as a stop for a personal errand on the way between a business delivery and the employee's home.)
4. The employee does not use the automobile for personal purposes, other than commuting and de minimis personal use.
5. If this vehicle is an automobile, the employee required to use it for commuting is not a control employee.

A **control employee** of a nongovernmental employer is any employee who (1) is a board-appointed, shareholder-appointed, confirmed, or elected officer of the employer whose compensation equals or exceeds $105,000, (2) is the director of the employer, (3) owns a one percent or greater equity, capital or profit interest in the employer, or (4) receives $215,000 or more in compensation. (IRS Publication 15-B, page 24)

● *100% Business Use Rule (Very Unlikely)*

If an employer **prohibited all personal use** and commuting by the employee, no value would be taxable to the employee. Without personal use, no log of business miles would be required.

All of the following conditions must be met:

1. The vehicle is owned or leased by the employer and is provided to an employee for use in the employer's trade or business.
2. The vehicle is kept on the employer's premises.
3. Only de minimis stop on the way between a business delivery and the employer's place of business.
4. The vehicle is not being used for personal purposes.
5. No employee using the vehicle lives at the employer's place of business.
6. There must be evidence that the vehicle meets all these conditions.

Withholding of Tax: When an auto is either owned or leased by the employer for an employee's use, the personal value of the automobile's use is a taxable fringe benefit subject to withholding of income tax and social security for the lay employee. The dual-status minister will incur the additional income tax and social security tax for estimated tax purposes.

When an employee pays the employer for personal use, the amount to be included in income is reduced by what the employee pays. If the proper amount is computed (general valuation rule or one of the three special valuation rules timely chosen) and paid to the employer, nothing would need to be shown on the W-2, nor any taxes withheld for the lay employee.

Library & Equipment Purchases

Capital purchases are major purchases of equipment that have an expected useful life of more than a year. IRS depreciation rules are easy to use to compute the right amount of allowable depreciation.

Usually when a minister begins his career he already owns a sizable library. The purchase of books and equipment during college and seminary that did not qualify for deductible educational expense or credits can begin to be depreciated when a minister begins receiving an income from their use. They become business property and are considered "placed in service." The **lesser of the cost or fair market value** of items that are converted from personal to business use should be inventoried and placed on the depreciation schedule. Sec. 179 expensing is not available for converted property.

New purchases of library, office furniture, typewriters, computers, printers, fax machines, overhead or video projectors, cameras, copiers, or cellular phones are examples of items that are capital and need to be depreciated or expensed under Sec. 179. **Tax plan according to your tax liability;** choose to "spread out" or depreciate capital assets in years of no tax liability and choose Sec. 179 expensing and/or bonus depreciation during years with a tax liability.

Sec. 168(k) Bonus Depreciation began in 2010 and has been available on **new purchases**. It is the default method and you have to include an election with your timely filed return if you did not want to use it. The election could be made for one class and not all classes of property. Sec. 168(k) Bonus Depreciation could create an NOL loss. If the asset percentage of business use falls below 50%, there is no recapture. The Protecting Americans from Tax Hikes (PATH) Act of 2015 extended bonus depreciation for property acquired and placed in service during 2015 through 2019.

Sec. 179 Expensing is available for both new and used purchases. It must be chosen and can be 100% of the purchase price or it can be a part of it. Sec. 179 Expensing cannot create a business loss, however, unused amounts carry over to future years. If the asset percentage of use falls below 50% there is a recapture to be computed and added to income.

If you are fully reimbursed for the purchase of a capital item in the year of purchase, it will be the same as choosing Sec. 168(k) bonus depreciation and/or Sec. 179 expensing. We recommend that a depreciation worksheet be completed to show each purchase and any election to expense capital assets.

To be reimbursed by your employer for library and equipment depreciation, compute what this year's depreciation will be for previous assets on your depreciation schedule, divide by 12 and use it as a monthly amount. Then in December, include an extra amount that is the depreciation for the current year's capital purchases.

• *Guidance and Discussion of Ownership of Equipment*

When the **employer makes the decision** to purchase equipment needed for ministry use, the items will be owned by the employer. When an **employee makes the decision** to purchase equipment needed for ministry use from his accountable reimbursement plan, the items will be owned by the employee.

This concept is best understood when we think of the use of an automobile for business. If the employer makes the decision to purchase an auto for an employee's use, it is titled in the employer's name. The rules provided for "employer provided autos" are followed for proper tax treatment. If an employee makes the decision to purchase an auto, it is titled in the employee's name. The rules for business use deductions or reimbursements are followed.

Reimbursement to an employee from an accountable plan for business purchases of library or any equipment is owned by the employee. **Ownership of them does not change to the employer.**

• *Computers*

Computers have become so capable, useful and affordable that almost everyone has entered into the age of technology. Bible research CD's, web-site promotions, E-mail with missionaries, word processing for sermon preparation and congregation data bases are examples of current ministry business use of computers.

Congress has made dual-use (part business and part personal) of computers complex by placing them in a category called "listed property." Complex depreciation treatment can be avoided by dedicating a computer to 100% business use. Now that the cost of owning a computer is more reasonable, it is advisable to purchase one for business use and a second one for the family and personal use. The computer for family and personal use can be deducted as parsonage allowance.

Employers should be willing to own and provide the business use computer for their employees. When the employer owns the computer and it is used exclusively for business use, no log of personal time needs be kept. The time spent learning how to manipulate the peripheral devices is to be counted as business use. (Keyboard and mouse exercises - Solitaire, Freecell, etc.)

When employees purchase and own a computer and it is used for both business and personal, a log of time must be kept to know the business use percentage. If less than 50% of computer use is business, you cannot choose Sec 168(k) Bonus Depreciation or Sec. 179 Expensing. The cost basis must be recovered over five years using the straight-line method and the half-year or mid-year convention.

Unreimbursed employee business use of computers has to qualify as being a **mandatory requirement** of the employer and a **condition of employment** to be allowable as an itemized deduction. IRS audit history has not been friendly to the employee. In Cadwallader, T.C. Memo 1989-356 the court allowed the deduction for 100% use. In Muline, T.C. Memo 1996-320 a sales manager convinced the court to allow her a deduction with the help of her supervisor as a witness.

- ● *MACRS Depreciation for Equipment Purchased After 12-31-86*
  Under Modified Accelerated Cost Recovery System (MACRS) the depreciation percentages are based on 200% declining balance method. Items in the 5-year class are computers, typewriters, copiers, and printing equipment. Items in the 7-year class are library, office furniture, and fixtures. The IRS depreciation tables have computed the mid-year and mid-quarter factors for the year of purchase automatically.
  Mid-year convention allows one half of the annual percentage available in the year of purchase and in the year of sale.
  Mid-quarter convention allows the mid-quarter computation percentage depending on which quarter the purchase or sale occurs. If more than **40% of the year's** depreciable assets are placed in service in the **final quarter**, then all non-realty assets for that year **must** be depreciated using "mid-quarter" convention instead of the normal mid-year convention.
  In our discussion of auto depreciation earlier in this chapter we included the MACRS percentages for 5-year class property. The MACRS percentages for both mid-year and mid-quarter for 7-year class property are listed below.

Depreciation Table - MACRS 7-year Class Property

Year	Mid-year	Mid-quarter			
		(1st)	(2nd)	(3rd)	(4th)
1	14.29%	25.00%	17.86%	10.71%	3.57%
2	24.49%	21.43%	23.47%	25.51%	27.55%
3	17.49%	15.31%	16.76%	18.22%	19.68%
4	12.49%	10.93%	11.97%	13.02%	14.06%
5	8.93%	8.75%	8.87%	9.30%	10.04%
6	8.92%	8.74%	8.87%	8.85%	8.73%
7	8.93%	8.75%	8.87%	8.86%	8.73%
8	4.46%	1.09%	3.33%	5.53%	7.64%

Travel

Ordinary and necessary travel expenses incurred in order to be able to earn income include: train, airplane, boat, bus fares, auto rental, taxi, hotel, motel, rooming house, meals, gratuities, telephone, fax, travel insurance, baggage charges, cleaning, and laundry costs. Unreimbursed meals and incidental expenses while away from home overnight are subject to a 50% limitation.

To substantiate your travel expenses, you must record the following at or near the time of the travel: the amount spent, the date of the business trip, the place traveled to, and the business reason or purpose of the trip. Receipts are always required for lodging. Receipts are also required for other expenses that are $75.00 or more. You may maintain an **account book or diary** for any **expense under $75.00**.

"Tax home" is defined as a taxpayer's place of business or employment where he earns most of his income regardless of where the family residence is maintained. Travel **away from home overnight** is necessary for travel expenses to be deductible. "Overnight" does not necessarily mean a 24-hour period but there must be enough time allowed for you to be released from activities for 6 hours of sleep, even if it is from noon to 6 p.m. **Do not** deduct or adequately account to your employer for **meal expenses when you are not away from home overnight.**

A **traveling evangelist** or conference speaker with a permanent tax home will incur deductible travel expenses for lodging and meals while on the road and use parsonage allowance exclusion for his permanent home. If he lives in a motor home or travel trailer and does not have a permanent home, he is considered a transient or itinerant. His tax home for tax purposes is wherever he "hangs his hat." His lodging and meal expenses **will not** be deductible as business travel expenses. He may treat the motor home as his parsonage but his meals **will not** be deductible. The cost of transportation between engagements **does qualify** as business transportation expense.

Temporary work location: If employment at a work location is realistically expected to last (and does in fact last) one year or less, the employment is temporary in the absence of facts and circumstances indicating otherwise. You can deduct transportation expenses to a temporary work location outside your metropolitan area.

Second Job: If you regularly work at two or more places in one day, you can deduct your transportation expenses of getting from one workplace to another.

A minister may incur away-from-home expenses for the following: attendance at a church convention, speaking engagements, lectures, travel to perform a wedding or a funeral, travel for pulpit supply, evangelistic meetings, deputation for missionaries, travel to youth camps, etc.

Most overseas travel will not qualify as deductible. The primary purpose of a trip has to be business and your employer has to send or require you to make the trip. Be sure the rules are satisfied before deducting or becoming reimbursed for overseas travel. No deduction is allowed for costs of travel claimed as a **form of education.** (Sec. 274(m)(2)) **For example, a trip to the Holy Land is not deductible.** Enrollment in a formal course of study in the Holy Land **may** qualify as an education expense.

If a trip is primarily for business and you extend your stay for a vacation or have other nonbusiness activities, you may deduct the travel expense to and from the business destination. You would not be able to deduct side-trip mileage or the extra cost of the meals and lodging for the personal time.

If a trip is primarily for business and you have weekend or off duty days, all of the meals and lodging will be deductible. Personal side-trip miles would not be deductible. Due to airline pricing policies, Saturday lodging and meals are deductible as an allowable business day when required to obtain a cheaper air fare.

If a trip is primarily for vacation or personal reasons, the entire cost of the trip is a nondeductible personal expense. However, you can deduct any expenses while there that are directly related to your business.

Travel expenses for business reasons are only allowable for the person earning an income. Expenses for a nonsalaried spouse and children to accompany you on a trip are personal and not allowable as business expenses. The single room rate can be used instead of one half of double room rate. Except for bona fide entertainment the spouse's meals are not deductible.

Reconciliation Act of 1993 added Sec. 274(m)(3) and states: "No deduction shall be allowed under this chapter for travel expenses paid or incurred with respect to a spouse, dependent, or other individual accompanying the taxpayer (or an officer or employee of the taxpayer) on business travel, unless--

(A) the spouse, dependent, or other individual is an employee of the taxpayer,

(B) the travel of the spouse, dependent, or other individual is for a bona fide business purpose, and

(C) such expenses would otherwise be deductible by the spouse, dependent, or other individual."

Volunteer workers, **including a non salaried spouse,** attending a convention, who are reimbursed for travel and ministry expenses can be reimbursed at the business standard mileage rate. The **2016** rate is **54¢.** (2017 the rate is 53½¢) A non salaried spouse must be attending a convention as an official delegate or representative of a church or organization. A volunteer must adequately account to the organization making the reimbursement to be a "bona fide volunteer." Unreimbursed lodging, meals, fares, and auto mileage at **14¢** per mile as a delegate are allowable as a contribution deduction on Schedule A.

CAUTION: When an employer reimburses an employee for non-business meals, overseas travel that does not qualify as business, or personal family members' travel expenses it must be reported as **income** on the employee's Form W-2, Box 1.

Lodging, Meal, And Incidental Expense Per Diem Rates

Periodically, the IRS publishes per diem rates that may be used by employers who reimburse employees for their traveling expenses. The IRS per diem rates are adjusted for inflation. These per diem rates include an individual's lodging, meals and incidental (M&IE) travel expenses. **Incidental expenses** covered by a per diem arrangement include: fees and tips given to porters, baggage carriers, hotel staff, and staff on ships. They do not include cab fares, business calls, fax, or other communication costs. An optional method of deducting for incidental expenses only, when no meal expenses are incurred, is **$5** a day.

The applicable per diem amount depends on the locality of travel. For travel within the continental United States (CONUS) and for foreign and non-foreign travel outside the continental 48 states (OCONUS), separate lodging and M&IE rates are published periodically. The standard rate for locations not listed is **$91** for lodging and **$51** for M&IE for a total of **$142.** By entering each city you have traveled to, you can access the federal per diem rates on the internet at: **http://www.gsa.gov/portal/content/104208**

How to prorate partial travel days: You can use either of the following methods to prorate the full-day rate for M&IE: (1) use ¾ of the M&IE rate for the day of departure and the day of arrival back home, or (2) use any method that you consistently apply and that is in accordance with reasonable business practice. For example, for travel away from home from 9 a.m. of one day to 5 p.m. of the next day can be treated as 2 full days of M&IE, even though federal employees are limited to 1½ days of M&IE.

Unreimbursed employees and self-employed individuals may only use the per diem rate established for meals and incidental expenses found in the IRS CONUS tables. The entire M&IE rate is subject to the 50% limitation on meal expenses. **Actual lodging** expenses must be used. The high-low rate available to employers with an accountable reimbursement plan, discussed below, **may not** be used by unreimbursed employees and self-employed individuals.

• *Alternative Method for Employers*

A **high-low per diem method** is available to simplify the administrative burden of determining the correct rate for an employee's particular areas of travel. Under the high-low per diem method, the IRS publishes a list of localities that are classified as high-cost areas. All other localities within the continental United States are classified as low-cost areas. The IRS then establishes a per diem rate for the two types of localities. The **2016** per diem rates are **$275** for high-cost localities and **$185** for low-cost localities. The M&IE portion of the alternative method is **$68** for high-cost localities and **$57** for low-cost localities. The remaining **$207 or $128** is the lodging portion of the per diem allowance. There is no optional standard lodging amount similar to the standard meal allowance, you can not combine actual meal cost and lodging high-low per diem rates.

The high-low method may not be used to reimburse an employee for M&IE expenses only. The employer can use the M&IE rate from the IRS tables if the employer pays for lodging, provides lodging or the employee does not incur lodging.

The **same method of reimbursement** must be used for the whole year of travel within the continental United States. Annually compare the four options for computing your best travel reimbursement and use the greater of:

1. Individual location rates from the CONUS or OCONUS tables
2. High-low per diem alternative method (both lodging & M&IE)
3. Your actual cost of lodging and M&IE from the CONUS or OCONUS tables
4. Your actual cost of lodging and actual cost of meals

Become reimbursed throughout the year according to the method you expect to be the greater, then at year end, calculate all three. If another method is greater, become reimbursed for the adjusting differential at the end of the year.

The high-cost locations listed on page 81 are eligible for the high cost rates. Some locations are high cost for **only a portion** of the year. Effective date for the list from **Notice 2015-63** was October 1, 2015. The IRS published Notice 2015-63 in 2015 for calendar year 2016. Transition rules state that an employer who used Notice 2015-63 for an employee during the first 9 months of calendar year 2016 may not use the rates in IRS Notice 2016-58 until January 1, 2017.

High-low Per Diem Rates

Effective Dates	Lodging & Meals	Lodging Only	Meals & Incidentals
10/1/16-12/31/17	$282 high/ $189 low	$214 high/ $132 low	$68 high/ $57 low
10/1/15-12/31/16	$275 high/ $185 low	$207 high/ $128 low	$68 high/ $57 low
10/1/14-12/31/15	$259 high/ $172 low	$194 high/ $120 low	$65 high/ $52 low
10/1/13-12/31/14	$251 high/ $170 low	$186 high/ $118 low	$65 high/ $52 low
10/1/12-12/31/13	$242 high/ $163 low	$177 high/ $111 low	$65 high/ $52 low
10/1/11-12/31/12	$242 high/ $163 low	$177 high/ $111 low	$65 high/ $52 low
10/1/10-12/31/11	$233 high/ $160 low	$168 high/ $108 low	$65 high/ $52 low

Entertainment

Entertainment expenses and meals for entertainment that are not reimbursed will be subject to the 50% limitation, then combined with other unreimbursed professional expenses and further limited by 2% of AGI and Sec. 265 allocation limitation as a deduction on Schedule A. An employee can be reimbursed for 100% of meal and entertainment expense. Employers will deduct only 50% of reimbursed meals and entertainment as a business expense. Nonprofit employers, who reimburse their employees, will not be affected since they have no tax liability.

Restrictive tests for meals and entertainment require that the event is directly related to the active conduct of your job and directly preceding or following a substantial and bona fide business discussion on a subject associated with the active conduct of your business or ministry.

The record-keeping rules for entertainment, **Sec. 274**, are very strict. The entertainment diary section in our **"Professional Tax Record Book"** is designed to help you record all of the necessary facts. **You must have the name of the persons entertained, their title or position, where the entertainment took place, what purpose or discussion took place and the amount of the expense.** Receipts are important if the expense is $75.00 or more. When the entertainment is in the home and the occasion is over the $75 threshold, keep the receipt from the grocery store.

By adopting an accountable reimbursement plan, you will be submitting your expense records to your employer. According to IRS Reg. 1.274-5T(c)(2)(ii)(D), because of the confidential nature of a minister's activity, only the **date and amount** of entertainment expense needs to be submitted for reimbursement under an accountable plan. To cover the confidential portion of the diary before making a photocopy is therefore recommended.

Most ministers are required to do substantial entertaining in their home. Since the cost of the home itself is nontaxable as parsonage allowance, the main expense of entertaining is the cost of meals provided. Special speakers, missionaries, board members, prospective faculty, etc., are entertained and a record of the number of meals provided in the home, multiplied by an average cost per meal, will result in a sizable deduction. A reasonable amount per meal, depending on your actual circumstances and service practices, might vary between **$10.00 to $15.00** per meal. Those afternoon meetings with refreshments, or after evening service snacks for the youth group, etc, might vary between **$4.50 to $5.50** per snack.

If the meals are eaten outside of the home, then the receipt for the actual cost of the meals is deductible. If you entertain business and non-business individuals at the same event, you must divide your entertainment expenses between business and non-business. For example, if you entertain a group of individuals that **includes yourself**, three business prospects, and seven social guests, 4/11 of the expenses qualifies for the deduction.

If your spouse is present during an occasion of entertainment because the spouse of the person being entertained is present, you may deduct the meal cost for both spouses. Meal expenses for your children are not business deductions.

Educational Expenses as an Employee

Educational expenses incurred for the purpose of maintaining or improving present job or professional skills or meeting the expressed requirements of an employer to retain the job are deductible. The deduction will not be allowed if the education qualifies you for a new trade or business or satisfies the minimum requirements of your present job.

For education costs to be deductible as a business expense, you are unable to be absent from your profession for more than a year. A minister who has not been gainfully employed as a minister will not be able to deduct his seminary education. Most seminary degrees require three or more years. Seminary students who have the opportunity to serve as a "part-time" minister while obtaining additional education will be more likely to qualify for the education expense deduction. IRS considers you to have changed careers if you work a secular job while obtaining additional education for a period of more than 12 months.

Tuition, fees, books and supplies, any transportation to attend school away from your hometown, meals and lodging (if necessary to be away from home overnight to attend classes) are typical educational expenses. Unreimbursed meals are only 50% deductible.

When possible, it is best to include qualified educational expenses in your accountable reimbursement plan with your employer.

No deduction is allowed for costs of travel claimed as a **form of education.** (Sec. 274(m)(2)) For example, a trip to the **Holy Land** is not deductible. Enrollment in a formal course of study in the Holy Land **may** qualify as an education expense.

According to Sec. 25, education tax-planning has become very important. Unreimbursed educational expenses deducted on Form 2106 are not eligible for either the American Opportunity Credit or Lifetime Learning Credits. Compute the tax benefits of education expenses that qualify for deduction. Compute the education credit that is available. Choose the method that provides the best tax benefit. (IRS Publication 970, "Tax Benefits for Higher Education")

Education Incentives for Taxpayer and Family

Who is Eligible for the American Opportunity Credit and Lifetime Learning Credits? You, your spouse, or any child claimed as your dependent. If the child is your dependent, the money is *considered* to be paid by you even if it *is* paid by the child.

Eligible Expenses for American Opportunity Credit and Lifetime Learning Credit: Qualified expenses for both credits include tuition and student activity fees that are required of all students for enrollment. Generally, the credit is allowed for adjusted qualified education expenses paid in 2016 for an academic period beginning in 2016 or beginning in the first 3 months of 2017. Course-related books, supplies and equipment:

1. Can be purchased privately for American Opportunity Credit.
2. Must be purchased from the educational institution for Lifetime Learning Credit.

The 2009 Recovery Act expanded the definition of qualified educational expenses to include the purchase of any computer technology or equipment or internet access and related services.

Non eligible expenses include room and board, insurance, student health fees, and transportation even if paid to the institution. Expenses for sports or hobby-related courses that are not part of the student's degree program do not qualify for the American Opportunity Credit but such non-degree courses qualify for the Lifetime Learning credit if they help the student acquire or improve job skills.

Qualified tuition and related expenses **must be reduced** by tax-free funds received from scholarships, Pell grants, employer-provided educational assistance, educational bonds, Coverdell distributions, and veterans' educational assistance.

• American Opportunity Credit - *Now Permanent! "Protecting Americans from Tax Hikes" (PATH Act)*
In **2016** you may be able to claim up to a **$2,500** credit per eligible student. Credit can be claimed for the first **four years** of post-secondary education. A student must be pursuing an undergraduate degree or other recognized education credential. A student must be enrolled at least half time for at least one academic period. There can be no felony drug conviction on a student's record.

Generally, 40% of the American Opportunity Credit is now a **refundable credit**, which means that you can receive up to **$1,000** even if you owe no taxes. However, none of the credit is refundable if the taxpayer claiming the credit is a child who: (1) is under age 18 (or a student who is at least age 18 and under age 24 and whose earned income does not exceed one-half of his own support,) (2) who has at least one living parent, and (3) who does not file a joint return.

Phase Out Thresholds for American Opportunity Credit: The credits phase out as your **2016** AGI ranges from $160,000 to $180,000 ($80,000 to $90,000 for single filers).

• *Lifetime Learning Credit*
You may be able to claim up to a **$2,000** credit per return, for the entire family. Credit is available for all years of postsecondary education and for courses to acquire or improve job skills for an unlimited number of years. A student does not need to be pursuing a degree or other recognized education credential and can be enrolled in one or more courses. Felony drug conviction rule does not apply.

Phase Out Thresholds for Lifetime Learning Credits. The credits phase out as your **2016** AGI ranges from $111,000 to $131,000 ($55,000 to $65,000 for single filers).

• Coverdell Education Savings Accounts - *American Taxpayer Relief Act of 2012* **- made the $2,000 contribution permanent**
The maximum annual contribution you can make to a Coverdell ESA is **$2,000**. Contributions must be for a child under age 18 or a special needs beneficiary. Contributions are *not deductible.* Saving and investing in a mutual fund could *compound and grow* to a significant amount if begun when the child is young. The money is *completely tax-free* when taken out if it is used to pay for qualifying elementary, secondary or post-secondary education expenses.

Contributions to a **Coverdell ESA** for any year can be made by the due date of your return for that year (not including extensions). If you file a joint return, the amount you can contribute to a Coverdell ESA will be **phased out** if your modified **2016** adjusted gross income is more than $190,000 but less than $220,000. ($95,000 to $110,000 for single filers.)

You can claim the Hope or Lifetime Learning Credit in the same year you take a tax-free distribution from a Coverdell ESA, provided that the distribution from the Coverdell ESA is not used for the same expenses for which the credit is claimed.

• *Qualified Tuition Programs (QTPs) - Sec 529 Plans*

One of the best ways to increase the affordability of your child's education is to take advantage of federal tax breaks aimed at families saving and paying for college. **Section 529** plans, allow you to prepay or establish a savings plan from which future higher education expenses can be paid. Plans vary from state to state and we recommend that you visit **www.savingforcollege.com** for the complex details.

• *Student Loan Interest - Permanent -The American Taxpayer Relief Act of 2012*

Up to **$2,500** can be deducted—even if you do not itemize. The deduction is allowed only for interest paid on qualified education loans. For joint filers the **2016** threshold for phase out is $130,000 to $160,000 and it is $65,000 to $80,000 for single filers. You can deduct interest paid during the remaining period of your student loan.

• *College Tuition Deduction - Extended for 2015 and 2016 - "Protecting Americans from Tax Hikes" (PATH Act)*

You may be able to deduct qualified education expenses for higher education paid during the year for yourself, your spouse, or your dependent(s). You cannot claim this deduction if your filing status is married filing separately or if another person can claim an exemption for you as a dependent on his or her tax return.

A **$4,000** "above the line deduction" can be claimed by joint filers whose modified adjusted gross income is less than $130,000. (Single filers - $65,000)

A **$2,000** "above the line deduction" can be claimed by joint filers whose modified adjusted gross income is less than $160,000. (Single filers - $80,000)

This deduction is taken as an adjustment to income. This means you can claim this deduction even if you do not itemize deductions on Schedule A (Form 1040). This deduction may be beneficial to you if you do not qualify for the American Opportunity or Lifetime Learning Credits. Expenses eligible for the deduction are reduced by any tax-free distribution from a Coverdell ESA.

Office Expense and Supplies

Typical expenses an employee might have in their ministry are stationery, pens, stapler, paper clips, record books, postage, copier supplies, computer supplies, etc. Any office furniture or equipment that have useful lives of more than one year can be depreciated. If you are fully reimbursed for the purchase of a capital item in the year of purchase, it will be the same as choosing Sec. 168(k) bonus depreciation or Sec. 179 expensing. We recommend that a depreciation worksheet be completed to show each purchase and any election to expense capital assets.

If you are required to provide an office outside of your home, any cost to you would be a deductible expense. Rent, furniture, utilities, etc., would be allowable expenses.

Office-In-Home deduction is not available if your employer provides an office on their premises. It is generally not available when you have 100% of your home expenses tax-free under Sec. 107 parsonage allowance. If you have a qualifying office-in-home and you failed to have a parsonage allowance designated, deduct office-in-home for that year and be sure to designate adequate parsonage allowance for the future.

A home office that is used regularly and exclusively as the principal place of business qualifies if: (1) the office is used by the taxpayer to conduct administrative or management activities of a trade or business, and (2) there is no other fixed location of the trade or business where the taxpayer conducts substantial administrative or management activities of the trade or business.

To compute the amount allowable, divide the square footage used as an office by the square footage in your entire home. Use this percentage of the allowable home expenses and depreciation. A qualified "office-in-the-home" deduction would reduce your social security base and if "adequately accounted" to your employer would not increase income tax. Qualifying office-in-the-home use results in the favorable absence of **personal commuting miles** for business use of the automobile.

Revenue Procedure 2013-13, provides a simplified option for computing "office-in-the-home" deduction. Since 2013, taxpayers may use a simplified option when figuring the deduction for business use of their home. Highlights of the simplified option:

(1) Standard deduction of $5 per square foot of home used for business (maximum 300 square feet).

(2) Allowable home-related itemized deductions claimed in full on Schedule A. (For example: Mortgage interest, real estate taxes).

(3) No home depreciation deduction or later recapture of depreciation for the years the simplified option is used.

Generally, it is best for you to have 100% of your home expenses be tax-free under Sec. 107 parsonage allowance.

Religious Materials

Many trips to the religious bookstore add up to considerable expense for most employees in the ministry. Tracts and booklets purchased for distribution in the visitation ministry, music and musical supplies for the choir; gifts for presentation at marriages, baptisms, or holidays; teaching aids, including DVD programs, are but a few of the usual expenses a dual-status or lay employee incurs.

Clothing for the minister is usually not deductible. Tax law states that if something is required as a condition of employment and is not adaptable for general wear, it is deductible. Suits and shirts that are adaptable for general wear **are not** deductible for a salesman, businessman, or a minister.

Pulpit robes or special shirt collars and their cleaning expense would qualify as a deduction.

Seminars And Dues

Fees charged to attend seminars or conference meetings and dues to professional organizations that are directly related to your profession are deductible.

Subscriptions, Paperbacks, and DVDs

A number of periodicals and journals find their way into your mail box. The cost of subscriptions that are directly related to your ministry is deductible. Magazines and local newspapers give the current events so necessary for sermon illustrations and provide news of the local community. Except for one subscription to a local newspaper (which the IRS claims must be personal), deduct the subscriptions you use directly in your ministry.

Small booklets, paperback books, and DVDs should be separate from regular library books and the whole cost deducted in full in the year of purchase. **DO NOT deduct** magazine subscriptions, books and DVDs that are purchased for **personal reasons and interests.**

Business Telephone

Long distance business calls need to be separated from the personal portion used in the parsonage allowance computation because as a business expense they will reduce income tax as well as social security and medicare tax. The base rate portion of your home telephone can never be used as a business expense. (Base rate and personal long distance cost is a parsonage allowance utility expense.)

The business portion of your cellular phone bill is a legitimate professional expense. Personal use of cellular phones is to be used as parsonage allowance.

The business portion of your internet connection is a legitimate professional expense. When used in the parsonage, the personal portion would be a utility for parsonage allowance expense.

Professional Gifts

Regulation 1.274-3 states: *"No deduction shall be allowed under section 162 or 212 for any expense for a gift made directly or indirectly by a taxpayer to any individual to the extent that such expense, when added to prior expenses of the taxpayer for gifts made to such individual during the taxpayer's taxable year, exceeds $25".*

Small gifts to members of the congregation for weddings, baptisms, births, etc, that cost less than $25 are legitimate professional gifts.

When an individual gives directly to a person because of a need, it is not a business expenses nor deductible as a contribution. Such benevolences should be handled through a church benevolence fund.

Earned Income Credit

Since 2001, the earned income that is included in the taxpayer's gross income is used to calculate earned income credit. The former inclusion of nontaxable earned income no longer applies. As a result, many ministers qualify for earned income credit!!

For **2016**, earned income credit is available for the low-income taxpayer who maintains a household in the U.S. for more than one-half of the taxable year and has taxable earned income of less than:

$20,430 (married joint) or **$14,880** (single) without a qualifying child;

$44,846 (married joint) or **$39,296** (single) with one qualifying child;

$50,198 (married joint) or **$44,648** (single) with two qualifying children;

$53,505 (married joint) or **$47,955** (single) with three or more qualifying children.

It is a refundable credit, if there is no tax liability, the government "refunds" it to the taxpayer.

The amount of the credit increases each year based on inflation indexing. The maximum basic credit for **2016** is **$506** without a qualifying child; **$3,373** with one qualifying child; **$5,572** with two qualifying children; and **$6,269** with three or more qualifying children.

Earned income credit will be denied for taxpayers who have "disqualified income" of over **$3,400** for the taxable year. "Disqualified income" consists of (a) interest (taxable and tax-exempt); (b) taxable dividends; (c) gross income from Schedule E less expenses; (d) capital gain net income; (e) net passive income that is not self-employment income.

A modified definition of AGI is used for phasing out the earned income credit by disregarding certain losses.

• *Definition of Earned Income for Ministers*

For tax years before 2002, earned income was based on modified AGI. Salary deferrals such as Sec. 403(b), 401(k) and salary reductions such as Sec. 125 cafeteria plans were treated as "earned income" for Earned Income Credit purposes. Sec. 107 parsonage allowance and Sec. 119 meals and lodging for the convenience of the employer were also treated as "earned income."

Since 2001, earned income no longer includes certain nontaxable employee compensation. Earned income credit will generally be figured using your AGI, **not** modified AGI. According to the instructions for Earned Income Credit, Sec. 107 parsonage allowance **is still included** as "earned income" for a minister subject to social security and **is not included** for an exempt minister who is an employee of an organization.

Sec. 32(c)(2)(A) says: "The term "earned income" means—

(i)   wages, salaries, tips, and other employee compensation, but only if such amounts are includible in gross income for the taxable year, plus

(ii)   the amount of the taxpayer's net earnings from self-employment for the taxable year (within the meaning of section 1402(a), but such net earnings shall be determined with regard to the deduction allowed to the taxpayer by section 164(f)."

Rev. Ruling 79-78 defines "earned income" for the dual-status minister to include parsonage allowance and to include the income of a minister who elected to be exempt from social security if he is **an employee.**

Use the following outline to guide you in determining if you are entitled to earned income credit.

1.   Ministers who are **subject** to social security and medicare tax:

    a.   An employee of an organization - Earned income includes wages, value of parsonage and/or parsonage allowance, and Schedule C net honorariums, less adjustment for one half of self-employment tax, Form 1040, line 27.

    b.   An independent evangelist - Earned income includes Schedule C net honorariums and parsonage allowance, less adjustment for one half of self-employment tax, Form 1040, line 27.

2.   Ministers who have become **exempt** from social security and medicare tax:

    a.   An employee of an organization - Earned income includes wages entered on Form 1040, line 7, including "excess parsonage allowance", **but not Schedule C net honorariums**.

    b.   An independent evangelist - **Sch C net honorariums do not qualify** for earned income credit.

IRS Publication 596 and Instructions for Form 1040, Pages 54 - 70, contains detailed instructions and worksheets to calculate the correct amount of earned income credit.

We show two more examples of completed tax returns in Chapter Seven. Returns for Rev. Pious will illustrate the effect of Earned Income Credit on lower income and whether the minister is subject to Social Security or whether the minister is exempt from Social Security.

High Cost Localities for High-Low Per Diem Method

State	Key City	County or other defined locations	Effective Dates 2016 (IRS Notice 2015-63)	Effective Dates 2017 (IRS Notice 2016-58)
AZ	Sedona	City Limits of Sedona	N/A	3/1-4/30
CA	Los Angeles	Los Angeles, Orange, Ventura, Edwards AFB	N/A	1/1-3/31
	Mammoth Lakes	Mono	12/1-2/29	N/A
	Mill Valley/San Rafael/Novato	Marin	N/A	10/1-10/31, 6/1-9/30
	Monterey	Monterey	7/1-8/31	7/1-8/31
	Napa	Napa	5/1-9/30, 10/1-10/31	5/1-9/30, 10/1-10/31
	San Francisco	San Francisco	All Year	All Year
	San Mateo	San Mateo/Foster City/Belmont	All Year	All Year
	Santa Barbara	Santa Barbara	All Year	All Year
	Santa Cruz	Santa Cruz	6/1-8/31	N/A
	Santa Monica	City limits of Santa Monica	All Year	All Year
	Sunnyvale/Palo Alto/San Jose	Santa Clara	All Year	All Year
CO	Aspen	Pitkin	12/1-3/31, 6/1-8/31	12/1-3/31, 6/1-8/31
	Denver/Aurora	Denver, Adams, Arapahoe, and Jefferson	All Year	10/1-11/30, 2/1-9/30
	Grand Lake	Grand	12/1-3/31	12/1-3/31
	Silverthorne/Breckenridge	Summit	12/1-3/31	12/1-3/31
	Steamboat Springs	Routt	12/1-3/31	12/1-3/31
	Telluride	San Miguel	12/1-3/31, 6/1-8/31	12/1-3/31, 6/1-8/31
	Vail	Eagle	12/1-03/31, 7/1-8/31	12/1-08/31
DC	Washington, D.C.	Cities of Alexandria, Falls Church and Fairfax, and counties of Arlington and Fairfax in VA; counties of Montgomery and Prince George's in MD	All Year	All Year
FL	Boca Raton/Delray Beach/Jupiter	Palm Beach/Hendry	1/1-4/30	1/1-4/30
	Fort Lauderdale	Broward	1/1-3/31	1/1-4/30
	Fort Walton Beach/De Funiak Springs	Okaloosa and Walton	6/1-7/31	6/1-7/31
	Key West	Monroe	All Year	All Year
	Miami	Miami-Dade	12/1-3/31	12/1-3/31
	Naples	Collier	1/1-4/30	12/1-4/30
	Vero Beach	Indian River	N/A	12/1-4/30

State	Key City	County or other defined locations	Effective Dates 2016 (IRS Notice 2015-63)	Effective Dates 2017 (IRS Notice 2016-58)
IL	Chicago	Cook and Lake	3/1-11/30	4/1-11/30
ME	Bar Harbor	Hancock	7/1-8/31	7/1-8/31
MD	Ocean City	Worcester	6/1-8/31	6/1-8/31
	DC Area	Montgomery & Prince George's Counties	All Year	All Year
MA	Boston/Cambridge	Suffolk, City of Cambridge	All Year	All Year
	Falmouth	City Limits of Falmouth	7/1-8/31	7/1-8/31
	Martha's Vineyard	Dukes	6/1-9/30	6/1-9/30
	Nantucket	Nantucket	6/1-12/31	6/1-12/31
MI	Traverse City/Leland	Grand Traverse and Leelanau	7/1-8/31	7/1-8/31
NY	Lake Placid	Essex	7/1-8/31	7/1-8/31
	New York City	Bronx, Kings, New York, Queens, Richmond	All Year	All Year
	Saratoga Springs/Schenectady	Saratoga and Schenectady	7/1-8/31	7/1-8/31
NC	Kill Devil	Dare	N/A	6/1-8/31
OR	Seaside	Clatsop	N/A	7/1-8/31
PA	Hershey	Hershey	6/1-8/31	6/1-8/31
	Philadelphia	Philadelphia	3/1-6/30, 9/1-11/30	4/1-6/30, 9/1-11/30
RI	Jamestown/Middletown/Newport	Newport	6/1-8/31	7/1-8/31
SC	Charleston	Charleston, Berkeley and Dorchester	3/1-11/30	3/1-11/30
TX	Midland	Midland	All Year	N/A
UT	Park City	Summit	12/1-3/31	12/1-3/31
VA	Virginia Beach	City of Virginia Beach	6/1-8/31	6/1-8/31
	Wallops Island	Accomack	7/1-8/31	7/1-8/31
	Washington, DC Metro Area	Alexandria, Fairfax, and Falls Church Arlington and Fairfax Counties	All Year	All Year
WA	Seattle	King	All Year	All Year
WY	Jackson/Pinedale	Teton and Sublette	6/1-9/30	7/1-8/31

CHAPTER FOUR

Social Security and Retirement Planning

Dual-status ministers are treated as self-employed individuals in the performance of ministerial services for social security purposes as a result of written law. Sec. 1402(a)(8) is an exception to the "common law" rules for determining whether a person is an employee or self-employed. **Dual-status means** that the minister is an **employee** for income reporting, fringe benefit, and expense deducting purposes and **self-employed** for social security purposes.

Social Security for Ministers and Missionaries

Dual-Status Minister

Detailed information presented in Chapter Two helps you determine your correct treatment for social security purposes. **Summary:** The same regulations for determining if a minister qualifies for self-employed status for social security purposes are used to determine if a minister is entitled to parsonage allowance. Generally, you must be employed by a church or an integral agency of a church, perform the duties of a minister, and be ordained or "the equivalent thereof" to be treated as if you were self-employed for social security purposes. Because Sec. 1402(e) and it's regulations say, "if you are a minister of the gospel," you are to be treated as self-employed for social security purposes; **it is mandatory**. It is a serious error for a church to withhold and match social security for a minister.

In the absence of a formal ordination, licensing, or commissioning, the date of hire by a church or an integral agency, becomes an important date at which the unique dual-status tax treatment begins. It is necessary for your church to have formally ordained, licensed, or commissioned you as a minister before they can "assign or designate" you to a position at a "non-integral agency" and qualify you for dual-status treatment. It is also necessary for your church to have formally ordained, licensed, or commissioned you as a minister if you conduct worship and administer ordinances or sacraments, but are an evangelist or a chaplain and are not employed by a church or an integral agency of a church.

Before 1968, services performed by ministers were exempt from social security unless they filed a certificate (Form 2031) stating that they wished to be covered by social security.

Since 1968, ministers are automatically covered under social security unless they file an application for exemption on the grounds of conscientious or religious opposition to social security and the government's involvement in public insurance. **If you choose to be covered under social security, YOU DO NOTHING**. You are automatically liable for paying social security on Schedule SE.

An individual who had elected to be covered by social security by filing Form 2031 (before 1968) made an irrevocable decision and could not file Form 4361 and elect to be exempt. Anyone engaged in the ministry at the time of the law change in 1968 had until April 15, 1970, to file Form 4361 and continue not being covered by social security. A minister is often unaware of his **opportunity to choose** between paying social security or becoming exempt from paying Social Security. Once a minister begins to pay social security and the time expires for filing Form 4361 **and he does not have a change of belief accompanied by a change to another faith**, there is no way for him to become exempt. (See discussion "When to File Form 4361 - Including 'New Belief' Opportunity")

Computation Of Social Security Base - "Worksheet to be Used with Form 2106"

In Chapter Six we have a chart showing the types of income common to a minister and indicate what is required to be entered as salary on Form 941, line 2, and Form W-2, Box 1. **Parsonage provided and/or parsonage allowance designated is to be omitted from Form W-2, Box 1.** (IRS Publication 15-A, page 11) However, both the parsonage provided and/or the parsonage allowance must be added to the taxable amount of salary for social security and medicare tax purposes. In Part C, the "Computation of Social Security Base" section of the "Worksheet to be Used with Form 2106," enter the value of the parsonage provided on line 2, and enter the parsonage allowance designated from Part D, line 16, on line 3.

Because a dual-status minister is treated as "self-employed" for social security purposes, you can subtract **all unreimbursed professional expenses** from your income to arrive at the amount of income upon which to compute social security. Rev. Ruling 80-110 clearly states that unreimbursed auto, travel, and professional expenses can be used to reduce the social security base for the dual-status minister. Based on Rev. Ruling 80-110, Sec. 1402(a) and Sec. 62(1), **it is correct to use the business percentage of auto interest and personal property tax as a subtraction** from a minister's social security base. The portion of tax preparation fee that is attributable to the reporting of ministry transactions can be a subtraction from a minister's social security base according to Rev. Ruling 92-29.

Qualified fringe benefits are not subject to social security and are correct to be omitted from the employee's Form W-2, Box 1. Nonqualified and taxable fringe benefits receive the same treatment as taxable salary. They are to be included in the employee's Form W-2, Box 1 and they are subject to social security.

Contributions to an employer's qualified retirement plan by a dual-status minister **are not subject** to social security according to **Rev. Ruling 68-395**.

If you have filed Form 4361 and are exempt from social security, write **"Exempt - Form 4361"** on the self-employment line, Form 1040, page 2. If you are exempt from social security on your earnings from the ministry, but have secular self-employment income, use Schedule SE, page 2. Check the box on Line A to report that you have filed Form 4361 and compute social security on your secular earnings.

- ### Social Security Deductions For Self-Employed
On Schedule SE the gross social security base is adjusted to allow one half of social security as a deduction. On Form 1040, page 1, an adjustment for one half of the social security paid by the self-employed taxpayer is allowed. This is similar to the way employees are treated under the tax laws, because the employer's share of the Social Security tax is not considered wages to the employee.

Social Security Exemption

Form 4361 includes a statement that, because of your religious principles, you are conscientiously opposed to accepting, for services performed as a member of the clergy, any public insurance (governmental insurance that makes payments in the event of death, disability, old age, or retirement). This includes public insurance established by the Social Security Act. Your conscientious opposition must be based on the institutional principles and discipline of your particular religious denomination **OR** it must be based on **your individual religious principles**. Opposition based on the general conscience or for economic reasons will not satisfy this requirement.

A dual-status minister must prayerfully make his/her own decision as to whether he/she wants ministry earnings to be covered by social security. After a personal study of the **scriptures for biblical principals** that would show opposition to public or government insurance, a minister choosing to be exempt from social security should informally make sufficient notes of his study and conclusions.

As tax professionals, our job is to inform and teach you that, as a dual-status minister, you have an important decision to make regarding social security. No tax professional can make the choice for you nor should they advise you either way. **You must prayerfully make your own decision**. If you choose to remain subject to social security, you will compute it on Schedule SE and timely prepay your estimate of income tax and social security and medicare tax liability. If you choose to become exempt from social security you must timely file Form 4361. If you choose to become exempt **it must be for the religious and conscientious grounds** stated above.

Ministers who have filed Form 4361 are opposed to **only public** insurance and must provide their own alternative to social security. They most certainly **can** and **should** have a private investment plan for retirement needs and private disability insurance coverage.

- ### Form 4361 Filed For Invalid Reason
You **may not** become exempt for solely economic reasons. If you file an application for exemption only for economic reasons, you have not made a valid election. In **Rev. Ruling 70-197** a minister established *"that his application was made as a result of erroneous advice and was predicated solely on a judgement determination that a private insurance program was preferable from an economic standpoint for his insurance needs over that of the social security program rather than because he was conscientiously opposed to, or because of religious principles opposed to, the acceptance of any public insurance as specified in the form."* Accordingly it was held that the minister did not qualify for the exemption and his net earnings from ministry was subject to social security.

Rev. Ruling 82-185 concluded that Social Security tax can not be assessed later than three years after the taxpayer files a Form 1040 and fully reports all income but makes no entry with respect to self-employment tax.

● *What Happens To What I Have Already Paid In?*

Form 4361 does not cause you to waive the right to receive social security benefits. Any secular employment or work that is **NOT** in the exercise of your ministry will be subject to either social security or self-employment tax. Any social security you pay on secular earnings will be credited to your account.

If vested, you will be entitled to receive social security benefits from all mandatory contributions on secular earnings. **Ten years or forty quarters** of social security contributions result in your being vested and eligible for benefits based on your lifetime average. You can find out the number of quarters you have been credited for by contacting the Social Security Administration. Since secular work is always subject to social security, it would be possible to earn additional quarters by performing secular work after filing Form 4361. Earnings required for a quarter of credit in **2016 is $1,260** and in **2017 is $1,300**. When you retire, you can choose the **greater source** of benefits, either from **your account** or **your spouse's** account.

If vested, or your spouse is also vested, Medicare Insurance Part A **will be provided** for you and your spouse.

If neither spouse is vested or a single person is not vested, Medicare Insurance Part A **can be purchased** by an exempt minister. In **2016** Medicare Part A costs **$411** a month **per person** if you have less than 30 quarters and **$226** a month per person if you have between 30 and 39 quarters. (2017 rates - $413/ 227)

This should bring **peace of mind** to exempt ministers who have been given **wrong** information and have been told they will not qualify for Medicare. Everyone pays for Medicare B.

www.medicare.gov/your-medicare-costs/

● *Disability Coverage*

Disability coverage under social security will discontinue after you become exempt. When it will discontinue for you, depends upon your age and the number of quarters of credit you have. Knowing how many credits you need to remain covered by social security disability is very important. You could obtain a secular job to add credits or you could purchase private disability insurance coverage. Foreign missionaries have difficulty obtaining comparable life and disability insurance coverages and may wish to remain covered by social security.

● *Irrevocable Unless Congress Creates a "Window" for Revocation*

The exemption, once obtained, is basically irrevocable. Except when Congress gives a "window" of time for an exempt minister to revoke it, the decision is permanent. Historically, there have been three times that Congress has made provisions for revocation. **Ministers who revoke their election can never become exempt again.** If filed by the due date of the 1978 return, Form 4361-A gave opportunity for ministers who were exempt to revoke their election. If filed by the due date of the 1987 return, Form 2031 gave the second opportunity for ministers who were exempt to revoke their election. If filed by the due date of 2001 return, Form 2031 gave the third opportunity for ministers who were exempt to revoke their election.

● *When To File Form 4361 - Including "New Belief" Opportunity*

When a minister has the belief of opposition to public insurance at the time he begins **his initial ministry** he will have until the due date (April 15th) of his tax return, including extensions, for the **second tax year** in which he has net self-employment **earnings of $400** or more from services as a minister to **timely file** Form 4361, "Application for Exemption." Net earnings is the salary and/or honorariums, minus unreimbursed business expenses, plus parsonage provided and/or parsonage allowance designated.

It is very important for a minister who wishes to become exempt from social security to be aware that the date his ministry begins is when he assumes the duties of the ministry. In the absence of a formal ordination, licensing or commissioning, it is the **date a church called or hired** you as their minister and gave you the authority to perform substantially all of the religious duties.

Here is a very important court definition of a "duly ordained, licensed, or commissioned" minister. In J.M. Ballinger, U.S. Court of Appeals, 10th Circuit, No. 82-1928, 3/7/84, it was stated:

> *"Not all churches or religions have a formally ordained ministry, whether because of the nature of their beliefs, the lack of a denominational structure or a variety of other reasons. Courts are not in a position to determine the merits of various churches... We interpret Congress' language providing an exemption for any individual who is `a duly ordained, commissioned, or licensed minister of a church' to mean that the **triggering event** is the assumption of the duties and functions of a minister."*

Several of the tax court cases we reviewed in Chapter Two were concerning ministers who wanted to become exempt from social security. After waiting until they received their formal or permanent credentials, they were denied exemption because their applications were untimely filed. Services they performed with temporary or limited credentials were still being performed **with the same employer** when they received their permanent credentials. Not realizing that their initial date of hire was the beginning of their ministry caused them to have their applications disapproved because of untimeliness. When an application to become exempt from social security is filed late, it will be disapproved. A minister who files untimely and has his application disapproved has no future opportunity to become exempt. **A timely filed Form 4361 will be approved.**

Example of timing: you had net earnings of $5,000 in 2015 and $38,000 in 2016, the deadline for filing Form 4361 would be April 18th, 2017. The two years need not be consecutive. If a minister had net earnings of $700 in 2009, less than $400 in 2010 through 2015, and $4,000 in 2016, the deadline for filing Form 4361 would be April 18th, 2017.

Change of belief accompanied by a change to another faith: When an individual enters the ministry anew in a new church, having adopted a new set of beliefs about the propriety of accepting public insurance, it is logical and consistent with the statutory language of section 1402(e) to characterize that individual as a "new" minister for the purposes of seeking an exemption.

When a minister does not have the belief of opposition to public insurance at the time of his initial date of hire, and does not file an application to be exempt, he may experience **another opportunity to become exempt**. It depends upon the church polity of his employing church. In a **connectional** (not self-governing) church polity, a minister is typically appointed to a congregation and generally is moved by an overseer to a different congregation within the denomination. In an **autonomous** (self-governing) church polity, a minister is typically hired or called directly by a congregation and generally makes his own decision as to when he wants to resign and change church employers.

1. A change of faith **does not happen** when an employee is transferred between connectional church congregations.
2. A change of faith **does happen** when a minister leaves a connectional church denomination and goes to another connectional church denomination or to an autonomous church employer.
3. A change of faith **does happen** when a minister resigns from one autonomous church and goes to another autonomous church or to a connectional church.

When a minister has the belief of opposition to public insurance at the time he begins **his "change of faith"** ministry, he will have until the due date (April 15th) of his tax return, including extensions, for the **second tax year** in which he has net self-employment **earnings of $400** or more from services as a minister to **timely file** Form 4361, "Application for Exemption." Net earnings is the salary and/or honorariums, minus unreimbursed business expenses, plus parsonage provided and/or parsonage allowance designated. No formal reordination or relicensing is necessary. In filling out a "new belief, new faith" Form 4361, enter the new date of hire in Box 3 and enter the year of hire as the first year on line 5.

The Ballinger and Hall tax court decisions require the Internal Revenue Service to approve "**change of belief accompanied by a change to another faith**" applications for social security exemption. We had communication with one service center that said they had no knowledge of this provision and sought help from the national IRS office on the issue. The Form 4361 that they had denied was resubmitted and finally approved. All Form 4361 applications are now being processed in one office rather than in several service centers.

A **summary** of the **two tax court cases** that have brought about the ability for a minister to have more than one "window" of time to acquire an opposition to social security follows:

J.M. Ballinger, U.S. Court of Appeals, 10th Circuit, No 82-1928, 3/7/84: Taxpayer was ordained as a minister of the First Missionary Baptist Church, on November 22, 1969. He became minister of the Maranatha Church in September 1973. He received net earnings from the ministry in excess of $400 during 1973, 1974 and 1975. On March 8, 1977 he incorrectly filed Form 4029 instead of Form 4361. It was disapproved by the IRS because he was not a member of a religious order described in Sec. 1402(g). On May 2, 1978 he was reordained by the Maranatha Church. On July 7, 1978 he filed the correct Form 4361 showing May 2, 1978 as the beginning of his ministry. The IRS initially approved the application. Upon discovery that Rev. Ballinger had first been ordained in 1969 and hired by Maranatha Church in September, 1973, the IRS revoked the exemption. Had Rev. Ballinger filed Form 4361 by April 15, 1975, the judges stated that it would have been a different case. The three judge panel said:

> "*The statute makes no distinction between a first ordination and subsequent ordinations Courts are not in a position to determine the merits of various churches nor an individual's conversion from one church to another. Nor can we hold that an individual who has a change of belief **accompanied** by a change to another faith is not entitled to the exemption.*"

Having **untimely filed** his Form 4361, the taxpayer's exemption from social security **was disapproved**.

James B. Hall, U.S. Court of Appeals, 10th Circuit, No 93-9027, 7/19/94: The same court ten years later upheld their decision and the three judge panel said, *"We anticipated a case like this when we decided Ballinger v. Commissioner."* Taxpayer was ordained as a deacon in the United Methodist Church in 1979 and earned more than $400 per year from his ministerial services in both 1980 and 1981. Taxpayer's activities as a deacon made him potentially eligible to apply for a 1402(e)exemption. At that time, however, the taxpayer was not religiously or conscientiously opposed to the acceptance of public insurance, thus he was not eligible and did not apply for an exemption. He left the ministry and spent five years as an engineer. Taxpayer was ordained by the Community Church and began a new ministry and accepted a new belief in opposition to public insurance. Rev. Hall applied for exemption in the first tax year immediately following his second ordination and the commencement of his new ministry. It was initially denied as untimely (after April 15, 1982.) A lower Tax Court affirmed this denial. The U.S. Court of Appeals judges said:

> *"We ultimately concluded that the statute permits all ministers who oppose public insurance on religious grounds to qualify and, as we interpret the statute, permits ministers who change churches to qualify."*

> They also stated: *"We are not concerned that our decision will open the floodgates for conniving Elmer Gantrys to dupe the Internal Revenue Service and opt out of the social security system without a sincere religious objection."*

Having **timely filed** his Form 4361, the taxpayer's exemption from social security **was approved**.

Private Letter Ruling 200404048: A minister who because of religious principles was opposed to the acceptance of public insurance, had filed Form 4361 untimely after his first date of hire. It had been denied as untimely. Upon changing faiths he filed a new Form 4361 and it was also denied. Both the Ballinger and Hall cases are discussed in the letter ruling. The minister had a change of faith **without** a change in belief. His belief of opposing the acceptance of public insurance was made evident when he filed the first Form 4361.

• *Exemption is Retroactive to Beginning of New Ministry*

An approved Form 4361 is retroactive back to the date your ministry or change of faith began. If you paid social security for the first year of your ministry or change of ministry and have chosen to file Form 4361 during the second year, you can receive a refund of the first year's social security payment. Upon receiving an approved Form 4361, file Form 1040X as a claim for your refund. Attach a photocopy of your approved Form 4361 to Form 1040X. **The IRS does not automatically send** social security refunds.

• *How To File Form 4361 and Attachments*

For efficient processing of your exemption application it is important to include all of the required attachments and information.

Attach proof of the beginning of your initial ministry or change of faith ministry: a copy of your certificate for ordination, license, commissioning or a letter from the church who hired you verifying the date you were hired as their minister.

Extra statements required for applicants without an ordination certificate: If your church or denomination both ordains and licenses ministers, Form 4361, line 6, requires that you attach a copy of the by-laws stating that a licensed or employed minister is invested with the authority to perform substantially all of the duties of the church or denomination. If no such by-laws exist, then type the following statement on your church's letterhead, have a person in authority sign it, and attach it to your application:

> *"Our church/denomination does not have specific by-laws regarding the powers of ordained, licensed, commissioned or employed ministers. We do give the same authority to perform all of the ecclesiastical duties to our licensed, commissioned or employed ministers as we do to those who are ordained."*

Notify church: The ordaining, licensing or commissioning body of your church must be informed that you are conscientiously opposed to or because of religious principles you are opposed to the acceptance of public insurance benefits based on ministerial service. In the absence of a formal ordination, licensing or commissioning, it is the church that hired you that you must notify. When you sign Form 4361 you are certifying (line 7) that you have performed this notification. Individual opposition is sufficient for a minister to be exempt; it does not matter that the position of the employer is different.

Prove your church is a church: You must establish that the organization that gave you the authority to do ministerial services **is a church**. The IRS requires the exemption applicant to establish or prove that the church that ordained him or "the equivalent thereof" is a religious organization described in **Sec. 501(c)(3)** and also in **Sec. 170(b)(1)(A)(i).**

IRS Publication 78, published quarterly, lists organizations, denominations or churches that have filed Form 1023 requesting exempt status. If your church is a part of a major denomination, your church will be under its group exempt status. If the church that ordained you or "the equivalent thereof" is independent or autonomous and voluntarily filed Form 1023 and received a determination letter, it is listed in IRS Publication 78. Attach a copy of their determination letter to your Form 4361.

Churches are not required to file and submit the information requested on Form 1023. Form 8718 must accompany the Form 1023 and requires either a $400 or a $850 fee to be paid to the IRS.

If the church on your application has not voluntarily filed Form 1023, you must provide proof that it is a church with your Form 4361. The national office to which you send your Form 4361 will accept the following types of information from you to establish that the church is a church:

1. On church stationery provide the name of organization, address, and Employer Identification Number. Make this statement: *"We are a church described in Sec. 501(c)(3) and also in Sec. 170(b)(1)(A)(i)."* Include a description of the characteristics that qualify the organization as a church such as regular worship, evangelism and membership. The statement should be signed by someone authorized to represent the church.

2. If your church is incorporated, attach copies of the organization's creating instrument and a copy of the constitution and bylaws.

3. Provide copies of church bulletins, newsletters, photos of the church and members, etc., to show the regular times of worship and other activities that are typical of a church.

• *How To Send Your Form 4361*

File your Form 4361 by itself. Never file it with your Form 1040. Make photocopies of the completed Form 4361 for your records and keep in two or three safe places. File the **original and two copies** with the attached documents we have discussed by **Certified Mail** so that you can prove that it was timely filed. Form 4361, page 2 instructions give the address to which it should be sent. All Form 4361s are to be sent to one national office.

Watch For Letter: The Secretary of Health and Human Services has the responsibility of communicating with the applicant to further verify that the applicant understands the grounds (basis) for exemption and is seeking the exemption on those grounds. Applicants receive a letter asking for their signature again, verifying that they understand the grounds under which they filed Form 4361. **The letter must be returned to the IRS within 90 days** or the effective date of the exemption will not begin until it is received by the IRS.

Eventually a copy is sent back to you marked **"approved"**. The process can take several months. If you fail to get an approved copy back in 6 to 8 months, call the IRS and ask that they put a tracer on it. Applications sometimes get lost and need to be refiled.

• *Put Your Approved Copy In Several Safe Places*

Once you receive your **"APPROVED COPY"** from the IRS — copy it, protect it, and treat it as a valuable document. We recommend making several copies. Give a copy to your tax accountant. If your approved copy has been misplaced or lost, request a copy from the Social Security Administration. Write to: Department of the Treasury, Internal Revenue Service Center, Philadelphia, PA 19255-0733.

• *What If You Timely Filed, But Have Never Received An Approved Copy From IRS*

Ministers who failed to receive their "Approved Copy" of Form 4361 should take steps to obtain one. Often during an audit event they are unable to prove their exempt status and are billed for social security in the audit report. Common reasons for not receiving the "Approved Copy" are (1) minister moved before receiving approval; (2) application got lost in the mail or in the processing system; (3) original application lacked complete information and was denied because of lack of information. **The Good news** is that anytime you **have proof** that Form 4361 was timely filed, you can refile it! By resubmitting a new Form 4361, containing correct original information, with a letter stating the history and proof of timely filing, many ministers have been successful in obtaining an "Approved Copy" back, effective to the original date ministry began. Any social security tax assessed can then be canceled or refunded.

Form **4361** (Rev. January 2011)
Department of the Treasury
Internal Revenue Service

Application for Exemption From Self-Employment Tax for Use by Ministers, Members of Religious Orders and Christian Science Practitioners

OMB No. 1545-0074

File Original and Two Copies

File original and two copies and attach supporting documents. This exemption is granted only if the IRS returns a copy to you marked "approved."

Please type or print

1 Name of taxpayer applying for exemption (as shown on Form 1040) | Social security number

Number and street (including apt. no.) | Telephone number (optional)

City or town, state, and ZIP code

2 Check **one** box:
☐ Christian Science practitioner
☐ Member of religious order not under a vow of poverty
☐ Ordained minister, priest, rabbi
☐ Commissioned or licensed minister (see line 6)

3 Date ordained, licensed, etc. (Attach supporting document. See instructions.)

4 Legal name of ordaining, licensing, or commissioning body or religious order

Number, street, and room or suite no. | Employer identification number

City or town, state, and ZIP code

5 Enter the first 2 years after the date shown on line 3 that you had net self-employment earnings of $400 or more, any of which came from services as a minister, priest, rabbi, etc.; member of a religious order; or Christian Science practitioner ▶

6 If you apply for the exemption as a licensed or commissioned minister and your denomination also ordains ministers, please indicate how your ecclesiastical powers differ from those of an ordained minister of your denomination. Attach a copy of your denomination's bylaws relating to the powers of ordained, commissioned, and licensed ministers.

7 I certify that I am conscientiously opposed to, or because of my religious principles I am opposed to, the acceptance (for services I perform as a minister, member of a religious order not under a vow of poverty, or Christian Science practitioner) of any public insurance that makes payments in the event of death, disability, old age, or retirement; or that makes payments toward the cost of, or provides services for, medical care. (Public insurance includes insurance systems established by the Social Security Act.)

I certify that as a duly ordained, commissioned, or licensed minister of a church or a member of a religious order not under a vow of poverty, I have informed the ordaining, commissioning, or licensing body of my church or order that I am conscientiously opposed to, or because of religious principles I am opposed to, the acceptance (for services I perform as a minister or as a member of a religious order) of any public insurance that makes payments in the event of death, disability, old age, or retirement; or that makes payments toward the cost of, or provides services for, medical care, including the benefits of any insurance system established by the Social Security Act.

I certify that I have never filed Form 2031 to revoke a previous exemption from social security coverage on earnings as a minister, member of a religious order not under a vow of poverty, or Christian Science practitioner.

I request to be exempted from paying self-employment tax on my earnings from services as a minister, member of a religious order not under a vow of poverty, or Christian Science practitioner, under section 1402(e) of the Internal Revenue Code. I understand that the exemption, if granted, will apply only to these earnings. Under penalties of perjury, I declare that I have examined this application and to the best of my knowledge and belief, it is true and correct.

Signature ▶   Date ▶

Caution: Form 4361 is **not proof** of the right to an exemption from federal income tax withholding or social security tax, the right to a parsonage allowance exclusion (section 107 of the Internal Revenue Code), assignment by your religious superiors to a particular job, or the exemption or church status of the ordaining, licensing, or commissioning body, or religious order.

For Internal Revenue Service Use
☐ Approved for exemption from self-employment tax on ministerial earnings
☐ Disapproved for exemption from self-employment tax on ministerial earnings

By
(Director's signature)   (Date)

Social Security & the Religious Sects Opposed to Insurance

A completely different set of rules apply to members of religious orders. **Sec. 1402(g)** allows any self-employed member of a religious order that opposes both private and public insurance to file **Form 4029** and be exempt from social security regardless of his work activity (farming, construction, etc.). Since November 10, 1988, **Form 4029** can be filed at any time. This exemption is a statement that the individual is opposed to both **public and private insurance** and **is an actual waiver** of ever receiving any benefits from social security. It is necessary that the religious order has a history and a plan to provide for the members when they become dependent through disability or old age. **It is also necessary that the order was organized before 1950.** New religious orders described in Sec. 1402(g) cannot be formed. If a member ceases to be a member of the order their exemption is revoked. Members who have filed Form 4029 for exemption from social security and have made contributions to a private retirement annuity revoke their exemption and will have to pay back-years' social security tax according to Rev. Ruling 77-88. According to Private Letter Ruling 8741002, funding of an IRA through a CD in a bank did not constitute insurance, and thus, did not disqualify the taxpayer from exemption. However, earnings exempt from Social Security under Sec. 1402(g) are not eligible earnings from which to make an IRA contribution.

Because Rev. Ruling 77-88 has often been taken out of context and thought to apply to **Sec. 1402(e)** for ministers who have filed Form 4361, it is important for you to know that it does not apply to ministers. Ministers who have filed Form 4361 are opposed to **only public** insurance and must provide their own alternative to social security. They **can** and **should have a private investment plan for retirement needs.**

Social Security and the Lay Employee

An employee who does not qualify for dual-status tax treatment must be treated as a lay employee of the employer for social security and medicare tax purposes. He does not have an individual choice of being exempt or subject to social security.

Prior to 1984, a nonprofit religious organization as described in Sec. 501(c)(3) had been automatically exempt from withholding social security from their employees and matching it with their share. So an organization that wished to remain exempt from withholding social security for all its employees did not have to file any form. Prior to 1984, if an organization and its employees desired to be covered by social security, they had to file Form SS-15.

Since January 1, 1984, the Social Security Amendments Act of 1983 extended social security coverage **on a mandatory** basis to all lay employees of nonprofit organizations.

Electing Churches - Form 8274

The Tax Reform Act of 1984 provided for an election by a church or qualified church-controlled organization that is **opposed for religious reasons** to the payment of social security taxes not to be subject to such taxes. (Sec. 3121(w)) The election merely **transfers** the social security liability **from the electing church to the lay employee**.

The electing church is required to withhold income tax and to report the compensation paid to each lay employee who earns **more than $108.28** on Form W-2. The electing church should withhold additional amounts of income tax so their employees will have an adequate amount of tax prepaid to cover the cost of the social security to be computed on their Schedule SE. Form 941, with the box on Line 4 marked, is the correct quarterly report for an electing church. The electing church **must communicate** to their employees their responsibility to compute and pay their own social security on their Form 1040, Schedule SE. In Chapter Six we show a filled out example of Form 941 and W-2's for an electing church. We recommend that a memo, "Electing church employee to pay social security on Schedule SE", be entered on the employee's Form W-2, Box 14.

- **When To Make The Election - Form 8274**

Church employers with lay employees, as of October 1, 1984, had until October 31, 1984 to file Form 8274. To become an "electing church," a church must file Form 8274 (two copies) before the first date on which a quarterly employment tax return would otherwise be due. Existing churches that have never had lay employees, only dual-status minister employees or volunteers, may file Form 8274 by the due date of the quarter in which they first hire a lay employee. Churches not aware of when to timely file for the election have no recourse. In Private Letter Ruling 199911025, a church asked for an extension of the time period for filing the Form 8274 and it was denied.

Example of timely filing: A church was organized many years ago and has had a dual-status minister as their only employee. On October 15, 2016, they hired a secretary to work in the office and based on opposition for religious reasons, they can timely file Form 8274 before January 31, 2017.

If an electing church fails to provide the required Form W-2's for two years and fails to furnish the information upon request by the IRS, the IRS will revoke their election.

Lay employees of "electing churches" do not qualify to claim exemption from paying social security by filing Form 4361. The wages subject to social security on Schedule SE are the wages in Box 1 of their Form W-2 plus any Sec. 403(b), 408(p), or 401(k) voluntary contributions. Such wages from an electing church can not be reduced by losses from other self-employment activity or unreimbursed employee business expenses. (Sec. 3121(b)(8); 3121(w)) (IRS Publication 557, page 13)

- **How To Revoke The Election - Form 8274**

The Tax Reform Act of 1986 **made it easy for electing churches to revoke their election**. By simply filing a Form 941 on or before its due date for the first quarter for which the revocation is to be effective, accompanied by payment in full of the social security taxes that would be due for the quarter, the election is revoked.

How To Do Correction For Wrong Treatment

Are you a dual-status minister but your employer **wrongly treated you as an employee for social security purposes**? When, according to the regulations, you are to be treated as self-employed for social security purposes, **dual-status tax treatment is mandatory**. For your employer to withhold and match social security is in error. This can be corrected for all three "open" years that allow amended returns to be filed.

Even though it is advisable to correct the wrong treatment of the minister's status, there has not been an underpayment or overpayment of tax liability. Some employers may choose to correct the wrong treatment for the current and future years.

We want to give adequate information for making corrections if you choose to correct the open years. The amount of social security matched by the employer is not required to be credited or paid to the employee. The social security withheld from the employee's salary must be paid back to the employee. If the employer chooses to allow their matched portion to be credited to their employee, it must be counted as extra salary on the W-2c in the year of the correction.

Because a dual-status minister can deduct unreimbursed employee business expenses from his social security base, the social security and medicare tax computed on Schedule SE may be less than the amount withheld and matched in error.

- *Two Ways To Handle The Corrections*
    1. When the employer is willing to count their matching portion as extra salary for the minister:
        a. Prepare 941X to reflect the changes made. You will not be requesting a refund on the 941X.
        b. Prepare W-2c and W-3c showing matching portion added to "Wages, tips, other compensation" as additional salary.
        c. Include total amount of social security withheld and matched as income tax withheld in "federal income tax withheld."
        d. Prepare an amended return for the minister. The minister will have credit on his 1040X for the total social security amount withheld and matched. Depending on the level of his total income, he may have a small refund or owe a small amount of additional tax, plus interest on the balance.
    2. When the employer wishes to keep their matching portion:
        a. Prepare 941X to reflect the changes made and claim a credit on the next quarter's 941 or claim a refund for the employer's matching portion.
        b. Prepare W-2c and W-3c showing original salary in "Wages, tips, other compensation."
        c. Include amount of social security withheld as income tax withholding in "federal income tax withheld."
        d. Prepare an amended return for the minister. The minister will have partial credit on his 1040X for social security computed on Schedule SE and will incur interest on the balance owed.

It is important when making changes to your federal Form 1040 to remember to amend your state income tax return when it is affected. **Do not hesitate to seek** professional accounting help in preparing corrections to payroll reports.

Should the Minister's Spouse be on the Payroll?

No one will dispute the fact that a minister's spouse works many hours for the church as a volunteer and receives no paycheck. To establish a salary, it is necessary that there is a true employer/employee relationship. The amount of the salary should be reasonable and paid on the basis of time spent in working for the employer. Employed ministers **should not personally pay** their spouse a salary. It is not allowed under the "assignment of income" portion of tax law according to Sec. 61 and Rev. Ruling 74-32.

Benefits - When Both Spouses Have Earned Income: When both spouses have income from salaries it qualifies them for claiming Child Care Credit on Form 2441 for babysitting expenses incurred while both are at work. Babysitting expense is **never to be treated** as an employee business expense.

Travel and professional expenses can be justified for both employed spouses. For a husband and wife to both be receiving a salary and conducting bona fide business activities, travel away from home expenses, auto travel, entertainment, etc., are able to be reimbursed or deducted.

At retirement the ability to receive two semi-retired salaries and be within the social security earnings limitation can be very advantageous. Those who retire early, between age 62 and full retirement age will benefit from this situation. The earnings limitation has been lifted for those who reach full retirement age!

Estimated Tax, Form 1040ES

It is necessary for all taxpayers to "prepay" their income tax and their social security tax. A lay employee has tax withheld from each paycheck and "prepaid" on Form 941 by the employer. **Withholding by the employer of a dual-status minister is optional.** The dual-status minister is generally required to "prepay" tax by making quarterly payments based on an estimate of the amount of tax he expects to owe for the year. The current year's estimate is to be calculated at the time you prepare the previous year's tax return and the first installment of ¼ of the total is due on **April 15th**. Other due dates are **June 15th, September 15th, and January 15th**. Instead of paying the final January 15th installment, you may elect to file your return early, by January 31st, and pay any tax due with the return.

If you or your spouse are an employee and earn other wages from which tax is withheld, you may be able to arrange to have enough withheld to cover your combined tax liability. To claim less exemptions or allowances at the other job is usually more convenient than to make quarterly payments. It makes no difference **how you prepay your tax liability;** either **estimated payments** or **adequate withholding** will meet the requirements. An estimate is exactly what the word means. No one can predict the correct amount of tax a year in advance. If you anticipate no tax or **less than $1,000** for the year, no estimate is necessary. If circumstances change during the year you may always amend or change your estimate and increase or decrease the quarterly payments.

- **Underpayment Penalties**

You may be charged a penalty for not paying enough estimated tax or for not making the payments on time. The amount of underpayment penalty is the same as the rate of interest the IRS charges on late payments and it is announced each quarter. For individuals (other than high-income individuals) the penalty does not apply if **each required payment is timely** and the total tax paid is based on:

1. 90% of the total tax liability due on the return for the current year (income tax, social security tax, early withdrawal penalties, alternative minimum tax, etc.) or;
2. 100% of your total tax liability shown on the previous year's return, commonly referred to as a **safe harbor estimate.** When you expect your tax liability will increase, pre-pay 100% of the liability shown on the previous year's return in timely installments, and pay any remaining balance with the return by April 15th and you will not incur a penalty.

Higher income taxpayers: If your adjusted gross income (AGI) was more than $150,000 ($75,000 for married separate), substitute 110% for 100% in (2) above.

File your estimated tax on **Form 1040ES** and keep in mind that the estimate includes income tax and social security/medicare tax.

- **Waiver of Penalty**

A waiver of penalty is available if you did not make a payment because of a casualty, disaster, or other unusual circumstance. Also, a waiver may be claimed if you retired (after reaching age 62) or became disabled during the tax year a payment was due or during the preceding tax year and your underpayment was not due to willful neglect. To claim the waiver, follow the instructions given for Form 2210 or in IRS Publication 505, page 56.

- **Optional Withholding Agreement**

A withholding agreement can be made between an employer and a dual-status minister. It is to be a written agreement. A Form W-4 can be prepared with the amount to be withheld each pay period entered on line 6 rather than claiming any allowances on line 5. The employer should withhold enough **income tax** to prepay the minister's total income tax and social security/medicare tax liability. Form W-2 will show the amount that has been withheld in Box 2.

Retirement Planning For Ministers and Missionaries

All ministers and missionaries should establish retirement plans to **supplement** social security income during retirement. Dual-status ministers who have become exempt from social security must have a disciplined savings plan for retirement to take the place of social security. **It would be FOOLISH to become exempt from social security and do nothing to provide for one's needs in retirement.**

We want to present some ideas and information that will make it possible to have the option to retire or semi-retire. Financial planning for retirement has been neglected by many ministers and missionaries. We can blame low compensation, busy work schedules, and even a hopeful expectation that the Lord will return before retirement, but the fact is many ministers and missionaries can not afford to retire.

Investments that are diversified are the best way to plan for meeting your needs during retirement. Through mutual funds it is possible to invest regular amounts in a diversified portfolio. The principle of investing regularly and over a long time horizon results in amazing compound growth. Investments in common stocks or stock funds have historically outperformed savings in fixed income investments. **You should never feel it is too late** to begin an investment plan. Most Americans do not begin to save regularly until the children are raised and the mortgage is nearly paid. The increase in life expectancy creates a greater need for investment planning and at the same time allows a longer time for the magic of compounding to function.

Let us give you an example of **the magic of compounding.** If you began investing at age 25 and invested $265.00 a month for 40 years and had a 8% rate of return, you would be a millionaire at age 65. If you began investing at age 45 and invested $1,650.00 a month for 20 years and had a 8% rate of return, you would also be a millionaire at age 65.

Mutual Funds

Over meaningful time spans of 10 years or more, well-managed stock funds have performed better than other investments. The growth of an investment in a mutual fund comes from two sources: income dividends and capital appreciation. While there have been times when the value of an investment in mutual funds have declined, over the years such an investment has produced much better results than savings deposits. There is no doubt that a savings account or certificate of deposit is a good place to put money you want to keep in reserve for short-term needs. However, well-managed stock funds are the best place for your long-term **investment** or retirement dollars.

Investing in the stock market can be confusing if you do not have much time to devote to it. Some publications would encourage you to try to "time" the market and to trade often. Most of us do not have the time to be watching the daily changes in the market place. Even investment professionals cannot always "buy low and sell high." Those who "buy high and sell low" become discouraged and often discontinue investing. A better strategy for investing is to invest regular amounts into a family of mutual funds and let your investment compound over a long period of time. This strategy is often called "dollar cost averaging."

A well managed mutual fund must charge the investors for management costs. Some mutual funds have "loads" or commissions up front or at the time of your investment. Other mutual funds advertised in the Wall Street Journal and financial magazines are "no load" or without a commission at the time of the investment. Generally, the "no load" funds have a higher annual management fee than the "loaded" funds. Some funds have a back end "load" if you do not own the fund long enough. **Before you make any investment in a mutual fund, you will be given a prospectus that fully explains the fees that particular fund will charge.** Choosing a "no load" mutual fund could actually end up costing more over the life of an investment because the annual management fees are charged on the compounded value of the investment. "Loaded" mutual funds typically have much lower annual management fees. "Loaded" mutual funds are marketed through registered representatives and having received a commission at the time of your investment, they are willing to answer your questions and help you monitor your investments.

Life Insurance

Life insurance is an important part of your portfolio because it provides risk protection for your family. One purpose of life insurance is to replace your earnings should you die prematurely. The amount of your debt, the ability of your spouse to earn a living, the age and number of dependent children are a few of the factors to consider in determining how much life insurance coverage you should have. There is no easy formula to use to decide whether it is best to have a term life policy, a universal life policy or a whole life policy. The facts and circumstances of your individual needs can be evaluated by an insurance professional. It is possible to combine life insurance protection and mutual fund investing within a variable life policy. Upon your death, life insurance benefits are not taxable to your beneficiaries on their Form 1040. However, the amount of benefits are to be included in your taxable estate and could cause estate tax.

Annuities

An annuity is a product of life insurance companies that is a contract which promises to pay you for the rest of your life in exchange for a stated cost of premium. A fixed annuity is invested in interest bearing investments and usually has a better rate of return than a bank certificate of deposit. A variable annuity is invested in the capital market through a group of mutual funds. An annuity's earnings are reinvested and are tax deferred, or not currently taxed. If you are receiving social security benefits, and you have a high adjusted gross income that causes a portion of your social security to be taxed, an unqualified annuity, funded with "after tax" dollars, is a good tax planning tool.

At age 65 you can annuitize the investment through several options. If you annuitize an annuity, and die early, the insurance company wins; if you live beyond life expectancy, you win. The option of choosing joint life is usually a good choice. If you choose to annuitize an annuity, an income factor of **about 3%** is used to calculate your monthly distribution.

An annuity does not have to be annuitized. Distributions can be withdrawn from the annuity as you need cash flow without annuitization. The contract can continue to earn at **a higher rate** and any principal remaining at your death can be passed on to your beneficiaries. The value will not be subject to probate expense. However, as the contract passes to your appointed beneficiary, the profit or gain in the contract will be taxable on your beneficiary's Form 1040.

Because annuities have an "end load" or cost if you take more than the allowed minimum withdrawal during the first six to eleven years of the investment, they should never be used as a short term investment. The taxable portion of withdrawals before age 59½ or disability do incur the 10% penalty assessed by the IRS. The taxable portion of withdrawals are also subject to regular tax.

- **Investments and annuities are available in unqualified plans and qualified plans.**

An unqualified plan means that the amount invested is not subtracted from your taxable income. A qualified plan means that the amount invested is subtracted or "sheltered" from your taxable income. To establish a qualified investment or annuity, it is usually a simple procedure of signing an extra document that establishes a custodian for the plan. See Chapter One for additional details for Tax Sheltered Accounts (TSAs), Employer Simple IRA Accounts and Individual Retirement Accounts (IRAs).

- **When Should You Have A Qualified Plan?**

When you have an income tax liability, it is good tax planning to consider making contributions to a sheltered or qualified retirement plan. Even when you have no income tax liability you may wish to contribute to a Sec. 403(b) retirement plan or a SIMPLE IRA plan 408(p) and reduce your social security base if you are a dual-status minister. In any year you have **no income tax** liability and if you are exempt from paying social security (Form 4361), it would be best to invest in a Roth IRA or an unqualified investment.

Contributions to an Employer's Qualified Retirement Plan by a dual-status minister **are not** subject to social security and medicare tax according to **Rev. Ruling 68-395**. However, contributions to an Employer's Qualified Retirement Plan by a lay employee **are** subject to social security and medicare tax withholding according to **Rev. Ruling 65-208**.

- **Tax Sheltered Account or 403(b) Plan**

Tax Sheltered Accounts are available to public school employees and employees of nonprofit organizations. Ministers employed by a nonprofit organization are eligible for making contributions to a Sec. 403(b) retirement account. Since January 1, 1997, a minister or chaplain, who in connection with the exercise of his ministry is a self-employed individual or is working for an employer that is not a qualified nonprofit organization, can also contribute to a TSA.

On July 23, 2007, the first comprehensive regulations in 43 years were issued. The general effective date is for taxable years beginning after **December 31, 2009**. Previously, individuals controlled their accounts exclusively. Under the new regulations, 403(b)s will be established and maintained by the employer. As a result, employers will need to take a much more active role in the plan oversight and management. **See Chapter One, pages 29-32 for complete discussion.**

- **Sec. 408(p) - Savings Incentive Match Plan for Employees (SIMPLE)**

Employers with less than 100 employees may want to consider establishing Sec. 408(p) SIMPLE plan instead of a 403(b). The IRS has provided the plan document. The contribution limitations are lower and the employer is required to match up to 3% of employee participation.

A SIMPLE retirement plan is a written salary reduction arrangement that allows a **small employer** (an employer with 100 or fewer employees) to make elective contributions to a simple retirement account (IRA) on behalf of each eligible employee. The plan document is provided by the IRS and is *"really"* **simple** to establish and administer by an employer.

For **2016**, an employee can contribute up to 100% of compensation limited to **$12,500** annually, with an additional **$3,000** available if age 50 or over by end of year. (2017 - $12,500, with an additional $3,000 available if age 50 or over by end of year.) The employer is required to match the employees' contributions on a dollar for dollar basis, up to 3% of compensation, or elect to make 2% nonelective contributions on behalf of all eligible employees. Eligible employees are those who earned at least $5,000 in compensation from the employer during any two prior years and who are reasonably expected to receive at least $5,000 in compensation during the year. The plan document allows an employer to choose between $0 and $5,000 for the compensation requirement and to choose between zero to two prior years for the time requirement.

Sec 408(a) - Individual Retirement Account

A qualified tax shelter that we are all familiar with is the Individual Retirement Account or the IRA. You can set up and make contributions to an IRA if you received taxable compensation during the year and have not reached age 70½ by the end of the year.

You can establish an IRA that is invested in mutual funds. You can establish an IRA with an insurance company that is an annuity contract. You can establish an IRA with a bank that is invested in a Certificate of Deposit. **IRAs** are now **flexible** and have the capability of being **qualified or unqualified.** You can choose to designate contributions to an IRA as "nondeductible" on Form 8606 in a year that you have no tax liability.

Contributions to a Roth IRA are nondeductible in the year of the contribution. Their earnings will accumulate tax free and qualified distributions will be tax free.

A Roth IRA is a wonderful choice for the non-tax paying minister's retirement planning. A Roth IRA invested in a mutual fund will capture the long term growth of the capital market. Qualified distributions are those made after a 5 year period, and in addition, made after age 59½, after death to a beneficiary, after becoming disabled or distributed to pay for "qualified first time home buyer expenses."

According to Reg. 1.219(b)(3), for IRA purposes, compensation does not include Sec. 911, foreign earned income and/or housing that is excluded from income and consequently contributions to an IRA are not allowed.

Retired Ministers & Parsonage Designation

A **retired minister** receiving an otherwise taxable distribution from a qualified Sec. 401(a), Sec. 401(k), Sec. 403(b), Sec. 408(k), Sec. 408(p) or Sec. 414(e) plan may have a **"parsonage allowance"** designated by the former employer or denominational pension board according to Rev. Ruling 63-156. We recommend that a perpetually worded designation state that 100% of the retirement income be designated as parsonage allowance and be tax free to the extent spent for housing. **(See sample wording in Chapter Two, page 53)** Language found in the Department of Labor Regulations under ERISA indicate that both types of contributions to a Sec. 403(b) plan (ERISA and Non-ERISA) are considered as contributions to an employer's plan and both types are eligible for parsonage allowance designation.

When a minister has a choice of receiving a lump-sum distribution, it is important to "roll over" by transfer trustee to trustee into a qualified retirement plan, **otherwise the vendor is required to withhold 20%** of the distribution for income tax withholding. Some vendors no longer offer transfer 403(b)s. They only offer "rollover" IRAs. To retain the proper identity of earnings from the ministry, and to preserve the opportunity for designated parsonage allowance, **never co-mingle** retirement funds from ministry earnings with retirement funds from secular earnings.

"Retired Minister" is recommended to be shown as "occupation" on Form 1040.

According to Rev. Ruling 72-249, the parsonage allowance exclusion **is not available** to the surviving spouse who continues to receive retirement income as a beneficiary.

Tax Planning for the Retired or Semi-retired Minister

Between the ages of 62 and full retirement age, most ministers consider the possibility of semi-retirement. **Between age 62 and full retirement age**, an employer can pay salary and parsonage value and/or allowance up to the limitation shown on the next page and the minister will receive all of his social security benefits. If his earned income is more than the limitation, his social security benefits will be reduced by $1 for each $2 of extra earned income. Sign up and receive all benefits available to you. Social Security will obtain the information from your tax return. Always have your tax advisor examine any Social Security proposed adjustments. Often they add your wages from Form 1040, line 7 and your Schedule SE earnings in error. The amount of the limitation is adjusted for inflation every year and is announced in October.

The Retirement Earnings Test **has been eliminated** for individuals when they **reach full retirement age.**

A modified test applies for the year an individual reaches full retirement age.

In the year an individual reaches full retirement age, the limitation shown below will only apply to the earnings for the months prior to attaining full retirement age. If his earned income is more than the limitation his social security benefits will be reduced by $1 for each $3 of extra earned income. **There is no limit on earnings beginning the month an individual attains** full retirement age.

After the year in which you reach full retirement age, and the earnings limitation ends, you can earn $1,000,000 and still draw your full social security benefits!

The amount of earnings a person can receive, before it affects the amount of social security benefits available, are as follows:

Year of Birth	Full Retirement Age
1937 or earlier	65
1938	65 & 2 months
1939	65 & 4 months
1940	65 & 6 months
1941	65 & 8 months
1942	65 & 10 months
1943-1954	66
1955	66 & 2 months
1956	66 & 4 months
1957	66 & 6 months
1958	66 & 8 months
1959	66 & 10 months
1960 & later	67

	2015	2016	2017
Before Full Retirement Age	$ 15,720	$15,720	$16,920
Year Reaches Full Retirement Age	$ 41,880	$41,880	$44,880

Definition of Earned Income

Salary and the value of a home provided and/or the parsonage allowance **ARE** considered "earned income" by social security.

Fringe benefits, an accountable employee business expense reimbursement plan, and nonforfeitable contributions to a salary reduction 403(b)(7) or 408(p) **ARE NOT** "earned income" and can be provided in addition to $15,720/$41,880 salary and housing limitation. Income from pensions, interest, dividends, rents and sale of property **ARE NOT** earned income. You can receive **unlimited** amounts of such **unearned income** and still receive all of your social security benefits.

Social Security Benefits are Sometimes Taxed

Social security benefits you receive may be taxable in some instances. You will receive Form SSA-1099 showing the total benefits paid to you during the year and the amount of any social security benefits you repaid during the year. For the first threshold of $32,000 ($25,000 for single) the maximum amount of your social security benefits that can be taxable is 50%. For the second threshold of $44,000 ($34,000 for single) the maximum amount of your social security benefits that can be taxable is 85%. The worksheet provided with Form 1040 helps you compute the "modified adjusted gross income", which for the first threshold is 50% of your social security benefits, plus other taxable income, plus tax-exempt interest, less adjustments. If this amount is less than the threshold of $32,000 ($25,000 for single) none of your benefits will be taxed. It is important for married taxpayers to file a joint return. The threshold for married separate returns is -0-. Married separate returns would cause unnecessary tax.

Is Your Social Security Earnings Record Correct?

The Social Security Administration has announced that it will resume mailing estimated benefit statements to most workers every five years. They encourage all workers to create a personalized Social Security account online that will allow them to access their benefit information at any time. You also may be able to estimate your retirement benefit using their online Retirement Estimator. It is very important to examine your statement and correct any errors in your account. Social Security's web site's address is: **www.ssa.gov**

Dual-status ministers often experience mistakes in their social security earnings record. The amount of earnings on Form 1040, line 7, is often combined with the social security base on Schedule SE. This mistake can lead to an overstatement of your earnings. If the amount of earnings on Form 1040, line 7, is recorded as your earnings and the parsonage allowance is omitted, your earnings will be understated. Ministers who begin to receive social security benefits while continuing to work often experience problems receiving correct amounts.

CHAPTER FIVE

Overseas Missionaries and Religious Orders

Missionaries Serving Overseas

Missionaries who are U.S. citizens serving overseas in a foreign country are subject to the same U.S. income tax laws as those living in the U.S. All income, worldwide, must be reported on their Form 1040. However, they may qualify for the **$101,300** foreign earned income exclusion provided in Sec. 911. Generally, your **initial choice** of the exclusion on Form 2555 **must be filed with a timely filed 1040 return**.

Missionaries are considered to be performing ministerial duties when evangelizing, conducting worship, teaching, etc. They are to be treated as dual-status ministers. You may want to reread Chapter Two for our detailed discussion defining dual-status and the special tax treatment for those who qualify.

When a dual-status minister, serving as a missionary overseas, has an "approved" Form 4361 and is exempt from social security, he is to write "Exempt Form 4361" on the self-employment line, Form 1040, page 2. Disability coverage under social security will discontinue after you become exempt. When it will discontinue for you depends upon your age and the number of quarters of credit you have. Overseas missionaries have difficulty obtaining comparable life and disability insurance coverages. If you are considering an overseas ministry, you may wish to choose being covered by social security.

Missionaries who do secular jobs (carpenters, physicians, nurses, pilots, computer technicians, cooks, mechanics, etc), are regular lay employees. When employed by an American employer they are subject to withholding and matching of social security and medicare tax. When employed by a foreign employer they are subject to that country's equivalent of social security, if they have one.

• Tax Increase Prevention and Reconciliation Act (TIPRA)

Its title is a misnomer for Americans working abroad. Starting in 2006, taxpayers who elect to exclude foreign earned income and/or foreign housing allowances, will be subject to a **higher tax rate** on income in excess of the exclusion amount and other sources of income. Such income is taxed for both regular and minimum tax purposes by applying to that income the tax rates that would have applied had the taxpayer not elected the exclusions. Previously, other income after deductions and exemptions was taxable in the lowest tax bracket.

• Statement For Claiming Benefits of Section 911

Lay employees that are eligible for the foreign earned income exclusion should sign and submit Form 673 to their employer. It permits the employer to not withhold federal income tax on foreign wages.

• Effect of Sec. 911 Foreign Earned Income Exclusion on Tax Sheltered Account and IRA Contributions

According to Reg. 1.403(b)-2(b)(11), foreign earned income counts as includible compensation if an employee wishes to make contributions to a Tax Sheltered Account.

According to Reg. 1.219(b)(3), for IRA purposes, compensation **does not include** foreign earned income and/or housing that is excluded from income and contributions to an IRA **are not allowed**.

• Social Security and Binational Agreements

U.S. Citizens living and working outside of the United States as dual-status ministers are subject to social security regardless of whether their employer is American or foreign. When they are employed by a foreign church or nonprofit organization or they are independent contractors, they may also be subject to that country's equivalent of social security. The United States has entered into **agreements** with several foreign countries to coordinate social security coverage and taxation. If the country you work in has entered into such an agreement, dual coverage and dual contributions (taxes) for the same work is eliminated. U. S. citizens who live and work in a foreign country **five years** or more may be subject to social security in the foreign country. A certificate of coverage issued by one country serves as proof of exemption from social security taxes on the same earnings in the other country.

Independent contractors doing secular jobs, living and working outside of the United States, are subject to social security. The binational agreements usually eliminate double coverage and double tax for them also.

IRS Publication 54, page 10, gives a list of countries and additional information. You can get more information on any specific agreement at **www.socialsecurity.gov/international**.

● *FinCEN Form 114 - FBAR Foreign Bank Account Report (*Previously Form TD F 90-22.1*)*

FinCEN Form 114 should be filed for all missionaries who have savings or checking accounts overseas which exceed $10,000 in aggregate value at any time during the calendar year. Since July 1, 2013 this form **MUST be e-filed** annually or a penalty will be assessed. The June 30 filing date may not be extended.

Failing to file an FBAR can carry a civil penalty of $10,000 for each non-willful violation. But if your violation is found to be willful, the penalty is the greater of $100,000 or 50 percent of the amount in the account for each violation.

http://bsaefiling.fincen.treas.gov/main.html

Bona Fide Residency and Physical Presence Rules

To qualify for Sec. 911 foreign earned income exclusion and/or foreign housing exclusion, the missionary must be able to satisfy the requirements of either bona fide residency or be physically present in a foreign country or countries for a total of at least 330 days during any period of 12 consecutive months.

To be considered a **bona fide resident** of a foreign country, you must have intentions to remain overseas for an indefinite stay and give evidence by words and acts as to the length and nature of your stay. You will not be treated as a bona fide resident of a foreign country if you have made a statement to the authorities of that country that you are not a resident and have been held not subject to its income tax. To establish your bona fide residency in a foreign country you must reside there for an uninterrupted period **which includes an entire tax year**. If you use the calendar year as your tax year, your entire tax year is the period beginning January 1 and ending December 31. The term "uninterrupted period" refers to your bona fide residence and not to your physical presence. Temporary absence for vacations or business trips is allowable.

The **physical presence test** does not apply to the type of residence you establish, to your intentions about returning, or to the nature and purpose of your stay overseas. It is concerned only with how long you stay in a foreign country or countries. If, during a period of 12 consecutive months, you are physically present in a foreign country 330 full days (approximately 11 months), you meet the physical presence test. ANY period of 12 consecutive months may be used. If 12 months during the middle of the stay overseas contains 330 days of physical presence, you will satisfy the requirement and be able to be exempt for the whole stay overseas.

Discussion of Form 2555 and Form 2555-EZ

The **IRS Publication 54, Form 2555, and Form 2555-EZ** are available on **www.irs.gov.** IRS Publication 54, "Tax Guide for U.S. Citizens and Resident Aliens Abroad" contains in depth information for missionaries. Form 2555-EZ can be filed if you are a U.S. citizen or resident alien; your income from earned wages/salaries in a foreign country is less than $101,300; you are filing a calendar year return that covers a 12-month period; there are no adjustments to your income such as one half of self-employment tax deduction; and you are not filing a Schedule C with expenses.

● *Sec. 911 - Foreign Earned Income Exclusion*

Individuals meeting either the bona fide residency test or the physical presence test can elect to exclude foreign earned income at the following annual rates:

2012	$95,100
2013	$97,600
2014	$99,200
2015	$100,800
2016	**$101,300**
2017	$102,100

If both you and your spouse work abroad and meet either test you can each choose the foreign earned income exclusion. Together, you and your spouse can exclude as much as $202,600 a year.

The foreign earned income exclusion **is voluntary**. Generally, your initial choice of the exclusion on Form 2555 must be filed with a timely filed return (including extensions), a return amending a timely filed return, or a late filed return (determined without regard to any extensions) filed within one year from the original due date of the return. The amending of Reg. 1.911-7 now provides a fourth time to make a valid election. If no federal tax is owed after taking into account the foreign earned income exclusion or housing cost amount, an election may be made at any time later than the times provided above whether or not the IRS has discovered the failure to make the election. The change applies to taxable years beginning after December 31, 1981. This provision had made it very important for missionaries to timely file their initial tax returns. The $75,000/$80,000 exclusion in 1982 and 1983 was denied a taxpayer, an American citizen, who worked abroad and failed to file timely returns. (William J. Faltesek, Docket No. 48522-86, 6-6-89)

Once you choose to exclude your foreign earned income, that choice remains in effect for that year and all later years unless you revoke it. If you revoke your choice for any tax year, you cannot claim the exclusion again for your next 5 tax years without the approval of the IRS. The government charges a fee for this request. In Private Letter Ruling 9625060, 3/28/96, a taxpayer, having revoked his foreign earned income exclusion election for 1993 and 1994 because taxes were higher in the United Kingdom, **was granted** permission to re-elect the foreign earned income exclusion for 1995. He had moved to Hong Kong and their tax rate was less than the United Kingdom. Several other private letter rulings have been submitted to the IRS requesting to re-elect Sec. 911 exclusion. They have all received a positive response.

Tax Planning: Missionaries with children and low income can actually benefit by **not choosing** to use IRS 911 exclusion. Child Tax Credit and College Credit are partly refundable. Facts and circumstances of each family should be considered and it is possible that by revoking Sec. 911 there could be refundable credits. A credit can be applied to Social Security/Medicare tax or refunded.

Earned Income Credit is not available while overseas.

• *Foreign Housing Exclusion*

In addition to the foreign earned income exclusion, you can separately claim an exclusion or a deduction from gross income for your housing amount if your tax home is in a foreign country and you qualify under either the bona fide residence test or the physical presence test.

For missionaries who earn considerably less than the $101,300 foreign earned income exclusion, it is not advisable for them to choose the foreign housing exclusion. In addition to a complex computation, **if chosen,** the foreign housing exclusion **must be used first** and fully before using the foreign earned income exclusion. In any year that a missionary earns over $101,300, he can initially choose and apply the foreign housing exclusion on a timely filed return by completing the appropriate section on Form 2555. The two exclusions available can be separately chosen and separately revoked. By attaching a statement to the return or an amended return for the first year that you do not wish to claim the exclusion(s), you can revoke either choice for any tax year.

Sec. 911 foreign housing exclusion is unique, and very different from Sec. 107 housing for ministers and Sec. 119 housing. Any year your income exceeds $101,300, take the time to study IRS Publication 54, pages 21-23. Being able to use the foreign earned income exclusion first makes your Form 2555 less complicated.

• *Vacation Computation*

According to Rev. Ruling 76-191, while home in the U. S., (unless on vacation ONLY), income earned is usually taxable on your federal return. Vacation time earned during the last year preceding your leave can be considered eligible Sec. 911 exclusion. If your mission gives you 6 months vacation (without work) for a four year term, one-fourth, or 45 days is eligible for the exclusion. If you are working and traveling on deputation all of your furlough, all of your leave would be taxable.

To determine the amount of U. S. income you should count the number of days in the U.S., subtract the vacation days, divide the result by 365 days, then multiply that percentage times the annual salary. For a missionary, who usually works a 7 day week, you would count 7 days for each week.

Example: Days in U.S.   75 days
                    Less vacation   (21 days)
                                                                      54 days
                    54 ÷ 365 =   14.79%
                    Taxable income for U.S. $35,500 X 14.79% =**$5,250.45**

Moving Expense — Overseas

• *Foreign Moves - Form 3903F*

If you move to a new principal place of work outside the United States and its possessions, it is a "foreign move." If all or part of the income you earn at the new foreign location is excluded under the foreign earned income exclusion, the part of the moving expense that is allocable to the excluded income is not deductible.

Qualified moving expenses are an above-the-line deduction subtracted from gross income in arriving at adjusted gross income under Sec. 62(a). More detailed discussion is included in Chapter One.

Qualified moving expenses **are limited** to the reasonable cost of:

1.   Moving household goods and personal effects from the former residence to the new residence; and

2.   Traveling, including lodging during the period of travel, from the former residence to the new place of residence. **Meal expenses while moving are non-deductible.**

A special moving rule applies to Form 3903-F: The cost of moving household goods is expanded to include the reasonable expenses of moving household goods and personal effects to and from storage and of storing them for all or part of the time the new workplace continues to be your principal workplace. If you moved in an earlier year and are claiming only storage fees during your absence from the United States, you can simply enter the allowable amount on the moving deduction line, Form 1040, page 1. Next to the amount write "Storage Fees."

● *Non-Foreign Move Form 3903*

A move from a foreign country to the U.S. is not a foreign move. The regular moving deduction rules apply. If you permanently retire and your principal place of work and former home were outside the U.S. and its possessions, you do not have to satisfy the 39 work week requirement. You may deduct the move back to the U.S., subject to all of the other requirements and limitations of Form 3903.

When and Where To File As An Overseas Missionary

There is an automatic extension of two months to June 15th for any U.S. citizen with **both their tax home and their abode** outside the U.S. on April 15th. This is an extension of time to file only, tax liability has to be paid by April 15th. If you take advantage of the automatic extension, you are required to attach a statement to your return showing you were residing outside the U.S. on the due date of your return. If additional time is required, the regular automatic six month extension, Form 4868, must be filed by April 15th to obtain the extra four months of extension.

File Form 2555 or Form 2555-EZ with Form 1040 and send to: **Department of Treasury, Internal Revenue Service Center, Austin, TX 73301-0215**

● *Special Extensions Of Time For Filing*

A new missionary arriving in an overseas country anytime during the year cannot file Form 2555 or Form 2555-EZ the first year and claim the foreign earned income exclusion. However, after he has established his bona fide residence or met the physical presence test, all of his income is eligible for the special tax treatment from the **date of his arrival.** There are two ways to handle the problem of filing:

1. **File Form 2350** by the due date of your return, requesting an extension of filing your return until after establishing foreign residence. It is necessary to pay any anticipated tax on U.S. income with Form 2350. Then, within 30 days after meeting the residency requirements, file your return along with a copy of the approved Form 2350.

    a.   An earlier first year return can often be filed by satisfying the physical presence rules.

    b.   After satisfying the bona fide residency rules, it is best to switch to bona fide resident because it does not have to be re-established after a furlough or vacation back in the U.S.

2. *(Not the best choice!)* File the current year's return and pay tax on all income, including income earned abroad. After meeting the residency requirements, file Form 1040X and Form 2555 or Form 2555-EZ within one year of the due date of the original return to claim a refund of taxes on earnings while overseas.

Independent Missionaries

If a missionary has a sponsoring mission or church, it is correct for that organization to treat the missionary as an employee under the "common law rules." Missionaries who perform ministerial duties and are employed by a US foreign mission board or an integral agency of a church are entitled to dual-status treatment. Missionaries who do secular jobs (carpenters, physicians, mechanics, etc.), are regular employees subject to withholding and matching of social security and medicare tax.

When a missionary does not have a sponsoring mission or church, the total gross income may include substantial funds for ministry projects. Entering large expenditures and building projects as Schedule C deductions creates a very high IRS audit exposure. Should an independent missionary be chosen for an audit, foreign IRS personnel are apt to be inexperienced concerning typical ministry endeavors. The experience can become costly, difficult, frustrating and time consuming.

We have included further instructions and recommendations for handling independent missionaries in Chapter Six.

● *Employers of Non-Resident Aliens* must verify that an individual whom they plan to employ is authorized to accept employment in the U.S. No alien may accept employment in the U.S. unless they have been authorized to do so. The website for U.S. Citizenship and Immigration Services provides forms and information to seek such authorization. **www.uscis.gov** Employers can call 1-800-375-5283 for information.

Religious Orders — Two Types

Vow of Poverty: Members of qualifying Religious Orders described in Sec. 1402(c)(4) and Sec. 1402(g) who perform services for a religious order in the exercise of duties required by such order are exempt from income tax or social security tax liability according to Sec. 3121(b)(8)(A). Members serving under a vow of poverty are typically held to a strict level of moral and spiritual discipline which requires daily prayer and communion with other members and prohibits the ownership of material possessions. Pro rata goods, services, and cash allowances received by members for their needs, whether disabled or able to perform services assigned to them, was deemed to be nontaxable. (Private Letter Rulings 199938013, 199937013, and 9752002)

Protestant Religious Orders Described in Sec. 1402(c)(4)

The idea of non-integral agency protestant ministries adopting the status of "religious order" was popular in the late 70's and early 80's. Some were advised to change their by-laws and declare their organization to be a "religious order." The Social Security Amendments Act of 1983, and the mandatory application of social security coverage to employees of nonprofit organizations made the idea flourish. In order to avoid the cost of withholding and matching social security, several non-integral agency protestant ministries began claiming the status of "religious order." So many requests for determination were received by IRS that they put a freeze on responding to them. During 1985 the IRS responded with letters stating that the question of what constitutes a religious order was under intensive study by the Service and that they would not be able to respond to the requests until their study was completed.

During 1991, IRS issued **Rev. Procedure 91-20, IRB 1991-10**. It established guidelines that are used by the IRS in determining whether an organization is a religious order for federal employment tax purposes. The IRS has identified from previous court cases the following characteristics:

1. The organization is described in Sec. 501(c)(3) of the Code.
2. The members of the organization vow to live under a strict set of rules requiring moral and spiritual self-sacrifice and dedication to the goals of the organization at the expense of their material well-being.
3. The members of the organization, after successful completion of the organization's training program and probationary period, make a long-term commitment to the organization (normally more than two years).
4. The organization is, directly or indirectly, under the control and supervision of a church or convention or association of churches, or is significantly funded by a church or convention or association of churches.
5. The members of the organization normally live together as part of a community and are held to a significantly stricter level of moral and religious discipline than that required of lay church members.
6. The members of the organization work or serve full-time on behalf of the religious, educational, or charitable goals of the organization.
7. The members of the organization participate regularly in activities such as public or private prayer, religious study, teaching, care of the aging, missionary work, or church reform or renewal.

Being a 501(c)(3) organization is required. Considering all the facts and circumstances about an organization, it is not necessary that all of the above characteristics be true. If most of the above characteristics are true, the organization will be treated as a religious order. In the absence of one or more of the above characteristics, Rev. Proc. 91-20 says that the IRS will contact the organization and carefully consider the organization's views concerning their status.

We are aware of and have read the IRS's favorable private letter rulings granting Sec. 1402(c)(4) status of religious order to two different organizations during 1992. Several organizations have received favorable private letter rulings affirming their status of a "religious order." (Private Letter Rulings 9322009, 9418012, 9434015, 9448017, 9630011, 199937013, 200106015, 200143017, 200546010 and 201340015)

If a non integral agency ministry wrongly claims the status of a "religious order," the underpayment of payroll taxes could be so overwhelming that the ministry could find it hard to survive.

- *Information Returns and Proper Tax Treatment for Sec. 1402(c)(4) Religious Orders*

The proper form to report the income paid to a member of a "religious order" is Form W-2. The practice of **issuing Form 1099** to employee-members **is incorrect**. To qualify as an "independent contractor" or a "non-employee" of a religious order would be impossible, due to the amount of control a religious order has over its members.

1. Member, ordained or "the equivalent thereof," doing duties of the ministry. Tax treatment is the same as a dual-status minister, eligible for parsonage allowance, self-employed for social security purposes and **must timely file Form 4361 to be exempt from social security.** Withholding of income tax is optional, Form W-2 is the proper form to show taxable salary.

2. Member, lay employee of order, performing services required by the order are not eligible for parsonage allowance. Earnings are treated as self-employment for social security purposes and **must timely file Form 4361 to be exempt from social security.** Withholding income tax is optional, Form W-2 is the proper form to show taxable salary.

3. Nonmember lay employees are automatically covered by social security, cannot become exempt, and are to receive a regular Form W-2 with income tax withholding.

4. Member, employee working for the order, doing duties required by the order, receives no salary, and has no income tax or social security tax liability, does not have to file any forms.

Religious Orders Described in Sec. 1402(g)

Sec. 1402(g) describes Religious Orders that are opposed to both private and public insurance. Examples of such orders are the Amish, Quakers and Catholic Monastic Orders. The term "religious order" is not well defined in IRS Code or regulations. In a 1969 tax court case, Eighth Street Baptist Church, Inc. v. U.S., 295 F. Supp. 1400 (D. Kan. 1969), the judge cited Webster's dictionary as his best source of a definition to determine that Eighth Street Baptist Church was not a religious order. Sec. 1402(g)(1)(E) gives the fact that a religious order or sect has to have been in existence at all times since December 31, 1950. In a court case for the year of 1976, a taxpayer argued that this provision was unconstitutional under the first amendment since it discriminates against religious sects not established prior to December 31, 1950. The judge stated that Congress has great latitude in limiting the exemptions by any general standards, (TC Memo 1980-284, Glen A. Ross, Docket No. 3593-79). Sec. 1402(g)(1)(D) states that a religious order described in Sec. 1402(g) must have for a substantial period of time been making reasonable provisions for its dependent members.

- *Information Returns and Proper Tax Treatment for Sec. 1402(g) Religious Orders*

1. Member, working outside of the order, earnings are given to the order, and duties are the kind that are ordinarily performed by members of the order and they are required to be exercised on the behalf of the religious order as its agent. Examples in Publication 517 indicate that being instructed to be a secretary qualified and being instructed to be a lawyer did not. According to Revenue Ruling 84-13, a psychologist did not qualify either.

    a. If duties qualify, the earnings are not taxable to the member and there are no tax liabilities.

    b. If duties do not qualify, even though the order receives the salary, the earnings are taxable to the member and subject to federal income tax withholding and social security tax withholding and matching.

2. Member, working outside of the order, self employed doing secular work, profits are subject to regular income tax and self-employment tax. An exemption is available from self-employment tax by filing **Form 4029 at any time.** To be able to file for this exemption, the member must be conscientiously opposed to accepting benefits of **any private or public insurance and waive all rights to ever receive any social security benefits.**

3. Since 1988, members or member partnerships who have filed Form 4029 and are exempt from social security, can employ other members who have also filed Form 4029 and be exempt from withholding and matching social security tax on their wages. An exempt employer will be required to withhold income tax and prepare Form W-2 for exempt employees. (IRS Publication 15-A, page 11)

4. Nonmember lay employees are automatically covered by social security, cannot become exempt, and are to receive a regular Form W-2 with income tax and social security tax withholding and matching.

CHAPTER SIX

Completed Payroll Reports

Now we are ready for the practical application of all the information presented in the preceding chapters! Though the tax laws are complex and every employer/employee relationship is unique, the examples shown in this Chapter are for the purpose of teaching the simplest approach to designing the best compensation package. **Regardless of what creative label** the employer might call money or property "paid" to an employee, **it is taxable** if a section of the Internal Revenue Code **does not exclude it.** Generally, the employee will be taxed on all remuneration that is not a qualified *fringe benefit* (Chapter One), *parsonage allowance* (Chapter Two), or *reimbursement for professional expenses* **under an accountable plan** (Chapter Three). Tax law excludes these categories of a compensation package from federal income tax. Fringe benefits and an accountable reimbursement plan for professional expenses are also excluded from social security and medicare tax.

The **payroll sheets** show extra columns for parsonage allowance, contributions to Tax Sheltered Accounts and a section to keep record of an accountable reimbursement plan. This is a tell and show chapter. You will benefit greatly by studying the "compensation agreement" and the payroll sheets and reports for Mission Community Church & Rev. H. Richard Snodgrass.

Steps in Establishing a Compensation Package

Whether by a denominational salary formula or simple budget determination, once the total compensation available is determined, we recommend the following four steps to arrive at the best tax treatment. For example, if the salary formula does not allow for enough housing, it is important to designate a different amount that is adequate. For tax and bookkeeping purposes, the compensation package may differ from the formula used to arrive at the total compensation available.

1. **Establish the fringe benefits that will be provided.** Contributions to a qualified pension plan, premiums for up to $50,000 group term life insurance, etc, generally are to be paid by the employer directly to the companies providing the plans. The ACA has dramatically complicated the once wonderful fringe benefit of providing medical insurance. See Chapter One, pages 19-20 explanations. The employer provided qualified fringe benefits are not to be included on the payroll record, quarterly reports, or in the W-2 at year end.

2. **Establish an accountable reimbursement plan** for auto and professional employee business expenses. Establish a written reimbursement plan for each employee using the suggested wordings in Chapter Three. Employees must "adequately account" their auto and professional expenses to the employer. The tax benefits to be gained by establishing an accountable reimbursement plan should convince employers to bear the burden of the "cost of doing ministry business." An employer should be willing to reimburse their employees for all auto and professional expenses over and above their salary. Employers who initially adjust the employee's salary and adopt a "fixed limit plan," according to Private Letter Ruling 9822044 can, prior to the start of a calendar year, determine the amount the "fixed limit" will be in the succeeding year. If the employer provides an auto for an employee, they must have a written plan and follow the IRS regulations to determine how much to include in the employee's income for personal use. The employee must maintain and submit a log of business miles to his employer.

3. **Determine the amount of the cash salary**. You may wish to obtain a copy of "compensation guidelines" provided by denominational handbooks or other organizations.

4. **Designate an adequate portion of salary as parsonage allowance in advance for the dual-status minister.** When a church or integral agency of a church owns the house in which the minister lives, they must designate a portion of his cash compensation as parsonage allowance for the additional home expenses he personally incurs. When a church or integral agency of a church does not provide the home and the minister rents or owns his own home, they must designate a portion of his cash compensation as parsonage allowance for the whole cost of providing the home. Use the "Suggested Wordings" in Chapter Two. The amount of **designated housing allowance**, divided by the number of pay periods is shown on the payroll record as a subtraction from salary and **is not to be shown** as taxable compensation on the **941 quarterly reports or W-2 at year end**. The minister is responsible to show any unused portion as income on his Form 1040, line 7.

Using our suggested wordings for designation of parsonage allowance and an accountable reimbursement arrangement, an employer can easily make the statements in the minutes of a business meeting. We have prepared a "Compensation Agreement" showing the 2016 compensation package Mission Community Church provided for Rev. H. Richard Snodgrass as a one page document. It shows the complete compensation arrangement with clarity.

2016 COMPENSATION AGREEMENT

1. Fringe Benefits: Employer agrees to provide the following fringe benefits:
    (a) Employer agrees to pay or reimburse, on the behalf of employee and his family, the premium for a group accident and health plan. The premium is **$16,421.04** or **$1,368.42** monthly.
    (b) Employer is providing $50,000 Group Term Life Insurance for employee. The premium is **$420.00** annually.
    (c) Employer has established a 403(b)(7) voluntary salary reduction retirement plan for employee. Employee's salary reduction agreement requests **$6,000** or **$500.00** a month to be contributed for the year.
2. Accountable Reimbursement Plan:
    (a) Whereas, according to Sec. 62(a)(2)(A), an employee that adequately accounts to the employer the details of their professional expenses, is allowed a deduction from gross income. Sec. 62(c) further requires an employee to return any excess reimbursement or advance to the employer within a reasonable time. Reg. 1.62-2(d)(3) further requires that no part of our employee's salary be recharacterized as being paid under this reimbursement arrangement.
    (b) Resolved that in addition to the salary provided our employee, we will reimburse him for auto, travel and professional expenses considered ordinary and necessary for him to carry out his duties. (The amount budgeted is **$14,000.00**)
    (c) Employer agrees that the reimbursement for auto mileage considered ordinary and necessary for him to carry out his duties will be at the IRS mileage allowance rate.
    (d) It is further understood that a person other than the employee will examine the adequately accounted records and that the records will be kept for at least four years by the employer.
3. Employer further agrees to pay employee an annual cash salary of **$51,000.00**.
    ($51,000 - $6,000.00 TSA = $45,000.00)
    $45,000.00 ÷ 24 bimonthly pay periods = **$1,875.00**
4. Parsonage Allowance Designation:
    (a) Whereas, under the tax law, a minister of the Gospel is not subject to federal income tax on the "parsonage allowance paid to him as a part of his compensation to the extent used by him to rent or provide a home."
    (b) Employer agrees to designate **$24,000.00** of employee's salary as parsonage allowance.
    (c) This amount of designated parsonage allowance shall apply to all future years until modified.

RECAP:		
	Fringe Benefits	$16,841.04
	403(b) voluntary Salary reduction	$ 6,000.00
	Budget Estimate of accountable reimbursement plan	$14,000.00
	Salary& Housing Allowance	$45,000.00
	Total Compensation	$81,841.04

This agreement was established on December 10th, 2015.

_____   _____
Timothy Buck II, Moderator   H. Richard Snodgrass, Pastor
Mission Community Church

Dual-Status Minister - Rev. Snodgrass' Compensation Package

Fringe Benefits Provided:

Hospital Plan Premiums	$ 16,421
Group Term Life Insurance ($50,000)	$ 420
Unlimited professional expense reimbursement policy	$ 13,864
Total Cash Compensation	$ 51,000
*Parsonage Allowance Designated	($24,000)
Contributions to Salary Reduction 403(b) Retirement	($ 6,000)
Taxable Salary on W-2	**$ 21,000**

* Rev. Snodgrass owns his own home. **The $24,000 parsonage allowance is not shown in Box 1 of his W-2.** As we illustrate on his tax return in Chapter 7, he is responsible to show the unused portion of $1,518 as income on Form 1040, line 7. Rev. Snodgrass will include the $24,000 parsonage allowance on his Schedule SE for social security purposes unless he has an approved Form 4361 exemption.

(When the parsonage is owned by the church employer, **do not include its value anywhere** on a W-2. It is the responsibility of the minister to include the value of parsonage provided on his Sch SE for social security purposes.)

Calculation for Amount of Paycheck: The contributions to the 403(b) retirement will be paid directly to a mutual fund or vendor by the employer. **$51,000 less $6,000 = $45,000** divided by the number of paydays in the year. Our sample payroll sheet illustrates semimonthly pay periods:

$45,000 ÷ 24 = **$1,875.00** per pay check.

Lay Employee - Joseph Mop's Compensation Package

Value of Home & Utilities Provided (Sec. 119)	$ 5,700
Fringe Benefits Provided:	
Group Hospital Plan Premiums	$ 14,268
Group Term Life Insurance ($50,000)	$ 276
Unlimited professional expense reimbursement policy	$ 1,654
Total Cash Compensation	$28,800
Contributions to Salary Reduction 403(b) Retirement	($ 1,800)
Taxable Salary on W-2	**$27,000**

When an employer provides housing and utilities for a lay employee that satisfies all three conditions of Sec. 119, the value is not to be shown on the payroll report, 941 quarterly reports, or W-2 at year end. It is free from federal income tax, social security, and medicare tax. When one of the three tests is not satisfied, the value of housing and utilities provided is subject to income tax, social security, and medicare tax and is to be shown as taxable compensation on the payroll reports. We illustrate Joseph Mop, the janitor, being provided Sec. 119 housing that satisfies all three conditions.

Calculation for Amount of Paycheck: The contributions to the 403(b) retirement will be paid directly to a mutual fund or vendor by the employer. **$28,800 less $1,800 = $27,000** divided by the number of paydays in the year. Our sample payroll sheet illustrates semimonthly pay periods:

$27,000 ÷ 24 = **$ 1,125.00** per pay check.

Organizations Must File Information Returns!

Gone are the days when an employer can get by with handing the minister a piece of paper stating the amount of money paid for his services during the year. The following quotes and facts are provided with the hope that nonprofit employers will take heed, *do what the law requires, and avoid* the frustration of penalties and problems with the IRS.

Who is An Employer?

It is important that a nonprofit organization practice responsible payroll accounting in a **business like manner**. Individuals to whom you make payments for services rendered are not to be given the "choice" of their status treatment. The correct reporting to the IRS of payments for services rendered is very well documented in IRS Publications. Employers have often suffered the consequence of listening to inaccurate opinion or counsel. IRS Publication 15-A "Employer's Supplemental Tax Guide", page 10, states:

"Many nonprofit organizations are exempt from federal income tax. Although they do not have to pay income tax themselves, they must still withhold federal income tax from the pay of their employees. However, there are special social security, Medicare, and federal unemployment (FUTA) tax rules that apply to the wages that they pay their employees."

In Chapter One, we discussed fully the "common law rules" that are used to determine if an individual who has been paid for services rendered is an employee or an independent contractor. According to **Sec. 3509**, employers who wrongly treat an employee as a non-employee **are liable** for income tax that should have been withheld and both the employer's and the employee's portion of social security tax and medicare tax.

In Chapter One we also discussed the "statutory employee" definition. It is a status limited to four occupational groups and **a status that is not available** for either dual-status ministers or lay employees of a church or organization.

Who Is An Employee?

Payment to janitors, secretaries, paid baby sitters, etc., for services rendered, are generally employees when the "common law rules" are applied. **Payment of $100 or more in a year** to a lay employee is subject to withholding and matching of social security and medicare tax. (IRS Publication 15-A, page 10) The threshold of **$100** annual applies to nonprofit employers. For-profit employers have a threshold of—**$50** per quarter; Farm employees—**$150** annual; Household employees—**$2,000** annual (2017 - $2,000). You must carefully study federal employment tax rules and timely file payroll reports and **Form W-2's**. The sample payroll reports in this chapter will guide you.

Who Is An Independent Contractor?

Payment to guest musicians, evangelists, skilled contractors, and others who provide occasional services usually qualify for "independent contractor" status. At the time of payment for services rendered, have each person provide their social security number on a Form W-9. You are required to prepare **Form 1099** for each "independent contractor" that you paid **$600** or more during the year. Form 1099s are not required for payments made to corporations.

Payments to evangelists and guest speakers can be designated as parsonage allowance in advance and you may reimburse them for adequately accounted travel expense diaries and/or receipts. At the time of payment for the engagement have them fill out a **Form W-9**. **Designated parsonage allowance and reimbursements are not to be shown on Form 1099.** Report the remaining taxable honorarium on Form 1099 if it is $600 or more for the year. If an evangelist or musical group is employed by a corporation and the check is written to the corporation, a Form 1099 is not required.

Suggestion: Churches often hire janitors and lawn care persons or companies. The **"common law rules"** we discussed in Chapter One must be the basis for your decision to treat payment for services rendered as employee wages and issue Form W-2 or as independent contractor payments and issue Form 1099. To contract janitorial or lawn care services that advertise in the yellow pages or the classified ads, perform the services for the general public and provide their own equipment, etc., would qualify for independent contractor treatment.

Informational Return Penalties

IRS's emphasis on informational reporting affects everyone, not just nonprofit organizations. Computer cross-matching of all informational returns with individuals' tax returns gives the IRS the ability to detect unreported income. Their current emphasis is on correct and timely filed information returns. Since 1982 there have been penalties for failure to submit W-2's and 1099's to the IRS. Information return penalties include failure to file electronically if filing 250 or more information returns including Form W-2s, 1099s, 1098s, etc. The penalty for failure to file information returns is provided for in Sec. 6721.

The penalty applies if you: (1) fail to file timely, (2) fail to include all information required to be shown on Form W-2, (3) include incorrect information on Form W-2, (4) file on paper forms when you are required to e-file, (5) report an incorrect TIN, (6) fail to report a TIN, or (7) fail to file paper Forms W-2 that are machine readable - must be typed with black ink.

The Trade Preferences Extension Act of 2015 made steep increases in information reporting penalties in Sec. 6721 for 2016.

In 2016 the amount of the penalty is based on how late the return is filed or when the failure is corrected. If filed after August 1st of any year, the penalty is $250 a return, maximum of $3,000,000 a year. If corrected by the 30th day after the due date, the penalty is $50 a return, maximum of $500,000 a year. If filed or corrected more than 30 days late but by August 1, the penalty is $100 a return, maximum of $1,500,000 a year.

Willful Or Intentional Disregard

Willful or intentional disregard causes very severe penalties. An example of a long-standing penalty for intentional disregard of doing payroll taxes from **Sec. 6672, is the 100% penalty.**

> *"Any person required to collect, truthfully account for, and pay over any tax imposed by this title who willfully fails to collect such tax, or truthfully account for and pay over such tax, or willfully attempts in any manner to evade or defeat any such tax or the payment thereof, shall, in addition to other penalties provided by law, be liable to a penalty equal to the total amount of the tax evaded, or not collected, or not accounted for and paid over."*

Failure to file informational returns due to intentional disregard of the filing requirements results in a penalty of **$500** per each failure or if greater - **10% of the amount** of the items required to be reported correctly.

Late payment penalties and interest are in addition to the above penalties. **Trustees or treasurers** of non-profit organizations, whether paid or volunteer, **can be held responsible when** the organization fails to pay their tax liability.

It is unfortunate that such severe penalties exist. **It is very important** for an employer to **fulfill the informational return filing requirements** rather than having to go before the board or congregation and ask for funds to be raised to pay penalties and interest that could have been avoided by filing timely returns.

United States v. Indianapolis Baptist Temple, USTC 1999-1 and USTC 1999-2: To satisfy a nearly **$6 million** payroll tax debt for the years spanning 1987 through 1992, a U.S. District judge in Indianapolis ordered the church properties to be seized in the fall of 2000. A summary judgement was ordered on June 29, 1999 for $5,319,750.27, plus interest and other penalty additions that had accrued after July 26, 1998. **On February 13, 2001**, dozens of federal marshals swarmed the building and a helicopter hovered overhead during **the peaceful seizure**. Rev. Greg Dixon Sr. and several others were carried out on stretchers. Indianapolis Baptist Temple appealed to the 7th Circuit in 2000 and lost. (USTC 2000-2)

The timely filing of Form 8274 and timely filed Form 941s and W-2s would have prevented years of court proceedings, unfortunate debt and loss of property.

Attitude Towards the IRS Should Be One of Cooperation

We recommend that the attitude of any organization towards the IRS or its agents should be one of cooperation. If your organization was not aware of your obligation to withhold income tax and withhold and match social security and medicare tax, it is our recommendation that for all wages paid within the three year statute of limitations, late reports should be filed and taxes paid. It is possible to write a letter and claim "reasonable cause" and lack of knowledge, rather than intentional disregard, and have the IRS forgive some or all of the penalties. Interest will be assessed on the late payments.

To be uncooperative may cause the IRS to suspect that your church is a fraudulent one. Avoid being considered as a "tax protest" church. There are those who are not religious or not actually ministers but become "ordained" by mail and establish fictitious nonprofit churches in their homes for the purpose of "tax avoidance" or "tax protest." As in Tweeddale v. Commissioner, 92 T.C. 501, the judge said, *"Petitioner was not a lone cowboy riding off on a wild stallion. He paid $1,200 for a set of documents constituting the plan or arrangement, purporting to establish a tax-exempt church with himself as a tax-exempt minister.....a totally meritless claim he abandoned on the eve of trial. Moreover, the organizer of this scheme went to jail for tax crimes as a result of it."* The judge cited United States v. Daly, 756 F.2d 1076 (5th Cir. 1985). Daly, who did not himself file Basic Bible Church returns, formed the Basic Bible Church chapters to have the appearance of religious organizations while disseminating information on how to file returns so as to hamper IRS investigation and detection of the tax scheme. The judge further said, *"We are bone-tired of seeing the Court's time, respondent's resources, and the national treasury wasted in litigating these phony vow of poverty cases."*

If you are aware of anyone involved in this type of "tax protest," go to the IRS website and download **Form 211**, report them, and **be eligible for up to 10%** of tax collected as a **reward** from the IRS!

How To Prepare Information Returns

The employer is responsible for filing informational reports, not the employee. However, **we recommend that the minister take an active part** in helping the treasurer prepare and timely file required reports. Treasurers hold a very responsible position; consider paying them wages for carrying out their duties. When a new person assumes the responsibility, be sure they are properly informed and taught the importance of timely and correctly filed payroll reports. **Do not hesitate to seek professional accounting help** in preparing the informational returns.

We would encourage the careful reading and study of the following:

IRS Publication 15, "Employer's Tax Guide"

IRS Publication 15-A, "Employer's Supplemental Tax Guide," contains information for exempt organizations and the "common law guidelines

IRS Publication 15-B, "Employer's Tax Guide to Fringe Benefits"

2016 Instructions for preparing Forms W-2 and W-3.

Go to **www.irs.gov** and download their pdf files. **Efficient :+)** There is an IRS toll free number in your phonebook. You can call and order publications and forms. **Inefficient :+(**

We will teach you how to prepare the proper payroll forms by example. Rev. Snodgrass and Joseph Mop are employed by Mission Community Church. We have used their sample "compensation packages," shown earlier in this chapter to prepare the reports. Refer to them often as we give you step by step instructions.

Obtain An Employer Identification Number

Does your organization or church have one? The bank where you have your organization's checking account has required you to furnish them with a Employer Identification Number. It looks like this: 00-0000000, nine digits. It is a Federal Identification Number for federal reports, and is not your state incorporation number or sales tax exempt number.

New churches and existing churches without a number should request one with Form SS-4. You can apply for an EIN online, by telephone, by fax or by mail depending on how soon you need to use the EIN. When you apply for your EIN online you can use it immediately to file a return or make a payment. Go the IRS website at **http://www.irs.gov/Businesses/Small-Businesses-&-Self-Employed/Apply-for-an-Employer-Identification-Number-(EIN)-Online**

Lay Employees

It is **important to understand** that dual-status ministers and lay employees are treated differently for withholding purposes.

A lay employee's income **IS** subject to income tax withholding and each lay employee must fill out a Form W-4. The status and number of allowances claimed will determine how much income tax is to be withheld. **IRS Publication 15** contains the tables showing how much income tax is required to be withheld. **IRS Publication 15-A** contains the tables showing a combination of income tax, social security tax, and medicare tax withholding.

Joseph Mop's W-4 shows he is married and wishes to claim "0" allowance. Turn to page 56 of IRS Publication 15 (2016) and find his semimonthly pay of $1,125.00 on the left-hand column. Under the "0" allowance column we see the proper amount to withhold is **$77.00**.

A lay employee's income **IS** subject to social security and medicare tax withholding and matching. **2016** combined rate to be withheld for employees was 7.65%. Employers pay an additional 7.65% when they file Form 941. **The 7.65% combined rate is made up of 6.2% rate for social security tax and 1.45% rate for medicare.**

The only exception to the above paragraph is for **electing churches** that have filed **Form 8274** and are exempt **because of religious reasons**, Sec. 3121(w). The election merely **transfers** the social security liability **from the church to the employee**. Churches who desire to be an electing church must file two copies of Form 8274 after they hire lay employees, but before the first date on which a quarterly employment tax return is due. (See more detailed discussion in Chapter Four.) Lay employees of churches that have filed Form 8274 are subject to paying social security at the **2015** self-employed rate of **15.3%** (less adjustments) on their personal return.

Dual-Status Ministers

A dual-status minister's income **IS NOT** subject to withholding income tax according to Sec. 3401(a)(9). The dual-status minister is to "prepay" his taxes by filing Form 1040ES, Estimated Tax for Individuals. When a dual-status minister prepays his taxes on Form 1040ES, we recommend that he does not prepare Form W-4 for the employer.

A dual-status minister's income **IS NOT** subject to withholding and matching for social security and medicare tax purposes. Sec. 1402(a)(8), an **exception** to the normal employer/employee common law rules, states that the dual-status minister is to be treated as self-employed for social security purposes. A dual-status minister who is conscientiously opposed to or because of religious principles opposed to the acceptance of public insurance based on ministerial service can timely file Form 4361 and become exempt from social security. This is discussed fully in Chapter Four. When the employer is a church or integral agency of a church, it is **NEVER correct** to treat a dual-status minister, doing the duties of a minister, **as an employee** for social security and medicare tax purposes.

For a minister who is serving part-time and is not fully supported by the employer, it is possible to **designate all or 100%** of his salary as parsonage allowance. Since parsonage allowance is not required to be shown on Form W-2, a **Form W-2 generally would not need to be prepared**. You may report a designated parsonage allowance in a separate statement.

Optional Withholding: When an employer and a dual-status minister agree to optional withholding as the means for prepaying the minister's tax liability, he should prepare a Form W-4. Entering the amount to be withheld each pay period on line 6 will satisfy the requirement that the agreement be written. (Status and number of allowances on line 5 should be left blank.) We recommend that the dual-status minister "estimate" his total tax liability — income tax, social security, and medicare tax; divide it by the number of pay periods (24 if paid semimonthly) and have the employer "withhold" that amount each payday as **federal income tax withholding**. The amount withheld will be shown as a credit in Box 2 of Form W-2.

This option would take the place of the dual-status minister prepaying his taxes on Form 1040ES. Rev. Snodgrass estimated he needed $6,000.00 prepaid and had $250.00 withheld each payday.($6,000.00 ÷ 24 = $250.00)

His other choice would have been to personally pay 4 estimated tax payments of $1,500.00 on Form 1040ES.

Independent Home and Foreign Missionaries

When an independent missionary **does not** have a sponsoring mission or church, the total gross income may include substantial funds for ministry projects. Entering large expenditures and building projects as Schedule C deductions creates a very high audit exposure. Should an independent minister/missionary be chosen for an audit, foreign IRS personnel are apt to be inexperienced concerning typical ministry endeavors. The communication between the taxpayer and the IRS agent can be difficult, frustrating, and time consuming.

The **ideal solution** to the Schedule C problem for the independent missionary is **to establish an employer/employee relationship with a church** in the U.S.

Every independent missionary needs to find a supporting organization or church to be willing to function as his employer. A carefully planned compensation plan with fringe benefits, designated parsonage allowance, an accountable reimbursement plan, and salary will provide the best tax advantages and **reduce audit exposure.** A church checking account should be set up with the missionary having signature privileges. **The missionary then advises all of his supporters to make their checks payable to the church**. As the missionary pays for "work projects" and employee business expenses, they become legitimate church ministry expenses of the organization. Copies of all of the financial transactions and detailed receipts should be submitted to the sponsoring church.

The income the missionary receives for his personal salary is recorded on a payroll record and included on the church's quarterly Form 941 and a **Form W-2 at year end**. The missionary's uncomplicated Form 1040 will reflect only his true personal earnings. If the missionary qualifies for dual-status treatment, he will be responsible for his own social security on Schedule SE, the same as any dual-status minister employed by a church or an integral agency of a church. If he does not qualify for dual-status treatment, the support received can be used to provide the necessary social security and medicare tax withholding and matching.

Prepare a Payroll Sheet for each Employee

Employers are responsible for accurate recording of the salary, deductions, and net pay for each individual employee. Computers are wonderful replacements of manual payroll! Most payroll software programs will allow modifications to handle the dual-status minister and the employee of "an electing church."

We have created and have available manual "Payroll Sheets" that contain extra columns needed to show parsonage allowance and voluntary salary reduction retirement plans. Memo columns on the right are provided to keep a record of the professional business expense reimbursements.

1. Begin entering a paycheck on the "Payroll Sheet" by entering the total cash salary (including parsonage allowance) in the "total" column in the middle. **Also enter** in this column: a bonus or love gift, salary to offset social security cost, any taxable fringe benefits, etc., as they are paid to the employee.

2. The columns to the right of the "total" column allow you to show income tax, social security tax, medicare tax, state income tax, and local income tax deductions. A dual-status minister who "prepays" his federal taxes on Form 1040ES and state taxes on the appropriate state forms will not use these columns.

3. The first column to the left of the "total" column allows you to subtract voluntary salary reduction retirement plans. Sec. 403(b) and 408(p) contributions **are subject** to social security and medicare tax withholding and matching for the lay employee according to Revenue Ruling 65-208. They are **not subject** to social security on Schedule SE for the dual-status employee according to Revenue Ruling 68-395. The total contribution is to be entered on Form W-2, Box 12 and omitted from Form W-2, Box 1.

4. The second column to the left of the "total" column allows you to subtract parsonage allowance for the dual-status minister. The parsonage allowance of **$24,000** for Rev. Snodgrass is divided by 24 pay periods to arrive at the semimonthly amount of **$1,000.00**.

5. Use the right hand column to record the checks written to reimburse an employee for adequately accounted employee business expenses. Study Chapter Three and **be sure you have adopted a written reimbursement plan** that satisfies the IRS Regulation 1.62-2.

Chart of Where to Show Transactions

Study our "**Chart of Where to Show Transactions**" shown on page 113. It will guide you as to what portions of the compensation package you are required to include and what portions you are not required to include on the payroll reports. The payroll sheet's "total" column for each employee should include any item from the chart with a "yes" in the "taxable income" column.

It is important that your computer or manual "payroll sheets," Form 941s (all four quarters), and the W-2s at year end **reconcile or balance.**

Make Payroll Tax Deposits as Required

The amount of payroll taxes you owe determines the frequency of deposits. You owe these taxes when you pay the wages. There are penalties for making late deposits. It is **mandatory to use EFTPS** to make deposits electronically or by telephone 24/7. (On January 1, 2011, Form 8109 deposit vouchers were eliminated.)

There are four deposit rules for determining when you deposit taxes: annually, quarterly, monthly or semi-weekly. The IRS will notify you each November whether you are a monthly or semiweekly depositor for the coming calendar year. This determination is made based on the aggregate amount of employment taxes reported during a "look back" period. The regulations define a **look back period** as the twelve-month period ending on the preceding June 30th.

Combine federal income tax withheld, social security and medicare tax withheld and matched, to determine total liability for each period.

$1,000 Annual Rule - Small employers, whose annual liability is **$1,000** or less will file **Form 944** and pay these taxes only once a year instead of every quarter. In general, if the IRS has notified you to file Form 944, then you must file Form 944 even if your liability exceeds $1,000. Unless you contacted the IRS by April 1, 2015 to request to file Form 941 instead and received written confirmation that your filing requirement was changed.

If you do not receive a notice to file Form 944 from the IRS, but estimate your employment tax liability for calendar year 2017 will be $1,000 or less, call the IRS at 1-800-829-4933 by April 1, 2017. The IRS will send you a written notice that your filing requirement has been changed to Form 944.

$2,500 Quarterly Rule - If an employer accumulates less than **$2,500** tax liability for the quarter, no deposit is needed and payment can be paid with Form 941 for the quarter.

Monthly Rule - An employer is a monthly depositor if the aggregate amount of employment taxes reported for the look back period is $50,000 or less. A monthly depositor must deposit employment taxes for payments made during a calendar month by the 15th day of the following month.

Semiweekly Rule - An employer is a semiweekly depositor if the aggregate amount of employment taxes reported for the look back period is more than **$50,000**. Under the semiweekly deposit rule, those paying wages on Wednesday, Thursday, and/or Friday must deposit employment taxes by the next Wednesday, while those paying wages on Saturday, Sunday, Monday, and/or Tuesday are required to deposit employment taxes on the following Friday.

If the total accumulated tax reaches **$100,000** or more on any given day, it must be deposited by the next banking day.

Deposits Penalty: It is important to make timely deposits for payroll taxes. The applicable percentage of penalty for late payment in **Sec. 6656** is:

(1) **2%** if not more than 5 days late,

(2) **5%** if not more than 15 days late, and

(3) **10%** if more than 15 days late.

(4) **15%** Amounts still unpaid more than 10 days after the date of the first notice the IRS sent asking for the tax due or the day on which you received notice and demand for immediate payment, whichever is earlier. It is possible to have the penalty waived if it occurs during the 1st quarter that a deposit was required.

- ## How To Make A Deposit

It is **mandatory to use EFTPS** and make deposits electronically or by telephone 24/7 at 1-800-555-4477. The Electronic Federal Tax Payment System® tax payment service is provided free by the U.S. Department of the Treasury. After you've enrolled and received your credentials, you can pay any tax due to the Internal Revenue Service (IRS) using this system. The website for information and making electronic deposits is: **www.eftps.gov**

- ## Example of Computing Monthly Deposits

Mission Community Church's Form 941 for the 4th quarter shows the monthly liabilities on line 15, Monthly Summary Record of Federal Tax Liability section. **We computed the monthly liabilities as follows:**

Joseph's Social Security tax - $2,400.00 X 12.4%=	297.60
Joseph's Medicare Tax - $2,400.00 X 2.9% =	69.60
Rev. Snodgrass' Federal Tax	500.00
Joseph's Federal Tax	154.00
October Total	**$ 1,021.20**
Joseph's taxable wage - $2,400.00 X 12.4% =	297.60
Joseph's Medicare Tax - $2,400.00 X 2.9% =	69.60
Rev. Snodgrass' Federal Tax	500.00
Joseph's Federal Tax	154.00
November Total	**$ 1,021.20**
Joseph's taxable wage - $2,400.00 X 12.4 =	297.60
Joseph's Medicare Tax - $2,400.00 X 2.9% =	69.60
Rev. Snodgrass' Federal Tax	500.00
Joseph's Federal Tax	154.00
December Total	**$ 1,021.20**

Prepare Quarterly Reports

- ## Form 941 - Instructions With Social Security

LINE 2   will include taxable salaries of both dual-status ministers and lay employees from the extreme left-hand column of the "Payroll Sheets".

LINE 3   Enter the income tax you withheld for lay employees and all optional withholding for dual-status employees.

LINE 5a   will only include taxable salaries plus voluntary salary reduction retirement plan contributions of lay employees. In our 2016 example, the employee's withheld social security tax of 6.2% and the employer's matching portion 6.2% is combined for a total tax of 12.4%.

LINE 5c   will only include taxable salaries plus voluntary salary reduction retirement plan contributions of lay employees. In our 2016 example, the employee's withheld medicare tax of 1.45% and the employer's matching portion 1.45% is combined for a total tax of 2.9%. The 2017 rate will be the same.

LINE 10   undeposited taxes due must be less than $2,500 or you will be billed up to a 10% penalty for not paying on time with EFTPS electronic deposits or by telephone 24/7.

- ## Form 941 - Instructions Without Social Security - Filed Form 8274

If an existing church filed Form 8274 by October 31, 1984 (a new church by the first date on which a quarterly tax return would be due), and for religious reasons became exempt from withholding and matching social security, they should use **Form 941 and mark the box** provided on line **4**. Their employees will be liable for paying social security and medicare tax at the combined rate of 15.3% (less adjustments) on their personal Schedule SE for 2016.

LINE 2   will include taxable salaries of both dual-status ministers and lay employees from the extreme left-hand column of the "Payroll Sheet".

LINE 3   Enter the income tax you withheld for lay employees and all optional withholding for dual-status employees.

LINE 4   Check the box.

LINE 5a   Leave blank - does not apply to electing churches.

LINE 5c   Leave blank - does not apply to electing churches.

LINE 10   undeposited taxes due must be less than $2,500 or you will be billed up to a 10% penalty for not paying on time with EFTPS electronic deposits or by telephone 24/7.

- **Due Dates for Quarterly Reports**

  January, February, and March ....due on April 30th

  April, May, and June ....due on July 31st

  July, August, and September ....due on October 31st

  October, November, and December ....due on January 31st.

- **941 Reports Are Required - Even When There is No Liability**

  Since 2011, according to **Instructions for Form 941, page 3**, *"After you file your first Form 941, you must file a return for each quarter, even if you have no taxes to report, unless you filed a final return...."* Employers with only dual-status employees will show the dual-status minister's taxable salary **on Line 2** and check the box on **Line 4.** Employers, who are electing churches (Form 8274), will show taxable salaries on **Line 2** and check the box on **Line 4**.

  Historically, when there was no liability, the IRS did not require you to file Form 941. When a church employer had only dual-status employees and was not withholding income tax, no quarterly Form 941 was required. It was important to report the taxable salary for a dual-status employee on Form W-2 annually.

Prepare Year End Reports

Form W-3 and Copy A of all Forms W-2 are to be sent to the Social Security Administration address shown on Form W-3. Since Copy A is imaged and character recognized by machines, **they must be typed with black ink.** Do not use script type, or make any white outs or strike overs. Use decimal points but not dollar signs or commas (00000.00). Specific line by line instructions are given in 2016 Instructions for the preparation of the W-3 and the W-2. If a box **does not apply,** instructions say to **leave it blank.** A dual-status minister's W-2 **must not** have any entry in **Boxes 3, 4, 5, and 6.** If the tax liability figures on the W-3 do not reconcile with the tax liability figures that have been reported quarterly on the 941, you will receive a computer print out from the IRS asking why they are different and a billing of tax liability they think you owe.

Form 941, Line 2	wages should match	= W-2, Box 1
Form 941, Line 3	tax should match	= W-2, Box 2
Form 941, Line 5a	wages should match	= W-2, Box 3
Form 941, Line 5a	column 2 tax should match	= W-2, Box 4 X 2 (odd cents okay)
Form 941, Line 5c	wages should match	= W-2, Box 5
Form 941, Line 5c	column 2 tax should match	= W-2, Box 6 X 2 (odd cents okay)

Year-end reports are to be prepared by January 31st. Employees are to be given their W-2 copies by January 31st. New due date for filing with SSA: the due date for filing 2016 Forms W-2 and W-3 with the Social Security Administration is now January 31, 2017. Some employers provide a W-2 to their employee, then fail to send Copy A to the Social Security Administration. Be sure to send Copy A to the Social Security Administration, so they can cross match it with your employees' returns. Avoid "failure to file" penalties!

- **Required entries on Form W-2**

  You will find in the **2016 Instructions for W-2 and W-3**, pages 14-23, a complete discussion, line by line, on how to prepare Form W-2 & W-3. We will list a few of the required entries on the W-2 that are typical for ministers and missionaries. Enter appropriate codes using capital letters, leave one space blank after the code and enter the dollar amount on the same line. Use decimal points but not dollar signs or commas.

Box 10:	Show total amount of dependent care benefits paid or incurred by you for your employee.	
Box 12:	C 1060	($1060 premium for over $50,000 group term life insurance)
	D 3600	($3,600 elective deferral to 401(k) plan)
	E 3600	($3,600 elective deferral to 403(b) plan)
	L 5400	($6,400 reimbursement for 10,000 miles @ 64¢, enter $1,000 in Box 1 as taxable)
	P 1690	($1690 reimbursement for qualified moving expenses)
	S 3600	($3,600 salary reduction contributions to 408(p) SIMPLE plan)
	W 2500	($2,500 employer contributions to a Health Savings Account)
	DD 8200	(Cost of Employer-Sponsored Health Coverage) **Required since 2015**
	No Entry	($5,400 reimbursement for 10,000 miles @54¢)
	No Entry	(All reimbursements with accountable plan at IRS rates or actual)

Box 14:   You may use this box for any other information you want to give your employee. Please label each item. Examples are parsonage allowance designated, moving expenses paid, or reminder for employee of an electing church to pay social security on Sch SE.

Box 14:   Show total value of taxable fringe benefits that are also shown in Box 1, such as the value of personal use of employer owned auto **or** provide a statement to employee of calculations.

State and Local Tax Withholding

Call your State and local Departments and ask for materials and instructions for withholding the proper amount of tax for your employees. Some states require that you withhold state tax for the dual-status minister as well as the lay employee.

Unemployment Taxes

Nonprofit employers **are not subject** to Federal Unemployment Taxes. IRS Publication 15-A, page 10, says *"An organization that is exempt from federal income tax under section 501(c)(3) of the Internal Revenue Code is also exempt from FUTA tax. This exemption cannot be waived. Do not file Form 940 to report wages paid by these organizations or pay the tax."*

Most states do not require nonprofit employers to pay state unemployment tax. Consult with your state unemployment office to be sure.

Workmen's Compensation Insurance

Most states **require** nonprofit employers to provide Workmen's Compensation Insurance coverage for both lay and dual-status minister employees. Consult with an insurance professional in your state to be sure.

Form I-9 - Employment Eligibility Verification

The Immigration Reform and Control Act of 1986 requires all employers to examine the applicant's documents proving identity and eligibility to work in the United States and complete Form I-9 **before hiring the applicant**. The law says that we cannot hire an alien if we know that the alien is not authorized to work in the U.S. The Form I-9 is not an IRS form, but can be obtained from the Bureau of Immigration and Customs Enforcement (ICE). Form I-9 and instructions is able to be filled in and printed for your files. Go to their website: **http://www.uscis.gov/i-9** - you will see a PDF of Form I-9.

Form I-9 is not required to be filed with USCIS or ICE. The employer is required to keep Form I-9 for possible audit. Fines for noncompliance are from $110 to $1,100 per employee for failure to maintain the necessary paperwork. Fines for hiring illegal aliens are from $375 to $16,000 per individual illegally employed.

New Hire Reporting Requirements

Within a few business days of a new employee's date of hire (20 days), all employers are to submit to their state unemployment department a report containing the following information:

(1)   the new employee's name, address, social security number, and date of hire; and

(2)   the employer's name, address and federal tax identification number.

The employer may submit the report by conveying to their state department a copy of the new employee's W-4 form or an alternative scannable W-4. Each State has a website to allow electronic reporting.

How To Correct Information Returns

The IRS provides Form W-2c, Form W-3c and Form 941X as the means of correcting mistakes on previously filed information returns. It is important to correct returns when you discover a mistake.

Annual Form 1096 and Form 1099

Prepare Form 1096 and Form 1099-Misc for payments to evangelists, musicians, janitors and contractors whom you paid more than $600. They are required to be given to the recipients by January 31st and submitted to your IRS Service Center by **January 31st**. You may be required to prepare and file Form 1099-INT for interest of $10 or more paid on bonds or loans from individuals. You may be required to prepare and file Form 1099-MISC for rents paid of $600 or more. It is important for payors to obtain **W-9s from each** payee at the time of service.

Form 1099 is not required for payments made to **corporations.**

Chart of Where to Show Transactions
For a dual-status employee, leave Form W-2, Boxes 3 and 5 blank.

Type of Transaction	*Taxable Income Box 1, W-2	Lay Employee FICA & Medicare Box 3 & 5, W-2	**Dual-Status Sch. SE Line 2	Show on Sch. C	Not to be shown anywhere	Deducted on Form 1040
INCOME						
Salary, Dual-status minister	Yes		Yes			
Soc. Security paid by employer, dual-status	Yes		Yes			
Salary, Lay employee	Yes	Yes				
Salary, Lay employee of electing church	Yes	No	***Yes			
Bonus or "love gift" from employer	Yes	Yes	Yes			
Pastor Appreciation or "love gifts from individuals and supporters			Yes	Yes		
Individual Medical Plan (When 2 or more full-time employees)	Yes	Yes	Yes			
Professional Income			Yes	Yes		
Gift from relative, etc	No	No	No		Yes	
FRINGES						
Employer qualified pension- 401a, SEP, 403b(9)	No	No	No		Yes	
Premium for $50,000 term life insurance	No	No	No		Yes	
Premium for over $50,000 term life insurance	Yes	Yes	Yes			
Permanent life, employee's beneficiary	Yes	Yes	Yes			
Group Medical plan paid by employer	No	No	No		Yes	
Individual Medical Plan or One person HRA plan that includes other medical expenses (When only one full-time employee)	No	No	No		Yes	
Qualified medical HRA or Sec. 125 Plan	No	No	No		Yes	
Qualified moving reimbursement	No	No	No		Yes	W-2, Box 12 (P)
Nonqualified moving reimbursement	Yes	Yes	Yes			
Employee, 403(b)(7) or 408(p) lay employee	No	Yes				
Employee, 403(b)(7) or 408(p) dual-status	No		No			
ADJ						
Employer payments to an IRA	Yes	Yes	Yes			1040, Ln. 32
Sep or Simple payments (Evangelist)						1040, Ln. 28
Unreimbursed qualified moving expenses						1040, Ln. 26
HOUSING						
Value of home provided, dual-status	No		Yes			
Parsonage Allowance, dual-status	No		Yes			
Value of home provided, lay employee (Sec.119 qualifications met)	No	No				
Value of home provided, lay employee (Sec. 119 qualifications not met)	Yes	Yes				
PROF EXP						
Auto reimbursement	No	No	No		Yes	
Employer provided auto, personal use	Yes	Yes	Yes			
Travel and professional reimbursement	No	No	No		Yes	
Expense allowance without adequate accounting to employer	Yes	Yes	Deduct			Sch. A, Ln. 21
Unreimbursed business expenses			Deduct			Sch. A, Ln. 21

*   Amounts in this column are to be shown in left-hand column of payroll sheets, line 2 of Form 941, and Box 1 of W-2.

**   If a dual-status employee is exempt because he has filed Form 4361, then he is to disregard the column for Social Security and write "Exempt—Form 4361" on the self-employment line of Form 1040, Page 2.

***   Lay employees of electing church report wage on Section B, Part I, Line 5a of Sch. SE

Report Date: 01/01/2016   Thru: 12/31/2016
Criteria: ExTags=U

SNODGRASS, H JAMES

Date	Sta	Gross	MCWH	SSWH	FITW	SITW	LITW	403(B)	HOUSING	ACCTREIM	Net
01/01	A10	2125.00	0.00	0.00	250.00	45.00	11.00	250.00	1000.00	990.91	1569.00
01/15	A10	2125.00	0.00	0.00	250.00	45.00	11.00	250.00	1000.00	0.00	1569.00
02/01	A10	2125.00	0.00	0.00	250.00	45.00	11.00	250.00	1000.00	936.59	1569.00
02/15	A10	2125.00	0.00	0.00	250.00	45.00	11.00	250.00	1000.00	0.00	1569.00
03/01	A10	2125.00	0.00	0.00	250.00	45.00	11.00	250.00	1000.00	1547.14	1569.00
03/15	A10	2125.00	0.00	0.00	250.00	45.00	11.00	250.00	1000.00	0.00	1569.00
Qtr 1		**12750.00**	**0.00**	**0.00**	**1500.00**	**270.00**	**66.00**	**1500.00**	**6000.00**	**3474.64**	**9414.00**
04/01	A10	2125.00	0.00	0.00	250.00	45.00	11.00	250.00	1000.00	1323.50	1569.00
04/15	A10	2125.00	0.00	0.00	250.00	45.00	11.00	250.00	1000.00	0.00	1569.00
05/01	A10	2125.00	0.00	0.00	250.00	45.00	11.00	250.00	1000.00	1045.24	1569.00
05/15	A10	2125.00	0.00	0.00	250.00	45.00	11.00	250.00	1000.00	0.00	1569.00
06/01	A10	2125.00	0.00	0.00	250.00	45.00	11.00	250.00	1000.00	997.03	1569.00
06/15	A10	2125.00	0.00	0.00	250.00	45.00	11.00	250.00	1000.00	0.00	1569.00
Qtr 2		**12750.00**	**0.00**	**0.00**	**1500.00**	**270.00**	**66.00**	**1500.00**	**6000.00**	**3365.77**	**9414.00**
07/01	A10	2125.00	0.00	0.00	250.00	45.00	11.00	250.00	1000.00	1134.49	1569.00
07/15	A10	2125.00	0.00	0.00	250.00	45.00	11.00	250.00	1000.00	0.00	1569.00
08/01	A10	2125.00	0.00	0.00	250.00	45.00	11.00	250.00	1000.00	1027.13	1569.00
08/15	A10	2125.00	0.00	0.00	250.00	45.00	11.00	250.00	1000.00	0.00	1569.00
09/01	A10	2125.00	0.00	0.00	250.00	45.00	11.00	250.00	1000.00	1667.47	1569.00
09/15	A10	2125.00	0.00	0.00	250.00	45.00	11.00	250.00	1000.00	0.00	1569.00
Qtr 3		**12750.00**	**0.00**	**0.00**	**1500.00**	**270.00**	**66.00**	**1500.00**	**6000.00**	**3829.09**	**9414.00**
10/01	A10	2125.00	0.00	0.00	250.00	45.00	11.00	250.00	1000.00	998.96	1569.00
10/15	A10	2125.00	0.00	0.00	250.00	45.00	11.00	250.00	1000.00	0.00	1569.00
11/01	A10	2125.00	0.00	0.00	250.00	45.00	11.00	250.00	1000.00	957.78	1569.00
11/15	A10	2125.00	0.00	0.00	250.00	45.00	11.00	250.00	1000.00	0.00	1569.00
12/01	A10	2125.00	0.00	0.00	250.00	45.00	11.00	250.00	1000.00	1238.24	1569.00
12/15	A10	2125.00	0.00	0.00	250.00	45.00	11.00	250.00	1000.00	0.00	1569.00
Qtr 4		**12750.00**	**0.00**	**0.00**	**1500.00**	**270.00**	**66.00**	**1500.00**	**6000.00**	**3194.98**	**9414.00**
Qtr 1		**12750.00**	**0.00**	**0.00**	**1500.00**	**270.00**	**66.00**	**1500.00**	**6000.00**	**3474.64**	**9414.00**
Qtr 2		**12750.00**	**0.00**	**0.00**	**1500.00**	**270.00**	**66.00**	**1500.00**	**6000.00**	**3365.77**	**9414.00**
Qtr 3		**12750.00**	**0.00**	**0.00**	**1500.00**	**270.00**	**66.00**	**1500.00**	**6000.00**	**3829.09**	**9414.00**
Qtr 4		**12750.00**	**0.00**	**0.00**	**1500.00**	**270.00**	**66.00**	**1500.00**	**6000.00**	**3194.98**	**9414.00**
Total		**51000.00**	**0.00**	**0.00**	**6000.00**	**1080.00**	**264.00**	**6000.00**	**24000.00**	**13864.48**	**37656.00**

Report Date: 01/01/2016   Thru: 12/31/2016
Criteria: ExTags=T

MOP, JOSEPH

Date	Sta	Gross	MCWH	SSWH	FITW	SITW	LITW	403(B)	HOUSING	ACCTREIM	Net
01/01	A10	1200.00	17.40	74.40	77.00	38.25	9.00	75.00	0.00	126.50	908.95
01/15	A10	1200.00	17.40	74.40	77.00	38.25	9.00	75.00	0.00	0.00	908.95
02/01	A10	1200.00	17.40	74.40	77.00	38.25	9.00	75.00	0.00	151.06	908.95
02/15	A10	1200.00	17.40	74.40	77.00	38.25	9.00	75.00	0.00	0.00	908.95
03/01	A10	1200.00	17.40	74.40	77.00	38.25	9.00	75.00	0.00	146.41	908.95
03/15	A10	1200.00	17.40	74.40	77.00	38.25	9.00	75.00	0.00	0.00	908.95
Qtr 1		**7200.00**	**104.40**	**446.40**	**462.00**	**229.50**	**54.00**	**450.00**	**0.00**	**423.97**	**5453.70**
04/01	A10	1200.00	17.40	74.40	77.00	38.25	9.00	75.00	0.00	149.77	908.95
04/15	A10	1200.00	17.40	74.40	77.00	38.25	9.00	75.00	0.00	0.00	908.95
05/01	A10	1200.00	17.40	74.40	77.00	38.25	9.00	75.00	0.00	130.46	908.95
05/15	A10	1200.00	17.40	74.40	77.00	38.25	9.00	75.00	0.00	0.00	908.95
06/01	A10	1200.00	17.40	74.40	77.00	38.25	9.00	75.00	0.00	151.58	908.95
06/15	A10	1200.00	17.40	74.40	77.00	38.25	9.00	75.00	0.00	0.00	908.95
Qtr 2		**7200.00**	**104.40**	**446.40**	**462.00**	**229.50**	**54.00**	**450.00**	**0.00**	**431.81**	**5453.70**
07/01	A10	1200.00	17.40	74.40	77.00	38.25	9.00	75.00	0.00	166.42	908.95
07/15	A10	1200.00	17.40	74.40	77.00	38.25	9.00	75.00	0.00	0.00	908.95
08/01	A10	1200.00	17.40	74.40	77.00	38.25	9.00	75.00	0.00	159.25	908.95
08/15	A10	1200.00	17.40	74.40	77.00	38.25	9.00	75.00	0.00	0.00	908.95
09/01	A10	1200.00	17.40	74.40	77.00	38.25	9.00	75.00	0.00	94.80	908.95
09/15	A10	1200.00	17.40	74.40	77.00	38.25	9.00	75.00	0.00	0.00	908.95
Qtr 3		**7200.00**	**104.40**	**446.40**	**462.00**	**229.50**	**54.00**	**450.00**	**0.00**	**420.47**	**5453.70**
10/01	A10	1200.00	17.40	74.40	77.00	38.25	9.00	75.00	0.00	133.36	908.95
10/15	A10	1200.00	17.40	74.40	77.00	38.25	9.00	75.00	0.00	0.00	908.95
11/01	A10	1200.00	17.40	74.40	77.00	38.25	9.00	75.00	0.00	128.50	908.95
11/15	A10	1200.00	17.40	74.40	77.00	38.25	9.00	75.00	0.00	0.00	908.95
12/01	A10	1200.00	17.40	74.40	77.00	38.25	9.00	75.00	0.00	116.33	908.95
12/15	A10	1200.00	17.40	74.40	77.00	38.25	9.00	75.00	0.00	0.00	908.95
Qtr 4		**7200.00**	**104.40**	**446.40**	**462.00**	**229.50**	**54.00**	**450.00**	**0.00**	**378.19**	**5453.70**
Qtr 1		7200.00	104.40	446.40	462.00	229.50	54.00	450.00	0.00	423.97	5453.70
Qtr 2		7200.00	104.40	446.40	462.00	229.50	54.00	450.00	0.00	431.81	5453.70
Qtr 3		7200.00	104.40	446.40	462.00	229.50	54.00	450.00	0.00	420.47	5453.70
Qtr 4		7200.00	104.40	446.40	462.00	229.50	54.00	450.00	0.00	378.19	5453.70
Total		28800.00	417.60	1785.60	1848.00	918.00	216.00	1800.00	0.00	1654.44	21814.80

Example, Nonelecting Church

Form 941

Form 941 for 2016: Employer's QUARTERLY Federal Tax Return 970114
(Rev. January 2016)   Department of the Treasury — Internal Revenue Service

1213   OMB No. 1545-0029

Employer identification number (EIN)   35-2938279

Name (not your trade name)   MISSION COMMUNITY CHURCH

Trade name (if any)

Address   1620 E JONES STREET
SOUTH BEND, IN 46617

Report for this Quarter of 2016 (Check one.)

- ☐ 1: January, February, March
- ☐ 2: April, May, June
- ☐ 3: July, August, September
- ☒ 4: October, November, December

Instructions and prior year forms are available at www.irs.gov/form941.

Read the separate instructions before you complete Form 941. Type or print within the boxes.

Part 1: Answer these questions for this quarter.

		Column 1		Column 2
1	Number of employees who received wages, tips, or other compensation for the pay period including: Mar. 12 (Quarter 1), June 12 (Quarter 2), Sept. 12 (Quarter 3), or Dec. 12 (Quarter 4) ... 1	2		
2	Wages, tips, and other compensation ... 2	12000.00		
3	Federal income tax withheld from wages, tips, and other compensation ... 3	1962.00		
4	If no wages, tips, and other compensation are subject to social security or Medicare tax ... ☐ Check and go to line 6.			
5a	Taxable social security wages ...	7200.00	× .124 =	892.80
5b	Taxable social security tips ...		× .124 =	
5c	Taxable Medicare wages & tips ...	7200.00	× .029 =	208.80
5d	Taxable wages & tips subject to Additional Medicare Tax withholding ...		× .009 =	
5e	Add Column 2 from lines 5a, 5b, 5c, and 5d ... 5e			1101.60
5f	Section 3121(q) Notice and Demand—Tax due on unreported tips (see instructions) ... 5f			
6	Total taxes before adjustments. Add lines 3, 5e, and 5f ... 6			3063.60
7	Current quarter's adjustment for fractions of cents ... 7			
8	Current quarter's adjustment for sick pay ... 8			
9	Current quarter's adjustments for tips and group-term life insurance ... 9			
10	Total taxes after adjustments. Combine lines 6 through 9 ... 10			3063.60
11	Total deposits for this quarter, including overpayment applied from a prior quarter and overpayments applied from Form 941-X, 941-X (PR), 944-X, 944-X (SP) filed in the current quarter ... 11			3063.60
12	Balance due. If line 10 is more than line 11, enter the difference and see instructions ... 12			
13	Overpayment. If line 11 is more than line 10, enter the difference [ ] Check one: ☐ Apply to next return. ☐ Send a refund.			

▶ You MUST complete both pages of Form 941 and SIGN it.

For Privacy Act and Paperwork Reduction Act Notice, see Payment Voucher.

CAT. No. 6 9411   NTF 25605.99   B16941   Copyright 2016 Greatland/Nelco - Forms Software Only

   Next ▶   Form **941** (Rev. 1-2016)

Form 941 (Rev. 1-2016) Page 2

Name (not your trade name)   MISSION COMMUNITY CHURCH

Employer identification number (EIN)   35-2938279

Part 2: Tell us about your deposit schedule and tax liability for this quarter.

If you are unsure about whether you are a monthly schedule depositor or a semiweekly schedule depositor, see section 11 of Pub. 15.

14 Check one:

☐ Line 10 on this return is less than $2,500 or line 10 on the return for the prior quarter was less than $2,500, and you did not incur a $100,000 next-day deposit obligation during the current quarter. If line 10 for the prior quarter was less than $2,500 but line 10 on this return is $100,000 or more, you must provide a record of your federal tax liability. If you are a monthly schedule depositor, complete the deposit schedule below; if you are a semiweekly schedule depositor, attach Schedule B (Form 941). Go to Part 3.

☒ You were a monthly schedule depositor for the entire quarter. Enter your tax liability for each month and total liability for the quarter, then go to Part 3.

Tax liability:		
Month 1		1021.20
Month 2		1021.20
Month 3		1021.20
Total liability for quarter		3063.60 Total must equal line 10.

☐ You were a semiweekly schedule depositor for any part of this quarter. Complete Schedule B (Form 941), Report of Tax Liability for Semiweekly Schedule Depositors, and attach it to Form 941.

Form W-3

DO NOT STAPLE

33333	a Control number		For Official Use Only ▶ OMB No. 1545-0008	

b Kind of Payer (Check one)   941 ☒   Military ☐   Hshld. emp. ☐   Medicare govt. emp. ☐   943 ☐   944 ☐   CT-1 ☐

Kind of Employer (Check one)   None apply ☐   501c non-govt. ☒   State/local non-501c ☐   State/local 501c ☐   Federal govt. ☐   Third-party sick pay ☐ (Check if applicable)

c Total no. of Forms W-2   2

d Establishment number

1 Wages, tips, other compensation 48000.00	2 Federal income tax withheld 7848.00
3 Social security wages 28800.00	4 Social security tax withheld 1785.60
5 Medicare wages and tips 28800.00	6 Medicare tax withheld 417.60
7 Social security tips	8 Allocated tips
9	10 Dependent care benefits
11 Nonqualified plans	12a Deferred compensation 7800.00
13 For third-party sick pay use only	12b
14 Income tax withheld by payer of third-party sick pay	

e Employer identification number (EIN)   35-2938279

f Employer's name   MISSION COMMUNITY CHURCH

1620 E JONES STREET
SOUTH BEND, IN 46617

g Employer's address and ZIP code

h Other EIN used this year

15 State IN Employer's state ID number 35-2938279		16 State wages, tips, etc. 48000.00	17 State income tax 1998.00
		18 Local wages, tips, etc. 48000.00	19 Local income tax 480.00

Employer's contact person

Employer's telephone number   For Official Use Only   0 0 0 0/1034

Employer's fax number

Employer's email address

Under penalties of perjury, I declare that I have examined this return and accompanying documents and, to the best of my knowledge and belief, they are true, correct, and complete.

Signature ▶   Title ▶   Date ▶

Form **W-3 Transmittal of Wage and Tax Statements**   **2016**

Department of the Treasury
Internal Revenue Service

Example, Nonelecting Church

W-2 Form #1

a Employee's social security no. 483-12-0200	Copy B—To Be Filed With Employee's FEDERAL Tax Return. OMB No. 1545-0008

b Employer identification number (EIN) 35-2938279

1 Wages, tips, other comp. 21000.00	2 Federal income tax withheld 6000.00

c Employer's name, address, and ZIP code
MISSION COMMUNITY CHURCH
1620 E JONES STREET
SOUTH BEND, IN 46617

3 Social security wages	4 Social security tax withheld
5 Medicare wages and tips	6 Medicare tax withheld
7 Social security tips	8 Allocated tips

d Control number

9	10 Dependent care benefits

e Employee's name, address, and ZIP code
H JAMES SNODGRASS

2309 E SMITH STREET
SOUTH BEND, IN 46617

11 Nonqualified plans	12a See instructions for box 12 E 6000.00
13 Statutory employee / Retirement plan [X] / Third-party sick pay	12b DD 16421.00
14 Other HOUSING ALLOWANCE 24000.00	12c
	12d

15 State	Employer's state ID number	16 State wages, tips, etc.	17 State income tax	18 Local wages, tips, etc.	19 Local income tax	20 Locality name
IN	35-2938279	21000.00	1080.00	21000.00	264.00	KOSCIUSKO

Form W-2 Wage and Tax Statement **2016** 38-2099803 Department of the Treasury -- Internal Revenue Service

This information is being furnished to the Internal Revenue Service.
6 BW2BC NTF 2580333 BW2EEBC Copyright 2016 Greatland/Nelco – Forms Software Only

---

W-2 Form #2

a Employee's social security no. 403-19-0000	Copy B—To Be Filed With Employee's FEDERAL Tax Return. OMB No. 1545-0008

b Employer identification number (EIN) 35-2938279

1 Wages, tips, other comp. 27000.00	2 Federal income tax withheld 1848.00

c Employer's name, address, and ZIP code
MISSION COMMUNITY CHURCH
1620 E JONES STREET
SOUTH BEND, IN 46617

3 Social security wages 28800.00	4 Social security tax withheld 1785.60
5 Medicare wages and tips 28800.00	6 Medicare tax withheld 417.60
7 Social security tips	8 Allocated tips

d Control number

9	10 Dependent care benefits

e Employee's name, address, and ZIP code
JOSEPH MOP

1620 E JONES STREET
SOUTH BEND, IN 46617

11 Nonqualified plans	12a See instructions for box 12 E 1800.00
13 Statutory employee / Retirement plan [X] / Third-party sick pay	12b DD 14268.00
14 Other	12c
	12d

15 State	Employer's state ID number	16 State wages, tips, etc.	17 State income tax	18 Local wages, tips, etc.	19 Local income tax	20 Locality name
IN	35-2938279	27000.00	918.00	27000.00	216.00	KOSCIUSKO

Form W-2 Wage and Tax Statement **2016** 38-2099803 Department of the Treasury -- Internal Revenue Service

This information is being furnished to the Internal Revenue Service.

Example, Electing Church (Filed Form 8274)

Form 941

Form **941 for 2016:** Employer's QUARTERLY Federal Tax Return
(Rev. January 2016)   Department of the Treasury — Internal Revenue Service

970114

OMB No. 1545-0029   1213

Employer identification number (EIN) 35-2938279

Name (not your trade name) MISSION COMMUNITY CHURCH

Trade name (if any)

Address 1620 E JONES STREET
SOUTH BEND, IN 46617

Report for this Quarter of 2016
(Check one.)
- [ ] 1: January, February, March
- [ ] 2: April, May, June
- [ ] 3: July, August, September
- [X] 4: October, November, December

Instructions and prior year forms are available at www.irs.gov/form941.

Read the separate instructions before you complete Form 941. Type or print within the boxes.

Part 1: Answer these questions for this quarter.

1 Number of employees who received wages, tips, or other compensation for the pay period including: Mar. 12 (Quarter 1), June 12 (Quarter 2), Sept. 12 (Quarter 3), or Dec. 12 (Quarter 4) ...... 1 | 2

2 Wages, tips, and other compensation. ...... 2 | 12000.00

3 Federal Income tax withheld from wages, tips, and other compensation. ...... 3 | 2847.60

4 If no wages, tips, and other compensation are subject to social security or Medicare tax. [X] Check and go to line 6.

	Column 1		Column 2
5a Taxable social security wages.		× .124 =	
5b Taxable social security tips.		× .124 =	
5c Taxable Medicare wages & tips.		× .029 =	
5d Taxable wages & tips subject to Additional Medicare Tax withholding.		× .009 =	

5e Add Column 2 from lines 5a, 5b, 5c, and 5d. 5e

5f Section 3121(q) Notice and Demand—Tax due on unreported tips (see instructions). 5f

6 Total taxes before adjustments. Add lines 3, 5e, and 5f ...... 6 | 2847.60

7 Current quarter's adjustment for fractions of cents 7

8 Current quarter's adjustment for sick pay 8

9 Current quarter's adjustments for tips and group-term life insurance. 9

10 Total taxes after adjustments. Combine lines 6 through 9. ...... 10 | 2847.60

11 Total deposits for this quarter, including overpayment applied from a prior quarter and overpayments applied from Form 941-X, 941-X (PR), 944-X, or 944-X (SP) filed in the current quarter. ...... 11 | 2847.60

12 Balance due. If line 10 is more than line 11, enter the difference and see instructions. 12

13 Overpayment. If line 11 is more than line 10, enter the difference. Check one: [ ] Apply to next return. [ ] Send a refund.

▶ You MUST complete both pages of Form 941 and SIGN it.
For Privacy Act and Paperwork Reduction Act Notice, see Payment Voucher.

Next ▶

CAA   6   9411   NTF 2580599   B16941   Copyright 2016 Greatland/Nelco — Forms Software Only   Form **941** (Rev. 1-2016)

Form 941

Form **941 for 2016:** Employer's QUARTERLY Federal Tax Return
(Rev. January 2016)   Department of the Treasury — Internal Revenue Service

970114

OMB No. 1545-0029   1213

Employer identification number (EIN) 35-2938279

Name (not your trade name) MISSION COMMUNITY CHURCH

Trade name (if any)

Address 1620 E JONES STREET
SOUTH BEND, IN 46617

Report for this Quarter of 2016
(Check one.)
- [ ] 1: January, February, March
- [ ] 2: April, May, June
- [ ] 3: July, August, September
- [X] 4: October, November, December

Instructions and prior year forms are available at www.irs.gov/form941.

Read the separate instructions before you complete Form 941. Type or print within the boxes.

Part 1: Answer these questions for this quarter.

1 Number of employees who received wages, tips, or other compensation for the pay period including: Mar. 12 (Quarter 1), June 12 (Quarter 2), Sept. 12 (Quarter 3), or Dec. 12 (Quarter 4) ...... 1 | 2

2 Wages, tips, and other compensation. ...... 2 | 12000.00

3 Federal Income tax withheld from wages, tips, and other compensation. ...... 3 | 2847.60

Form W-3

DO NOT STAPLE

33333	a Control number		For Official Use Only ▶ OMB No. 1545-0008

b Kind of Payer (Check one)
- [X] 941
- [ ] Military
- [ ] 943
- [ ] 944
- [ ] CT-1
- [ ] Hshld. emp.
- [ ] Medicare govt. emp.

Kind of Employer (Check one)
- [ ] None apply
- [X] 501c non-govt.
- [ ] State/local non-501c
- [ ] State/local 501c
- [ ] Federal govt.

[ ] Third-party sick pay (Check if applicable)

c Total no. of Forms W-2 2   d Establishment number

e Employer identification number (EIN) 35-2938279

f Employer's name MISSION COMMUNITY CHURCH

g Employer's address and ZIP code 1620 E JONES STREET SOUTH BEND, IN 46617

h Other EIN used this year

1 Wages, tips, other compensation 48000.00	2 Federal income tax withheld 11390.40
3 Social security wages 48000.00	4 Social security tax withheld
5 Medicare wages and tips	6 Medicare tax withheld
7 Social security tips	8 Allocated tips
9	10 Dependent care benefits
11 Nonqualified plans	12a Deferred compensation 7800.00
13 For third-party sick pay use only	12b
14 Income tax withheld by payer of third-party sick pay	

15 State IN Employer's state ID number 35-2938279

16 State wages, tips, etc. 48000.00	17 State income tax 1998.00	18 Local wages, tips, etc. 48000.00	19 Local income tax 480.00

Employer's contact person

Employer's telephone number

For Official Use Only 0 0 0/1034

Employer's fax number

Employer's email address

Under penalties of perjury, I declare that I have examined this return and accompanying documents and, to the best of my knowledge and belief, they are true, correct, and complete.

Signature ▶   Title ▶   Date ▶

Form **W-3** Transmittal of Wage and Tax Statements   **2016**

Department of the Treasury
Internal Revenue Service

Example, Electing Church (Filed Form 8274)

a Employee's social security no. 483-12-0200	Copy B—To Be Filed With Employee's FEDERAL Tax Return. OMB No. 1545-0008	
b Employer identification number (EIN) 35-2938279	**1** Wages, tips, other comp. 21000.00	**2** Federal income tax withheld 6000.00
c Employer's name, address, and ZIP code MISSION COMMUNITY CHURCH 1620 E JONES STREET SOUTH BEND, IN 46617	**3** Social security wages	**4** Social security tax withheld
	5 Medicare wages and tips	**6** Medicare tax withheld
	7 Social security tips	**8** Allocated tips
d Control number	**9**	**10** Dependent care benefits
e Employee's name, address, and ZIP code H JAMES SNODGRASS 2309 E SMITH STREET SOUTH BEND, IN 46617	**11** Nonqualified plans	**12a** See instructions for box 12 E 6000.00
	13 Statutory employee / Retirement plan [X] / Third-party sick pay	**12b** DD 16421.00
	14 Other HOUSI 24000.00 ALLOW ANCE	**12c**
		12d

15 State Employer's state ID number IN 35-2938279	**16** State wages, tips, etc. 21000.00	**17** State income tax 1080.00	**18** Local wages, tips, etc. 21000.00	**19** Local income tax 264.00	**20** Locality name KOSCIUSKO

Form **W-2** Wage and Tax Statement   **2016**   38-2099803   Department of the Treasury -- Internal Revenue Service

This information is being furnished to the Internal Revenue Service.

6 **BW2BC**   NTF 2580333   **BW2EEBC**   Copyright 2016 Greatland/Nelco – Forms Software Only

---

a Employee's social security no. 403-19-0000	Copy B—To Be Filed With Employee's FEDERAL Tax Return. OMB No. 1545-0008	
b Employer identification number (EIN) 35-2938279	**1** Wages, tips, other comp. 27000.00	**2** Federal income tax withheld 5390.40
c Employer's name, address, and ZIP code MISSION COMMUNITY CHURCH 1620 E JONES STREET SOUTH BEND, IN 46617	**3** Social security wages	**4** Social security tax withheld
	5 Medicare wages and tips	**6** Medicare tax withheld
	7 Social security tips	**8** Allocated tips
d Control number	**9**	**10** Dependent care benefits
e Employee's name, address, and ZIP code JOSEPH MOP 1620 E JONES STREET SOUTH BEND, IN 46617	**11** Nonqualified plans	**12a** See instructions for box 12 E 1800.00
	13 Statutory employee / Retirement plan [X] / Third-party sick pay	**12b** DD 14268.00
	14 Other ELECT CHURCH PAY SS ON SE	**12c**
		12d

15 State Employer's state ID number IN 35-2938279	**16** State wages, tips, etc. 27000.00	**17** State income tax 918.00	**18** Local wages, tips, etc. 27000.00	**19** Local income tax 216.00	**20** Locality name KOSCIUSKO

Form **W-2** Wage and Tax Statement   **2016**   38-2099803   Department of the Treasury -- Internal Revenue Service

This information is being furnished to the Internal Revenue Service.

6 **BW2BC**   NTF 2580333   **BW2EEBC**   Copyright 2016 Greatland/Nelco – Forms Software Only

Note: Joseph Mop's W-2, Box 2 above includes additional federal withholdings to cover self-employment tax liability that he will incur as an employee of an electing church. The Form 941 on the previous page reflects additional federal withholdings on line 3 for the fourth quarter.

CHAPTER SEVEN

Completed Income Tax Return

A typical problem with the actual tax forms filled out seems to be the most practical way to further explain the tax law as it applies to the minister. So study the following information about Rev. Snodgrass and how it is to be shown on the tax forms. We have added two more examples to illustrate the Church owning the parsonage.

To illustrate that **$1,198.00 difference** in tax liability resulted from Rev. Snodgrass having an accountable reimbursement plan, we have prepared his return both ways.

Rev. Snodgrass's employer provides Group Health Insurance and the box on Line 61 is marked to indicate that.

The proration of unreimbursed employee business expenses, according to the Dalan Case is also illustrated. His W-2 would show **$35,529** without reimbursement, and as shown in Chapter Six, **$21,000** with reimbursement.

Facts of the Problem

Rev. H. James Snodgrass and Mary T., live at 2309 E. Smith St., South Bend, Indiana 46617. Rev. Snodgrass' S.S.# is 483-12-0200; Mary's S.S.# is 483-15-3200. They have three children, Ruth, Thomas and Samuel, ages 17,15 & 12. Children under 17 qualify for the Child Tax Credit.

Rev. Snodgrass is minister of Mission Community Church and Mrs. Snodgrass is a nurse at a local hospital. Mary's wage on her W-2 is **$50,278** with **$3,580** federal tax withheld, $3,117 social security tax, $729 medicare tax, **$1,702** State tax and **$406** Local tax withheld. Combine his salary of **$21,000/$35,529** and her salary of **$50,278** on line 7, Form 1040. His federal, state & local withholdings are shown on his W-2. (Page 117)

During the year Rev. Snodgrass received **$690** professional income from weddings and funerals. In earning this income, Rev. Snodgrass spent **$114** for booklets & **$12** for Schedule C tax prep fee.

The Snodgrasses own their own home (purchased 6-10-04) and they make payments of **$826.33** a month. Their interest was **$8,081** and principal payments were **$1,835**. Real estate taxes were **$1,182**. Insurance was **$840**, and repairs were **$3,292**. They bought new furniture for **$2,409**. Decorator items (oval rug for living room) cost **$463**. Utilities and personal phone were **$3,738**. Miscellaneous household expenses Mary kept a record of came to **$642**.

Professional expenses are as follows: Tuition for class at seminary **$345**, Office Supplies **$86**, Religious Materials **$327**, Subscriptions **$132**, Home entertainment meals **$881**. He purchased **$548** worth of books this year and also bought a fax machine for **$329**. Rev. Snodgrass was reimbursed for the depreciation factor of **$991**. Sec. 179 expensing was used for this year's purchases of books. Travel expenses are as follows: Lodging **$363**, Meals away from home **$357**, Tips for meals **$48**, Cleaning while away from home **$22**. Local transportation expenses are as follows: Parking **$11**, Tolls **$34**. The total year's reimbursement for professional and travel expenses was **$3,597** as shown on the payroll sheet.

Business auto mileage from his log book was **19,013** miles. Total miles driven for the year was **26,410** The church reimbursed mileage allowance of **54¢** a mile. Total reimbursement for mileage was **$10,267**. Actual expenses for the Honda amount to less than **54¢** per mile for reimbursement. The return showing non-reimbursed expenses shows the actual expenses for each auto on "Worksheet for Form 2106." Without reimbursement, vehicle #1 is computed by actual method as required (MACRS chosen in year of purchase), and vehicle #2 is computed by optional which is best. Details of their auto trade are shown on the "Auto Basis Worksheets."

Itemized deductions are as follows: Medical expenses were not greater than 10% of AGI. Additional State tax last spring of **$152**, Real Estate Tax is used again **$1,182**, personal property tax on the family auto of **$78**, personal property tax of **$456** on vehicle #2 must be deducted on Schedule A as taxes. He can not use auto interest of $639 on Schedule A (vehicle #1 $158 & vehicle #2 $481). Interest on home is used again **$8,081**. Personal interest of $753 can not be used. Contributions were to Mission Community Church **$5,308**, Central Bible College **$200**. Total tax return preparation fee **$165/205** less Schedule C portion - $12=**$153/193**, Nursing license **$135**, Uniforms, shoes, nylons and cost of cleaning them **$375**.

Due to the fact a minister is self-employed for social security purposes, we are able to use the business percentage of personal property tax & auto interest **$842** and the business portion of tax preparation fee **$63/87** as a reduction of S.S. base.

Study the completed forms on the following pages to see how the Snodgrass return is prepared.

Without Accountable Reimbursement Plan

Form 1040 (2016) H JAMES & MARY T SNODGRASS 483-12-0200 — Page 2

Tax and Credits

38	Amount from line 37 (adjusted gross income)	84,707
39a	Check: You were born before January 2, 1952 [ ]; Blind [ ]; Spouse was born before January 2, 1952 [ ]; Blind [ ]. Total boxes checked ▶ 39a	
b	If your spouse itemizes on a separate return or you were a dual-status alien, check here ▶ 39b	
40	Itemized deductions (from Schedule A) or your standard deduction (see left margin)	26,350
41	Subtract line 40 from line 38	58,357
42	Exemptions. If line 38 is $155,650 or less, multiply $4,050 by the number on line 6d. Otherwise, see instructions	20,250
43	Taxable income. Subtract line 42 from line 41. If line 42 is more than line 41, enter -0-	38,107
44	Tax (see instructions). Check if any from: a [ ] Form(s) 8814 b [ ] Form 4972 c [ ]	4,791
45	Alternative minimum tax (see instructions). Attach Form 6251	
46	Excess advance premium tax credit repayment. Attach Form 8962	
47	Add lines 44, 45, and 46	4,791
48	Foreign tax credit. Attach Form 1116 if required	
49	Credit for child and dependent care expenses. Attach Form 2441	
50	Education credits from Form 8863, line 19	
51	Retirement savings contributions credit. Attach Form 8880	
52	Child tax credit. Attach Schedule 8812, if required	2,000
53	Residential energy credit. Attach Form 5695	
54	Other credits from Form: a [ ] 3800 b [ ] 8801 c [ ]	
55	Add lines 48 through 54. These are your total credits	2,000
56	Subtract line 55 from line 47. If line 55 is more than line 47, enter -0-	2,791

Other Taxes

Line	Description	Amount
57	Self-employment tax. Attach Schedule SE	6,458
58	Unreported social security and Medicare tax from Form: a [ ] 4137 b [ ] 8919	
59	Additional tax on IRAs, other qualified retirement plans, etc. Attach Form 5329 if required	
60a	Household employment taxes from Schedule H	
60b	First-time homebuyer credit repayment. Attach Form 5405 if required	
61	Health care: individual responsibility (see instructions) Full-year coverage [X]	
62	Taxes from: a [ ] Form 8959 b [ ] Form 8960 c [ ] instructions, enter code(s)	
63	Add lines 56 through 62. This is your total tax	9,249

Payments

64	Federal income tax withheld from Forms W-2 and 1099	
65	2016 estimated tax payments and amount applied from 2015 return	
66a	Earned income credit (EIC)	
b	Nontaxable combat pay election 66b	
67	Additional child tax credit. Attach Schedule 8812	
68	American opportunity credit from Form 8863, line 8	
69	Net premium tax credit. Attach Form 8962	
70	Amount paid with request for extension to file	
71	Excess social security and tier 1 RRTA tax withheld	
72	Credit for federal tax on fuels. Attach Form 4136	
73	Credits from Form: a [ ] 2439 b [ ] Reserved c [ ] 8885 d [ ]	
74	Add lines 64, 65, 66a, and 67 through 73. These are your total payments	9,580

Refund

75	If line 74 is more than line 63, subtract line 63 from line 74. This is the amount you overpaid	331
76a	Amount of line 75 you want refunded to you. If Form 8888 is attached, check here ▶ [ ]	331
b	Routing number _____ ▶ c Type: [ ] Checking [ ] Savings	
d	Account number	
77	Amount of line 75 you want applied to your 2017 estimated tax ▶ 77	

Amount You Owe

78	Amount you owe. Subtract line 74 from line 63. For details on how to pay, see instructions	
79	Estimated tax penalty (see instructions)	

Third Party Designee: Do you want to allow another person to discuss this return with the IRS (see instructions)? [ ] Yes. Complete below. [X] No

Sign Here: Your occupation MINISTER. Spouse's occupation RN. Date 12-03-2016

Paid Preparer Use Only: Print/Type preparer's name Beverly J Worth — PTIN P00106320 — Firm's name ▶ Worth Financial Service — Firm's EIN ▶ 48-0733498 — Firm's address ▶ PO Box 242, Winona Lake, IN 46590 — Phone no. 574-269-2121

CLERGY

Form 1040 (2016)

Form 1040 — U.S. Individual Income Tax Return 2016

Department of the Treasury - Internal Revenue Service (99) OMB No. 1545-0074

For the year Jan. 1-Dec. 31, 2016, or other tax year beginning , 2016, ending , 20

Your first name and initial: H JAMES — Last name: SNODGRASS — Your social security number: 483-12-0200

If a joint return, spouse's first name and initial: MARY T — Last name: SNODGRASS — Spouse's social security number: 483-35-3200

Home address (number and street): 2309 E SMITH ST — Apt. no.

City, town or post office, state, and ZIP code: SOUTH BEND IN 46617

Presidential Election Campaign

Filing Status
2 [X] Married filing jointly (even if only one had income)

Exemptions
6a [X] Yourself
6b [X] Spouse

Dependents:

(1) First name	Last name	(2) Dependent's social security number	(3) Dependent's relationship to you	(4) Chk if child under age 17 qualifying for child tax credit
RUTH	SNODGRASS	483-13-0000	DAUGHTER	
THOMAS	SNODGRASS	483-14-0000	SON	[X]
SAMUEL	SNODGRASS	483-15-0000	SON	[X]

Boxes checked on 6a and 6b: 2
No. of children on 6c who lived with you: 3
Add numbers on lines above: 5

Income

7	Wages, salaries, tips, etc. Attach Form(s) W-2 · · · Excess Allowance · · · Rev Snodgrass -1,518 $35,529 / Excess Parsonage Mrs. Snodgrass $50,278 $1,518	87,325
8a	Taxable interest. Attach Schedule B if required	
8b	Tax-exempt interest. Do not include on line 8a	
9a	Ordinary dividends. Attach Schedule B if required	
9b	Qualified dividends	
10	Taxable refunds, credits, or offsets of state and local income taxes	
11	Alimony received	
12	Business income or (loss). Attach Schedule C or C-EZ	611
13	Capital gain or (loss). Attach Schedule D if required. If not required, check here ▶	
14	Other gains or (losses). Attach Form 4797	
15a	IRA distributions 15a b Taxable amount	
16a	Pensions and annuities 16a b Taxable amount	
17	Rental real estate, royalties, partnerships, S corporations, trusts, etc. Attach Schedule E	
18	Farm income or (loss). Attach Schedule F	
19	Unemployment compensation	
20a	Social security benefits 20a b Taxable amount	
21	Other income	
22	Combine the amounts in the far right column for lines 7 through 21. This is your total income ▶	87,936

Adjusted Gross Income

23	Educator expenses	
24	Certain business expenses of reservists, performing artists, and fee-basis government officials. Attach Form 2106 or 2106-EZ	
25	Health savings account deduction. Attach Form 8889	
26	Moving expenses. Attach Form 3903	
27	Deductible part of self-employment tax. Attach Schedule SE	3,229
28	Self-employed SEP, SIMPLE, and qualified plans	
29	Self-employed health insurance deduction	
30	Penalty on early withdrawal of savings	
31a	Alimony paid b Recipient's SSN ▶	
32	IRA deduction	
33	Student loan interest deduction	
34	Tuition and fees. Attach Form 8917	
35	Domestic production activities deduction. Attach Form 8903	
36	Add lines 23 through 35	3,229
37	Subtract line 36 from line 22. This is your adjusted gross income ▶	84,707

For Disclosure, Privacy Act, and Paperwork Reduction Act Notice, see separate instructions.

Form 1040 (2016)

EEA

Without Accountable Reimbursement Plan

SCHEDULE C (Form 1040) — Profit or Loss From Business
(Sole Proprietorship)

Department of the Treasury Internal Revenue Service (99)

▶ Information about Schedule C and its separate instructions is at *www.irs.gov/schedulec*.
▶ Attach to Form 1040, 1040NR, or 1041; partnerships generally must file Form 1065.

OMB No. 1545-0074 — 2016 — Attachment Sequence No. 09

Name of proprietor: H JAMES SNODGRASS — Social security number (SSN): 483-12-0200

A Principal business or profession: HONORARIUMS
B Enter code from instructions ▶ 813000
C Business name. If no separate business name, leave blank.
E Business address: 2309 E SMITH ST — City: SOUTH BEND, IN 46617
F Accounting method: (1) ☒ Cash (2) ☐ Accrual (3) ☐ Other
G Did you "materially participate"... ☒ Yes ☐ No
I Did you make any payments... ☐ Yes ☒ No
J If "Yes," did you or will you file required Forms 1099? ☐ Yes ☐ No

Part I — Income
1 Gross receipts or sales	690
2 Returns and allowances	0
3 Subtract line 2 from line 1	690
5 Gross profit	690
7 Gross income	690

Part II — Expenses
22 Supplies	114
27a Other expenses	12
28 Total expenses	79
31 Net profit or (loss) — SEE CLERGY ATTACHMENT	611

For Paperwork Reduction Act Notice, see the separate instructions.   Schedule C (Form 1040) 2016

SCHEDULE A (Form 1040) — Itemized Deductions

Department of the Treasury Internal Revenue Service (99)

▶ Information about Schedule A and its separate instructions is at *www.irs.gov/schedulea*.
▶ Attach to Form 1040.

OMB No. 1545-0074 — 2016 — Attachment Sequence No. 07

Name(s) shown on Form 1040: H JAMES & MARY T SNODGRASS — Your social security number: 483-12-0200

Medical and Dental Expenses
Caution: Do not include expenses reimbursed or paid by others.

Taxes You Paid
5 State and local income taxes (☒ a)	3,604
6 Real estate taxes	1,182
7 Personal property taxes	534
9 Add lines 5 through 8	5,320

Interest You Paid
10 Home mortgage interest and points	8,081
15 Add lines 10 through 14	8,081

Gifts to Charity
16 Gifts by cash or check	5,508
19 Add lines 16 through 18	5,508

Job Expenses and Certain Miscellaneous Deductions
21 Unreimbursed employee expenses ▶ FORM 2106-EZ	8,432
22 Tax preparation fees	193
23 Other expenses ▶ NURSING EXPENSES 510	510
24 Add lines 21 through 23	9,135
25 Enter amount from Form 1040, line 38	84,707
26 Multiply line 25 by 2% (0.02)	1,694
27 Subtract line 26 from line 24	7,441

Total Itemized Deductions
29	26,350

29 Is Form 1040, line 38, over $155,650? ☒ No.

For Paperwork Reduction Act Notice, see Form 1040 instructions.   Schedule A (Form 1040) 2016

Without Accountable Reimbursement Plan

Form 2106-EZ — Unreimbursed Employee Business Expenses

Form **2106-EZ**	OMB No. 1545-0074 **2016**
Department of the Treasury Internal Revenue Service (99)	Attachment Sequence No. **129A**

▶ Attach to Form 1040 or Form 1040NR.
▶ Information about Form 2106-EZ and its instructions is available at *www.irs.gov/form2106ez*.

Your name	Occupation in which you incurred expenses	Social security number
H JAMES SNODGRASS	MINISTER	483-12-0200

You Can Use This Form Only if All of the Following Apply.

• You are an employee deducting ordinary and necessary expenses attributable to your job. An ordinary expense is one that is common and accepted in your field of trade, business, or profession. A necessary expense is one that is helpful and appropriate for your business. An expense doesn't have to be required to be considered necessary.

• You **don't** get reimbursed by your employer for any expenses (amounts your employer included in box 1 of your Form W-2 aren't considered reimbursements for this purpose).

• If you are claiming vehicle expense, you are using the standard mileage rate for 2016.

Caution: *You can use the standard mileage rate for 2016 only if: (a) you owned the vehicle and used the standard mileage rate for the first year you placed the vehicle in service, or (b) you leased the vehicle and used the standard mileage rate for the portion of the lease period after 1997.*

Part I — Figure Your Expenses

1	Complete Part II. Multiply line 8a by 54 cents (0.54). Enter the result here	1 10,501
2	Parking fees, tolls, and transportation, including train, bus, etc., that **didn't** involve overnight travel or commuting to and from work	2 45
3	Travel expense while away from home overnight, including lodging, airplane, car rental, etc. **Don't** include meals and entertainment	3 385
4	Business expenses not included on lines 1 through 3. **Don't** include meals and entertainment	4 1,881
5	Meals and entertainment expenses: $ ___1,286___ x 50% (.50). (Employees subject to Department of Transportation (DOT) hours of service limits: Multiply meal expenses incurred while away from home on business by 80% (.80) instead of 50%. For details, see instructions.)	5 643
6	**Total expenses.** Add lines 1 through 5. Enter here and on **Schedule A (Form 1040), line 21** (or on **Schedule A (Form 1040NR), line 7**). (Armed Forces reservists, fee-basis state or local government officials, qualified performing artists, and individuals with disabilities: See the instructions for special rules on where to enter this amount.)	6 SEE CLERGY ATTACHMENT 8,432

Part II — Information on Your Vehicle. Complete this part only if you are claiming vehicle expense on line 1.

7	When did you place your vehicle in service for business use? (month, day, year) ▶	
8	Of the total number of miles you drove your vehicle during 2016, enter the number of miles you used your vehicle for:	
a	Business _____ b Commuting (see instructions) _____ c Other _____	
9	Was your vehicle available for personal use during off-duty hours?	☒ Yes ☐ No
10	Do you (or your spouse) have another vehicle available for personal use?	☒ Yes ☐ No
11a	Do you have evidence to support your deduction?	☒ Yes ☐ No
b	If "Yes," is the evidence written?	☒ Yes ☐ No

For Paperwork Reduction Act Notice, see your tax return instructions.   Form **2106-EZ** (2016)

Schedule SE (Form 1040) — Self-Employment Tax

SCHEDULE SE (Form 1040)		OMB No. 1545-0074 **2016**
Department of the Treasury Internal Revenue Service (99)	▶ Information about Schedule SE and its separate instructions is at *www.irs.gov/scheduylese*. ▶ Attach to Form 1040 or Form 1040NR.	Attachment Sequence No. **17**

Name of person with **self-employment** income (as shown on Form 1040 or Form 1040NR)	Social security number of person with **self-employment** income ▶
H JAMES SNODGRASS	483-12-0200

Before you begin: To determine if you must file Schedule SE, see the instructions.

May I Use Short Schedule SE or Must I Use Long Schedule SE?

Note. Use this flowchart *only* if you must file Schedule SE. If unsure, see *Who Must File Schedule SE* in the instructions.

Did you receive wages or tips in 2016?

Are you a minister, member of a religious order, or Christian Science practitioner who received IRS approval **not** to be taxed on earnings from these sources, **but** you owe self-employment tax on other earnings? — No / Yes

Are you using one of the optional methods to figure your net earnings (see instructions)? — No / Yes

Did you receive church employee income (see instructions) reported on Form W-2 of $108.28 or more? — No / Yes

You may use Short Schedule SE below

Was the total of your wages and tips subject to social security or railroad retirement (tier 1) tax **plus** your net earnings from self-employment more than $118,500? — Yes / No

Did you receive tips subject to social security or Medicare tax that you **didn't** report to your employer? — No / Yes

Did you report any wages on Form 8919, Uncollected Social Security and Medicare Tax on Wages? — No / Yes

You must use Long Schedule SE on page 2

Section A – Short Schedule SE. Caution. Read above to see if you can use Short Schedule SE.

1a	Net farm profit or (loss) from Schedule F, line 34, and farm partnerships, Schedule K-1 (Form 1065), box 14, code A	1a
b	If you received social security retirement or disability benefits, enter the amount of Conservation Reserve Program payments included on Schedule F, line 4b, or listed on Schedule K-1 (Form 1065), box 20, code Z	1b ( )
2	Net profit or (loss) from Schedule C, line 31; Schedule C-EZ, line 3; Schedule K-1 (Form 1065), box 14, code A (other than farming); and Schedule K-1 (Form 1065-B), box 9, code J1. Ministers and members of religious orders, see instructions for types of income to report on this line. See instructions for other income SEE CLERGY ATTACHMENT	2 45,709
3	Combine lines 1a, 1b, and 2	3 45,709
4	Multiply line 3 by 92.35% (0.9235). If less than $400, you do not owe self-employment tax; **don't** file this schedule unless you have an amount on line 1b **Note.** If line 4 is less than $400 due to Conservation Reserve Program payments on line 1b, see instructions.	4 42,212
5	**Self-employment tax.** If the amount on line 4 is: • $118,500 or less, multiply line 4 by 15.3% (0.153). Enter the result here and on **Form 1040, line 57,** or **Form 1040NR, line 55** • More than $118,500, multiply line 4 by 2.9% (0.029). Then, add $14,694 to the result. Enter the total here and on **Form 1040, line 57,** or **Form 1040NR, line 55**	5 6,458
6	**Deduction for one-half of self-employment tax.** Multiply line 5 by 50% (0.50). Enter the result here and on **Form 1040, line 27,** or **Form 1040NR, line 27**	6 3,229

$45,098 from "Worksheet to be Used with Form 2106" + $611 Sch C

For Paperwork Reduction Act Notice, see your tax return instructions.   Schedule SE (Form 1040) 2016

Without Accountable Reimbursement Plan

WORKSHEET TO BE USED WITH FORM 2106

	Year **2016**

Name **H. James Snodgrass**	Social Security Number **483 12 0000**	Filed Form 4361? Yes ☐ No ☑

Part A - Computation of Business Expenses ● *Use this section in conjunction with Form 2106 (or 2106-EZ) or to figure your net social security base.*

Auto Expense	Vehicle 1	Vehicle 2
1. Total Miles Driven	5,029	19,581
2. Total Business Miles	4,085	14,928
3. % of Business Use *(Line 1/Line 2)*	81.22 %	76.24 %
4. Lease Payments		
5. Inclusion Amount		
6. Subtract Line 5 from Line 4		
7. Gas, Oil, Lubrication	598	1,682
8. Repairs	1,200	242
9. Tires & Batteries	84	
10. Insurance & Auto Club	161	389
11. Miscellaneous		13
12. Washing & Polishing	24	120
13. License *(Registration Only)*		
14. Add Lines 6 through 13	2,067	2,446
15. Multiply Line 14 by Line 3	1,679	1,865
16. Depreciation	761	2,409
17. Total Actual Exp (Line 15 + 16)	2,440	4,274
18. Optional Method *(Line 2 x Standard Mileage Rate)*		8,061
19. Interest	158	481
20. Personal Property Tax		456
21. Line 19 + Line 20	158	937
22. Line 21 x Line 3 *(To Line 6 of Social Security Base Computation)*	128	714

Local Travel Expense	Amount
23. Parking	11
24. Tolls	34
25. Fares	
26. Total	45

Enter on Form 2106-EZ, Part II, Ln2 or Form 2106, Part I Ln 2

Overnight Travel Exp.	Amount
27. Auto Rental, Taxi	
28. Fares (air, train, bus)	
29. Parking & Tolls	
30. Laundry & Cleaning	22
31. Lodging	363
32. Telephone, Postage, Fax, etc.	
33. Tips other than meals	
34. Total	385

Enter on Form 2106-EZ, Part II, Ln 3 or Form 2106, Part I Ln 3

Meals & Entertainment	Amount
35. Meals Away Overnight ☑ Actual ☐ Per Diem	357
36. Entertainment Meals	881
37. Entertainment, Other	
38. Tips for Meals	48
39. Total	1,286

Enter on Form 2106-EZ, Part II, Ln 5 or Form 2106, Part I Ln 5

Professional Expense	Amount
40. Business-In-Home	
41. Education Expense	345
42. Equipment Depreciation	991
43. Office Supplies & Postage	86
44. Religious Materials	327
45. Seminars & Dues	
46. Subscriptions & Paperbacks	132
47. Business Telephone & Internet Use	
48. Gifts	
49. Other	
50. Total	1,881

Enter on Form 2106-EZ, Part II, Ln 4 or Form 2106, Part I Ln 4

Unreimbursed Expenses	Amount
51. Auto Expense (Ln 17 or Ln 18)	10,501
52. Local Travel (Ln 26)	45
53. Overnight Travel (Ln 34)	385
54. Professional Expense (Ln 50)	1,881
55. Total of Lines 51 through 54	12,812
56. Reimbursement for Auto, Travel, & Prof.	(0)
57. Unreimbursed Auto Travel & Prof (Ln 55-Ln 56)	12,812
58. Meals & Entertainment (Ln 39)	1,286
59. Reimbursement for M & E	(0)
60. Unreimbursed M & E (Ln 58 - Ln 59)	1,286
61. Deductible M&E (½ of Ln 60)	643
62. Total Unreimbursed Exp (Ln 57+Ln 61)	13,455

Part B - Unreimbursed Expense Allocation (Sec. 265)
Use if Filing Form 2106 or Sch. C or C-EZ and claiming expense deductions

	A. Taxable Compensation	B. Total Compensation
1. Wages from W-2	35,529	35,529
2. Unused Parsonage Allowance	1,518	
3. Parsonage Allowance Designated		24,000
4. FRV of Parsonage Provided		
5. Gross Income / Sch C or C-EZ	690	690
6. Recapture of Auto Depreciation		
7. Total for Columns A & B	37,737	60,219
8. Inclusion Percentage *(Ln 7 Col. A Divided by Col. B)*		0.63 %

Employee Business Expenses	Amount
9. Expense from Form 2106-EZ, Ln 6 or Form 2106, Ln 10	13,455
10. Inclusion % from Ln 8	0.63 %
11. Deductible Expenses to Sch A, Ln 20 (Ln 9 x Ln 10)	8,432
12. Expenses Disallowed *(Ln 9 - Ln 11)*	5,023

Sch C or Sch C-EZ	Amount
13. Total Expense from Sch C or C-EZ	126
14. Inclusion % from Ln 8	0.63 %
15. Deductible Expense (Ln 13 x Ln 14)	79
16. Expenses Disallowed (Ln 13 - Ln 15)	47

Part C - Computation of Social Security Base
If exempt, omit

	Amount
1. Salary from W-2	35,529
2. Value of Parsonage Provided	
3. Parsonage Allowance (Part D, Ln 16)	24,000
4. Recapture of Auto Depreciation	
5. Less Business Portion of Tax Prep	(87)
6. Less Business % of Auto Int & Tax (Part A, Ln 22)	(842)
7. Less Disallowed Exp on Sch C (Part B, Ln 16)	(47)
8. Less Unreimbursed Bus Exp (Form 2106 or Part A, Ln 62)	(13,455)
9. Total *(Enter on Sch SE)*	45,098

Part D - Computation of Parsonage Allowance
If you own your home, use both Columns A & B. Otherwise, use Column B only.

	First Home		Second Home	
Value of Parsonage Provided by Church	$		$	
FMV of Home Owned	$ 150,000		$	
	Column A FRV Computation	Column B Expenses Paid by Minister	Column A FRV Computation	Column B Expenses Paid by Minister
1. Fair Rental Value of Home Owned	18,000			
2. Fair Rental Value of Furnishings	5,400			
3. Rent Paid				
4. Closing Costs / Downpayment				
5. Principal Payments		1,835		
6. Real Estate Taxes		1,182		
7. Mortgage Interest		8,081		
8. Insurance		840		
9. Repairs & Upkeep		3,292		
10. Furniture, Appliances, etc.		2,409		
11. Decorator Items	463	463		
12. Utilities	3,738	3,738		
13. Miscellaneous Supplies	642	642		
14. Total	28,243	22,482		
15. Lesser of Line 14, Column A (if applicable) or Column B		22,482		
16. Amount Designated Pension ☐ *(Pension not subject to Self-Employment tax)*		24,000	Pension ☐	
17. If Line 16 is greater than Ln 15, enter the difference here and as income on Form 1040, Line 7; or If amount designated is included in error on W-2, obtain a corrected Form W-2C		1,518		

Without Accountable Reimbursement Plan

Form 8824 — Like-Kind Exchanges (and section 1043 conflict-of-interest sales)

Form 8824
Department of the Treasury
Internal Revenue Service
▶ Information about Form 8824 and its separate instructions is at www.irs.gov/form8824.
▶ Attach to your tax return.

OMB No. 1545-1190
2016
Attachment Sequence No. 109

Name(s) shown on tax return
H JAMES & MARY T SNODGRASS

Identifying number
483-12-0200

Part I — Information on the Like-Kind Exchange

Note: If the property described on line 1 or line 2 is real or personal property located outside the United States, indicate the country.

1 Description of like-kind property given up:
BUICK LASBRE

2 Description of like-kind property received:
HONDA ACCORD

3 Date like-kind property given up was originally acquired (month, day, year)	3	01-06-2013
4 Date you actually transferred your property to other party (month, day, year)	4	03-10-2016
5 Date like-kind property you received was identified by written notice to another party (month, day, year). See instructions for 45-day written identification requirement	5	03-10-2016
6 Date you actually received the like-kind property from other party (month, day, year). See instructions	6	03-10-2016

7 Was the exchange of the property given up or received made with a related party, either directly or indirectly (such as through an intermediary)? See instructions. If "Yes," complete Part II. If "No," go to Part III ☐ Yes ☒ No

Note: Do not file this form if a related party sold property into the exchange, directly or indirectly (such as through an intermediary); that property became your replacement property; and none of the exceptions in line 11 applies to the exchange. Instead, report on this disposition of the property as if the exchange had been a sale. If one of the exceptions on line 11 applies to the exchange, complete Part II.

Part II — Related Party Exchange Information

8 Name of related party | Relationship to you | Related party's identifying number

Address (no., street, and apt., room, or suite no., city or town, state, and ZIP code)

9 During this tax year (and before the date that is 2 years after the last transfer of property that was part of the exchange), did the related party sell or dispose of any part of the like-kind property received from you (or an intermediary) in the exchange? ☐ Yes ☐ No

10 During this tax year (and before the date that is 2 years after the last transfer of property that was part of the exchange), did you sell or dispose of any part of the like-kind property you received? ☐ Yes ☐ No

If both lines 9 and 10 are "No" and this is the year of the exchange, go to Part III. If both lines 9 and 10 are "No" and this is not the year of the exchange, stop here. If either line 9 or line 10 is "Yes," complete Part III and report on this year's tax return the deferred gain or (loss) from line 24 unless one of the exceptions on line 11 applies.

11 If one of the exceptions below applies to the disposition, check the applicable box.
a ☐ The disposition was after the death of either of the related parties.
b ☐ The disposition was an involuntary conversion, and the threat of conversion occurred after the exchange.
c ☐ You can establish to the satisfaction of the IRS that neither the exchange nor the disposition had tax avoidance as one of its principal purposes. If this box is checked, attach an explanation. See instructions.

For Paperwork Reduction Act Notice, see the instructions.

Form 8824 (2016)

Form 8824 (2016)
Page 2

Name(s) shown on tax return. Do not enter name and social security number if shown on page 1.
H JAMES & MARY T SNODGRASS

Your social security number
483-12-0200

Part III — Realized Gain or (Loss), Recognized Gain, and Basis of Like-Kind Property Received

Caution: If you transferred and received (a) more than one group of like-kind properties or (b) cash or other (not like-kind) property, see Reporting of multi-asset exchanges in the instructions.

Note: Complete lines 12 through 14 only if you gave up property that was not like-kind. Otherwise, go to line 15.

12 Fair market value (FMV) of other property given up	12	
13 Adjusted basis of other property given up	13	
14 Gain or (loss) recognized on other property given up. Subtract line 13 from line 12. Report the gain or (loss) in the same manner as if the exchange had been a sale	14	

Caution: If the property given up was used previously or partly as a home, see Property used as home in the instructions.

15 Cash received, FMV of other property received, plus net liabilities assumed by other party, reduced (but not below zero) by any exchange expenses you incurred. See instructions	15	
16 FMV of like-kind property you received **Auto Basis Worksheet - Honda Line F**	16	21,901
17 Add lines 15 and 16	17	21,901
18 Adjusted basis of like-kind property you gave up, net amounts paid to other party, plus any exchange expenses not used on line 15. See instructions **Auto Basis Worksheet - Honda Line G**	18	24,799
19 Realized gain or (loss). Subtract line 18 from line 17	19	(2,898)
20 Enter the smaller of line 15 or line 19, but not less than zero	20	
21 Ordinary income under recapture rules. Enter here and on Form 4797, line 16. See instructions	21	
22 Subtract line 21 from line 20. If zero or less, enter -0-. If more than zero, enter here and on Schedule D or Form 4797, unless the installment method applies. See instructions	22	
23 Recognized gain. Add lines 21 and 22	23	
24 Deferred gain or (loss). Subtract line 23 from line 19. If a related party exchange, see instructions	24	(2,898)
25 Basis of like-kind property received. Subtract line 15 from the sum of lines 18 and 23	25	24,799

Part IV — Deferral of Gain From Section 1043 Conflict-of-Interest Sales

Note: This part is to be used only by officers or employees of the executive branch of the Federal Government or judicial officers of the Federal Government (including certain spouses, minor or dependent children, and trustees as described in section 1043) for reporting nonrecognition of gain under section 1043 on the sale of property to comply with the conflict-of-interest requirements. This part can be used only if the cost of the replacement property is more than the basis of the divested property.

26 Enter the number from the upper right corner of your certificate of divestiture. (Do not attach a copy of your certificate. Keep the certificate with your records.) ▶

27 Description of divested property ▶

28 Description of replacement property ▶

29 Date divested property was sold (month, day, year)	29	
30 Sales price of divested property. See instructions	30	
31 Basis of divested property	31	
32 Realized gain. Subtract line 31 from line 30	32	
33 Cost of replacement property purchased within 60 days after date of sale	33	
34 Subtract line 33 from line 30. If zero or less, enter -0-	34	
35 Ordinary income under recapture rules. Enter here and on Form 4797, line 10. See instructions	35	
36 Subtract line 35 from line 34. If zero or less, enter -0-. If more than zero, enter here and on Schedule D or Form 4797. See instructions	36	
37 Deferred gain. Subtract the sum of lines 35 and 36 from line 32	37	
38 Basis of replacement property. Subtract line 37 from line 33	38	

EEA

Form 8824 (2016)

Without Accountable Reimbursement Plan

W 12/16

STATEMENT OF DEPRECIATION AND COST RECOVERY

Attach to Schedule or Form__________

Description of Property	N or U	Date Acquired	Cost or Other Basis	Bus %	Business Basis	Sec 179 Exp.	Basis Before Bonus Depreciation Allowance	50%/100% Bonus Depr. Allowance	Adjusted Basis	Prior Depr.	Class Life	Method Used	Life or Rec'y Period	Year 2016	%	Year 20__	%	Year 20__	%
Total Amount of Sec. 179 Expensing, 50%or 100% Bonus Depreciation Claimed Each Year														548					
Library		01/01/12	533	100%	533				533	366	7	DDB½		48					
Library		01/01/13	400	100%	400				400	225	7	DDB½		50					
Library		01/01/14	366	100	366				366	142	7	DDB½		64					
Equipment		08/11/14	538	100%	538				538	209	7	DDB½		94					
Library		01/01/15	496	100%	496				496	71	7	DDB½		121					
Library		01/01/16	548	100%	548			548	0	0	7	DDB½		0					
Fax Machine		07/17/16	329	100%	329				329	0	5	DDB½		66					
		TOTAL											TOTAL	991					

Note: Land cannot be depreciated. Enter Land value on separate line in *"Cost or Other Basis"* column only.

Form **4562**

Department of the Treasury
Internal Revenue Service (99)

Depreciation and Amortization
(Including Information on Listed Property)

▶ Attach to your tax return.

▶ **Information about Form 4562 and its separate instructions is at *www.irs.gov/form4562*.**

OMB No. 1545-0172

2016

Attachment Sequence No. **179**

Name(s) shown on return	Business or activity to which this form relates	Identifying number
H JAMES & MARY T SNODGRASS	Form 2106 - 1	483-12-0200

Part I **Election To Expense Certain Property Under Section 179**

Note: If you have any listed property, complete Part V before you complete Part I.

1	Maximum amount (see instructions)	1	500,000
2	Total cost of section 179 property placed in service (see instructions)	2	877
3	Threshold cost of section 179 property before reduction in limitation (see instructions)	3	2,010,000
4	Reduction in limitation. Subtract line 3 from line 2. If zero or less, enter -0-	4	0
5	Dollar limitation for tax year. Subtract line 4 from line 1. If zero or less, enter -0-. If married filing separately, see instructions	5	500,000

6	(a) Description of property	(b) Cost (business use only)	(c) Elected cost
	LIBRARY	548	548

7	Listed property. Enter the amount from line 29	7	
8	Total elected cost of section 179 property. Add amounts in column (c), lines 6 and 7	8	548
9	Tentative deduction. Enter the **smaller** of line 5 or line 8	9	548
10	Carryover of disallowed deduction from line 13 of your 2015 Form 4562	10	
11	Business income limitation. Enter the smaller of business income (not less than zero) or line 5 (see instructions)	11	86,371
12	Section 179 expense deduction. Add lines 9 and 10, but don't enter more than line 11	12	548
13	Carryover of disallowed deduction to 2017. Add lines 9 and 10, less line 12 ▶	13	

Note: Don't use Part II or Part III below for listed property. Instead, use Part V.

Part II **Special Depreciation Allowance and Other Depreciation** (**Don't** include listed property.) (See instructions.)

14	Special depreciation allowance for qualified property (other than listed property) placed in service during the tax year (see instructions)	14	0
15	Property subject to section 168(f)(1) election	15	
16	Other depreciation (including ACRS)	16	

Part III **MACRS Depreciation** (**Don't** include listed property.) (See instructions.)

Section A

17	MACRS deductions for assets placed in service in tax years beginning before 2016	17	377
18	If you are electing to group any assets placed in service during the tax year into one or more general asset accounts, check here ▶ ☐		

Section B - Assets Placed in Service During 2016 Tax Year Using the General Depreciation System

(a) Classification of property	(b) Month and year placed in service	(c) Basis for depreciation (business/investment use only-see instructions)	(d) Recovery period	(e) Convention	(f) Method	(g) Depreciation deduction
19a 3-year property						
b 5-year property		329	5	HY	200 DB	66
c 7-year property						
d 10-year property						
e 15-year property						
f 20-year property						
g 25-year property			25 yrs.		S/L	
h Residential rental property			27.5 yrs.	MM	S/L	
			27.5 yrs.	MM	S/L	
i Nonresidential real property			39 yrs.	MM	S/L	
				MM	S/L	

Section C - Assets Placed in Service During 2016 Tax Year Using the Alternative Depreciation System

(a)	(b)	(c)	(d)	(e)	(f)	(g)
20a Class life					S/L	
b 12-year			12 yrs.		S/L	
c 40-year			40 yrs.	MM	S/L	

Part IV **Summary** (See instructions.)

21	Listed property. Enter amount from line 28	21	
22	**Total.** Add amounts from line 12, lines 14 through 17, lines 19 and 20 in column (g), and line 21. Enter here and on the appropriate lines of your return. Partnerships and S corporations - see instructions	22	991
23	For assets shown above and placed in service during the current year, enter the portion of the basis attributable to section 263A costs	23	

For Paperwork Reduction Act Notice, see separate instructions. Form **4562** (2016)

Without Accountable Reimbursement Plan

W 12/16

WORKSHEET TO COMPUTE AUTO BASIS

DESCRIPTION OF AUTO	
DATE ACQUIRED	01/06/2013
YEAR	2013
MAKE	Buick LaSabre
	☒ NEW OR ☐ USED *(Check one)*

FORMULA FOR COMPUTING GAIN OR LOSS WHEN USE IS PART BUSINESS AND PART PERSONAL:

1. Odometer reading when traded *(old car)* .... 86,206 Miles
2. Odometer reading when acquired *(old car)* .... 80 Miles
3. Total miles driven while owned *(line 1 less line 2)* .... 86,216 Miles
4. Business miles driven while owned *(line D)* .... 64,780 Miles
5. Average business % while owned *(line 4 divided by line 3)* .... .7522 %
6. Purchase price of old car *(list price)* .... $ 18,650
7. Trade-in allowance towards new car or Sales price .... $(7,000)
8. **Difference** *(line 6 less line 7)* .... $(11,650)
9. Business portion *(line 8 times line 5)* .... $ 8,763
10. Gain or loss on previous trade-in *(if none, enter zero)* .... $ 0
11. Balance of lines 9 and 10 *(subtract gain or add loss)* .... $ 8,763
12. Depreciation and expensing allowed or allowable *(use worksheet below)* .... $ 9,717
13. Gain or loss on business portion .... $ 954 ☒ Gain or ☐ Loss *(Check one)*
    (Gain when line 12 is greater than line 11)
    (Loss when line 11 is greater than line 12)
14. Purchase price of new car .... $ 24,300 + $ 1,450 = $ 25,790
       List price   Sales Tax   Total

A. Odometer reading end of year ....
B. Odometer reading beginning of year ....
C. Total miles driven during year *(A minus B)* ....
D. Business miles from log ....
E. Business % *(D divided by C)* ....
F. Multiply line 14 by E ....
G. Basis for depreciation ....
   (Balance of line 13 and F, Subtract gain, Add loss)

	2013 1st Year	2014 2nd Year	2015 3rd Year	2016 4th Year	5th Year	6th Year
A.	23,700	49,572	72,482	77,511		
B.	80	23,700	49,572	72,482		
C.	23,620	25,872	22,910	5,029		
D.	18,003	18,804	17,712	4,085		
E.	.7622 %	.7268 %	.7731 %	.8122 %	%	%
F.	$ 19,567	$ 18,744	$ 19,938	$ 20,946	$	$
G.	$ 18,703	$ 17,790	$ 18,984	$ 19,992	$	$

Year	Basis From (G)	(H) Expensing Sec. 179	(I) Adjusted Basis	(J) Bonus Depr.	(K) Adjusted Basis	(L) Class Life	(M) Method Used	(N) Life or RP	(O) Act Opt	(P) Depreciation Computed	(Q) Depreciation Limit	(R) Depreciation Allowed	(S) Depreciation Recapture
2013	18,703		18,703		18,703	5	DDB½	20.00	9,717	3,741	2,409	2,409	
2014	17,790		17,790		17,790	5	DDB½	32.00		5,693	3,707	3,707	
2015	18,984		18,984		18,984	5	DDB½	19.20	9,717	3,845	2,358	2,358	
2016	19,992		19,992		19,992	5	DDB½	11.52		1,152	761	761	

General Instructions:

Lines 1 through 11: Enter information from **previous auto's** worksheet if there has been a trade. Leave blank if newly acquired auto is the result of an outright purchase.

Line 12: Depreciation allowed or allowable is computed as follows:
- Actual Depreciation or optional "factor" *[see ¶ (P)]* .... $ 9,717
- Plus Expensing - Sec. 179 & Special Depreciation Allowance .... $
- Total to be taken to line 12 .... $ 9,717

Line 13: If auto is sold, take Gain or Loss to Form 4797. If trade, complete form 8824.

(H) An election in year of purchase, reduce basis each year by amount claimed in year of purchase. Since 6-18-84, luxury auto rules severely limit the use of Code Sec. 179 expensing for autos. Current 100% Bonus Depreciation basically puts Sec. 179 on hold for new property.

(I) Adjusted basis - Line G minus Column (H).

(J) 50% or 100% of Column (I) in the year of purchase, up to **$8,000** for autos. A 50% or 100% special bonus depreciation allowance deduction is available. To qualify, the auto must have been: (1) bought new; (2) bought after 12-31-2007 and before 1-1-20; (3) used more than 50% qualified business use. If taxpayer does not want to use the bonus depreciation, then an "election out" is required.

(K) Adjusted basis - Column (I) minus Column (J). (Basis used for depreciation computation.)

(L) When actual expenses are used, enter "5" for autos purchased after 12-31-86. When optional method is used, leave blank.

(M) Indicate MACRS percentage method by using "DDB".
Indicate conventions by "½" or "¼". If 40% of purchases are after 9-30, you must use mid-quarter convention.
Indicate Straight Line method by "SL".

(N) When MACRS percentage method is chosen, enter % used.
When MACRS straight line is chosen, enter 5 years.
When optional method was chosen in 1st year and you have switched to actual, enter the life chosen according to useful life.

(O) Indicate whether depreciation computation in Column (P) is actual method "A" or optional method "O". If optional, indicate whether, 21¢, 22¢, 23¢ or 24¢ rate is used. ("O-21" or "O-24").

(P) COMPUTE ACTUAL DEPRECIATION AS FOLLOWS:
MACRS percentage method: After 12-31-86 - Column (I) multiplied by:

Year	Mid-year	Mid-quarter (1st)	Mid-quarter (2nd)	Mid-quarter (3rd)	Mid-quarter (4th)
1	20%	35%	25%	15%	5%
2	32%	26%	30%	34%	38%
3	19.20%	15.60%	18%	20.40%	22.80%
4	11.52%	11.01%	11.37%	12.24%	13.68%
5	11.52%	11.01%	11.37%	11.30%	10.94%
6	5.76%	1.38%	4.26%	7.06%	9.58%

MACRS straight line method: Column (I) divided by 5 years. First year is either ½ year or mid-quarter convention.
When business use is 50% or less, only 5 year straight line can be computed for autos purchased since 6-18-84.
If Code Sec. 179 expensing has been elected, add Column (H) to actual depreciation.
Since 1-1-81, if you choose actual depreciation in year of purchase, you must continue to use actual as long as you own that car.

COMPUTE OPTIONAL DEPRECIATION FACTOR AS FOLLOWS:
2009 thru 2015 All business miles multiplied by 21¢ in 2009; 23¢ in 2010; 22¢ in 2011; 23¢ in 2012-2013; 22¢ in 2014; 24¢ in 2015.
2016 All business miles multiplied by **24¢**.

If optional method is elected in the 1st year, it carries with it the election to exclude the auto from the MACRS method of depreciation.
As "non-recovery" property, depreciation is required to be computed as straight line over the useful life in any year election is changed to actual method.
As "non-recovery" property, you may choose actual or optional method each year.

(Q) Luxury auto limitations for depreciation:

Date Auto Placed in Service

	01-01-09 thru 12-31-09	01-01-10 thru 12-31-10	01-01-11 thru 12-31-11	01-01-12 thru 12-31-12	01/01/13 thru 12/31/13	01/01/14 thru 12/31/14	01/01/15 thru 12/31/15	01/01/16 thru 12-31-16
Special Bonus Allowance	10,960		11,060	11,160	11,160	11,160	11,160	11,160
No Bonus Depreciation	2,960	3,060	3,060	3,160	3,160	3,160	3,160	3,160
2nd year	4,800	4,900	4,900	5,100	5,100	5,100	5,100	5,100
3rd year	2,850	2,950	2,950	3,050	3,050	3,050	3,050	3,050
4th-6th	1,775	1,775	1,775	1,875	1,875	1,875	1,875	1,875

Date Auto Placed in Service 01/06/12

# of Years Owned Year	Amount from Table	Business %	Depr. Limit	Year	Amount from Table	Business %	Depr. Limit
1st	$ 3,160	X .7622 % =	$ 2,409	4th	$ 1,875	X .8122 % =	$ 761
2nd	$ 5,100	X .7268 % =	$ 3,707	5th	$	X	$
3rd	$ 3,050	X .7731 % =	$ 2,358	6th	$	X % =	$

"Half-Year Convention: $761"

(R) Enter the smallest of Column (P) or (Q). In year of purchase, the smallest of Columns (H) + (J) + (P) or (Q). Also, enter this amount on Form 2106.

(S) Autos purchased after 6-18-84: Depreciation Recapture or "pay back" is to be computed if an auto was more than 50% business use in year of purchase, but drops below 50% business use in any future year when a method of accelerated depreciation was used. You must include in gross income the difference between depreciation and Code Section 179 expensing claimed and the amount of depreciation recomputed after the 5 year straight line method. You must continue using 5 year straight line even if business use rises back above 50%. (Bonus Depreciation does not have to be recaptured.)

When this happens, get another worksheet, figure the 5 year SL on it and use it for the rest of the auto's life. Employees enter the income on Form 1040, line 21; Ministers also include in computation for Social Security; Self employed taxpayers on Sch. C, line 6; Farmers on Sch. F, line 10.

Without Accountable Reimbursement Plan

(H) An election in year of purchase, reduce basis each year by amount claimed in year of purchase. Since 6-18-84, luxury auto rules severely limit the use of Code Sec. 179 expensing for autos. Current 100% Bonus Depreciation basically puts Sec. 179 on hold for new property.

(I) Adjusted basis - Line G minus Column (H).

(J) 50% or 100% of Column (I) in the year of purchase, up to **$8,000** for autos. A 50% or 100% special bonus depreciation allowance deduction is available. To qualify, the auto must have been: (1) bought new; (2) bought after 12-31-2007 and before 1-1-20; (3) used more than 50% qualified business use. If taxpayer does not want to use the bonus depreciation, then an "election out" is required.

(K) Adjusted basis - Column (I) minus Column (J). (Basis used for depreciation computation.)

(L) When actual expenses are used, enter "5" for autos purchased after 12-31-86. When optional method is used, leave blank.

(M) Indicate MACRS percentage method by using "DDB".
Indicate conventions by "½" or "¼". If 40% of purchases are after 9-30, you must use mid-quarter convention.
Indicate Straight Line method by "SL".

(N) When MACRS percentage method is chosen, enter % used.
When MACRS straight line is chosen, enter 5 years.

(O) Indicate whether depreciation computation in Column (P) is actual method "A" or optional method "O". If optional, indicate whether 21¢, 22¢, 23¢ or 24¢ rate is used. ("O-21" or "O-24").

(P) **COMPUTE ACTUAL DEPRECIATION AS FOLLOWS:**

MACRS percentage method: After 12-31-86 - Column (I) multiplied by:

Year	Mid-year	Mid-quarter (1st)	Mid-quarter (2nd)	Mid-quarter (3rd)	Mid-quarter (4th)
1	20%	35%	25%	15%	5%
2	32%	26%	30%	34%	38%
3	19.20%	15.60%	18%	20.40%	22.80%
4	11.52%	11.01%	11.37%	12.24%	13.68%
5	11.52%	11.01%	11.37%	11.30%	10.94%
6	5.76%	1.38%	4.26%	7.06%	9.58%

MACRS straight line method: Column (I) divided by 5 years. First year is either ½ year or mid-quarter convention.

When business use is 50% or less, only 5 year straight line can be computed for autos purchased since 6-18-84.

If Code Sec. 179 expensing has been elected, add Column (H) to actual depreciation.

Since 1-1-81, if you choose actual depreciation in year of purchase, you must continue to use actual as long as you own that car.

COMPUTE OPTIONAL DEPRECIATION FACTOR AS FOLLOWS:

2009 thru 2015 All business miles multiplied by 21¢ in 2009; 23¢ in 2010; 22¢ in 2011; 23¢ in 2012-2013; 22¢ in 2014; 24¢ in 2015.

2016 All business miles multiplied by **24¢**.

If optional method is elected in the 1st year, it carries with it the election to exclude the auto from the MACRS method of depreciation.

As "non-recovery" property, depreciation is required to be computed as straight line over the useful life in any year election is changed to actual method.

As "non-recovery" property, you may choose actual or optional method each year.

(Q) Luxury auto limitations for depreciation:

Date Auto Placed in Service

# of Years Owned	01-01-09 thru 12-31-09	01-01-10 thru 12-31-10	01-01-11 thru 12-31-11	01-01-12 thru 12-31-12	01-01-13 thru 12-31-13	01-01-14 thru 12-31-14	01-01-15 thru 12-31-15	01-01-16 thru 112-31-16
50% or 100% Bonus Depreciation	10,960	11,060	11,060	11,160	11,160	11,160	11,160	11,160
No Bonus Allowance	2,960	3,060	3,060	3,160	3,160	3,160	3,160	3,160
2nd year	4,800	4,900	4,900	5,100	5,100	5,100	5,100	5,100
3rd year	2,850	2,950	2,950	3,050	3,050	3,050	3,050	3,050
4th-6th	1,775	1,775	1,775	1,875	1,875	1,875	1,875	1,875

Date Auto Placed in Service 3 / 10 / 16			Date Auto Placed in Service 3 / 10 / 16		
Year	Amount from Table	Business %	Depr. Limit	Year	Amount from Table
1st $ 3,160	X .7624	% = $ 2,409	4th $	X	% = $
2nd $	X	% = $	5th $	X	% = $
3rd $	X	% = $	6th $	X	% = $

Year	Amount from Table	Business %	Depr. Limit
1st $ 3,160	X	%	= $
2nd $	X	%	= $
3rd $	X	%	= $

(R) Enter the smallest of Column (P) or (Q). In year of purchase, the smallest of Columns (H) + (J) + (P) or (Q). Also, enter this amount on Form 2106.

(S) Autos purchased after 6-18-84: Depreciation Recapture or "pay back" is to be computed if an auto was more than 50% business use in year of purchase, but drops below 50% business use in any future year when a method of accelerated depreciation was used. You must include in gross income the difference between depreciation and Code Section 179 expensing claimed and the amount of depreciation recomputed at the 5 year straight line method. You must continue using 5 year straight line even if business use rises back above 50%. (Bonus Depreciation does not have to be recaptured.)

When this happens, get another worksheet, figure the 5 year SL on it and use it for the rest of the auto's life. Employees enter the income on Form 1040, line 21; Ministers also include in computation for Social Security; Self employed taxpayers on Sch. C, line 6; Farmers on Sch. F, line 10.

W 12/16

WORKSHEET TO COMPUTE AUTO BASIS

FORMULA FOR COMPUTING GAIN OR LOSS WHEN USE IS PART BUSINESS AND PART PERSONAL:

		DESCRIPTION OF AUTO

1. Odometer reading when traded *(old car)*. . . . . 77,511 Miles

DATE ACQUIRED 03/10/2016

2. Odometer reading when acquired *(old car)*. . . . . 80 Miles

3. Total miles driven while owned *(line 1 less line 2)*. . . . . 77,431 Miles

YEAR 2016

4. Business miles driven while owned *(line D)*. . . . . 58,604 Miles

5. Average business % while owned *(line 4 divided by line 3)*. . . . . . .7569 %

MAKE Honda Accord

6. Purchase price of old car *(list price)*. . . . . $ 25,790

☐ NEW OR ☐ USED *(Check one)*

7. Trade-in allowance towards new car or Sales price. . . . . . $(8,500)

8. **Difference** *(line 6 less line 7)*. . . . . $ 17,290

9. Business portion *(line 8 times line 5)*. . . . . $ 13,087

x

10. Gain or loss on previous trade-in *(if none, enter zero)*. . . . . $ 954

11. Balance of lines 9 and 10 *(subtract gain or add loss)*. . . . . $ 12,133

12. Depreciation and expensing allowed or allowable *(use worksheet below)*. . . $ 9,235

13. Gain or loss on business portion. . . . . $ 2,888 ☐ Gain *or* ☐ Loss *(Check one)*
(Gain when line 12 is greater than line 11)
(Loss when line 11 is greater than line 12)

14. Purchase price of new car. . . . . $ 27,100 + $ 1,626 = $ 28,726
List price Sales Tax Total

	2016 1st Year	2nd Year	3rd Year	4th Year	5th Year	6th Year
A. Odometer reading end of year. . . .	19,601					
B. Odometer reading beginning of year. . .	20					
C. Total miles driven during year *(A minus B)*. . .	19,581					
D. Business miles from log. . .	14,928					
E. Business % *(D divided by C)*. . .	.7624 %	%	%	%	%	%
F. Multiply line 14 by E. . .	$ 21,901	$	$	$	$	$
G. Basis for depreciation. . . *(Balance of line 13 and F; Subtract gain, Add loss)*	$ 24,799	$	$	$	$	$

Year	Basis From (G)	(H) Expensing Sec. 179	(I) Adjusted Basis	(J) Bonus Depr.	(K) Adjusted Basis	(L) Class Life	(M) Method Used	(N) Life or RP	(O) Act Opt	(P) Depreciation Computed	(Q) Depreciation Limit	(R) Depreciation Allowed	(S) Depreciation Recapture
2016	24,799		24,799		24,799	5			OPT	3,583		3,583	
2016	24,799		24,799		24,799	5	SL½	10%	ACT	2,480	2,409	2,409	

General Instructions:

Lines 1 through 11: Enter information from previous auto's worksheet if there has been a trade. Leave blank if newly acquired auto is the result of an outright purchase.

Line 12: Depreciation allowed or allowable is computed as follows:

Actual Depreciation or optional "factor" [see ¶ (P)]. . . . . $ 9,235

Plus Expensing - Sec. 179 & Special Depreciation Allowance. . . . . $

Total to be taken to line 12 . . . . $ 9,235

Line 13: If auto is sold, take Gain or Loss to Form 4797. If trade, complete form 8824.

With Accountable Reimbursement Plan

Form 1040 (Page 1)

Form 1040 Department of the Treasury - Internal Revenue Service (99)
U.S. Individual Income Tax Return **2016** OMB No. 1545-0074 IRS Use Only-Do not write or staple in this space.

For the year Jan. 1-Dec. 31, 2016, or other tax year beginning , 2016, ending , 20

Your first name and initial: H JAMES — Last name: SNODGRASS
Your social security number: 483-12-0200

If a joint return, spouse's first name and initial: MARY T — Last name: SNODGRASS
Spouse's social security number: 483-35-3200

Home address (number and street): 2309 E SMITH ST — Apt. no.:

City, town or post office, state, and ZIP code: SOUTH BEND IN 46617

Make sure the SSN(s) above and on line 6c are correct.

Presidential Election Campaign — Check here if you, or your spouse if filing jointly, want $3 to go to this fund. Checking a box below will not change your tax or refund. You [ ] Spouse [ ]

Filing Status
1 [ ] Single
2 [X] Married filing jointly (even if only one had income)
3 [ ] Married filing separately. Enter spouse's SSN above and full name here.
4 [ ] Head of household (with qualifying person).
5 [ ] Qualifying widow(er) with dependent child

Exemptions
6a [X] Yourself. If someone can claim you as a dependent, do not check box 6a
6b [X] Spouse
Boxes checked on 6a and 6b: 2
c Dependents:

(1) First name	Last name	(2) social security number	(3) relationship to you	(4) ✓ if child under age 17 qualifying for child tax credit
RUTH	SNODGRASS	483-13-0000	DAUGHTER	
THOMAS	SNODGRASS	483-14-0000	SON	X
SAMUEL	SNODGRASS	483-15-0000	SON	X

No. of children on 6c who: lived with you 3; did not live with you due to divorce or separation

d Total number of exemptions claimed — Add numbers on lines above: 5

Income
7 Wages, salaries, tips, etc. Attach Form(s) W-2 ... **Excess Allowance** ..... 1,518 → 7 — 72,796
  - Rev Snodgrass.........$21,000
  - Mrs. Snodgrass.........$50,278
  - Excess Parsonage.......$1,518
8a Taxable interest. Attach Schedule B if required ... 8a
b Tax-exempt interest. Do not include on line 8a ... 8b
9a Ordinary dividends. Attach Schedule B if required ... 9a
b Qualified dividends ... 9b
10 Taxable refunds, credits, or offsets of state and local income taxes ... 10
11 Alimony received ... 11
12 Business income or (loss). Attach Schedule C or C-EZ ... 12 — 626
13 Capital gain or (loss). Attach Schedule D if required. If not required, check here ... 13
14 Other gains or (losses). Attach Form 4797 ... 14
15a IRA distributions ... 15a b Taxable amount ... 15b
16a Pensions and annuities ... 16a b Taxable amount ... 16b
17 Rental real estate, royalties, partnerships, S corporations, trusts, etc. Attach Schedule E ... 17
18 Farm income or (loss). Attach Schedule F ... 18
19 Unemployment compensation ... 19
20a Social security benefits ... 20a b Taxable amount ... 20b
21 Other income ... 21
22 Combine the amounts in the far right column for lines 7 through 21. This is your **total income** ... 22 — 73,422

Adjusted Gross Income
23 Educator expenses ... 23
24 Certain business expenses of reservists, performing artists, and fee-basis government officials. Attach Form 2106 or 2106-EZ ... 24
25 Health savings account deduction. Attach Form 8889 ... 25
26 Moving expenses. Attach Form 3903 ... 26
27 Deductible part of self-employment tax. Attach Schedule SE ... 27 — 3,155
28 Self-employed SEP, SIMPLE, and qualified plans ... 28
29 Self-employed health insurance deduction ... 29
30 Penalty on early withdrawal of savings ... 30
31a Alimony paid b Recipient's SSN ▶ ... 31a
32 IRA deduction ... 32
33 Student loan interest deduction ... 33
34 Tuition and fees. Attach Form 8917 ... 34
35 Domestic production activities deduction. Attach Form 8903 ... 35
36 Add lines 23 through 35 ... 36 — 3,155
37 Subtract line 36 from line 22. This is your **adjusted gross income** ... 37 — 70,267

For Disclosure, Privacy Act, and Paperwork Reduction Act Notice, see separate instructions. — Form **1040** (2016)

Form 1040 (Page 2)

Form 1040 (2016) H JAMES & MARY T SNODGRASS 483-12-0200 Page 2

Tax and Credits
38 Amount from line 37 (adjusted gross income) ... 38 — 70,267
39a Check if: [ ] You were born before January 2, 1952, [ ] Blind. [ ] Spouse was born before January 2, 1952, [ ] Blind. Total boxes checked ▶ 39a
b If your spouse itemizes on a separate return or you were a dual-status alien, check here ▶ 39b

Standard Deduction for—
- People who check any box on line 39a or 39b or who can be claimed as a dependent, see instructions.
- All others: Single or Married filing separately, $6,300; Married filing jointly or Qualifying widow(er), $12,600; Head of household, $9,300.

40 Itemized deductions (from Schedule A) or your standard deduction (see left margin) ... 40 — 18,909
41 Subtract line 40 from line 38 ... 41 — 51,358
42 Exemptions. If line 38 is $155,650 or less, multiply $4,050 by the number on line 6d. Otherwise, see instructions ... 42 — 20,250
43 Taxable income. Subtract line 42 from line 41. If line 42 is more than line 41, enter -0- ... 43 — 31,108
44 Tax (see instructions). Check if any from: a [ ] Form(s) 8814 b [ ] Form 4972 c [ ] ... 44 — 3,741
45 Alternative minimum tax (see instructions). Attach Form 6251 ... 45
46 Excess advance premium tax credit repayment. Attach Form 8962 ... 46
47 Add lines 44, 45, and 46 ... 47 — 3,741
48 Foreign tax credit. Attach Form 1116 if required ... 48
49 Credit for child and dependent care expenses. Attach Form 2441 ... 49
50 Education credits from Form 8863, line 19 ... 50
51 Retirement savings contributions credit. Attach Form 8880 ... 51
52 Child tax credit. Attach Schedule 8812, if required ... 52 — 2,000
53 Residential energy credit. Attach Form 5695 ... 53
54 Other credits from Form a [ ] 3800 b [ ] 8801 c [ ] ... 54
55 Add lines 48 through 54. These are your **total credits** ... 55 — 2,000
56 Subtract line 55 from line 47. If line 55 is more than line 47, enter -0- ... 56 — 1,741

Other Taxes
57 Self-employment tax. Attach Schedule SE ... 57 — 6,310
58 Unreported social security and Medicare tax from Form: a [ ] 4137 b [ ] 8919 ... 58
59 Additional tax on IRAs, other qualified retirement plans, etc. Attach Form 5329 if required ... 59
60a Household employment taxes from Schedule H ... 60a
60b First-time homebuyer credit repayment. Attach Form 5405 if required ... 60b
61 Health care: individual responsibility (see instructions) Full-year coverage [X] ... 61
62 Taxes from: a [ ] Form 8959 b [ ] Form 8960 c [ ] instructions; enter code(s) ... 62
63 Add lines 56 through 62. This is your **total tax** ... 63 — 8,051

Payments
64 Federal income tax withheld from Forms W-2 and 1099 ... 64 — 9,580
65 2016 estimated tax payments and amount applied from 2015 return ... 65
66a Earned income credit (EIC) ... 66a
b Nontaxable combat pay election ... 66b
67 Additional child tax credit. Attach Schedule 8812 ... 67
68 American opportunity credit from Form 8863, line 8 ... 68
69 Net premium tax credit. Attach Form 8962 ... 69
70 Amount paid with request for extension to file ... 70
71 Excess social security and tier 1 RRTA tax withheld ... 71
72 Credit for federal tax on fuels. Attach Form 4136 ... 72
73 Credits from Form: a [ ] 2439 b [ ] Reserved c [ ] 8885 d [ ] ... 73
74 Add lines 64, 65, 66a, and 67 through 73. These are your **total payments** ... 74 — 9,580

Refund
75 If line 74 is more than line 63, subtract line 63 from line 74. This is the amount you **overpaid** ... 75 — 1,529
76a Amount of line 75 you want **refunded to you**. If Form 8888 is attached, check here ▶ [ ] ... 76a — 1,529
b Routing number ... c Type: [ ] Checking [ ] Savings
d Account number
77 Amount of line 75 you want **applied to your 2017 estimated tax** ▶ 77

Amount You Owe
78 **Amount you owe.** Subtract line 74 from line 63. For details on how to pay, see instructions ▶ 78
79 Estimated tax penalty (see instructions) ... 79

Third Party Designee
Do you want to allow another person to discuss this return with the IRS (see instructions)? [X] Yes. Complete below. [ ] No
Designee's name ▶ Phone no. ▶ Personal identification number (PIN) ▶

Sign Here
Under penalties of perjury, I declare that I have examined this return and accompanying schedules and statements, and to the best of my knowledge and belief, they are true, correct, and complete. Declaration of preparer (other than taxpayer) is based on all information of which preparer has any knowledge.
Your signature — Date — Your occupation: MINISTER — Daytime phone number
Spouse's signature. If a joint return, both must sign. — Date — Spouse's occupation: RN — Identity Protection PIN (see inst.)

Paid Preparer Use Only
Print/Type preparer's name: Beverly J Worth — Preparer's signature — Date 12-03-2016 — Check [X] self-employed — PTIN P00106320
Firm's name ▶ Worth Financial Service — Firm's EIN ▶ 48-0733498
Firm's address ▶ PO Box 242, Winona Lake, IN 46590 — Phone no. 574-269-2121

Form **1040** (2016)

CLERGY

EEA

With Accountable Reimbursement Plan

SCHEDULE C (Form 1040)

Department of the Treasury
Internal Revenue Service (99)

OMB No. 1545-0074

2016

Attachment Sequence No. **09**

Profit or Loss From Business
(Sole Proprietorship)

▶ Information about Schedule C and its separate instructions is at *www.irs.gov/schedulec.*
▶ Attach to Form 1040, 1040NR, or 1041; partnerships generally must file Form 1065.

Name of proprietor **H JAMES SNODGRASS**

Social security number (SSN) **483-12-0200**

A Principal business or profession, including product or service (see instructions) **HONORARIUMS**

B Enter code from instructions ▶ **813000**

C Business name. If no separate business name, leave blank.

D Employer ID number (EIN), (see instr.)

E Business address (including suite or room no.) ▶ **2309 E SMITH ST**
   City, town or post office, state, and ZIP code **SOUTH BEND, IN 46617**

F Accounting method: (1) ☒ Cash (2) ☐ Accrual (3) ☐ Other (specify) ▶

G Did you "materially participate" in the operation of this business during 2016? If "No," see instructions for limit on losses ☒ Yes ☐ No

H If you started or acquired this business during 2016, check here ▶ ☐

I Did you make any payments in 2016 that would require you to file Form(s) 1099? (see instructions) ☐ Yes ☒ No

J If "Yes," did you or will you file required Forms 1099? ☐ Yes ☐ No

Part I Income

1 Gross receipts or sales. See instructions for line 1 and check the box if this income was reported to you on Form W-2 and the "Statutory employee" box on that form was checked ▶ ☐	1	690
2 Returns and allowances	2	0
3 Subtract line 2 from line 1	3	690
4 Cost of goods sold (from line 42)	4	
5 Gross profit. Subtract line 4 from line 3	5	690
6 Other income, including federal and state gasoline or fuel tax credit or refund (see instructions)	6	
7 Gross income. Add lines 5 and 6 ▶	7	690

Part II Expenses. Enter expenses for business use of your home only on line 30.

8 Advertising	8		18 Office expense (see instructions)	18	
9 Car and truck expenses (see instructions)	9		19 Pension and profit-sharing plans	19	
10 Commissions and fees	10		20 Rent or lease (see instructions):		
11 Contract labor (see instructions)	11		a Vehicles, machinery, and equipment	20a	
12 Depletion	12		b Other business property	20b	
13 Depreciation and section 179 expense deduction (not included in Part III) (see instructions)	13		21 Repairs and maintenance	21	
			22 Supplies (not included in Part III)	22	
			23 Taxes and licenses	23	
14 Employee benefit programs (other than on line 19)	14		24 Travel, meals, and entertainment:		
15 Insurance (other than health)	15		a Travel	24a	
16 Interest:			b Deductible meals and entertainment (see instructions)	24b	
a Mortgage (paid to banks, etc.)	16a		25 Utilities	25	
b Other	16b		26 Wages (less employment credits)	26	
17 Legal and professional services	17		27 a Other expenses (from line 48)	27a	114
			b Reserved for future use	27b	

28 Total expenses before expenses for business use of home. Add lines 8 through 27a ▶	28	64
29 Tentative profit or (loss). Subtract line 28 from line 7	29	626
30 Expenses for business use of your home. Do not report these expenses elsewhere. Attach Form 8829 unless using the simplified method (see instructions). Simplified method filers only: enter the total square footage of: (a) your home: _____ and (b) the part of your home used for business: 12 . Use the Simplified Method Worksheet in the instructions to figure the amount to enter on line 30	30	
31 Net profit or (loss). Subtract line 30 from line 29. (If a profit, enter on both Form 1040, line 12 (or Form 1040NR, line 13) and on Schedule SE, line 2. (If you checked the box on line 1, see instructions). Estates and trusts, enter on Form 1041, line 3. • If a loss, you must go to line 32.	31	626

32 If you have a loss, check the box that describes your investment in this activity (see instructions).
• If you checked 32a, enter the loss on both Form 1040, line 12, (or Form 1040NR, line 13) and on Schedule SE, line 2. (If you checked the box on line 1, see the line 31 instructions). Estates and trusts, enter on Form 1041, line 3.
• If you checked 32b, you must attach Form 6198. Your loss may be limited.

SEE CLERGY ATTACHMENT

32a ☐ All investment is at risk.
32b ☐ Some investment is not at risk.

For Paperwork Reduction Act Notice, see the separate instructions.   Schedule C (Form 1040) 2016

SCHEDULE A (Form 1040)

Department of the Treasury
Internal Revenue Service (99)

OMB No. 1545-0074

2016

Attachment Sequence No. **07**

Itemized Deductions

▶ Information about Schedule A and its separate instructions is at *www.irs.gov/schedulea.*
▶ Attach to Form 1040.

Name(s) shown on Form 1040 **H JAMES & MARY T SNODGRASS**

Your social security number **483-12-0200**

Medical and Dental Expenses

Caution: Do not include expenses reimbursed or paid by others.

1 Medical and dental expenses (see instructions)	1		
2 Enter amount from Form 1040, line 38	2		
3 Multiply line 2 by 10% (0.10). But if either you or your spouse was born before January 2, 1952, multiply line 2 by 7.5% (0.075) instead	3		
4 Subtract line 3 from line 1. If line 3 is more than line 1, enter -0-		4	

Taxes You Paid

5 State and local (check only one box): a ☒ Income taxes, or b ☐ General sales taxes	5	3,604	
6 Real estate taxes (see instructions)	6	1,182	
7 Personal property taxes	7	534	
8 Other taxes. List type and amount ▶	8		
9 Add lines 5 through 8		9	5,320

Interest You Paid

Note: Your mortgage interest deduction may be limited (see instructions).

10 Home mortgage interest and points reported to you on Form 1098	10	8,081	
11 Home mortgage interest not reported to you on Form 1098. If paid to the person from whom you bought the home, see instructions and show that person's name, identifying no., and address ▶	11		
12 Points not reported to you on Form 1098. See instructions for special rules	12		
13 Mortgage insurance premiums (see instructions)	13		
14 Investment interest. Attach Form 4952 if required. (See instructions.)	14		
15 Add lines 10 through 14		15	8,081

Gifts to Charity

If you made a gift and got a benefit for it, see instructions.

16 Gifts by cash or check. If you made any gift of $250 or more, see instructions	16	5,508	
17 Other than by cash or check. If any gift of $250 or more, see instructions. You must attach Form 8283 if over $500	17		
18 Carryover from prior year	18		
19 Add lines 16 through 18		19	5,508

Casualty and Theft Losses

20 Casualty or theft loss(es). Attach Form 4684. (See instructions.)	20	

Job Expenses and Certain Miscellaneous Deductions

21 Unreimbursed employee expenses - job travel, union dues, job education, etc. Attach Form 2106 or 2106-EZ if required. (See instr.) ▶	21	193	
22 Tax preparation fees	22		
23 Other expenses - investment, safe deposit box, etc. List type and amount ▶ NURSING EXPENSES	23	510	
24 Add lines 21 through 23	24	703	
25 Enter amount from Form 1040, line 38	25	70,267	
26 Multiply line 25 by 2% (0.02)	26	1,405	
27 Subtract line 26 from line 24. If line 26 is more than line 24, enter -0-		27	0

Other Miscellaneous Deductions

28 Other - from list in instructions. List type and amount ▶	28	

Total Itemized Deductions

29 Is Form 1040, line 38, over $155,650? ☐ No. Your deduction is not limited. Add the amounts in the far right column for lines 4 through 28. Also, enter this amount on Form 1040, line 40 ☐ Yes. Your deduction may be limited. See the Itemized Deductions Worksheet in the instructions to figure the amount to enter.	29	18,909

30 If you elect to itemize deductions even though they are less than your standard deduction, check here ▶ ☐

For Paperwork Reduction Act Notice, see Form 1040 instructions.   Schedule A (Form 1040) 2016

With Accountable Reimbursement Plan

SCHEDULE SE (Form 1040)

Department of the Treasury
Internal Revenue Service (99)

Self-Employment Tax

▶ Information about Schedule SE and its separate instructions is at *www.irs.gov/schedulese.*
▶ Attach to Form 1040 or Form 1040NR.

OMB No. 1545-0074
2016
Attachment Sequence No. 17

Name of person with **self-employment** income (as shown on Form 1040 or Form 1040NR)
H JAMES SNODGRASS

Social security number of person with **self-employment** income ▶ 483-12-0200

Before you begin: To determine if you must file Schedule SE, see the instructions.

May I Use Short Schedule SE or Must I Use Long Schedule SE?

Note. Use this flowchart only if you must file Schedule SE. If unsure, see *Who Must File Schedule SE* in the instructions.

- Did you receive wages or tips in 2016?
  - No → Are you a minister, member of a religious order, or Christian Science practitioner who received IRS approval **not** to be taxed on earnings from these sources, **but** you owe self-employment tax on other earnings?
    - No → Are you using one of the optional methods to figure your net earnings (see instructions)?
      - No → Did you receive church employee income (see instructions) reported on Form W-2 of $108.28 or more?
        - No → **You may use Short Schedule SE below**
        - Yes → **You must use Long Schedule SE**
      - Yes → **You must use Long Schedule SE**
    - Yes → **You must use Long Schedule SE**
  - Yes → Was the total of your wages and tips subject to social security or railroad retirement (tier 1) tax, plus your net earnings from self-employment more than $118,500?
    - Yes → **You must use Long Schedule SE**
    - No → Did you receive tips subject to social security or Medicare tax that you **didn't** report to your employer?
      - Yes → **You must use Long Schedule SE**
      - No → Did you report any wages on Form 8919, Uncollected Social Security and Medicare Tax on Wages?
        - Yes → **You must use Long Schedule SE**
        - No → **You may use Short Schedule SE below**

Section A – Short Schedule SE. Caution. Read above to see if you can use Short Schedule SE.

1a	Net farm profit or (loss) from Schedule F, line 34, and farm partnerships, Schedule K-1 (Form 1065), box 14, code A	1a
b	If you received social security retirement or disability benefits, enter the amount of Conservation Reserve Program payments included on Schedule F, line 4b, or listed on Schedule K-1 (Form 1065), box 20, code Z	1b ( )
2	Net profit or (loss) from Schedule C, line 31; Schedule C-EZ, line 3; Schedule K-1 (Form 1065), box 14, code A (other than farming); and Schedule K-1 (Form 1065-B), box 9, code J1. Ministers and members of religious orders, see instructions for types of income to report on this line. See instructions for other income to report SEE CLERGY ATTACHMENT	2	44,659
3	Combine lines 1a, 1b, and 2	3	44,659
4	Multiply line 3 by 92.35% (0.9235). If less than $400, you do not owe self-employment tax; **don't** file this schedule unless you have an amount on line 1b . . . . $44,033 from "Worksheet to Be Used with Form 2106" + $626 from Sch. C	4	41,243
	Note. If line 4 is less than $400 due to Conservation Reserve Program payments on line 1b, see instructions.		
5	**Self-employment tax.** If the amount on line 4 is:		
	• $118,500 or less, multiply line 4 by 15.3% (0.153). Enter the result on line 57, or Form 1040NR, line 55		
	• More than $118,500, multiply line 4 by 2.9% (0.029). Then, add $14,694 to the result. Enter the total here and on **Form 1040, line 57,** or **Form 1040NR, line 55**	5	6,310
6	**Deduction for one-half of self-employment tax.** Multiply line 5 by 50% (0.50). Enter the result here and on **Form 1040, line 27, or Form 1040NR, line 27**	6	3,155

For Paperwork Reduction Act Notice, see your tax return instructions. **Schedule SE (Form 1040) 2016**

WORKSHEET TO BE USED WITH FORM 2106

Name: **H. James Snodgrass**
Social Security Number: 483 | 12 | 0200
Year 2015
Filed Form 4361? Yes ☐ No ☑

Part A - Computation of Business Expenses ●

Use this section in conjunction with Form 2106 (or 2106-EZ) to figure your net social security base.

Auto Expense

	Vehicle 1	Vehicle 2
1. Total Miles Driven	5,029	19,581
2. Total Business Miles	4,085	14,928
3. % of Business Use (Line 1/Line 2)	81.22%	76.24%
4. Lease Payments		
5. Inclusion Amount		
6. Subtract Line 5 from Line 4		
7. Gas, Oil, Lubrication		
8. Repairs		
9. Tires & Batteries		
10. Insurance & Auto Club		
11. Miscellaneous		
12. Washing & Polishing		
13. License (Registration Only)		
14. Add Lines 6 through 13		
15. Multiply Line 14 by Line 3		
16. Depreciation		
17. Total Actual Exp (Line 15 + 16)		
18. Optional Method (Line 2 x Standard Mileage Rate)		
19. Interest	158	481
20. Personal Property Tax		456
21. Line 19 + Line 20	158	937
22. Line 21 x Line 3 (To Line 6 of Social Security Base Computation)	128	714

Local Travel Expense

	Amount
23. Parking	
24. Tolls	
25. Fares	
26. Total	

Enter on Form 2106-EZ, Part II, Ln 2 or Form 2106, Part I, Ln 2

Overnight Travel Exp.

	Amount
27. Auto Rental, Taxi	
28. Fares (air, train, bus)	
29. Parking & Tolls	
30. Laundry & Cleaning	
31. Lodging	
32. Telephone, Postage, Fax, etc.	
33. Tips other than meals	
34. Total	

Enter on Form 2106-EZ, Part II, Ln 3 or Form 2106, Part I, Ln 3

Meals & Entertainment

	Amount
35. Meals Away Overnight ☐ Actual ☐ Per Diem	
36. Entertainment Meals	
37. Entertainment, Other	
38. Tips for Meals	
39. Total	

Enter on Form 2106-EZ, Part II, Ln 5 or Form 2106, Part I, Ln 5

Professional Expense

	Amount
40. Business-In-Home	
41. Education Expense	
42. Equipment Depreciation	
43. Office Supplies & Postage	
44. Religious Materials	
45. Seminars & Dues	
46. Subscriptions & Paperbacks	
47. Business Telephone & Internet Use	
48. Gifts	
49. Other	
50. Total	

Enter on Form 2106-EZ, Part II, Ln 4 or Form 2106, Part I, Ln 4

Unreimbursed Expenses

	Amount
51. Auto Expense (Ln 17 or Ln 18)	
52. Local Travel (Ln 26)	
53. Overnight Travel (Ln 34)	
54. Professional Expense (Ln 50)	
55. Total of Lines 51 through 54	
56. Reimbursement for Auto, Travel, & Prof (Ln 57 Unreimbursed Auto Travel & Prof (Ln 55-Ln 56)	
57. Unreimbursed Auto Travel & Prof (Ln 55-Ln 56)	
58. Meals & Entertainment (Ln 39)	
59. Reimbursement for M & E	
60. Unreimbursed M & E (Ln 58 - Ln 59)	
61. Deductible M&E (% of Ln 60)	
62. Total Unreimbursed Exp (Ln 57+Ln 61)	

Part B - Unreimbursed Expense Allocation (Sec. 265)

Use if filing Form 2106 or Sch. C or C-EZ and claiming expense deductions

	A. Taxable Compensation	B. Total Compensation
1. Wages from W-2	21,000	21,000
2. Unused Parsonage Allowance	1,518	
3. Parsonage Allowance Designated		24,000
4. FRV of Parsonage Provided		
5. Gross Income / Sch C or C-EZ	690	690
6. Recapture of Auto Depreciation		
7. Total for Columns A & B	23,208	45,690
8. Inclusion Percentage (Ln 7 Col A Divided by Col B)	50.79%	50.79%

Employee Business Expenses

	Amount
9. Expense from Form 2106-EZ, Ln 6 or Form 2106, Ln 10	
10. Inclusion % from Ln 8	50.79%
11. Deductible Expense to Sch A Ln 20 (Ln 9 x Ln 10)	
12. Expenses Disallowed (Ln 9 - Ln 11)	

Sch C or Sch C-EZ

	Amount
13. Total Expense from Sch C or C-EZ	690
14. Inclusion % from Ln 8	50.79%
15. Deductible Expense (Ln 13 x Ln 14)	126
16. Expenses Disallowed (Ln 13 - Ln 15)	64

Part C - Computation of Social Security Base

If exempt, omit

	Amount
1. Salary from W-2	21,000
2. Value of Parsonage Provided	
3. Parsonage Allowance (Part D)	24,000
4. Recapture of Auto Depreciation	
5. Less Business Portion of Tax Prep	(63)
6. Less Business % of Auto Int & Tax (Part A, Ln 22)	(842)
7. Less Disallowed Exp on Sch C (Part B, Ln 16)	(62)
8. Less Unreimbursed Bus Exp (Form 2106 or Part A, Ln 62)	
9. Total (Enter on Sch SE)	44,033

Part D - Computation of Parsonage Allowance

If you own your home, use both Columns A & B. Otherwise, use Column B only.

	First Home		Second Home	
	Column A FRV Computation	Column B Expenses Paid by Minister	Column A FRV Computation	Column B Expenses Paid by Minister
Value of Parsonage Provided by Church	$	$		
FMV of Home Owned	$ 150,000			
1. Fair Rental Value of Home Owned	18,000			
2. Fair Rental Value of Furnishings	5,400			
3. Rent Paid				
4. Closing Costs / Downpayment		1,835		
5. Principal Payments		1,182		
6. Real Estate Taxes		8,081		
7. Mortgage Interest		3,292		
8. Insurance		2,409		
9. Repairs & Upkeep		840		
10. Furniture, Appliances, etc.		463		
11. Decorator Items		463		
12. Utilities	3,738	3,738		
13. Miscellaneous Supplies	642	642		
14. Total	28,243	22,482		
15. Lesser of Line 14, Column A (if applicable) or Column B		22,482		
16. Amount Designated ☐ Pension (Pension not subject to Self-Employment tax)	24,000	☐ Pension		
17. If Line 16 is greater than Ln 15, enter the difference here and as income on Form 1040, Line 7, or If amount designated is included in error on W-2, enter the lesser of Line 15 or Line 16 as a deduction on Form 1040, Line 21.		1,518		

Examples - When the Church Owns the Parsonage

The tax returns for Rev. Jonathan Pious will illustrate when the church owns the parsonage and when the minister has chosen to be exempt from Social Security. You will see how the earned income credit and child tax credits are calculated.

Facts of the problem:

Rev. Jonathan J Pious and Jane J, live at 2450 N 35th Street, Indianapolis, IN 46205. Rev. Pious's SS# is 555-22-8888; Janes's SS# is 555-22-8889. They have three children, Julie J, Justin J, and Jacob J, ages 12, 9 & 7. Children under 17 qualify for the Child Tax Credit.

Rev. Pious is the minister of 38th Street Harmony Church and Mrs. Pious is a homemaker. Rev. Pious's Form W-2 is shown below.

During the year Rev. Pious received $420 professional income from weddings and funerals. He did not incur any expenses.

18th Street Harmony Church owns and provides the parsonage for Rev. Pious and his family. Rev. Pious states that it's rental value is $700 a month or $8400 for the year. (Do not enter this value anywhere on Form W-2.) There was a designation of $6,000 for Rev. Pious's additional home expenses. Insurance on the contents was $269. They bought new furniture and appliances for $2,623. Decorator items cost $759, extra utilities and personal phone expense was $456. Miscellaneous household expenses were $573.

Rev. Pious has an accountable reimbursement plan for all of his professional expenses. He was reimbursed 100% for all of his expenses.

Without home interest and taxes, we know that the standard deduction exceeds their itemized deductions.

Rev. Pious and his entire family did not have medical coverage all year. Their Shared Responsibility Payment is entered on Form 1040, page 2, line 61.

First we show Rev. Pious subject to Social Security. (Pages 133-138)

Second we show Rev. Pious having an exemption from Social Security. Pages 139-142)

a Employee's social security no. 555-22-8888	Copy B--To Be Filed With Employee's FEDERAL Tax Return. OMB No. 1545-0008	
b Employer identification number (EIN) 35-9888888	**1** Wages, tips, other comp. 42000.00	**2** Federal income tax withheld 6500.00
c Employer's name, address, and ZIP code 18TH STREET HARMONY CHURCH 2460 E 38TH STREET INDIANAPOLIS, IN 46205	**3** Social security wages	**4** Social security tax withheld
	5 Medicare wages and tips	**6** Medicare tax withheld
	7 Social security tips	**8** Allocated tips
d Control number	**9**	**10** Dependent care benefits
e Employee's name, address, and ZIP code JONATHAN J PIOUS 2450 E 38TH STREET INDIANAPOLIS, IN 46205	**11** Nonqualified plans	**12a** See instructions for box 12
	13 Statutory employee Retirement plan Third-party sick pay	**12b**
	14 Other HOUSI 6000.00 ALLOW ANCE	**12c**
		12d

15 State Employer's state ID number	**16** State wages, tips, etc.	**17** State income tax	**18** Local wages, tips, etc.	**19** Local income tax	**20** Locality name
IN | 35-9888888	42000.00	1026.00	42000.00	428.00	MARION

Form **W-2** **Wage and Tax Statement**   **2016**   38-2099803   Department of the Treasury -- Internal Revenue Service

This information is being furnished to the Internal Revenue Service.

6 BW2BC   NTF 2580333   BW2EEBC   Copyright 2016 Greatland/Nelco – Forms Software Only

With Parsonage Provided and Subject to SS

Form 1040 (2016) JONATHAN J & JANE J PIOUS — 400-00-1048 — Page 2

Tax and Credits

38	Amount from line 37 (adjusted gross income)	39,726
39a	Blind/born before Jan 2 1952 — Total boxes checked ▶ 39a	
40	Itemized deductions or standard deduction	12,600
41	Subtract line 40 from line 38	27,126
42	Exemptions	20,250
43	Taxable income	6,876
44	Tax	688
45	Alternative minimum tax	
46	Excess advance premium tax credit repayment	
47	Add lines 44, 45, and 46	688
48	Foreign tax credit	
49	Credit for child and dependent care expenses	
50	Education credits	
51	Retirement savings contributions credit	
52	Child tax credit	688
53	Residential energy credit	
54	Other credits	
55	Add lines 48 through 54. Total credits	688
56	Subtract line 55 from line 47	0

Other Taxes

57	Self-employment tax. Attach Schedule SE	8,028
58	Unreported social security and Medicare tax	
59	Additional tax on IRAs	
60a	Household employment taxes	
60b	First-time homebuyer credit repayment	
61	Health care: individual responsibility / Full-year coverage	2,085
62	Taxes from Form 8959/8960	
63	Add lines 56 through 62. This is your total tax	10,113

Payments

64	Federal income tax withheld from Forms W-2 and 1099	
65	2016 estimated tax payments	6,500
66a	Earned income credit (EIC)	143
67	Additional child tax credit. Attach Schedule 8812	2,312
68	American opportunity credit Form 8863, line 8	
69	Net premium tax credit. Attach Form 8962	
70	Amount paid with request for extension to file	
71	Excess social security and tier 1 RRTA tax withheld	
72	Credit for federal tax on fuels. Attach Form 4136	
73	Credits from Form:	
74	Add lines 64, 65, 66a, and 67 through 73. These are your total payments	8,955

Refund

75	If line 74 is more than line 63, subtract. This is the amount you overpaid	
76a	Amount of line 75 you want refunded to you	
77	Amount applied to your 2017 estimated tax	

Amount You Owe

| 78 | Amount you owe | 1,158 |
| 79 | Estimated tax penalty | |

Third Party Designee: No

Sign Here: Your occupation: MINISTER. Spouse's occupation: HOUSEWIFE. Date 12-02-2016

Paid Preparer Use Only: Beverly J Worth — Worth Financial Service, PO Box 242, Winona Lake, IN 46590. PTIN P00106320. Firm's EIN 48-0733498. Phone no. 574-269-2121

Form 1040 (2016)

Form 1040 U.S. Individual Income Tax Return 2016 OMB No. 1545-0074

JONATHAN J PIOUS — SSN 400-00-1048
JANE J PIOUS — Spouse SSN 458-12-4715
Home address: 2450 E 38TH ST, INDIANAPOLIS, IN 46205

Filing Status: 2 — Married filing jointly (X)

Exemptions:
Dependents	SSN	Relationship
JULIE PIOUS	555-22-8879	DAUGHTER
JUSTIN PIOUS	555-22-8880	SON
JACOB PIOUS	555-22-8881	SON

Total number of exemptions claimed: 5

Income

7	Wages, salaries, tips — Excess Allowance	-1,320
8a	Taxable interest	
12	Business income (loss). Attach Schedule C	420
22	Total income	43,740
27	Deductible part of self-employment tax. Attach Schedule SE	4,014
36	Add lines 23 through 35	4,014
37	Adjusted gross income	39,726

For Disclosure, Privacy Act, and Paperwork Reduction Act Notice, see separate instructions. Form 1040 (2016)

With Parsonage Provided and Subject to SS

SCHEDULE SE
(Form 1040)

Department of the Treasury
Internal Revenue Service (99)

Self-Employment Tax

▶ Information about Schedule SE and its separate instructions is at *www.irs.gov/schedulese*.

▶ Attach to Form 1040 or Form 1040NR.

OMB No. 1545-0074

2016

Attachment
Sequence No. **17**

Name of person with **self-employment** income (as shown on Form 1040 or Form 1040NR)
JONATHAN J PIOUS

Social security number of person
with **self-employment** income ▶ 400-00-1048

Before you begin: To determine if you must file Schedule SE, see the instructions.

May I Use Short Schedule SE or Must I Use Long Schedule SE?

Note. *Use this flowchart only if you must file Schedule SE. If unsure, see Who Must File Schedule SE in the instructions.*

Did you receive wages or tips in 2016?

↓ No

Are you a minister, member of a religious order, or Christian Science practitioner who received IRS approval **not** to be taxed on earnings from these sources, **but** you owe self-employment tax on other earnings?
→ Yes → [to Yes box]

↓ No

Are you using one of the optional methods to figure your net earnings (see instructions)?
→ Yes → [to You may use Short Schedule SE]

↓ No

Did you receive church employee income (see instructions) reported on Form W-2 of $108.28 or more?
→ Yes → [to You must use Long Schedule SE]

↓ No

You may use Short Schedule SE below

Was the total of your wages and tips subject to social security or railroad retirement (tier 1) tax **plus** your net earnings from self-employment more than $118,500?
→ Yes → [to Long Schedule SE]

↓ No

Did you receive tips subject to social security or Medicare tax that you **didn't** report to your employer?
→ Yes → [to Long Schedule SE]

↓ No

Did you report any wages on Form 8919, Uncollected Social Security and Medicare Tax on Wages?
→ Yes

You must use Long Schedule SE on page 2

Section A - Short Schedule SE. Caution. Read above to see if you can use Short Schedule SE.

1a Net farm profit or (loss) from Schedule F, line 34, and farm partnerships, Schedule K-1 (Form 1065), box 14, code A	**1a**	
b If you received social security retirement or disability benefits, enter the amount of Conservation Reserve Program payments included on Schedule F, line 4b, or listed on Schedule K-1 (Form 1065), box 20, code Z	**1b**	( )
2 Net profit or (loss) from Schedule C, line 31; Schedule C-EZ, line 3; Schedule K-1 (Form 1065), box 14, code A (other than farming); and Schedule K-1 (Form 1065-B), box 9, code J1. Ministers and members of religious orders, see instructions for types of income to report on this line. See instructions for other income to report	**2**	56,820
3 Combine lines 1a, 1b, and 2	**3**	56,820
4 Multiply line 3 by 92.35% (0.9235). If less than $400, you do not owe self-employment tax; **don't** file this schedule unless you have an amount on line 1b	**4**	52,473
Note. If line 4 is less than $400 due to Conservation Reserve Program payments on line 1b, see instructions.		
5 **Self-employment tax.** If the amount on line 4 is:		
• $118,500 or less, multiply line 4 by 15.3% (0.153). Enter the result here and on **Form 1040, line 57,** or **Form 1040NR, line 55**		
• More than $118,500, multiply line 4 by 2.9% (0.029). Then, add $14,694 to the result. Enter the total here and on **Form 1040, line 57,** or **Form 1040NR, line 55**	**5**	8,028
6 **Deduction for one-half of self-employment tax.** Multiply line 5 by 50% (0.50). Enter the result here and on **Form 1040, line 27,** or **Form 1040NR, line 27**	**6**	4,014

For Paperwork Reduction Act Notice, see your tax return instructions.

Schedule SE (Form 1040) 2016

SCHEDULE C-EZ
(Form 1040)

Department of the Treasury
Internal Revenue Service (99)

Net Profit From Business

(Sole Proprietorship)

▶ Partnerships, joint ventures, etc., generally must file Form 1065 or 1065-B.

▶ Attach to Form 1040, 1040NR, or 1041. ▶ See instructions.

OMB No. 1545-0074

2016

Attachment
Sequence No. **09A**

Name of proprietor
JONATHAN J PIOUS

Social security number (SSN)
400-00-1048

Part I   General Information

**You May Use
Schedule C-EZ
Instead of
Schedule C
Only If You:**

- Had business expenses of $5,000 or less.
- Use the cash method of accounting.
- Did not have an inventory at any time during the year.
- Did not have a net loss from your business.
- Had only one business as either a sole proprietor, qualified joint venture, or statutory employee.

And You:

- Had no employees during the year.
- Do not deduct expenses for business use of your home.
- Do not have prior year unallowed passive activity losses from this business, and
- Are not required to file **Form 4562,** Depreciation and Amortization, for this business. See the instructions for Schedule C, line 13, to find out if you must file.

A Principal business or profession, including product or service	**B** Enter business code (see page 2) ▶	
C Business name. If no separate business name, leave blank.	**D** Enter your EIN (see page 2)	
E Business address (including suite or room no.). Address not required if same as on page 1 of your tax return.		
2450 E 38TH ST		
City, town or post office, state, and ZIP code		
INDIANAPOLIS, IN 46205		
F Did you make any payments in 2016 that would require you to file Form(s) 1099? (see the Instructions for Schedule C)	☐ Yes	☐ No
G If "Yes," did you or will you file required Forms 1099?	☐ Yes	☐ No

Part II   Figure Your Net Profit

1 **Gross receipts.** **Caution:** If this income was reported to you on Form W-2 and the "Statutory employee" box on that form was checked, see *Statutory employees* in the instructions for Schedule C, line 1, and check here ▶ ☐	**1**	420
2 **Total expenses** (see instructions). If more than $5,000, you **must** use Schedule C	**2**	
3 **Net profit.** Subtract line 2 from line 1. If less than zero, you **must** use Schedule C. Enter on both **Form 1040, line 12,** and **Schedule SE, line 2,** or on **Form 1040NR, line 13,** and **Schedule SE, line 2** (see instructions). (Statutory employees **do not** report this amount on Schedule SE, line 2.) Estates and trusts, enter on **Form 1041, line 3**	**3**	420

Part III   Information on Your Vehicle.   Complete this part **only** if you are claiming car or truck expenses on line 2.

4 When did you place your vehicle in service for business purposes? (month, day, year) ▶	
5 Of the total number of miles you drove your vehicle during 2016, enter the number of miles you used your vehicle for:	
a Business _____ **b** Commuting (see instructions) _____ **c** Other _____	
6 Was your vehicle available for personal use during off-duty hours?	☐ Yes ☐ No
7 Do you (or your spouse) have another vehicle available for personal use?	☐ Yes ☐ No
8a Do you have evidence to support your deduction?	☐ Yes ☐ No
b If "Yes," is the evidence written?	☐ Yes ☐ No

For Paperwork Reduction Act Notice, see the separate instructions for Schedule C (Form 1040).

Schedule C-EZ (Form 1040) 2016

With Parsonage Provided and Subject to SS

SCHEDULE 8812 (Form 1040A or 1040)

Department of the Treasury
Internal Revenue Service (99)

Child Tax Credit

▶ Attach to Form 1040, Form 1040A, or Form 1040NR.
▶ Information about Schedule 8812 and its separate instructions is at www.irs.gov/schedule8812.

OMB No. 1545-0074
2016
Attachment Sequence No. 47

Names(s) shown on return: JONATHAN J & JANE J PIOUS
Your social security number: 400-00-1048

Part I Filers Who Have Certain Child Dependent(s) with an ITIN (Individual Taxpayer Identification Number)

Complete this part only for each dependent who has an ITIN and for whom you are claiming the child tax credit.

CAUTION If your dependent is not a qualifying child for the credit, you cannot include that dependent in the calculation of this credit.

Answer the following questions for each dependent listed on Form 1040, line 6c; Form 1040A, line 6c; or Form 1040NR, line 7c, who has an ITIN (Individual Taxpayer Identification Number) and that you indicated is a qualifying child for the child tax credit by checking column (4) for that dependent.

A For the first dependent identified with an ITIN and listed as a qualifying child for the child tax credit, did this child meet the substantial presence test? See separate instructions.
☐ Yes ☐ No

B For the second dependent identified with an ITIN and listed as a qualifying child for the child tax credit, did this child meet the substantial presence test? See separate instructions.
☐ Yes ☐ No

C For the third dependent identified with an ITIN and listed as a qualifying child for the child tax credit, did this child meet the substantial presence test? See separate instructions.
☐ Yes ☐ No

D For the fourth dependent identified with an ITIN and listed as a qualifying child for the child tax credit, did this child meet the substantial presence test? See separate instructions.
☐ Yes ☐ No

Note: If you have more than four dependents identified with an ITIN and listed as a qualifying child for the child tax credit, see separate instructions and check here . . . . ▶ ☐

Part II Additional Child Tax Credit Filers

1 If you file Form 2555 or 2555-EZ stop here, you cannot claim the additional child tax credit.

If you are required to use the worksheet in Pub. 972, enter the amount from line 8 of the Child Tax Credit Worksheet in the publication. Otherwise:

1040 filers: Enter the amount from line 6 of your Child Tax Credit Worksheet (see the Instructions for Form 1040, line 52).
1040A filers: Enter the amount from line 6 of your Child Tax Credit Worksheet (see the Instructions for Form 1040A, line 35).
1040NR filers: Enter the amount from line 6 of your Child Tax Credit Worksheet (see the Instructions for Form 1040NR, line 49). | **1** | 3,000 |

2 Enter the amount from Form 1040, line 52; Form 1040A, line 35; or Form 1040NR, line 49 | **2** | 688 |
3 Subtract line 2 from line 1. If zero, stop here; you cannot claim this credit | **3** | 2,312 |
4a Earned income (see separate instructions) | **4a** | 39,726 |
b Nontaxable combat pay (see separate instructions) | **4b** | |
5 Is the amount on line 4a more than $3,000?
☐ No. Leave line 5 blank and enter -0- on line 6.
☒ Yes. Subtract $3,000 from the amount on line 4a. Enter the result | **5** | 36,726 |
6 Multiply the amount on line 5 by 15% (0.15) and enter the result | **6** | 5,509 |
Next. Do you have three or more qualifying children?
☐ No. If line 6 is zero, stop here; you cannot claim this credit. Otherwise, skip Part III and enter the smaller of line 3 or line 6 on line 13.
☒ Yes. If line 6 is equal to or more than line 3, skip Part III and enter the amount from line 3 on line 13. Otherwise, go to line 7.

For Paperwork Reduction Act Notice, see your tax return instructions.
Schedule 8812 (Form 1040A or 1040) 2016

WORKSHEET TO BE USED WITH FORM 2106

Name: JONATHAN J PIOUS
Social Security Number: 555 22 8888
Year 2016
Filed Form 4361? Yes ☐ No ☑

Part A - Computation of Business Expenses ●

Use this section in conjunction with Form 2106 (or 2106-EZ) to figure your net social security base.

Auto Expense (Vehicle 1 / Vehicle 2)

1. Total Miles Driven
2. Total Business Miles
3. % of Business Use (Line 1/Line 2) %
4. Lease Payments
5. Inclusion Amount
6. Subtract Line 5 from Line 4
7. Gas, Oil, Lubrication
8. Repairs
9. Tires & Batteries
10. Insurance & Auto Club
11. Miscellaneous
12. Washing & Polishing
13. License (Registration Only)
14. Add Lines 6 through 13
15. Multiply Line 14 by Line 3
16. Depreciation
17. Total Actual Exp (Line 15 + 16)
18. Optional Method (Line 2 x Standard Mileage Rate)
19. Interest
20. Personal Property Tax
21. Line 19 + Line 20
22. Line 21 x Line 3 (To Line 6 of Social Security Base Computation)

Local Travel Expense (Amount)
23. Parking
24. Tolls
25. Fares
26. Total *Enter on Form 2106-EZ Part II, Ln 2 or Form 2106, Part II, Line 2*

Overnight Travel Exp. (Amount)
27. Auto Rental, Taxi
28. Fares (air, train, bus)
29. Parking & Tolls
30. Laundry & Cleaning
31. Lodging
32. Telephone, Postage, Fax, etc.
33. Other than meals
34. Total *Enter on Form 2106-EZ Part II, Ln 3 or Form 2106, Part II, Line 3*

Meals & Entertainment (Amount)
35. Meals Away Overnight ☐ Actual ☐ Per Diem
36. Entertainment Meals
37. Entertainment, Other
38. Tips for Meals
39. Total *Enter on Form 2106-EZ Part II, Ln 5 or Form 2106, Part II, Line 5*

Professional Expense (Amount)
40. Business-In-Home
41. Education Expense
42. Equipment Depreciation
43. Office Supplies & Postage
44. Religious Materials
45. Seminars & Dues
46. Subscriptions & Paperbacks
47. Business Telephone & Internet Use
48. Gifts
49. Other
50. Total *Enter on Form 2106-EZ Part II, Ln 4 or Form 2106, Part II, Line 4*

Unreimbursed Expenses (Amount)
51. Auto Expense (Ln 17 or Ln 18)
52. Local Travel (Ln 26)
53. Overnight Travel (Ln 34)
54. Professional Expense (Ln 50)
55. Total of Lines 51 through 54
56. Reimbursement for Auto, Travel, & Prof. (Line 57-Ln 55)
57. Unreimbursed Auto Travel & Prof (Ln 55-Ln 56)
58. Meals & Entertainment (Ln 39)
59. Reimbursement for M & E
60. Unreimbursed M & E (Ln 58 - Ln 59)
61. Deductible M&E (½ of Ln 60)
62. Total Unreimbursed Exp (Ln 57+Ln 61)

Part B - Unreimbursed Expense Allocation (Sec. 265)

Use if Filing Form 2106 or Sch. C or C-EZ and claiming expense deductions.

	A. Taxable Compensation	B. Total Compensation
1. Wages from W-2		
2. Unused Parsonage Allowance		
3. Parsonage Allowance Designated		
4. FRV of Parsonage Provided		
5. Gross Income / Sch C or C-EZ		
6. Recapture of Auto Depreciation		
7. Total for Columns A & B		
8. Inclusion Percentage (Ln 7 Col. A Divided by Col. B)		%

Employee Business Expenses (Amount)
9. Expense from Form 2106-EZ, Ln 6 or Form 2106, Ln 10
10. Inclusion % from Ln 8 %
11. Deductible Expense to Sch A, Ln 20 (Ln 9 x Ln 10)
12. Expenses Disallowed (Ln 9 - Ln 11)

Sch C or Sch C-EZ (Amount)
13. Total Expense from Sch C or C-EZ
14. Inclusion % from Ln 8 %
15. Deductible Expense (Ln 13 x Ln 14)
16. Expenses Disallowed (Ln 13 - Ln 15)

Part D - Computation of Parsonage Allowance

If you own your home, use both Columns A & B. Otherwise, use Column B only.

	First Home		Second Home	
	Column A FRV Computation	Column B Expenses Paid by Minister	Column A FRV Computation	Column B Expenses Paid by Minister
Value of Parsonage Provided by Church	$ 8,400	$	$	$
FMV of Home Owned				
1. Fair Rental Value of Home Owned				
2. Fair Rental Value of Furnishings				
3. Rent Paid				
4. Closing Costs / Downpayment				
5. Principal Payments				
6. Real Estate Taxes				
7. Mortgage Interest				
8. Insurance		269		
9. Repairs & Upkeep		2,623		
10. Furniture, Appliances, etc.		759		
11. Decorator Items		456		
12. Utilities		573		
13. Miscellaneous Supplies				
14. Total		4,680		
15. Lesser of Line 14, Column A (if applicable) or Column B		4,680		
16. Amount Designated Pension ☐ (Pension not subject to Self-Employment tax)		6,000		Pension ☐
17. If Line 16 is greater than Ln 15, enter the difference here and as income on Form 1040, Line 7; or If amount designated is included in error on W-2, obtain a corrected Form W-2C		1,320		

Part C - Computation of Social Security Base

If exempt, omit.

	Amount
1. Salary from W-2	42,000
2. Value of Parsonage Provided	8,400
3. Parsonage Allowance (Part D, Ln 16)	6,000
4. Recapture of Auto Depreciation	
5. Less Business Portion of Tax Prep	
6. Less Business % of Auto Int & Tax (Part A, Ln 22)	
7. Less Disallowed Exp on Sch C (Part B, Ln 16)	
8. Less Unreimbursed Bus Exp (Form 2106 or Part A, Ln 62)	
9. Total (Enter on Sch SE)	56,400

With Parsonage Provided and Subject to SS

Earned Income Credit Worksheet - Form 1040, line 66a, Form 1040A, line 42a, or Form 1040EZ, line 8a

(Keep for your records)

Name(s) as shown on return: JONATHAN J & JANE J PIOUS

Tax ID Number: 400-00-1048

2016

1. Enter the amount from Form 1040 or Form 1040A, line 7, or Form 1040EZ, line 1 plus any nontaxable combat pay elected to be included in earned income **1.** 52,806

2. If you received a taxable scholarship or fellowship grant that was not reported on a W-2 form, enter that amount here, plus any amounts received for work performed while an inmate in a penal institution, plus any amounts received as a pension or annuity from a nonqualified deferred compensation plan or a nongovernmental section 457 plan .... **2.**

3. Subtract line 2 from line 1 .... **3.** 52,806

4. If you were self-employed or used Schedule C or C-EZ as a statutory employee, enter the amount from the worksheet for self employed taxpayers **4.** 143

5. Add lines 3 and 4 .... **5.** 52,806

6. Look up the amount on line 5 above in the EIC Table on pages 52-68 to find your credit. Enter the credit here. If line 6 is zero, **stop.** You **cannot** take the credit. Enter "**No**" directly to the right of Form 1040, line 66a, Form 1040A, line 38a, or Form 1040EZ, Line 8a. **6.** 143

7. Enter your AGI or Form 1040EZ, line 4 .... **7.** 39,726

8. Is line 7 less than -
   * $8,250 if you do not have a qualifying child? ($13,750 if married filing joint)
   * $18,150 if you have at least one qualifying child? ($23,650 if married filing joint)

   [ ] **Yes.** Go to line 9 now.
   [X] **No.** Look up the amount on line 7 above in the EIC Table to find your credit. Enter the credit here **8.** 2,902

9. Earned income credit.
   * If you checked "Yes" on line 8, enter the amount from line 6.
   * If you checked "No" on line 8, enter the **smaller** of line 6 or line 8 .... **9.** 143

   For additional information on the EIC calculation see the form instructions or IRS Publication 596

SCHEDULE EIC (Form 1040A or 1040)

Earned Income Credit
Qualifying Child Information

Department of the Treasury
Internal Revenue Service (99)

▲ Complete and attach to Form 1040A or 1040 only if you have a qualifying child.
▲ Information about Schedule EIC (Form 1040A or 1040) and its instructions is at www.irs.gov/schedule/eic.

OMB No. 1545-0074

2016

Attachment Sequence No **43**

Name(s) shown on return: JONATHAN J & JANE J PIOUS

Your social security number: 400-00-1048

Before you begin:
* See the instructions for Form 1040A, lines 42a and 42b, or Form 1040, lines 66a and 66b, to make sure that **(a)** you can take the EIC, and **(b)** you have a qualifying child
* Be sure the child's name on line 1 and social security number (SSN) on line 2 agree with the child's social security card. Otherwise, at the time we process your return, we may reduce or disallow your EIC. If the name or SSN on the child's social security card is not correct, call the Social Security Administration at 1-800-772-1213.

CAUTION!
* You can't claim the EIC for a child who didn't live with you for more than half of the year.
* If you take the EIC even though you are not eligible, you may not be allowed to take the credit for up to 10 years. See the instructions for details.
* It will take us longer to process your return and issue your refund if you do not fill in all lines that apply for each qualifying child

Qualifying Child Information

	Child 1		Child 2		Child 3	
1 Child's name If you have more than three qualifying children, you have to list only three to get the maximum credit.	First name: JACOB	Last name: PIOUS	First name: JUSTIN	Last name: PIOUS	First name: JULIE	Last name: PIOUS
2 Child's SSN The child must have an SSN as defined in the instructions for Form 1040A, lines 42a and 42b, or Form 1040, lines 66a and 66b, unless the child was born and died in 2016. If your child was born and died in 2016 and did not have an SSN, enter "Died" on this line and attach a copy of the child's birth certificate, death certificate, or hospital medical records.	555-22-8881		555-22-8880		555-22-8879	
3 Child's year of birth	Year 2009 If born after 1997 **and** the child is younger than you (or your spouse, if filing jointly), skip lines 4a and 4b; go to line 5.<ip>		Year 2007 If born after 1997 **and** the child is younger than you (or your spouse, if filing jointly), skip lines 4a and 4b; go to line 5.<ip>		Year 2004 If born after 1997 **and** the child is younger than you (or your spouse, if filing jointly), skip lines 4a and 4b; go to line 5.<ip>	
4a Was the child under age 24 at the end of 2016, a student, and younger than you (or your spouse, if filing jointly)?	[ ] **Yes.** **Go to line 5.**	[ ] **No.** **Go to line 4b.**	[ ] **Yes.** **Go to line 5.**	[ ] **No.** **Go to line 4b.**	[ ] **Yes.** **Go to line 5.**	[ ] **No.** **Go to line 4b.**
b Was the child permanently and totally disabled during any part of 2016?	[ ] **Yes.** **Go to line 5.**	[ ] **No.** The child is not a qualifying child.	[ ] **Yes.** **Go to line 5.**	[ ] **No.** The child is not a qualifying child.	[ ] **Yes.** **Go to line 5.**	[ ] **No.** The child is not a qualifying child.
5 Child's relationship to you (for example, son, daughter, grandchild, niece, nephew, foster child, etc.)	SON		SON		DAUGHTER	
6 Number of months child lived with you in the United States during 2016 • If the child lived with you for more than half of 2016 but less than 7 months, enter "7." • If the child was born or died in 2016 and your home was the child's home for more than half the time he or she was alive during 2016, enter "12."	12 months Do not enter more than 12 months.		12 months Do not enter more than 12 months.		12 months Do not enter more than 12 months.	

For Paperwork Reduction Act Notice, see your tax return instructions.

Schedule EIC (Form 1040A or 1040) 2016

EEA

With Parsonage Provided and Subject to SS

Form 8867 (2016) JONATHAN J & JANE J PIOUS   400-00-1048   Page 2

Due Diligence Questions for Returns Claiming EIC (If the return does not claim EIC, go to question 10.)

	EIC	CTC/ACTC	AOTC
9a Did you explain to the taxpayer the rules about claiming the EIC when a child is the qualifying child of more than one person (tie-breaker rules), and have you determined that this taxpayer is, in fact, eligible to claim the EIC for the number of children for whom the EIC is claimed?	☒ Yes ☐ No		
b Did you explain to the taxpayer that he/she may not claim the EIC if the taxpayer has not lived with the child for over half the year, even if the taxpayer has supported the child?	☒ Yes ☐ No		

Due Diligence Questions for Returns Claiming CTC and/or additional CTC (If the return does not claim CTC or Additional CTC, go to question 11.)

	EIC	CTC/ACTC	AOTC
10a Does the child reside with the taxpayer who is claiming the CTC/ACTC? (If "Yes," go to question 10c. If "No," answer question 10b.)		☒ Yes ☐ No	
b Did you ask if there is an active Form 8332, Release/Revocation of Claim to Exemption for Child by Custodial Parent, or a similar statement in place and, if applicable, did you attach it to the return?		☒ Yes ☐ No	
c Have you determined that the taxpayer has not released the claim to another person?		☒ Yes ☐ No	

Due Diligence Questions for Returns Claiming AOTC (If the return does not claim AOTC, go to *Credit Eligibility Certification*.)

	AOTC
11 Did the taxpayer provide substantiation such as a Form 1098-T and receipts for the qualified tuition and related expenses for the claimed AOTC?	☐ Yes ☐ No

▶ **You have complied with all due diligence requirements with respect to the credits claimed on the return of the taxpayer identified above if you:**

A. Complete this Form 8867 truthfully and accurately and complete the actions described in this checklist for all credits claimed;

B. Submit Form 8867 in the manner required;

C. Interview the taxpayer, ask adequate questions, document the taxpayer's responses on the return or in your notes, review adequate information to determine if the taxpayer is eligible to claim the credit(s) and in what amount(s); **and**

D. Keep all five of the following records for 3 years from the latest of the dates specified in the Form 8867 instructions under *Document Retention.*
 1. A copy of Form 8867,
 2. The applicable worksheet(s) or your own worksheet(s) for any credits claimed,
 3. Copies of any taxpayer documents you may have relied upon to determine eligibility for and the amount of the credit(s),
 4. A record of how, when, and from whom the information used to prepare this form and worksheet(s) was obtained, and
 5. A record of any additional questions you may have asked to determine eligibility for and amount of the credits, and the taxpayer's answers.

▶ **If you have not complied with all due diligence requirements for all credits claimed, you may have to pay a $510 penalty for each credit for which you have failed to comply.**

Credit Eligibility Certification

12 Do you certify that all of the answers on this Form 8867 are, to the best of your knowledge, true, correct and complete?	☒ Yes ☐ No

EEA   Form **8867** (2016)

Form **8867**	**Paid Preparer's Due Diligence Checklist**	OMB No. 1545-1629
	Earned Income Credit (EIC), Child Tax Credit (CTC), and American Opportunity Tax Credit (AOTC)	**2016**
Department of the Treasury Internal Revenue Service	▶ To be completed by preparer and filed with Form 1040, 1040A, 1040EZ, 1040NR, 1040SS, or 1040PR. ▶ Information about Form 8867 and its separate instructions is at www.irs.gov/form8867.	Attachment Sequence No. **70**

Taxpayer name(s) shown on return: JONATHAN J & JANE J PIOUS
Taxpayer identification number: 400-00-1048

Enter preparer's name and PTIN: Beverly J Worth   P00106320

Due Diligence Requirements

Please complete the appropriate column for all credits claimed on this return (check all that apply).

	EIC	CTC/ACTC	AOTC
1 Did you complete the return based on information for tax year 2016 provided by the taxpayer or reasonably obtained by you?	☒ Yes ☐ No	☒ Yes ☐ No	☐ Yes ☐ No
2 Did you complete the applicable EIC and/or CTC/ACTC worksheets found in the Form 1040, 1040A, 1040EZ, or 1040NR instructions, and/or the AOTC worksheet found in the Form 8863 instructions, or your own worksheet(s) that provides the same information, and all related forms and schedules for each credit claimed?	☒ Yes ☐ No	☒ Yes ☐ No	☐ Yes ☐ No
3 Did you satisfy the knowledge requirement? Answer "Yes" only if you can answer "Yes" to both 3a and 3b. To meet the knowledge requirement, did you . . .	☒ Yes ☐ No	☒ Yes ☐ No	☐ Yes ☐ No
a Interview the taxpayer, ask adequate questions, and document the taxpayer's responses to determine that the taxpayer is eligible to claim the credit(s)?	☒ Yes ☐ No	☒ Yes ☐ No	☐ Yes ☐ No
b Review adequate information to determine that the taxpayer is eligible to claim the credit(s) and in what amount?	☒ Yes ☐ No	☒ Yes ☐ No	☐ Yes ☐ No
4 Did any information provided by the taxpayer, a third party, or reasonably known to you in connection with preparing the return appear to be incorrect, incomplete, or inconsistent? (If "Yes," answer questions 4a and 4b. If "No," go to question 5.)	☐ Yes ☒ No	☐ Yes ☒ No	☐ Yes ☐ No
a Did you make reasonable inquiries to determine the correct or complete information?	☐ Yes ☐ No	☐ Yes ☐ No	☐ Yes ☐ No
b Did you document your inquiries? (Documentation should include the questions you asked, whom you asked, when you asked, the information that was provided, and the impact the information had on your preparation of the return.)	☐ Yes ☐ No	☐ Yes ☐ No	☐ Yes ☐ No
5 Did you satisfy the record retention requirement? To meet the record retention requirement, did you keep a copy of any document(s) provided by the taxpayer that you relied on to determine eligibility or to compute the amount for the credit(s)?	☒ Yes ☐ No	☒ Yes ☐ No	☐ Yes ☐ No

In addition to your notes from the interview with the taxpayer, list those documents, if any, that you relied on.

Form 8867, School Records, Healthcare Statement, Medical Records

	EIC	CTC/ACTC	AOTC
6 Did you ask the taxpayer whether he/she could provide documentation to substantiate eligibility for and the amount of the credit(s) claimed on the return?	☒ Yes ☐ No	☒ Yes ☐ No	☐ Yes ☐ No
7 Did you ask the taxpayer if any of these credits were disallowed or reduced in a previous year? (If credits were disallowed or reduced, go to question 7a. If not, go to question 8.)	☒ Yes ☐ No	☒ Yes ☐ No	☐ Yes ☐ No
a Did you complete the required recertification form(s)?	☐ Yes ☐ No	☐ Yes ☐ No	☐ Yes ☐ No
8 If the taxpayer is reporting self-employment income, did you ask adequate questions to prepare a complete and correct Form 1040, Schedule C?	☒ Yes ☐ No	☒ Yes ☐ No	☐ Yes ☐ No

For Paperwork Reduction Act Notice, see separate instructions.   Form **8867** (2016)

With Parsonage Provided and Subject to SS

EIC Due Diligence Assistant
(Keep for your records)

Name(s) as shown on return: JONATHAN J & JANE J PIOUS   2016   Tax ID Number 400-00-1048

Part I — All Taxpayers

1	Enter preparer's name and PTIN ▶ Beverly J Worth P00106320		
2	Is the taxpayer's filing status married filing separately?	☐ Yes	☒ No
	▶ If you checked "Yes" on line 2, stop; the taxpayer cannot take the EIC. Otherwise, continue.		
3	Does the taxpayer (and the taxpayer's spouse if filing jointly) have a social security number (SSN) that allows him or her to work and is valid for EIC purposes? See the instructions before answering.	☒ Yes	☐ No
	▶ If you checked "No" on line 3, stop; the taxpayer cannot take the EIC. Otherwise, continue.		
4	Is the taxpayer (or the taxpayer's spouse if filing jointly) filing Form 2555 or 2555-EZ (relating to the exclusion of foreign earned income)?	☐ Yes	☒ No
	▶ If you checked "Yes" on line 4, stop; the taxpayer cannot take the EIC. Otherwise, continue.		
5a	Was the taxpayer (or the taxpayer's spouse) a nonresident alien for any part of 2016?	☐ Yes	☒ No
	▶ If you checked "Yes" on line 5a go to line 5b Otherwise, skip line 5b and go to line 6		
5b	Is the taxpayer's filing status married filing jointly?	☐ Yes	☐ No
	▶ If you checked "Yes" on line 5a and "No" on line 5b, stop; the taxpayer cannot take the EIC. Otherwise, continue.		
6	Is the taxpayer's investment income more than $3,400?	☐ Yes	☒ No
	▶ If you checked "Yes" on line 6, stop; the taxpayer cannot take the EIC. Otherwise, continue.		
7	Could the taxpayer be a qualifying child of another person for 2016? If the taxpayer's filing status is married filing jointly, check "No."	☐ Yes	☒ No
	▶ If you checked "Yes" on line 7, stop; the taxpayer cannot take the EIC. Otherwise, go to Part II or Part III, whichever applies.		

EIC Due Diligence Assistant
(Keep for your records)

Name(s) as shown on return: JONATHAN J & JANE J PIOUS   2016   Tax ID Number 400-00-1048

Part II — Taxpayers With a Child

Caution: If there is more than one child, complete lines 8 through 14 for one child before going to the next column.

#	Question	Child 1	Child 2	Child 3
8	Child's name	JACOB PIOUS	JUSTIN PIOUS	JULIE PIOUS
9	Is the child the taxpayer's son, daughter, stepchild, foster child, brother, sister, stepbrother, stepsister, half brother, half sister, or a descendant of any of them?	☒ Yes ☐ No	☒ Yes ☐ No	☒ Yes ☐ No
10	Was the child unmarried at the end of 2016?	☒ Yes ☐ No	☒ Yes ☐ No	☒ Yes ☐ No
	If "No" and the child filed a return for any reason other than to claim a refund, the child is not the taxpayer's qualifying child.			
11	Did the child live with the taxpayer in the United States for over half of 2016?	☒ Yes ☐ No	☒ Yes ☐ No	☒ Yes ☐ No
12	Was the child (at the end of 2016) – • Under age 19 and younger than the taxpayer (or the taxpayer's spouse, if the taxpayer files jointly). • Under age 24, a student (defined in the instructions), and younger than the taxpayer (or the taxpayer's spouse, if the taxpayer files jointly), or • Any age and permanently and totally disabled?	☒ Yes ☐ No	☒ Yes ☐ No	☒ Yes ☐ No
	▶ If you checked "Yes" on lines 9, 10, 11, and 12, the child is the taxpayer's qualifying child; go to line 13a. If you checked "No" on line 9, 10, 11, or 12, the child is not the taxpayer's qualifying child.			
13a	Do you or the taxpayer know of another person who could check "Yes" on lines 9, 10, 11, and 12 for the child?	☐ Yes ☒ No	☐ Yes ☒ No	☐ Yes ☒ No
	▶ If you checked "No" on line 13a, go to line 14. Otherwise, go to line 13b			
b	Enter the child's relationship to the other person(s)			
c	Under the tiebreaker rules, is the child treated as the taxpayer's qualifying child?	☐ Yes ☐ No ☐ Don't know	☐ Yes ☐ No ☐ Don't know	☐ Yes ☐ No ☐ Don't know
	▶ If you checked "Yes" on line 13c, go to line 14. If you checked "No," the taxpayer cannot take the EIC based on this child and cannot take the EIC for taxpayers who do not have a qualifying child. If you checked "Don't know," explain to the taxpayer that, under the tiebreaker rules, the taxpayer's EIC and other tax benefits may be disallowed. Then, if the taxpayer wants to take the EIC based on this child, complete lines 14 and 15. If not, and there are no other qualifying children, complete lines 14 and 15, including the EIC for taxpayers without a qualifying child; do not complete Part III.			
14	Does the qualifying child have an SSN that allows him or her to work and is valid for EIC purposes?	☒ Yes ☐ No	☒ Yes ☐ No	☒ Yes ☐ No
	▶ If you checked "No" on line 14, the taxpayer cannot take the EIC based on this child and cannot take the EIC available to taxpayers without a qualifying child. If there is more than one child, complete lines 8 through 14 for the other child(ren) (but for no more than three qualifying children). If you checked "Yes" on line 14, continue.			
15	If the qualifying child was not the taxpayer's son or daughter, do you know or did you ask why the parents were not claiming the child?	☐ Yes ☒ Does not apply	☐ Yes ☒ Does not apply	☐ Yes ☒ Does not apply
16	Are the taxpayer's earned income and adjusted gross income each less than the limit that applies to the taxpayer for 2016?	☒ Yes ☐ No		

▶ If you checked "No" on line 15, stop; the taxpayer cannot take the EIC. If you checked "Yes" on line 15, the taxpayer can take the EIC. Complete Schedule EIC and attach it to the taxpayer's return. If there are two or three qualifying children with valid SSNs, list them on Schedule EIC in the same order as they are listed here. If the taxpayer's EIC was reduced or disallowed for a year after 1996, see Pub. 596 to see if Form 8862 must be filed.

With Parsonage Provided and Subject to SS

Figuring Net Self-Employment Income for Schedule SE (Form 1040)

(Keep for your records)

Worksheet 4

Name(s) as shown on return: JONATHAN J PIOUS   2016   Tax ID Number 400-00-1048

1	W-2 salary as a minister (from box 1 of Form W-2)	42,000
2	Net profit from Schedule C, line 31, or Schedule C-EZ, line 3	
3a	Parsonage or rental allowance (from Worksheet 1, line 3a or 4a)	8,400
b	Utility allowance (from Worksheet 1, line 3b or 4b)	6,000
c	Total allowance (add lines 3a and 3b)	14,400
4	Add lines 1, 2, and 3c	56,400
5	Schedule C or C-EZ expenses allocable to tax-free income (from Worksheet 2, line 6)	
6	Total unreimbursed employee business expenses after the 50% reduction for meals and entertainment (from Worksheet 3, line 9)	
7	Total business expenses not deducted in lines 1 and 2 above (add lines 5 and 6)	
8	Net self-employment income. Subtract line 7 from line 4. Enter here and on Schedule SE, Section A, line 2, or Section B, line 2	56,400

Shared Responsibility Payment Worksheet

(Keep for your records)

Name(s) as shown on return: JONATHAN J PIOUS   2016   Tax ID Number 400-00-1048

This worksheet is a combination of Steps 2-5, Worksheets A and B, and the Shared Responsibility Payment Worksheet shown in the instructions for Form 8965.

If you or another member of your tax household had neither minimum essential coverage nor a coverage exemption for any month during 2016, use the Shared Responsibility Payment Worksheet, below, to figure your shared responsibility payment.

Complete the monthly columns by placing "X's" in each month in which you or another member of your tax household had neither minimum essential coverage nor a coverage exemption.

Name	Jan	Feb	Mar	Apr	May	Jun	Jul	Aug	Sep	Oct	Nov	Dec
JONATHAN J PIOUS	X	X	X	X	X	X	X	X	X	X	X	X
JANE J PIOUS	X	X	X	X	X	X	X	X	X	X	X	X
JULIE PIOUS	X	X	X	X	X	X	X	X	X	X	X	X
JUSTIN PIOUS	X	X	X	X	X	X	X	X	X	X	X	X
JACOB PIOUS	X	X	X	X	X	X	X	X	X	X	X	X

		Jan	Feb	Mar	Apr	May	Jun	Jul	Aug	Sep	Oct	Nov	Dec
1.	Total number of X's in a month. If 5 or more, enter 5	5	5	5	5	5	5	5	5	5	5	5	5
2.	Total number of X's in a month for individuals 18 or over*	2	2	2	2	2	2	2	2	2	2	2	2
3.	One-half the number of X's in a month for individuals under 18*	1.5	1.5	1.5	1.5	1.5	1.5	1.5	1.5	1.5	1.5	1.5	1.5
4.	Add lines 2 and 3 for each month	3.5	3.5	3.5	3.5	3.5	3.5	3.5	3.5	3.5	3.5	3.5	3.5
5.	Multiply line 4 by $695 for each month. If $2,085 or more, enter $2,085	2,085.0	2,085.0	2,085.0	2,085.0	2,085.0	2,085.0	2,085.0	2,085.0	2,085.0	2,085.0	2,085.0	2,085.0

6.	Sum of the monthly amounts entered on line 1	60
7.	Enter your household income (see Household income)	39,726.00
8.	Enter your filing threshold (see Filing Thresholds For Most People)	20,700.00
9.	Subtract line 8 from line 7	19,026.00
10.	Multiply line 9 by 2.5% (.025)	475.65
11.	Is line 10 more than $2,085?	
	☐ Yes. Multiply line 10 by the number of months for which line 1 is more than zero	
	☒ No. Enter the amount from line 14 of the Flat Dollar Amount Worksheet	25,020.00
12.	Divide line 11 by 12.0	2,085.00
13.	Multiply line 6 by $223**	13,380.00
14.	Enter the smaller of line 12 or line 13 here and on Form 1040, line 61; Form 1040A, line 38; or Form 1040EZ, line 11. This is your shared responsibility payment	2,085.00
	Rounded amount will carry to main form	2,085

*For purposes of figuring the shared responsibility payment, an individual is considered under 18 for an entire month if he or she did not turn 18 before the first day of the month. An individual turns 18 on the anniversary of the day the individual was born. For example, someone born on March 1, 1999, is considered age 18 on March 1, 2017, and therefore, is not considered age 18 for purposes of the shared responsibility payment until April 2017.

**$223 is the 2016 national average premium for a bronze level health plan available through the Marketplace for one individual and should not be changed.

WK_89651.LD

With Parsonage Provided and Exempt from SS

Form 1040 (2016) — Page 2

JONATHAN J & JANE J PIOUS   400-00-1048

Tax and Credits

Line	Description	Amount
38	Amount from line 37 (adjusted gross income)	43,740
39a	Check if: You were born before January 2, 1952 □ Blind; Spouse was born before January 2, 1952 □ Blind. Total boxes checked ▶39a	
39b	If your spouse itemizes on a separate return or you were a dual-status alien, check here ▶39b	
40	Itemized deductions (from Schedule A) or your standard deduction	12,600
41	Subtract line 40 from line 38	31,140
42	Exemptions. If line 38 is $155,650 or less, multiply $4,050 by the number on line 6d	20,250
43	Taxable income. Subtract line 42 from line 41	10,890
44	Tax (see instructions). Check if any from: a □ Form(s) 8814 b □ Form 4972 c □	1,088
45	Alternative minimum tax (see instructions). Attach Form 6251	
46	Excess advance premium tax credit repayment. Attach Form 8962	
47	Add lines 44, 45, and 46	1,088
48	Foreign tax credit. Attach Form 1116 if required	
49	Credit for child and dependent care expenses. Attach Form 2441	
50	Education credits from Form 8863, line 19	
51	Retirement savings contributions credit. Attach Form 8880	
52	Child tax credit. Attach Schedule 8812, if required	1,088
53	Residential energy credit. Attach Form 5695	
54	Other credits from Form: a □ 3800 b □ 8801 c □	
55	Add lines 48 through 54. These are your total credits	1,088
56	Subtract line 55 from line 47. If line 55 is more than line 47, enter -0-	0

Other Taxes

Line	Description	Amount
57	Self-employment tax. Attach Schedule SE F4361	0
58	Unreported social security and Medicare tax from Form: a □ 4137 b □ 8919	
59	Additional tax on IRAs, other qualified retirement plans, etc. Attach Form 5329 if required	
60a	Household employment taxes from Schedule H	
60b	First-time homebuyer credit repayment. Attach Form 5405 if required	
61	Health care: individual responsibility (see instructions) Full-year coverage □	
62	Taxes from: a □ Form 8959 b □ Form 8960 c □ Instructions; enter code(s)	2,085
63	Add lines 56 through 62. This is your total tax	2,085

Payments

Line	Description	Amount
64	Federal income tax withheld from Forms W-2 and 1099	
65	2016 estimated tax payments and amount applied from 2015 return	6,500
66a	Earned income credit (EIC)	2,060
66b	Nontaxable combat pay election	
67	Additional child tax credit. Attach Schedule 8812	1,912
68	American opportunity credit from Form 8863, line 8	
69	Net premium tax credit. Attach Form 8962	
70	Amount paid with request for extension to file	
71	Excess social security and tier 1 RRTA tax withheld	
72	Credit for federal tax on fuels. Attach Form 4136	
73	Credits from Form: a □ 2439 b □ Reserved c □ 8885 d □	
74	Add lines 64, 65, 66a, and 67 through 73. These are your total payments	10,472

Refund

75	If line 74 is more than line 63, subtract line 63 from line 74. This is the amount you overpaid	8,387
76a	Amount of line 75 you want refunded to you. If Form 8888 is attached, check here ▶ □	8,387
77	Amount of line 75 you want applied to your 2017 estimated tax ▶	

Amount You Owe

78	Amount you owe. Subtract line 74 from line 63. For details on how to pay, see instructions ▶
79	Estimated tax penalty (see instructions)

Third Party Designee: Do you want to allow another person to discuss this return with the IRS? Yes / No ☒

Sign Here

Your occupation: MINISTER
Spouse's occupation: HOUSEWIFE
Date: 12-02-2016
Identity Protection PIN: P00106320

Paid Preparer Use Only

Print/Type preparer's name: Beverly J Worth
Firm's name: Worth Financial Service
Firm's address: PO Box 242, Winona Lake, IN 46590
Firm's EIN: 48-0733498
Phone no.: 574-269-2121
Self-employed ☒

EEA   Form 1040 (2016)

CLERGY

Form 1040 (2016) — Page 1

Form **1040** Department of the Treasury - Internal Revenue Service (99) U.S. Individual Income Tax Return **2016**   OMB No. 1545-0074   IRS Use Only—Do not write or staple in this space

For the year Jan. 1-Dec. 31, 2016, or other tax year beginning _____, 2016, ending _____, 20___

Your first name and initial: **JONATHAN J** Last name: **PIOUS**
Your social security number: **400-00-1048**

If a joint return, spouse's first name and initial: **JANE J** Last name: **PIOUS**
Spouse's social security number: **458-12-4715**

Home address (number and street): **2450 E 38TH ST** Apt. no.

City, town or post office, state, and ZIP code: **INDIANAPOLIS   IN   46205**

Presidential Election Campaign: You □ Spouse □

Filing Status
1 □ Single
2 ☒ Married filing jointly (even if only one had income)
3 □ Married filing separately
4 □ Head of household
5 □ Qualifying widow(er) with dependent child

Exemptions
6a ☒ Yourself
6b ☒ Spouse

Boxes checked on 6a and 6b: **2**

Dependents:

(1) First name	Last name	(2) Dependent's social security number	(3) Dependent's relationship to you	(4) ✓ if child under age 17 qualifying for child tax credit
JULIE	PIOUS	555-22-8879	DAUGHTER	☒
JUSTIN	PIOUS	555-22-8880	SON	☒
JACOB	PIOUS	555-22-8881	SON	☒

No. of children on 6c who lived with you: **3**
Add numbers on lines above ▶ **5**

Income

7	Wages, salaries, tips, etc. Attach Form(s) W-2 · Excess Allowance ·	-1,320
8a	Taxable interest. Attach Schedule B if required	
8b	Tax-exempt interest. Do not include on line 8a	
9a	Ordinary dividends. Attach Schedule B if required	
9b	Qualified dividends	
10	Taxable refunds, credits, or offsets of state and local income taxes	
11	Alimony received	
12	Business income or (loss). Attach Schedule C or C-EZ	420
13	Capital gain or (loss). Attach Schedule D if required. If not required, check here ▶ □	
14	Other gains or (losses). Attach Form 4797	
15a	IRA distributions / 15b Taxable amount	
16a	Pensions and annuities / 16b Taxable amount	
17	Rental real estate, royalties, partnerships, S corporations, trusts, etc. Attach Schedule E	
18	Farm income or (loss). Attach Schedule F	
19	Unemployment compensation	
20a	Social security benefits / 20b Taxable amount	
21	Other income	
22	Combine the amounts in the far right column for lines 7 through 21. This is your total income ▶	43,740

Adjusted Gross Income

23	Educator expenses	
24	Certain business expenses of reservists, performing artists, and fee-basis government officials. Attach Form 2106 or 2106-EZ	
25	Health savings account deduction. Attach Form 8889	
26	Moving expenses. Attach Form 3903	
27	Deductible part of self-employment tax. Attach Schedule SE	
28	Self-employed SEP, SIMPLE, and qualified plans	
29	Self-employed health insurance deduction	
30	Penalty on early withdrawal of savings	
31a	Alimony paid b Recipient's SSN ▶	
32	IRA deduction	
33	Student loan interest deduction	
34	Tuition and fees. Attach Form 8917	
35	Domestic production activities deduction. Attach Form 8903	
36	Add lines 23 through 35	
37	Subtract line 36 from line 22. This is your adjusted gross income ▶	43,740

For Disclosure, Privacy Act, and Paperwork Reduction Act Notice, see separate instructions.   Form **1040** (2016)

With Parsonage Provided and Exempt from SS

SCHEDULE 8812 (Form 1040A or 1040)

OMB No. 1545-0074
2016
Attachment Sequence No. 47

Department of the Treasury
Internal Revenue Service (99)

Child Tax Credit

▶ Attach to Form 1040, Form 1040A, or Form 1040NR.
▶ Information about Schedule 8812 and its separate instructions is at *www.irs.gov/schedule8812*.

Name(s) shown on return: JONATHAN J & JANE J PIOUS
Your social security number: 400-00-1048

Part I Filers Who Have Certain Child Dependent(s) with an ITIN (Individual Taxpayer Identification Number)

Complete this part only for each dependent who has an ITIN and for whom you are claiming the child tax credit. If your dependent is not a qualifying child for the credit, you cannot include that dependent in the calculation of this credit.

CAUTION

Answer the following questions for each dependent listed on Form 1040, line 6c; Form 1040A, line 6c; or Form 1040NR, line 7c, who has an ITIN (Individual Taxpayer Identification Number) and that you indicated is a qualifying child for the child tax credit by checking column (4) for that dependent.

A For the first dependent identified with an ITIN and listed as a qualifying child for the child tax credit, did this child meet the substantial presence test? See separate instructions.
☐ Yes   ☐ No

B For the second dependent identified with an ITIN and listed as a qualifying child for the child tax credit, did this child meet the substantial presence test? See separate instructions.
☐ Yes   ☐ No

C For the third dependent identified with an ITIN and listed as a qualifying child for the child tax credit, did this child meet the substantial presence test? See separate instructions.
☐ Yes   ☐ No

D For the fourth dependent identified with an ITIN and listed as a qualifying child for the child tax credit, did this child meet the substantial presence test? See separate instructions.
☐ Yes   ☐ No

Note: If you have more than four dependents identified with an ITIN and listed as a qualifying child for the child tax credit, see separate instructions and check here ▶ ☐

Part II Additional Child Tax Credit Filers

1 If you file Form 2555 or 2555-EZ *stop* here, you cannot claim the additional child tax credit.
If you are required to use the worksheet in **Pub. 972**, enter the amount from line 8 of the Child Tax Credit Worksheet in the publication. Otherwise:
- **1040 filers:** Enter the amount from line 6 of your Child Tax Credit Worksheet (see the Instructions for Form 1040, line 52).
- **1040A filers:** Enter the amount from line 6 of your Child Tax Credit Worksheet (see the Instructions for Form 1040A, line 35).
- **1040NR filers:** Enter the amount from line 6 of your Child Tax Credit Worksheet (see the Instructions for Form 1040NR, line 49).
1 3,000

2 Enter the amount from Form 1040, line 52; Form 1040A, line 35; or Form 1040NR, line 49 **2** 1,088
3 Subtract line 2 from line 1. If zero, *stop* here, you cannot claim this credit **3** 1,912
4a Earned income (see separate instructions) **4a** 43,740
b Nontaxable combat pay (see instructions) **4b**
5 Is the amount on line 4a more than $3,000?
☐ No. Leave line 5 blank and enter -0- on line 6.
☒ Yes. Subtract $3,000 from the amount on line 4a. Enter the result **5** 40,740
6 Multiply the amount on line 5 by 15% (0.15) and enter the result **6** 6,111
Next. Do you have three or more qualifying children?
☐ No. If line 6 is zero, *stop* here, you cannot claim this credit. Otherwise, skip Part III and enter the **smaller** of line 3 or line 6 on line 13.
☒ Yes. If line 6 is equal to or more than line 3, skip Part III and enter the amount from line 3 on line 13. Otherwise, go to line 7.

For Paperwork Reduction Act Notice, see your tax return instructions. Schedule 8812 (Form 1040A or 1040) 2016

SCHEDULE C-EZ (Form 1040)

OMB No. 1545-0074
2016
Attachment Sequence No. 09A

Department of the Treasury
Internal Revenue Service (99)

Net Profit From Business
(Sole Proprietorship)

▶ Partnerships, joint ventures, etc., generally must file Form 1065 or 1065-B.
▶ Attach to Form 1040, 1040NR, or 1041.   ▶ See instructions.

Name of proprietor: JONATHAN J PIOUS
Social security number (SSN): 400-00-1048

Part I General Information

You May Use Schedule C-EZ Instead of Schedule C Only If You:
- Had business expenses of $5,000 or less,
- Use the cash method of accounting,
- Did not have an inventory at any time during the year,
- Did not have a net loss from your business,
- Had only one business as either a sole proprietor, qualified joint venture, or statutory employee,

And You:
- Had no employees during the year,
- Do not deduct expenses for business use of your home,
- Do not have prior year unallowed passive activity losses from this business, and
- Are not required to file Form 4562, Depreciation and Amortization, for this business. See the instructions for Schedule C, line 13, to find out if you must file.

A Principal business or profession, including product or service
B Enter business code (see page 2)
C Business name. If no separate business name, leave blank.
D Enter your EIN (see page 2)
E Business address (including suite or room no.). Address not required if same as on page 1 of your tax return.
2450 E 38TH ST
City, town or post office, state, and ZIP code
INDIANAPOLIS, IN 46205
F Did you make any payments in 2016 that would require you to file Form(s) 1099? (see the instructions for Schedule C)   ☐ Yes ☐ No
G If "Yes," did you or will you file required Forms 1099?   ☐ Yes ☐ No

Part II Figure Your Net Profit

1 Gross receipts. Caution: If this income was reported to you on Form W-2 and the "Statutory employee" box on that form was checked, see *Statutory employees* in the instructions for Schedule C, line 1, and check here ▶ ☐ **1** 420
2 Total expenses (see instructions). If more than $5,000, you **must** use Schedule C **2**
3 Net profit. Subtract line 2 from line 1. If less than zero, you **must** use Schedule C. Enter on both Form 1040, line 12, and Schedule SE, line 2, or on Form 1040NR, line 13, and Schedule SE, line 2 (see instructions). (Statutory employees do not report this amount on Schedule SE, line 2.) Estates and trusts, enter on Form 1041, line 3 **3** 420

Part III Information on Your Vehicle. Complete this part only if you are claiming car or truck expenses on line 2.

4 When did you place your vehicle in service for business purposes? (month, day, year) ▶
5 Of the total number of miles you drove your vehicle during 2016, enter the number of miles you used your vehicle for:
a Business ____ b Commuting (see instructions) ____ c Other ____
6 Was your vehicle available for personal use during off-duty hours?   ☐ Yes ☐ No
7 Do you (or your spouse) have another vehicle available for personal use?   ☐ Yes ☐ No
8a Do you have evidence to support your deduction?   ☐ Yes ☐ No
b If "Yes," is the evidence written?   ☐ Yes ☐ No

For Paperwork Reduction Act Notice, see the separate instructions for Schedule C (Form 1040). Schedule C-EZ (Form 1040) 2016

Earned Income Credit Worksheet - Form 1040, line 66a, Form 1040A, line 42a, or Form 1040EZ, line 8a

(Keep for your records)

Name(s) as shown on return	Tax ID Number
JONATHAN J & JANE J PIOUS	400-00-1048
	2016

1. Enter the amount from Form 1040 or Form 1040A, line 7, or Form 1040EZ, line 1 plus any nontaxable combat pay elected to be included in earned income 1. **43,320**

2. If you received a taxable scholarship or fellowship grant that was not reported on a W-2 form, enter that amount here, plus any amounts received for work performed while an inmate in a penal institution, plus any amounts received as a pension or annuity from a nonqualified deferred compensation plan or a nongovernmental section 457 plan . . . . 2.

3. Subtract line 2 from line 1 . . . . 3. **43,320**

4. If you were self-employed **or** used Schedule C or C-EZ as a statutory employee, enter the amount from the worksheet for self employed taxpayers 4. **420**

5. Add lines 3 and 4 . . . . 5. **43,740**

6. Look up the amount on **line 5** above in the **EIC Table** on pages **62-68** to find your credit. Enter the credit here. If line 6 is zero, **stop.** You **cannot** take the credit. Enter "**No**" directly to the right of Form 1040, line 66a, Form 1040A, line 38a, or Form 1040EZ, Line 8a 6. **2,060**

7. Enter your **AGI** or Form 1040EZ, line 4 . . . . 7. **43,740**

8. Is line 7 less than –
   - $8,250 if you do not have a qualifying child ($13,750 if married filing joint)
   - $18,150 if you have at least one qualifying child? ($23,650 if married filing joint)

   [X] **Yes.** Go to line 9 now.

   [ ] **No.** Look up the amount on **line 7** above in the **EIC Table** to find your credit.
   Enter the credit here 8. **2,060**

9. **Earned income credit.**
   - If you checked "Yes" on line 8, enter the amount from line 6.
   - If you checked "No" on line 8, enter the **smaller** of line 6 or line 8 . . . . 9. **2,060**

   For additional information on the EIC calculation see the form instructions or IRS Publication 596.

SCHEDULE EIC
(Form 1040A or 1040)

Department of the Treasury
Internal Revenue Service (99)

Earned Income Credit

Qualifying Child Information

▶ **Complete and attach to Form 1040A or 1040 only if you have a qualifying child.**
▶ **Information about Schedule EIC (Form 1040A or 1040) and its instructions is at www.irs.gov/scheduleeic.**

OMB No. 1545-0074

2016

Attachment Sequence No. **43**

Name(s) shown on return
JONATHAN J & JANE J PIOUS

Your social security number
400-00-1048

Before you begin:
- See the instructions for Form 1040A, lines 42a and 42b, or Form 1040, lines 66a and 66b, to make sure that **(a)** you can take the EIC, and **(b)** you have a qualifying child.
- Be sure the child's name on line 1 and social security number (SSN) on line 2 agree with the child's social security card. Otherwise, at the time we process your return, we may reduce or disallow your EIC. If the name or SSN on the child's social security card is not correct, call the Social Security Administration at 1-800-772-1213.

CAUTION!
- You can't claim the EIC for a child who didn't live with you for more than half of the year.
- If you take the EIC even though you are not eligible, you may not be allowed to take the credit for up to 10 years. See the instructions for details.
- It will take us longer to process your return and issue your refund if you do not fill in all lines that apply for each qualifying child.

Qualifying Child Information

	Child 1		Child 2		Child 3	
1 Child's name If you have more than three qualifying children, you have to list only three to get the maximum credit.	First name JACOB	Last name PIOUS	First name JUSTIN	Last name PIOUS	First name JULIE	Last name PIOUS
2 Child's SSN The child must have an SSN as defined in the instructions for Form 1040A, lines 42a and 42b, or Form 1040, lines 66a and 66b, unless the child was born and died in 2016. If your child was born and died in 2016 and did not have an SSN, enter "Died" on this line and attach a copy of the child's birth certificate, death certificate, or hospital medical records.	555-22-8881		555-22-8880		555-22-8879	
3 Child's year of birth	Year 2009 If born after 1997 **and** the child is younger than you (or your spouse, if filing jointly), skip lines 4a and 4b; go to line 5. ◁▷		Year 2007 If born after 1997 **and** the child is younger than you (or your spouse, if filing jointly), skip lines 4a and 4b; go to line 5. ◁▷		Year 2004 If born after 1997 **and** the child is younger than you (or your spouse, if filing jointly), skip lines 4a and 4b; go to line 5. ◁▷	
4a Was the child under age 24 at the end of 2016, a student, and younger than you (or your spouse, if filing jointly)?	[ ] **Yes.** *Go to line 5.*	[ ] **No.** *Go to line 4b.*	[ ] **Yes.** *Go to line 5.*	[ ] **No.** *Go to line 4b.*	[ ] **Yes.** *Go to line 5.*	[ ] **No.** *Go to line 4b.*
b Was the child permanently and totally disabled during any part of 2016?	[ ] **Yes.** *Go to line 5.*	[ ] **No.** The child is not a qualifying child.	[ ] **Yes.** *Go to line 5.*	[ ] **No.** The child is not a qualifying child.	[ ] **Yes.** *Go to line 5.*	[ ] **No.** The child is not a qualifying child.
5 Child's relationship to you (for example, son, daughter, grandchild, niece, nephew, foster child, etc.)	SON		SON		DAUGHTER	
6 Number of months child lived with you in the United States during 2016 • If the child lived with you for more than half of 2016 but less than 7 months, enter "7." • If the child was born or died in 2016 and your home was the child's home for more than half the time he or she was alive during 2016, enter "12."	12 months Do not enter more than 12 months.		12 months Do not enter more than 12 months.		12 months Do not enter more than 12 months.	

For Paperwork Reduction Act Notice, see your tax return instructions.

Schedule EIC (Form 1040A or 1040) 2016

34th Annual

TAX SEMINAR
for Clergy and
NonProfit Organizations

Seminar Information

It's a Jungle Out There!

This seminar is a must for clergy, spouses, treasurers, board members, and accountants to attend.
Register NOW and YOU won't be disappointed!!

WORTH FINANCIAL SERVICE

1-574-269-2121 • Fax: 1-888-483-7350

● **E-Mail: bjworth1040@gmail.com** ● **Website: www.worthfinancial.com**

Topics to be Covered . . .

● The Affordable Health Care Act and its gradual implementation has caused major changes in the tax arena.

● Parsonage Allowance — Who can have parsonage allowance, what is includible and how to establish it legally.

● How an accountable plan for employee business expenses can save tax and reduce audit exposure.

● How to properly report a minister's compensation on payroll reports by the employer.

● Social Security Exemption — when to file, including "New Belief" opportunity.

● Retirement Planning — yes ministers need to plan — tax sheltered employer retirement plans are an excellent way to
*invest for retirement.

SEMINAR REGISTRATION INFORMATION

This seminar has been presented annually throughout the United States. Beverly J Worth
will present this seminar in person at the locations and times listed on the enclosed Registration Form. Registration for this seminar is only $129 per person when pre-registered
($139 at the door). $20 off seminar fee to spouse or additional persons from the same firm
or organization.

Registration includes: coffee breaks and copy of
"Worth's Income Tax Guide for Ministers".
Lunch will be "on your own."

Other Books and Supplies will be Available

$129

ALL SEMINAR SESSIONS are from 9:00 a.m. to 5:00 p.m.
(Registration at 8:45 a.m.)

● This is a basic tax course requiring no
prerequisites and no advanced preparation.

● Recommended for 8 hours CPE credits

● Taxation

● Delivery method: Group Live

● Tax deductible under revised law

100% MONEY BACK GUARANTEE
*If you are dissatisfied with this
program for any reason a full-
tuition refund will be issued upon
written request at the seminar.*

Cancellations received three (3) days before the seminar are refundable, minus a $20 registration service charge.
After that, you may attend another workshop or receive a DVD recording of a seminar if available. Substitutions may be made at any time.
Contact Information: For more information regarding administrative policies such as complaint and refund, please contact our office at (574) 269-2121

To register: FAX or Mail the enclosed registration form today
Call 1-574-269-2121 (Phone Answered EST 9:00 a.m. - 5:00 p.m. M-F)
Fax 1-888-483-7350 (24 hours a day, 7 days a week)
To Register online: www.worthfinancial.com or E-Mail: bjworth1040@gmail.com

The Speaker In Person

Mrs. Beverly Worth will personally teach the seminar. "Mrs. Beverly J. Worth is recognized in Christian circles as one of the foremost authorities in the area of Income Tax as it relates to ministers and religious workers. Mrs. Worth has been involved in income tax preparation since 1964 and began Worth Financial Service in 1972.

She has authored the annual publication "Worth's Income Tax Guide for Ministers" since 1973, the Professional Tax Record Book" since 1981 and has created numerous worksheets. Mrs. Worth has taught the "Tax Seminar for Clergy and NonProfit Organizations" in many locations since 1983. A graduate of Calvary Bible College, Beverly was honored as a Distinguished Alumna in 1988. The NRCC Business Advisory Council presented to Beverly a "2004 Businesswoman of the Year" award. Mrs. Worth is enrolled to practice before the IRS (EA), an Accredited Tax Advisor (ATA), a Certified Tax Professional (CTP) and a registered representative of HD Vest Financial Services. She is a member of the following professional organizations: National Association of Enrolled Agents, National Association of Tax Practitioners, National Society of Tax Professionals. She and her husband Jack live in Warsaw, Indiana and have two grown children, Elle and Jack II, and two grandchildren, Sara and Quentin. Her husband, Jack is the pastor of Dutchtown Brethren Church.

Beverly J. Worth, EA, ATA, CTP
*Seminar attendees are usually thrilled to find out some **simple steps** to take that can often **eliminate** or **greatly reduce** their income tax liability."*

Professional ... but affordable service since 1973

It's a Jungle Out There!

Grapevine or word of mouth sharing of tax strategies are often dangerously inaccurate. Grabbing the wrong vine might land you in quicksand, not on the river bank.

But understanding the financial aspects of your ministry can save you money and reduce your risk of IRS audits. That is why Worth Financial Service holds annual seminars around the country to benefit and educate ministers and other officers within churches and religious organizations.

Not knowing about the various applications of tax law to your ministry means you may be paying too much income taxes. Or worse, it could jeopardize the ministry itself if you are not paying enough.

Although the dangers are real, the purpose of these seminars is to take a positive approach to informing you about current tax law, and equipping you to handle the ministry's finances in the proper manner.

Our approach is upbeat and informative, giving you assurance that your ministry is doing things right. And we give you plenty of information to take home with you, so you can stay current year-round on changes in tax law that affect nonprofit organizations.

Testimonials

"Beverly J Worth shares her up-to-date knowledge of income tax preparation in a clear and precise manner. After attending her seminar for "Worth's Income Tax Guide for Ministers", there is no doubt in my mind that any CPA, professional accountant, or lay person will come away with the invaluable information needed to prepare a tax return correctly. I highly recommend any of B. J. Worth's programs in any form available."

...Linda G, Cartersville, GA

"I get so much accurate and valuable information from B J Worth's seminars that I keep coming back year after year for an update! She is not only very knowledgebable, but always smartly incorporates God's principles in her seminars, teaching in such a clear and understandaable style."

...Marleen G, Fort Wayne, IN

"I have attended the Worth Tax Seminars for many years and find that they always add insight and confidence when I'm working with the complicated rules set out by the government. Church tax rules are so different from the population's in general, that without guiidance, no one would be able to get them right"

...Janet B, Flat Rock, IN

"With several new clergy clients, including a foreign missionary, Beverly's seminar was not only instructive but set my mind at ease. I am now confident in the service I will provide to our full time ministers."

...Rob B, Lewis Center, OH

Dates and Locations - 2016 & 2017

www.worthfinancial.com
• Register online

Tuesday, December 06, 2016

Chattanooga/Hamilton, TN
Hilton Garden Inn
2343 Shallowford Village Dr
(423) 308-4400
I-75, Exit 5, Shallowford Exit

Thursday, December 8, 2016

Indianapolis/Fishers, IN
Holiday Inn Express
9791 North by Northeast Blvd,
(317) 558-4100
I-69 N, Exit 3, turn right onto 96th St, then left at the 1st stoplight (N by NE Blvd.)

Monday, December 12, 2016

Columbus/Dublin, OH
Holiday Inn Express
5500 Tuttle Crossing Blvd
(614) 793-5500
I-270, Exit 15, go west on Tuttle Crossing Blvd. - hotel will be on the right.

Thursday, December 15, 2016

Bloomington/Normal, IL
Holiday Inn Express
1715 Parkway Plaza Drive
(309) 862-1600
I-55 North. Take Exit 167, turn right onto Veterans Parkway at stop light. Continue for 2 miles, turn left onto Parkway Plaza Dr., hotel on the right.

Monday, December 19, 2016

Warsaw. IN 46580
Hampton Inn
115 Robmar Drive
574-268-2600
Take US 30 to Center Street in Warsaw IN From the West - turn right, From the East - turn left. Hotel is 1/4 mile on right.

Wednesday, January 04, 2017

Grand Rapids, MI 46548
Holiday Inn Express
6569 Clay Ave SW
616-871-9700
US 131, Exit at the 68th St Exit, go East to first stoplight and turn left on Clay Ave

APPROVED
CONTINUING EDUCATION
PROVIDER

Recommended for 8 hours of CPE credits
This seminar provides an overview of clergy taxes. No prerequisites required.

Worth Financial Service is registered with the National Association of State Boards of Accountancy (NASBA) as a sponsor of continuing professional education on the National Registry of CPE Sponsors. State boards of accountancy have final authority on the acceptance of individual courses for CPE credit. Complaints regarding registered sponsors may be submitted to the National Registry of CPE Sponsors through its website: **www.nasbaregistry.org**

- -

Cut Here and Mail Today to: Worth Financial Service, P.O. Box 242, Winona Lake, IN 46590 or Fax to (888) 483-7350 or Call (574)269-2121

S E M I N A R   R E G I S T R A T I O N   F O R M
This seminar is a must for clergy, spouses, treasurers, board members, and accountants to attend.

Church or Company Name: 2nd Attendee Name:

Name_____   Name_____

Address_____   Address_____

City_____ ST_____   City_____ ST_____

Phone_____ Zip_____   Phone_____ Zip_____

E-Mail_____   E-Mail_____

1st Attendee Name: 3rd Attendee Name:

Name_____   Name_____

Address_____   Address_____

City_____ ST_____   City_____ ST_____

Phone_____ Zip_____   Phone_____ Zip_____

E-Mail_____   E-Mail_____

Check box for method of payment.

Check box for seminar you wish to attend.
- ☐ Chattanooga, TN - December 6, 2016
- ☐ Indianapolis, IN - December 8, 2016
- ☐ Columbus, OH - December 12, 2016
- ☐ Bloomington, IL - December 15, 2016
- ☐ Warsaw, IN - December 19, 2016
- ☐ Grand Rapids, MI - January 4, 2017

Check box for amount enclosed.
- ☐ $129 for One Person
- ☐ $238 for Two Persons
- ☐ $347 for Three Persons
- ☐ Add $109 per each Additional Person

☐ Check enclosed. Make payable to: Worth Financial Service.
☐ Charge to my credit card. Visa, MasterCard, American Express, and Discover accepted. Enter phone number above.

Charge this order to my Charge Account
as I have indicated, to be paid according   V-Code_____
to the current terms of that account.

Expiration
Month   Year

2017 Edition
WORTH'S INCOME TAX GUIDE
FOR MINISTERS
(Revised annually since 1973)
Includes Affordable Care Act Information

Worth's Income Tax Guide
for Ministers
CD - PDF format
Without encryption
You will like the search feature!

A Practical How To guide with filled out Examples

Ministers quite often have difficulty communicating to their officials how they, the church, can assist the minister in paying the least amount of tax possible. Put THIS BOOK in the hands of the church officials!

1 to 2	$24.99
3 to 14	$21.25
15 to 99	$19.99
100 to 999	$14.99
1000 or more	call

152 pages
Order Online: worthfinancial.com

1 to 2	$24.99
3 to 14	$21.25
15 to 99	$19.99
100 or more	$14.99

PROFESSIONAL TAX RECORD BOOK

This record book is designed to provide you with a convenient way to keep the detailed and accurate records necessary to pay the least tax possible. Includes discussion about the current definition of an accountable reimbursement plan in Treasury Decision 8324.

You will find the following sections in which you can keep all the detailed records IRS requires:

- Business Mileage Log
- Auto Expenses
- Travel Expenses
- Professional Expenses
- Entertainment Diary
- Housing Expenses
- Professional Income
- Monthly Summary

There is room in the binder for you to add compatible inserts for Appointments, Addresses, Calendars, etc.

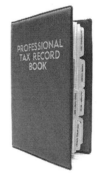

Complete Book with Binder

1 to 2	$24.99
3 to 14	$21.25
15 to 99	$19.99
100 or more	$14.99

Refill Pages & Tabs without Binder

1 to 2	$17.99
3 to 14	$15.30
15 to 99	$14.40
100 or more	$10.80

Vinyl Binder with Pockets
Looseleaf - 160 Pages
6 Rings - Tab Dividers
Page Size — 3¾ X 6½

AUDIO CD

MINISTERS COMPENSATION PACKAGE
TAX AND FINANCIAL PLANNING
WITH B.J. WORTH

ONE HOUR AUDIO PRESENTATION of how to arrange a compensation package that promotes good steward-ship and teaches how to legally lessen your tax burden. Ideal length for use at board meetings. Quickly teaches everyone enough to understand how to designate housing allowance and how to adopt an accountable reimbursement plan for business expense.

Financial planning for retirement has been neglected by many ministers. Today is the day to begin! Hear B.J. Worth, the most sought after speaker on clergy tax.

1 to 2	$10.99
3 to 14	$9.50
15 to 99	$8.80
100 or more	$6.60

Minister's Audio Presentation

Payroll Sheets for Employees of Nonprofit Organizations

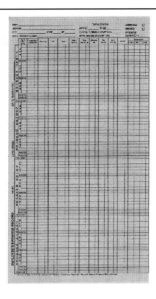

1 Sheet	50¢
25 Sheets	$ 6.00
50 Sheets	$10.80
100 Sheets	$18.00

Auto Log Book

Business Mileage Log and Auto Expense Only
Durable Cover - 48 pages
Handy Pocket Size

1 to 2	$ 5.99
3 to 14	$ 5.10
15 to 99	$ 4.80
100 or more	$ 3.60

Worksheet for Form 2106 for Ministers

Worksheet to Compute Auto Basis (2 sided)

Statement of Depreciation and Cost Recovery

Tax Organizer for All Taxpayers
Free of Charge to Our Clients

Prices to accountants
(Use your business stamp or label)

1 to 24	75¢
25 to 99	65¢
100 to 499	55¢
500 or more	50¢

1 Form	25¢	50 Forms	$5.40
25 Forms	$3.00	100 Forms	$9.00

Cut along this line

2017 ORDER FORM
FAX, CALL, OR MAIL TODAY
Order on Line - worthfinancial.com

Your Name _____
Company or
Church Name _____
Street Address _____
City _____ State _____
_____ Zip _____
Phone ( ) _____
☐ Residential or ☐ Commercial Address

Quantity	Description	Unit Price	Total Price
		Total	
		7% Sales Tax (Indiana Only)	
		*Postage & Handling	
		Grand Total	

Send Order To:
Worth Financial Service
PO Box 242, Winona Lake, IN 46590

Fax: (888) 483-7350
Office: (574) 269-2121
E-mail: bjworth1040@gmail.com

METHOD OF PAYMENT
☐ Check enclosed. Make payable to: Worth Financial Service.
☐ Charge to my credit card. Visa, MasterCard, American Express, and Discover accepted. Enter phone number above.

Charge this order to my Charge Account as I have indicated, to be paid according to the current terms of that account.

Expiration Month _____ Year _____
V-Code _____

*Postage and handling schedule @ retail cost

$ 0.00 - $ 5.00	$2.20
$ 5.01 - $ 50.00	$6.90
$ 50.01 - $ 75.00	$9.90
$ 75.01 - $100.00	$12.30
$100.01 - $150.00	$14.50
$150.01 - $200.00	$16.70
Over $ 200.00	$20.00

Self Study
Minister's Income Tax

An excellent training tool for clergy, spouses, treasurers, board members, and accountants. Plan a group training session or allow individuals to study on their own schedule.

No need to spend the time and money for travel to our live seminars.

Attending a live presentation seminar and getting all of your questions answered by B.J. Worth is definitely the best learning environment. However, we cannot always schedule in your area. If you are unable to attend one of our live seminars, consider ordering our DVD video of a live presentation.

Without CPE Credit
1 to 2 .... $99.00
3 to 6 .... $85.00

Includes a copy of "Worth's Income Tax Guide for Ministers" as your textbook

Recorded Annually by B. J. Worth

CONSULTATIONS

We encourage your reading "Worth's Income Tax Guide For Ministers" in its entirety. It will answer most of your questions.

We are available for consultation throughout the year and whether you are able to come to our office for an appointment or need to conduct the consultation by phone, or by letter, it is necessary for us to charge for our time. Our fee is $75.00 per hour for consultation.

We prefer phone consultations. Experience has shown us that requests for information and consultation by letter do not provide us with adequate facts. It is often necessary to call and ask for background and facts to give you the correct answer.

Up to 12 minutes - $15.00
13 to 24 minutes - $30.00
25 to 36 minutes - $45.00
37 to 48 minutes - $60.00
49 to 60 minutes - $75.00

Please have your charge card number available or be prompt to send amount consultant requests. For brief informational calls there will be no charge.

Service provided by:

WORTH FINANCIAL SERVICE

P.O. Box 242 • Winona Lake, IN 46590
Location: 3201 E Center St, Warsaw, IN 46582
(574) 269-2121
(888) 483-7350 (Fax) Alternate Fax (574) 269-4321
E-mail: bjworth1040@gmail.com
worthfinancial.com

INDEX

WORTH FINANCIAL SERVICE

P.O. Box 242 • Winona Lake, IN 46590
Location: 3201 E Center St, Warsaw, IN 46582
(574) 269-2121
(888) 483-7350 (Fax) Alternate Fax (574) 269-4321
E-mail: bjworth1040@gmail.com
worthfinancial.com

Made in the USA
Lexington, KY
27 March 2017